THE PENGUIN SPORTS LIBRARY

General Editor: Dick Schaap

BABE

Robert W. Creamer is a senior writer for *Sports Illustrated* and has been a member of the staff of that magazine since its inception in 1954. He is currently at work on a biography of Casey Stengel. Mr. Creamer is married and has five children.

BABE

THE LEGEND COMES TO LIFE

ROBERT W. CREAMER

PENGUIN BOOKS

PENGUIN BOOKS
Published by the Penguin Group
Viking Penguin Inc., 40 West 23rd Street,
New York, New York 10010, U.S.A.
Penguin Books Ltd, 27 Wrights Lane,
London W8 5TZ, England
Penguin Books Australia Ltd, Ringwood,
Victoria, Australia
Penguin Books Canada Ltd, 2801 John Street,
Markham, Ontario, Canada L3R 1B4
Penguin Books (N.Z.) Ltd, 182–190 Wairau Road,
Auckland 10, New Zealand

Penguin Books Ltd, Registered Offices:
Harmondsworth, Middlesex, England

First published in the United States of America by
Simon and Schuster 1974
Published in Penguin Books 1983
Reprinted 1983, 1984, 1985, 1986 (twice), 1988

LIBRARY OF CONGRESS CATALOGING IN PUBLICATION DATA
Creamer, Robert W.
Babe, the legend comes to life.
(The Penguin sports library)
Reprint. Originally published: New York: Simon and
Schuster, 1974.
1. Ruth, Babe, 1895–1948.   2. Baseball players—
United States—Biography.   I. Title.   II. Series.
GV865.R8C73   1983   796.357′092′4   [B]   83-10527
ISBN 0 14 00.6859 7

Printed in the United States of America by
R. R. Donnelley & Sons Company, Harrisonburg, Virginia
Set in Granjon

THE PENGUIN SPORTS LIBRARY

The purpose of this series of sports books is simple: It is to make available in paperback, at a reasonable price, some of the finest books that have been written about sports, books that otherwise might not be in print. There is only one basic requirement for a book to be considered for this series: It has to be good. It has to be pleasurable reading. It can be fiction or nonfiction. It can be a play. It can be angry or funny or, better yet, a blend of both. The author can be famous or obscure. He can be an athlete or an academic. He can write about the beauty of boxing or the brutality of chess. He can be a cynic or a cheerleader. He can be anything but dull.

A secondary requirement for a book to be selected for this series is that I must read it. This is my pleasure. The wonderful thing about reading and rereading the truly outstanding books about sports is that they are about so many things besides sports.

—Dick Schaap
New York City

FOR
MIGGY SCHELZ

Contents

Part One
1894–1919

Part Two
1920–1948

Photographs appear after page 214.

AUTHOR'S NOTE

A certain flatness of perspective may be evident in some of the descriptions of Ruth's adventures, but I did not want to invent motive and detail when I could not be sure of the facts. I have tried to keep surmise, conjecture and amateur psychoanalysis to a minimum. In a few instances I have edited stilted dialogue from old accounts to make it sound the way it probably was spoken, but I have not imagined any conversations or thoughts. All derive from one source or another.

Some of the baseball detail may prove tedious to the casual reader, who is given permission to skip such passages. Baseball fans are expected to wade through the whole thing.

ROBERT W. CREAMER

PART ONE

1894-1919

CHAPTER 1

Legend and Truth:
Babe Ruth Lives

I apologize for not having talked to everybody. There were so many. Each week I would think, There, now I've finished with that section. Now I know all there is to know about *that*. And a few days later I would learn of someone new or someone I had not thought of or someone I never would have thought of, and he would have one more window on the past for me to raise. A quick insight, an illuminating moment. Pete Appleton, for instance. The only thing I remembered about Pete Appleton was that his real name was Pete Jablonski, and I was wrong about that; it turned out to be Jablonowski. I had to look up his record to learn that he had pitched in the major leagues off and on for fourteen seasons. The clipping that came to my desk had Pete Appleton telling of Ruth phoning down to a hotel lobby from his room, asking the switchboard to page "any Yankee player that's around down there." Appleton, who was new to the ball club, took the call, and Ruth said, "Hey, keed, how about coming up and playing some cards with me?" He was lonesome, Appleton explained. He could not come downstairs to the lobby because he'd be mobbed by people, especially women. This was 1933. (Where was Claire?) There was nothing in Appleton's little story about booze and broads and gluttony and raising hell. Just an edgy, lonesome man in a hotel room.

And, said Appleton, "He had the prettiest swing of all." The "prettiest." An odd but strikingly accurate word to describe what Ruth did so much better than anyone else. Have you ever seen that old film clip of Ruth taking batting practice? If you like baseball you remember the pretty things about the game—the individual moments of craftsmanship and, sometimes, artistry within the mathematical precision of three strikes, three outs, four balls, four bases, nine innings, nine men. Ruth, easing along at three-quarter speed in batting practice, stepping into the pitch, flicking the bat around, meeting the ball cleanly, cocking the bat back for the next pitch, is for me—and maybe Pete Appleton—the epitome of baseball, its ideal expression.

This book had its genesis, I suppose, in my memory, because I saw Ruth when I was a boy. I saw him hit home runs in Yankee Stadium, and I remember that they all seemed to be a hundred feet high in the air as they passed first base. I remember watching him swing and miss, his huge torso twisting violently so that he ended up with his face more than 180 degrees around from the plate, staring intently up into the stands, right at me. God, how I remember that feeling: Babe Ruth is looking right at *me*. I remember him in right field one day when a little dying-quail hit began to fall into no man's land, that point of inaccessibility at the extreme range of center fielder, right fielder and second baseman, and I can still see Ruth waddling in from right field and *in* and *in* as he tried to get to the ball. (I think now that maybe the second baseman and the center fielder held up a little, giving way to the king.) He had his right arm extended, the glove held low, and after his long, inept run the ball glanced off the heel of his glove and fell safely. That was in 1933 too, when he was thirty-nine and his fat was old; I learned later that those who had played with him in his prime hated it when people like me, who saw him only in those last years, recalled him like that. They remembered when he could run (he stole fifty bases his first four seasons with the Yankees) and field and throw and do everything on a ballfield.

Correspondence followed with Peter Schwed of Simon and Schuster, in the course of which it was decided that I would attempt a thorough, detailed biography of the Babe. There had been several books written about him, all of them informative to varying degrees, but all necessarily limited in scope, one way or the other. His auto-biography, done with Bob Considine and Fred Lieb, was written when Ruth was desperately ill, at a time when it was difficult for him to speak and awkward for his collaborators to press him for nitpicking details and specific information. Two "unauthorized" biographies appeared at about the same time, one in 1947 and the other in 1948. The first, by Tom Meany, was lively and entertaining, but it was more a colorful portrait than a biography. The second, by Martin Weldon, was earnest and detailed but contained assumptions and mistakes that were surprising in a book so thoroughly re-searched. Ruth's widow wrote a memoir of her husband with Bill Slocum, Jr., in 1959 that shed a good deal of light on aspects of his personal life, but it degenerated into a philippic against organized baseball for its rejection of the Babe after his playing days were over. Lee Allen, the baseball historian, wrote a book for boys in 1966 that was a meticulous account of Ruth's playing days but which glossed over the unsavory episodes. Daniel M. Daniel wrote an early "authorized" biography in 1930 that contained firsthand material. Louis J. Leisman published a 36-page pamphlet in 1956 called *I Was with Babe Ruth at St. Mary's* that was of considerable help in under-standing what Ruth's boyhood was like. In 1959 Roger Kahn did a piece for *Esquire* that punctured some of the fatuous myths about Ruth and reaffirmed with fresh testimony the extraordinary impact and continuing hold he had on the people of his generation. By far the most revealing and rewarding work on Ruth was a novella-length soft-cover memoir written in 1948 by Waite Hoyt, who had been the Babe's teammate for more than a decade during the heroic years.

What I have tried to do in this book is go beyond the gentle inaccuracies and omissions of the earlier accounts and produce a total biography, one that, hopefully, would present all the facts and myths, the statistical details and personal exuberance, the obvious and subtle things that combined to make the man born George Ruth a unique figure in the social history of the United States. For more than any other man, Babe Ruth transcended sport, moved far beyond the artificial limits of baselines and outfield fences and sports pages. As I write this, he is dead and buried for more than twenty-five years, and it is nearly forty years since he played his last major league game. Yet almost every day, certainly several times a week, you read and hear about him. As Henry Aaron moved toward Ruth's career record of 714 home runs, he said, "I can't recall a day this year or last when I did not hear the name of Babe Ruth." Sometimes the references come in comic profusion. When Willie Sutton was released from prison, amid the odd adulation we Americans like to give to excrescences on the fabric of society, *Time* reminded us that he was known as "the Babe Ruth of bank robbers." A caption in *The New York Times* under a photograph of Enrico Caruso, illustrating a story on Franco Corelli, the singer, dubbed Caruso "the Babe Ruth of operatic tenors." A press release from Long Beach, California, said that Chuck Stearns was "the Babe Ruth of water skiing." John Lahr, in his thanks to those who helped him as he wrote the biography of his father, Bert Lahr, called Suzi Arensberg of Alfred A. Knopf "the Babe Ruth of copy editors." Someone at Simon and Schuster may disagree, but there it is.

It goes on and on. Philippe Halsman photographed his hundredth cover for *Life* and declared, "This is the high point of my career. It has taken me 27 years to achieve this record and I like to think of it as the equal of, maybe the superior of, Babe Ruth's." The New York Mets brought up a promising young slugger named Mike Jorgensen, who said, with a cheerful nod toward the concept of transmigration of souls, that he couldn't miss as a major leaguer because he was born August 16, 1948, the day Babe Ruth died.

Thus, Ruth lives, all around us, which is a matter of satisfaction to some, irritation to others, disinterest to a few. When Marianne Moore, the baseball fan, was asked about Ruth she said, "I never particularly liked him. He was tough." Roger Maris, when in 1961 he pursued and broke Ruth's sacrosanct record of 60 home runs in one season, was subjected to a continuing stream of abuse from spectators, sportswriters, letter writers, people in the street, people who for some reason deeply resented what Maris was doing and who felt impelled to act as surrogates for Ruth in trying to defend his record. Maris broke it anyhow, with a laudable display of sustained skill and athletic courage, yet a decade later only a handful of people knew where Roger was or what he was doing, while tenors and bank robbers and photographers and God knows who all else were still being measured against an indefinable standard of superiority called Babe Ruth. What will you bet that people, and not just those who attacked Maris, will write in after reading this and point out with some acerbity that Maris did *not* break Ruth's record, that Ruth hit his 60 in the old 154-game season and that Roger had only 59 after 154 games and needed the extra times at bat of the expanded 162-game season to get to 60, let alone 61? The phrase "with an asterisk," meaning a qualified success, came into common American usage after that 1961 season because of diehard insistence that Maris did not really break the Babe's record.

Maris himself never said a word against Ruth, so far as I know, but, Lord, he must have tired of hearing Babe Ruth's name. So have others. Or, at any rate, they have tired of hearing of Ruth as hero. Leonard Shecter, in his book *The Jocks,* a somewhat sophomoric attempt to tell the ungilded truth about sport, tried to undo the popular image of Ruth as a jolly, lovable, funmaking giant. Shecter wrote, "In fact, he was a gross man of gargantuan, undisciplined appetites for food, whiskey and women. . . . Ruth was never the playful, outgoing man he was supposed to be. . . . It does not take much research to find out what the Babe was really like. It doesn't matter. The fake Babe Ruth is more palatable than the real one."

And I hurry to blunt Shecter's comments because Ruth is alive for me too, and I know he is more complex than that, and I want *my* idea of the total truth about him to be known.

How many people dead a quarter of a century can arouse so much continuing interest, so much passion? Granted, we make special folk heroes of those highly proficient in sport. But very few people care, one way or the other, that Ty Cobb was a psychotic or that Honus Wagner as an old man coaching with Pittsburgh used to swipe baseballs and trade them for beers. Yet many insist that Cobb was a better ballplayer than Ruth, and Wagner may have been better than both of them. Does it matter about Cobb or Wagner? No. Yet Ruth matters. At seventy, Waite Hoyt, a member of baseball's Hall of Fame at Cooperstown, an urbane, intelligent, caustic, unsentimental veteran of a notably unserene life, talked of Ruth with intensity and fire. "I am almost convinced," Hoyt wrote to me, "that you will never learn the truth on Ruth. I roomed with Joe Dugan. He was a good friend of Babe's. But he will see Ruth in a different light than I did. Dugan's own opinion will be one in which Dugan revels in Ruth's crudities, and so on. While I can easily recognize all of this and admit it freely, yet there was buried in Ruth humanitarianism beyond belief, an intelligence he was never given credit for, a childish desire to be over-virile, living up to credits given his home-run power—and yet a need for intimate affection and respect, and a feverish desire to play baseball, perform, act and live a life he didn't and couldn't take time to understand."

Along with an abiding interest in Ruth the hero, Ruth the outsize man, I found in the people who knew him, most of whom are elderly now, a warm affection. You would ask about Ruth, and the first thing they would do, remembering, looking off into the past, would be to smile. I have a good friend named Jim Russell who is a lifelong baseball fan; one day after I had begun to write this book I had lunch with him. We got to talking about Ruth and about the various things I had learned. Finally he asked, "Have you found out what he was like? I mean, what kind of guy was he really?" It took me a moment to realize what he was getting at. I said, "Do you mean, underneath it all, was he a shit?" He said, "Yes. Was he?"

I told him about Ernie Shore and Bob Shawkey, neither of whom had any reason to be particularly fond of Ruth. Shore pitched in the minor leagues with him at Baltimore and was a better pitcher then than the Babe; yet Ruth was adulated far more than Shore. When the two of them were sold together to the Boston Red Sox, newspaper comment of the day said that the transaction could not help but be a good one for the Red Sox because of Ruth. But with Boston it was Shore who moved right in as a starting pitcher, while Ruth faltered and was sent back to the minor leagues again for a time. A year later, after the Red Sox had won the pennant, Shore pitched the opening game of the World Series against Grover Cleveland Alexander and started and won a second game; Ruth did not play at all, except to pinch-hit once. In 1917 Shore pitched a perfect game, one of the rarest feats in baseball. The Babe started that game and was thrown out of it by the plate umpire before getting anyone out. Shore, sent hurriedly to the mound in Ruth's place, did not allow anyone to reach first base in the nine full innings that followed and was credited with a perfect game. Baseball fans are more aware of that game because of Ruth than because of Shore. Even then, on his biggest day in baseball, Shore's solid accomplishment was overshadowed by the Babe's personality. Shore was a college man who later became a sheriff in his native North Carolina; Ruth was a reform school product. They roomed together in Boston, and the story is told that the Babe used Shore's toothbrush to brush his own teeth, and that Shore went to the manager of the ball club and insisted on being given a new roommate. Shore went into the armed forces in 1918 during World War I, but Ruth, who was married by then, did not; Shore was not the same pitcher after the war, and by 1921 his big league career was all over, just as Ruth was moving into the big, big money.

If ever a man had reason to be disenchanted by the Hero Ruth, it would appear to be Ernie Shore. Yet he too chuckled when he was asked about the Babe. He said the unhappy roommate story was not true. It wasn't a toothbrush at all, it was a shaving brush. The Babe didn't wash it out after he had used it, that was all. "Hell, I roomed with him in 1920 when we were both with the Yankees," Shore said. "I was the only one he would listen to." Asked what Ruth was like in those early days in Baltimore and Boston and New York, Shore replied with fervor, if not originality, "He was the best-hearted fellow who ever lived. He'd give you the shirt off his back."

Bob Shawkey was an outstanding pitcher in the American League for the first dozen years of Ruth's career. He had pitched against him in the beginning and later was his teammate on the superlative Yankee teams of the 1920s. In 1930 he was named manager of the Yankees and thus became Ruth's boss (for one season; he was deposed in favor of Joe McCarthy in 1931). Ruth had a burning ambition to be made the Yankee manager, and there were reports that he resented Shawkey getting the job. Shawkey told me some lively stories about Ruth, about fights he had had on the bench and in the clubhouse with teammates, about the time Miller Huggins, then the Yankee manager, fined Ruth $5000 for general misconduct, about an uproarious pennant celebration on a train coming back from Boston when Ruth and Bob Meusel, another Yankee out-fielder, banged on the door of Huggins' compartment and said they were going to throw him off the train. Shawkey impressed me as a gentle, decent man, sure of himself without making a big fuss over it, the kind of man who as a ballplayer might have resented a show-boat and troublemaker and flamboyant type like Ruth. Again I felt that I might have come across a vein of anti-Ruth feeling, and I asked, "Why did some people dislike the Babe?" Shawkey looked surprised and said, "People sometimes got mad at him, but I never heard of anybody who didn't *like* Babe Ruth."

I told this to Jim Russell at lunch and said that I had found the same sense of affection in all the oldtimers I talked to. Many of them had been specific—sometimes startlingly specific—in discussing the details of the things Ruth had done: the fights, the drinking, the eating, the girl chasing, the arrogance, his "indigestion" in 1925, his hypochondria late in his career, his bitterness and almost maudlin self-pity when he could not get the jobs he wanted in baseball after he was through as a player, the disastrous mistakes he made; but through it all there was a flow, a warmth, a delight as they talked about Ruth. He had been fun to be around. They *liked* him. Russell said he was glad to hear that. I was too.

I don't suppose it is necessary to declare that this is not intended to be a book for boys. But neither is it a sensational exposé. Ruth's sins, while many and glaring, were not terribly purple. He went to bed with a great many women, but he did not make public capital of it, nor was he ever involved in an ugly bedroom scandal. There were two or three putative paternity suits in the early years, but they came to nothing. He could drink extravagant amounts of liquor, and he got drunk a lot and raised hell, especially in the earlier years. He awed people with the amount of food he could eat. (Shore, asked if Ruth had a big appetite back in 1914, said, "Oh, my God. Oh, lord-a-mighty.") He disliked rules, objected to authority and most of his adult life did what he damned well wanted to. Yet, when he had to, he could discipline himself, and he had a continuing sense of responsibility to certain people and certain things, among them his own position as Hero.

His headlined troubles usually had to do with his flouting of ordinary standards of behavior, principally baseball's rules of discipline, and not with sex or drunkenness or gluttony as such. A considerable part of his headline-making propensity was the result of his extraordinary visibility. He could not hide. Ruth incognito was a contradiction in terms. Even in that era before television and mass-circulation picture magazines (the Sunday rotogravure was the big thing then), *everyone* knew and recognized Ruth's huge, round, flat-nosed, wide-mouthed face, his hulking body, his beaming grin, his unhappy pout. Wherever he went, the Babe was on public display, and few, if any, of his peccadillos went unnoticed.

Almost everyone from that era has a Babe Ruth story. Story multiplied by story becomes legend. Like all legends, Ruth's had a strong vein of truth in it—and an equally strong vein of baloney. Researching this book was an exploration into a curious world of misleading fact, perceptive misstatement, contradictory truth, substantiating myth. It was like going to live for the first time in a huge city, one that changes with the weather and the seasons as you get to know it. There were many dead-end streets and confusing neighborhoods, and at the end I could not possibly say that I knew all there was to know about Babe Ruth, any more than one man can say he *knows* New York or London, but I did learn some things about this odd, appealing, truly unique man.

Max Eastman wrote, "The mind should approach a body of knowledge as the eyes approach an object, seeing it in gross outline first, and then by gradual steps, without losing the outline, discovering the details." Has there ever been a grosser outline than that of Babe Ruth? Ask anyone. Babe Ruth? Baseball player. Home run hitter. Big fat guy, moon face, huge torso, skinny legs. Hit 60 home runs one year. Hit more home runs than anybody else. Tremendous home run hitter. Ate a lot of hot dogs. Loved kids.

Babe Ruth? Born in Baltimore. Grew up in an orphanage, signed out of the orphanage to play for the old minor league Baltimore Orioles. Went up to the Boston Red Sox, was a fine pitcher first and then became an outfielder, a home run star. Red Sox sold him to the New York Yankees. With Ruth, the Yankees became the greatest baseball team ever. Won pennants, World Series, everything. Babe Ruth and Lou Gehrig, the home run twins. Scared other teams. Scared the Pittsburgh Pirates in batting practice before the 1927 World Series, and the Pirates died in four straight. Ruth was the showman, always did things in the World Series. In 1932 against the Chicago Cubs he pointed to a spot in the center field bleachers and on the next pitch he hit a home run to the exact spot. You could look it up.

Babe Ruth? Glutton, drunkard, hellraiser, but beloved by all— except the Japanese during World War II. The Japs shouted, "To hell with Babe Ruth!" the ultimate insult, to GIs on Guadalcanal. Or Cape Gloucester. Or New Guinea. Or Peleliu. Someplace. They yelled it all right.

Hollywood made a movie about him, starring William Bendix, who should have had more sense. Terrible movie. Ran out all the myths and extended them to their illogical conclusions and then invented a dozen new ones. For thousands of people, maybe millions, William Bendix in a baseball suit is what Babe Ruth looked like. Which is a terrible shame, because lots of men look like William Bendix, but nobody else ever looked like Babe Ruth. Or behaved like him. Or did all the things he did in his repressed, explosive, truncated life.

CHAPTER 2

The Bad Kid:
Baltimore at the Turn
of the Century

The first twenty years of Ruth's existence are a shifting melange of elusive facts, erratic data, supposition and unsubstantiated invention. There are a few hooks to hang things on, but mists of ignorance obscure concrete knowledge until late in February 1914, when he came out into the world and became a professional baseball player. Even his name has been suspect. Halfway through his career it was an accepted fact among sportswriters that his surname was not Ruth at all but either Erhardt or Gerhardt, depending on whose column you read. When he became seriously ill in 1947 *The New York Times* referred to him as George Herman Erhardt Ruth, and Tom Meany, who was dependable if somewhat imaginative, wrote that in 1924, when newspapermen were commenting on the similarity of his alleged last name and that of a Brooklyn Dodger rookie named Rube Ehrhardt, Ruth supposedly remarked, "Mine has only one 'h.'"

But Ruth rejected the Erhardt-Gerhardt theory in his autobiography, and his sister and his widow have denied that either was ever his name. Ruth was a common surname in German Baltimore, and evidence of the Babe's family is reasonably plentiful in the more obscure records of the city. The facts, painstakingly dug out by historians like James H. Bready of the *Baltimore Sun,* indicate quite clearly that George Herman Ruth of baseball was the son of George Herman Ruth, Sr., of Baltimore. As the first-born son and oldest child, he was named after his father. His mother's maiden name was Katherine Schamberger. She was the daughter of an upholsterer named Pius Schamberger who had been born in Germany in 1833. Pius was an active trade unionist and for a time had served as vice-president of Woodworkers Local No. 6, although earlier, just after the Civil War, he had been a grocer and then a saloonkeeper on Pratt Street in Baltimore.

Ruth's paternal grandfather was another Baltimorean named John Ruth, who in 1873 (according to Baltimore city records) was in the business of making lightning rods. Lightning rods were the things to have on your house in that era, just as television antennas were a century later. The lightning rod dodge was the sort of work a man who shifts around a lot would take a stab at, and John Ruth tended to move from job to job, from business to business. He eventually left lightning rods and ended up with a combination grocery store and saloon on Frederick Avenue, not far from Pratt Street, near the Baltimore waterfront. His son George had worked with him for a while in the lightning rod business, and then George became successively a horse driver, an agent (agent for what is not known), a salesman (what he sold is obscured too by time), a grip-man on the streetcars and ultimately a bartender. In the 1890s George worked as a counterman in the family grocery and saloon on Frederick Avenue, and he was still living there with his family when he married Kate Schamberger and became a father.

Details of the marriage are not known and would not be of particular interest except for some curious complications. Babe Ruth was a well-publicized Catholic, but his father and mother were Lutherans, although not avid churchgoers. Family tradition says the Ruths were originally Pennsylvania Dutch; Baltimore is only about 60 miles south of the Pennsylvania Dutch country. John Ruth's father, Peter, is said to have been born in Bucks County in 1801 and his mother, Kaziah Reager, in Lancaster in 1805. The family spoke

German as readily as English, and around the house German was the first language. Fred Lieb, the sportswriter, told of exchanging a few sentences in German one day with Lou Gehrig, who was the son of German immigrants; Ruth, standing nearby, joined readily in the conversation.

The Schamberger side of the family was more complex, or obscure. Ruth always believed that his mother was Irish, or "mainly Irish," and his sister said that she thought her mother was partly Irish. The Irish background seems farfetched, since nineteenth-century immigrants tended to marry their own kind, but she may well have been a Catholic. Certainly Grandfather Schamberger's first name, Pius, has more a Catholic than a Protestant ring to it. On the other hand, marriage between Protestant and Catholic was neither commonplace nor casual in that time of strong religious bias. However, going a step further in this essentially fruitless speculation, it is at least possible that Pius Schamberger, even newly come from Germany, did marry an Irish girl, maybe an Irish Catholic girl, and that either his wife or, later, his daughter drifted away from the Catholic Church.

In any case George Ruth and Kate Schamberger married and had eight children. For her first lying-in Kate went home to her father's house at 216 Emory Street, just off Pratt Street and several blocks east of the home she and her husband shared with his family over the grocery and saloon. There, one February day in the mid-1890s, a neighborhood midwife named Minnie Graf helped her deliver a lusty son. The precise date, like so many of the details of Ruth's early years, is confused. For the first forty years of his life he assumed he had been born on February 7, 1894. In 1934 he needed a birth certificate in order to get a passport for a trip he was taking to Japan (his first time out of the country except for short sojourns to Canada and Cuba). The certificate that came from Baltimore stated that he had been born on February 6, 1895, or a year later and a day earlier than he had always thought. Ruth generally ignored this new data, continued to celebrate his birthday on February 7 and never bothered to take the year off his age. "What the hell difference does it make?" he'd growl. (In this book the earlier date is used throughout as the measure of Ruth's years, since that was the age he and those around him assumed was his for most of his life.)

And the 1895 birth date is not necessarily the right one. The birth record in Baltimore says only that a male child was born that day to George and Katherine Ruth. No name is given. Of the seven children the Ruths had after their oldest son (including two sets of twins), only one, a girl, lived past infancy. It is possible that one of the unfortunate babies was the male child born in February 1895. On the other hand, no record has been found of a male child born to the Ruths a year earlier. Speculation that Ruth was a foundling, an adopted child, is unwarranted. A photograph of Ruth with his father, taken about 1916, shows a startling resemblance. They look like twins themselves. His sister too bore a marked resemblance to the Babe.

The house on Emory Street where Ruth was born was one part of a four-unit row house. Each unit was 12½ feet wide and the house was about 60 feet deep, with a small back yard and a front door opening directly on the sidewalk. Although the house is now a museum and a monument to Ruth's memory, the infant lived there only until his mother felt strong enough to return to Frederick Avenue and her home with her in-laws. Little George (which is what he was called by the family; his father was Big George) learned to walk and play in the grocery store and the saloon. These were not totally dismal, poverty-stricken days for the family. Despite the legends that Ruth had a junglelike existence as a small boy, the family appears to have enjoyed some of the amenities of lower-middle-class life. There is, for example, a photograph of a "family picnic," taken sometime around 1896 or 1897. Whether it is a family picnic or not is uncertain, since there are more than eighty men, women and children in the picture, but in any case it is a cheerful, rather well-dressed group, the men mostly in ties, shirtsleeves and straw hats, the women in white dresses. Two of the men are holding what seem to be guitars. They are all gathered in front of a white clapboard building, possibly a house, possibly a school, possibly a meeting hall of some kind. Ruth's mother, fairly young, her hair up in a bun, is sitting at one end of the front row, gazing solemnly at the camera. Her son, no more than two or three, is standing by her knee, looking either bored or distressed, and his mother's hand is subtly but firmly against his cheek, turning his face toward the camera. Ruth's father is in the front row too, three or four places away, more toward the middle of the photograph. He is chunky, swarthy, wearing an open vest over his white shirt, a bow tie, a straw hat pushed back on his head; he is holding a pipe with a very long curved stem. Another photo in the family archives shows the Babe at three, this time in a formal studio portrait all his own. His lustrous dark hair is neatly groomed, as it so often was throughout his life; his expression is serious, somber, resigned.

By the time the boy was five the peripatetic father had taken his small family and moved out on his own, this time a few blocks south to Woodyear Street, where he and his brother John opened their own lightning rod business. This was another row house, several doors in from a corner saloon. Kate Ruth was still bearing and losing babies, and Little George was six when twin girls were born in August 1900. One of them was Mary Margaret, called Mamie, and, happily, she survived. Not long after her birth, George Ruth gave up lightning rods again and went back into the saloon trade, this time running his own place. He moved his wife, son and baby daughter to West Camden Street, where they lived upstairs over the bar. The neighborhood—still the same south side of Baltimore, close to the center of the city and the waterfront—was poor, rough and energetic, and young George took on its characteristics. His father and mother worked long hard hours—the saloon was open all day and a good part of the night—and there was not much time to pay attention to a hyperactive seven-year-old boy. He avoided school with a passion. He roamed the streets. Almost certainly he began to play baseball, for in those days little boys and youths and grown men played the game whenever they could. More often he hid in the alleys, ran with other tough little kids and became more and more difficult to control. "The truckdrivers, cops and store-keepers were our enemies," Ruth said in later years. "I learned to fear and hate the coppers and to throw apples and eggs at the truck-drivers." Legend says he chewed tobacco, drank whiskey and stole, and the odds are that he at least dabbled in all three. "I was a bum when I was a kid," he told Considine.

His father was beset with the problems of running the tavern, and his mother was tired and usually sick, perhaps as a result of her frequent and unhappy pregnancies; too, she had a toddling baby girl to take care of. What ultimately brought the Ruths to the final drastic step is impossible to determine, but on June 13, 1902, a Friday the 13th, when George was not yet eight and a half years old, he was committed by his parents to St. Mary's Industrial School for Boys. He was listed as "incorrigible" when he entered the Home, as it was usually called, and Ruth later admitted this, adding that whenever he wanted something in those days he took it, usually from his parents. "Looking back on my boyhood," he said in his autobiography, "I honestly don't remember being aware of the difference between right and wrong." As a grown man Ruth was usually meticulously honest in money matters, but otherwise that carefree attitude toward moral and social codes remained. His excesses occasionally brought him to his knees, figuratively if not literally, but in the words of sportswriter John Drebinger, "He was the most uninhibited human being I have ever known. He just did things."

Whatever Little George did in the late spring of 1902, it was enough to send him for the first time on the long trolley ride out to the Home. St. Mary's was primarily what its name said it was: an industrial training school for boys. But it was more than that. In later years it was to become solely a reform school, and a boy who was sent to St. Mary's was labeled bad. In Ruth's day it was a reform school too, but only partly; it harbored orphans and boys whose homes had been broken by divorce or death or serious illness, and it also took in poor boys whose families could not afford to take care of them. St. Mary's was four miles southwest of downtown Baltimore, a stunning distance for a small boy whose lifetime had been encompassed by a few city blocks. It was on the outskirts of the city, not out in the real countryside, but near enough to it so that its surroundings were a good deal greener and airier than the crowded, boisterous waterfront—except perhaps on overcast days when rain threatened and the east wind brought souvenirs of the stockyards half a mile away down Wilkens Avenue. St. Mary's was on a height of land on the southeast corner of Wilkens and Caton avenues. From the windows of the school buildings young Ruth could look over the iron fence and down Wilkens Avenue and watch the car tracks run straight as an arrow back toward the heart of Baltimore, clearly visible in the distance. There were 800 boys at St. Mary's, and George Ruth, at eight, was one of the youngest.

St. Mary's was a complex operation. It was run by the Xaverian Brothers, a Catholic order, but it received financial support from the city of Baltimore and the state of Maryland, and it took in boys from other religions (singer Al Jolson, a Jew, was, except for Ruth, its most famous alumnus), although in southern-oriented Baltimore it did not include Negro children in its embrace. The inmates (the boys used that term) ranged in age from seven to twenty-one. Discipline was strict, infractions quickly punished. The boys received religious training; Ruth became a practicing Catholic at St. Mary's and an altar boy who served mass for the chaplain, Father Francis. There was regular classroom work and a strong dose of industrial training.

There have been attempts, none of them conclusive, to pinpoint the reason why Ruth was sent to St. Mary's. His sister Mamie always insisted that he was put there simply because he would not go to school, and since he apparently was not able to read or write when he went into the Home, that must have been part of the reason. But Mamie was not yet two years old in June 1902, and her testimony is necessarily hearsay. Moreover, June is at the end of the school year and seems an illogical time to take action because of truancy, especially since most accounts agree that George stayed at St. Mary's only about a month that first time. He went in again for a month the following November but was back with his family by Christmas and stayed at home then until sometime in 1904.

Another story, the origins of which are vague, says that one day during a brawl in the Ruth saloon a shot was fired. No one was hurt, but an indignant neighbor got in touch with city authorities, declaring that the saloon was not a fit place to raise a child. As a result either the city insisted or the parents themselves decided that the increasingly wayward boy should be removed from his unwholesome environment. A variation of this holds that Ruth's father paid $15 a month to board the boy at St. Mary's, at least at first. But $15 a month was a substantial amount of money at the turn of the century; men supported families on ten dollars a week and less. If George Ruth did indeed pay $15 to send his boy to St. Mary's, it was a considerable sacrifice. Perhaps he did. Perhaps with his sick wife worse than usual in June and again in November and the saloon demanding all his time, he could find no neighbor or relative willing to take on the responsibility of looking after his wild young son.

The real incarceration in St. Mary's took place in 1904, when the boy was ten. This time he stayed in the Home for four years. His father was still a saloonkeeper, but he kept moving from place to place, from Camden Street to Hanover to Clement and eventually to Conway, at the corner of Charles, a block from Baltimore's inner harbor. Young George was fourteen when he came out of St. Mary's in 1908, and he remained out then until after his mother's death on August 23, 1910, when he was sixteen and Mamie only ten. Then he was put back in again. When Considine asked him why he would be returned to St. Mary's, the Babe shrugged and said, "You know, I'd do things." What things? "Drinkin'," the Babe said succinctly. A cousin, John Ruth, slightly older but a boyhood companion, said, "His mother missed him when he was in the Home and she would cry and ask her husband to get him out. Then when he came home she'd have trouble with him and hit him, and his father would put him back in again." John Ruth added, "He really liked his father," the implication being that he did not get along with his mother. But if the listed schedule of Ruth's arrivals and departures at St. Mary's is correct, he was there only for those two one-month terms in 1902 before the long four-year stretch from 1904 to 1908. Otherwise he was at home until after his mother died.

Considine had the impression that Ruth liked his mother and did not care for his father. Mamie Ruth—Mrs. Willard Moberly— remembered both her parents with affection and said her brother got along with both. ("He just wouldn't go to school.") In his pamphlet on Ruth at St. Mary's, Lou Leisman recalled a Sunday visiting day around 1912 when he, Leisman, was feeling sorry for himself because his father was dead, his mother was ill and he had had no visitors for two years; the eighteen-year-old Ruth, who had had no visitors himself, said, perhaps in a rough effort to console the younger boy, "You're lucky, Fats. I haven't seen my father in ten years." On another visitorless Sunday Ruth said, "I guess I'm too big and ugly to have visitors. Maybe next time." Next time never came, according to Leisman. But Mamie recalled, "We could visit him once a month. We used to ride out on the trolley. We had to change cars, there at the convent." So someone was visiting the boy.

After his mother died—some accounts say he was let out of St. Mary's only for her funeral—Ruth remained in the Home for another year. In 1911 he was released, but in 1912 he went back in for the last time and stayed until 1914, when at twenty he left to join the Baltimore Orioles. Leisman's little pamphlet raises some question about all this. In it is reproduced a letter from Associated Catholic Charities of Baltimore affirming that both Leisman and Ruth had been at St. Mary's at the same time. The letter says that Ruth "was resident there" from June 13, 1902, until February 27, 1914, and makes no mention of absences with or without leave. However, the boys used the term "parole" in reference to those who were out of the Home temporarily on probation; this would help to explain the multiple arrivals and departures of young Ruth.

It is all vague and confusing. But whatever the exact dates, it seems certain that Ruth spent at least seven of the ten years between 1904 and 1914, or from the time he was ten until he was twenty, behind the big gates at St. Mary's. He grew up there, and even though it was in a real sense a prison for a growing boy, he looked back on St. Mary's later with a warmth and nostalgia he never felt for the places he lived with his family. St. Mary's was his home.

CHAPTER 3

Early Exile:
Niggerlips in St. Mary's

For the uninitiated, it should be noted that brothers are not priests, although their garb is similar and people, Catholic and non-Catholic alike, are forever calling them "father." Brothers are, in effect, male nuns. They take religious vows, generally live in communal groups and are obliged to live holy lives, but they do not have the religious prerogatives of priests. They cannot say mass, for example, nor hear confession. They teach, they nurse, they give succor, they contemplate, they meditate, they labor in the vineyards of the Lord. There have been a fair number of god-awful people in their ranks: refugees from reality, neurotics, psychotics, losers, imperfect men to one degree or another. But the winners have been numerous too; for every brother who has occasionally belted a recalcitrant teenager (Catholic schools are filled with such stories, most of them splendidly exaggerated), there are dozens of decent dedicated men who in simple truth devote their lives to the welfare of their charges.

The twenty or thirty brothers at St. Mary's Industrial School had as many as 800 boys in their care at times, an outsize proportion of them blessed with a built-in gift for misbehavior. The brothers had to house the boys, feed them, clothe them, give them religious instruction and a basic classroom education and teach them a trade.

To do all this, they kept the boys under close control. St. Mary's was not a school you walked in and out of at will. Once in, you stayed in, and trips beyond the gates were special occasions. Inside, you were under the strict and constant supervision of the Xaverians. Even boys committed through no fault of their own were subject to the stringent rules. They went to bed at eight and arose at six. They washed, dressed, attended mass, ate breakfast and were in their classrooms by seven-thirty. Except for lunch, they were in classes or workshops all day until late afternoon. Then they had an hour or two of recreation time outside in the "yard" until supper. After supper a little canteen, or candy shop, opened for about an hour. The boys did not have cash, but they could earn credit in the workshops and charge candy, cakes, peanuts and the like against their accounts. Then it was back to the dormitories—there were four dormitories, each with about 200 cots—and a night's sleep before going through another day of the same closely supervised routine.

Such a regimen is never much fun (boys ran away from St. Mary's regularly), and in many places of confinement the discipline becomes extremely arbitrary and unfair. In Ruth's day at St. Mary's the prefect of discipline, the brother with overall responsibility for the boys' behavior, was an extraordinary man who managed to exert almost complete control over his wild 800 while still retaining their continuing respect and even affection. His Xaverian name was Matthias, and he was a huge man, nearly six feet six inches tall and probably over 250 pounds in weight. On one of the occasions in the 1920s when Ruth brought some of his New York Yankee teammates to St. Mary's for a visit, a photograph was taken of the half-dozen ballplayers with three or four of the brothers. Brother Matthias loomed distinctly taller and wider than Ruth, who was six feet two and weighed about 220 then, and Bob Meusel, who was six feet three and a half and 195. Brother Matthias was shaped something like a pear, with a relatively slight face and sloping shoulders descending into a heavy body with thick legs. He had blond hair and pale blue eyes, a somewhat receding jaw with a slight double chin, and a calm, expressionless face that could turn icy cold when he was dis-

pleased. Although Brother Paul, a small neat man who later became
head of the Xaverian Order, was superintendent of the school, the
boys referred to Brother Matthias as the Boss.

The boys were scared of the Boss, but he had qualities that
endeared him to them. He was immensely strong, stronger than any
of them, and that impressed them. He never ranted or shouted. He
was always calm, always consistent, always fair—and they appreciated that. If they misbehaved or broke a rule, they were punished.
As Leisman said, "He gave everyone a fair break but, brother, if you
ever crossed him you sure were in trouble." There is no testimony
that Matthias administered corporal punishment. Usually, a boy was
deprived of certain of the meager privileges allowed at the school,
like freedom during the recreation periods or the right to play ball
on one of the many organized teams, and he would be made to
stand through long hours of punishment time. When the punishment was over, the incident was over too as far as Brother Matthias
was concerned; and this the boys looked upon as eminently just.

Two stories are part of Brother Matthias' legend. One day a brawl
started among some of the older boys in the yard and soon developed into a small riot. Matthias was away from the school at the
time, but he was quickly sent for, hurried back, strode into the yard,
climbed onto a small elevation and simply stood there, looking
coldly out over the tumultuous throng of boys. Almost at once the
yard grew quiet and the fighting stopped. Another time a new boy
named Jerry DeLay, who had been committed to St. Mary's by the
Baltimore juvenile court, was brought into the yard and told to join
the other boys there. George Ruth wandered over and asked the
truculent newcomer if he wanted to have a catch. DeLay, who had
the build of a middleweight, told Ruth to mind his own business
and threw a punch at him. Ruth responded in kind, the two
tumbled to the ground fighting, and three or four other boys
scrambled in, either to break up the fight or to take a cheap shot or
two at DeLay, the stranger. Suddenly, seemingly from nowhere,
Brother Matthias appeared, dove into the pile, pulled out DeLay,
tucked him under one arm like a bag of laundry and carried him

off. A day or so later, after a more tractable DeLay had returned to the yard, the new boy and Ruth were seen playing catch. "The Babe was never one to hold a grudge," said Leisman, and while that seems like nostalgic gilding of the lily it was nonetheless a marked characteristic of Ruth through most—though not all—of his life. He bruised easy, as they used to say, but he healed quick.

Ruth revered Brother Matthias—"He was the greatest man I've ever known," he would often say—at St. Mary's and for the rest of his life, which is remarkable, considering that Matthias was in charge of making boys behave and that Ruth was one of the great natural misbehavers of all time. But Ruth—homely, overgrown, loud, boisterous, aggressive, probably annoying and irritating, certainly badly behaved—was graced with undeniable charm. He had it later, God knows, and he probably had the same infectious appeal when he was a boy. For all his faults, he was easy to like; and Catholic nuns and brothers have always been partial to the lovable rowdies in the back of the class, the Jimmy Breslins who raise a little ruckus now and then but who bring spirit and fire and, well, glamour to what all too often is a drab and unexciting life.

George Ruth caught Brother Matthias' attention early, and the calm, considerate attention the big man gave the young hellraiser from the waterfront struck a spark of response in the boy's soul. The spark did not seem to do much in the way of making Ruth into a polished soft-spoken gentleman, but it may have pulled some of the sharper claws and blunted a few of the more savage teeth in the gross man whom I have heard at least a half-dozen of his baseball contemporaries describe with admiring awe and wonder as "an animal."

Early in his years at St. Mary's the animal looked with his own awe and wonder at Brother Matthias as the Boss stood at one end of the yard and batted out fungoes (a fungo is tossing a ball up in the air and hitting it yourself). Matthias would hit tremendous fungoes, long towering fly balls, and he would hit them swinging the bat with one hand. Ruth said, "I think I was born as a hitter the first day I ever saw him hit a baseball." In later years Matthias would work for hours with George, when both had the time, hitting the boy grounder after grounder. "I could hit the first time I picked up a bat," Ruth also said, "but Brother Matthias made me a fielder."

With Matthias in his corner, Ruth got along pretty well at St. Mary's. Leisman says the fight with Jerry DeLay was the only one he ever heard of Ruth having in the years he knew him. But Leisman also wrote that Ruth's nickname all the time he was in the school was Niggerlips, and another old St. Mary's inmate named Lawton Stenersen said, "Any time you called him that you could get yourself a fight." Stenersen, who sold tip sheets outside racetracks along the East Coast and was known professionally as Clocker Lawton, said his own nickname at St. Mary's was Scoffer, because he liked to eat. (Brendan Behan used the verb "scoff" for "eat" in *Borstal Boy*.) One day around 1930 Stenersen ran into Ruth in Madison Square Garden in New York before a fight. Ruth, recognizing him, said "Hello, Scoffer," and added quickly, "Now don't call me Niggerlips, or I'll break your arm."

Ruth was an indifferent student in the classroom, though he developed an astonishingly graceful handwriting, but in vocational training he was proficient. He is said to have learned some carpentry and even so esoteric a skill as rolling cigars, which seems a reach for a boys' school. Eventually he settled in the tailor shop working on shirts. The tailor shop was divided between the second (called the low city tailor) and the third (the high city tailor) floors of the four-story building that housed the school's laundry on its first floor. Stenersen said, "I worked alongside Ruth in the shirt factory. I was a joiner and he put the collars on. We got six cents a shirt from the Oppenheim Shirt Company." That sort of contract labor was later prohibited by law, but Ruth seemed to enjoy the work, possibly as much for the creative satisfaction it gave him as for the credit he was amassing in his school account. His widow said that one of the fascinating sights of her married life was watching her husband, when he was making $80,000 a year, carefully turning the collars of his $30 Sulka shirts by himself, and doing a perfect job.

The account money he earned in the tailor shop was important to young Ruth. With it he would buy gobs of candy at the little store and distribute it to smaller boys, particularly those who were orphans and had no relatives or friends. This apparently is not legend, for his largesse stuck in the memory of those who knew him at the Home. Leisman grew rhapsodic about his kindness. He told a story about an eight-year-old boy with the rather graphic name of Loads Clark, who burst into frightened tears one day because he had broken a window in the laundry. He was terrified by the prospect of the punishment he would receive. Ruth, sixteen at the time, calmed and soothed the younger boy and told him, "Go on, get out of here. Take it on the lam." Loads did and Ruth took the blame for the window and accepted the punishment. According to the devoted Leisman, "He made life a little more livable when life seemed unbearable." Stenersen remembered Ruth at St. Mary's as popular, unpredictable, stubborn, reckless and, above all else, generous. When they met at Madison Square Garden that day, Ruth asked him if he had seen any of the old gang around Baltimore. Stenersen answered that he had recently run across Congo Kirby and Dope Flaherty. Ruth asked how they were doing, and Stenersen told him that Flaherty was driving a moving van with his own name on it. Ruth gave Stenersen a big wink and moved on into the Garden. A couple of months later Stenersen happened to meet Flaherty again and discovered that Ruth had loaned him the money to start his moving business. It seemed in character.

Equally in character was a small disaster that occurred at one point in Ruth's career at St. Mary's. The Xaverian Brothers also ran a place in Baltimore called St. James' Home, where older boys lived while they worked at regular jobs on a trial basis. It was a probationary period for them, a tentative nosing about in the outer world. The boys had to turn over their paychecks to the brothers, who would deduct room, board, laundry and insurance fees, return a small amount for spending money and put the rest in a savings account. Ruth was given a chance at St. James', but, whatever the job was that he had been put into, the experiment failed; in a couple of months he came back through the gates of St. Mary's wearing a gray suit, a blue baseball cap and a glum expression. He was popular with the boys at the school, but as he walked unhappily down through the yard they could not resist shouting sardonically, "Welcome back, Niggerlips!"

CHAPTER 4

The Star of the School: Enter Jack Dunn

By the time he was sixteen, Ruth was tall and rangy, a smooth-muscled, broad-shouldered youth with long arms and long legs. Even in his later years, when his weight ballooned and he developed the massive paunch that became one of his trademarks, his arms and legs had the lithe, smooth muscles of the athlete rather than the bunchy muscles of the strongman. The famous "skinny" legs looked skinny only because they were supporting a beer-barrel torso. His home run swing came from coordination and total commitment as much as it did from sheer strength.

At sixteen he wore his hair cropped short, and that and his swarthy skin and pushed-in nose and wide mouth made him look rough and mean. He *was* rough, but he was the other way from mean. In the winter, when the boys were out in the yard for their recreation hour, they would run around shouting and sliding to keep warm; some of the smaller boys could not cope with the cold and would begin to shiver and cry. Ruth, for his part, did not seem to mind the freezing weather. Brother Paul found him outside in midwinter in shirtsleeves and cautioned him about catching cold. "Not me, Brother," said Ruth. "I'm too tough." On chill-ridden days he would run from one shivering younger boy to another, rubbing their hands and blowing on their fingers to help get them warm.

The winter recreation period was part of the athletic program at the school. Physical exercise was considered very important, the brothers believing as so many keepers at large institutions do that it not only enhanced good health but served to reduce the incidence of moral and social turpitude. The boys had two playing fields, the Big Yard for older boys and the Little Yard for the younger ones, joined by a small curving road. The favorite sport was baseball, which they played almost constantly from March into October, but there were also football, soccer, handball, volleyball, basketball; they ran races, had boxing and wrestling matches, and in wintertime skated and slid on the ice in the yard. In warm weather two boys would play what they called pokenins, their version of the familiar boys' game in which one player with a bat stands in front of a wall while the other pitches to him. (Rules vary, but the batter stays up until the pitcher gets him out; then they switch positions.) Ruth played it by the hour.

Baseball was, beyond all others, the preferred sport, as it was almost everywhere else in America in that era. In Baltimore hundreds of amateur and semiprofessional teams played regularly scheduled games all spring and summer and even into the fall. At St. Mary's, with its 800 boys, there were more than forty teams organized at all age levels. Ruth usually played on teams with boys three and four years older than he was. When he first came to the school, a Xaverian named Brother Herman was the director of athletics; he was probably the first to put the boy into an organized game. When Ruth was fifteen or sixteen and becoming really proficient, Brother Albin was the coach of baseball, with Brother Matthias, who was in charge of all physical activity, keeping a supervisory eye on things. Albin and Matthias organized the oldest and best players in the school into a formal league and gave the teams major league nicknames like Red Sox, White Sox, Cubs,

Giants. Albin, who was in his twenties, was a fine athlete himself and played first base for one of the school teams; Matthias kept to the sidelines and his one-armed fungo hitting.

Ruth became a star in this fast league. He was a catcher, and a lefthanded catcher at that, a baseball rarity. He usually wore the catcher's mitt, made for a righthander, on his left, or throwing, hand. After he caught the ball, he shoved the mitt under his right arm, grabbed the ball with his left hand and threw it, with great effect. In 1912, when Ruth played with the Red Sox team that won the school championship, a team photograph of the victors shows him with the catcher's mitt on his left hand. However, a more informal photo of Ruth in catching regalia, grinning down at another boy, apparently his pitcher, reveals the mitt on his right (or wrong) hand, which would have made it easier for him to throw after catching. In all likelihood he probably used the mitt on either hand, depending on the game, the opponents and his mood, as most lefthanded kids stuck with a righthanded glove have done since Abner Doubleday invented Roger Bresnahan.

But Ruth was definitely a catcher when he first came into his own as a ballplayer. Leisman wrote that he became aware of Ruth for the first time because of a baseball game. He had not been at St. Mary's a very long time when he sensed great excitement in the air.

"What's going on?" he asked.

"Number 2 dormitory is going to play Number 3," he was told— Number 2 was for boys fifteen and over, Number 3 for boys under fifteen—"and Niggerlips is going to catch for Number 3!"

Leisman was curious as to who this superman was and went over to watch the game. He describes in explicit detail the way Ruth caught with the mitt on his left hand but adds nothing more about the game itself. However, a 1912 box score from the school paper, the *Saturday Evening Star,* shows that in one game Ruth caught, played third base (another interesting position for a lefthander) and pitched. He had one of the three doubles hit in the game, one of the two triples and the only home run. He also struck out six men. He was eighteen by then, just about the biggest boy in the school and by far the best ballplayer.

Still primarily a catcher, Ruth took to pitching because he was big and lefthanded and could throw hard. One story says that it happened when Congo Kirby, the regular Red Sox pitcher, was sidelined for several days because of a disciplinary problem and George persuaded Brother Albin to let him pitch in Kirby's place. Ruth himself said that Brother Matthias made him a pitcher. He said he was catching one day when his team was being beaten unmercifully and he began laughing at his pitcher, poking rough fun at his ineptitude.

"What are you laughing at, George?" Brother Matthias asked.

Ruth, somewhat abashed, admitted that he thought the pitching was pretty funny.

Matthias looked at him deliberately for a moment or two without speaking and then said, "All right, George. You pitch."

"Me?" said Ruth. "I don't know how to pitch."

"Oh, you must know a lot about it," Matthias said quietly. "You know enough to know that your friend here isn't any good. Go ahead out there and show us how it's done."

And Ruth did and turned out to be pretty good at it, although catching and hitting continued to be his fortes. He hit tremendous home runs in St. Mary's yard and caught more often than he pitched. In an interview that appeared in *Baseball Magazine* in February 1918, the twenty-four-year-old Ruth, who was the best lefthanded pitcher in baseball but who had hit only nine home runs in his four American League seasons, said of his days at St. Mary's: "I wasn't a pitcher in those days until I was pretty nearly through my course. My main job was catching, though I also played first base and the outfield. I used to hit .450 and .500. I kept track one season and found that I made over 60 home runs. The last two years I pitched and got along pretty well, but I never lost my taste for hitting and don't ever expect to." At this point, precisely four years after he had left St. Mary's, Ruth had never been in a major league game as anything but a pitcher, except for appearances as a pinch-hitter, and not for ten seasons would he hit his famous 60 homers in one year.

In his last year of playing baseball at St. Mary's, Ruth hit a home run in almost every game he played, and when he pitched he was undefeated. His name first appeared on a sports page (aside from the school paper) on June 8, 1913, when the *Baltimore American* in a brief note reported that at St. Mary's Industrial School the St. Mary's Stars defeated the White Sox, 10–3. Both were St. Mary's teams, with the Stars being just what they sounded like: a collection of the best players in the school. There was no description of the game and no box score, but the paper did list the batteries. Button, who had been Ruth's opposing catcher in the game noted in the school paper in 1912, was the pitcher for the Stars, and Ruth was the catcher. The Baltimore papers in those days ran column after column of reports on local games between schools and amateurs and semipros, and one of the Xaverian Brothers with an eye for publicity had taken it upon himself to send in a report of the game. It served too as an advertisement for St. Mary's baseball, since a line at the end of the account said: "For games, address XYZ, St. Mary's Industrial School." Amateur ball teams were always looking for opponents.

When Ruth was not playing ball at the Home during the summer of 1913, he had permission to go outside St. Mary's on weekends to play with amateur and semipro teams. A week after the little item appeared about the game at St. Mary's, the papers noted that St. Patrick's Catholic Club expected to pitch "Roth, the speed boy" against the powerful Northwestern A.C. A year earlier, in June 1912, a pitcher named Roth worked for the Mount Washington Club of Baltimore against Mount St. Mary's College of Emmitsburg, Maryland, and had won, 4–3. He had struck out six men and got a hit himself. Now, in June 1913, St. Patrick's Roth pitched a one-hit shutout against Northwestern, struck out twelve and got two hits, one a double. A week later he lost, 4–3, although he struck out fourteen men. He pitched once more for St. Patrick's and won, 2–1, but after that "Roth" disappears from the newspaper accounts.

On Sunday, August 3, Ruth, this time with a "u," appears in the lineup of another crack club, the Bayonnes. He caught both games of a doubleheader and had three hits. Three weeks later he played left field for the Bayonnes as they crushed the Sparrows Point Marines, 18–2. He had a perfect day at bat with a walk, a single, two doubles and a home run, and a newspaper report commented, "Ruth, the Bayonne fence buster, was there with the willow." In September he caught for the Bayonnes as they won, 12–11, and he hit another home run. He was nineteen years old and beginning to earn a reputation for himself around Baltimore, at least among the Xaverian Brothers.

The Xaverians also ran Mount St. Joseph's College in Baltimore. (The numbing similarity of the names St. Mary's, Mount St. Mary's and Mount St. Joseph's contributes to the imprecision of details about Ruth's life in this period.) Mount St. Joseph's varsity baseball team played colleges such as Villanova, Manhattan, Western Maryland and Seton Hall. Its star in 1912 and 1913 was a tall righthanded pitcher named Bill Morrisette, a Baltimore boy. In 1912 Morrisette attracted attention by carrying a no-hitter into the seventh inning against Washington College of Chestertown, Maryland, and by striking out a dozen men. In the spring of 1913 he pitched a one-hitter against Western Maryland. The Xaverians at Mount St. Joseph's, particularly Brother Gilbert, the baseball coach, did a little fraternal boasting to their confreres at the Industrial School about young Morrisette. The brothers at the Home countered by talking up young George Ruth. Inevitably, according to the old stories, the brothers arranged a game between the two institutions, with Morrisette and Ruth to meet *mano a mano*.

Enter Jack Dunn. Dunn was the owner and manager of the Baltimore Orioles, then of the International League. Part of his ball club's income came, of course, from gate receipts, but another and considerable source of money was derived from the sale of his players to major league teams. Minor league clubs were independently owned, for the most part, and only a few players in the minors had strings tying them to a major league team. The major leaguers could draft players from the minors in the off-season, paying a set sum for each player so drafted, but a minor league operator could and usually did sell outstanding players for better prices before the draft got them. To assure a steady supply of talent for their teams and eventually for the big league market, shrewd operators like Dunn were constantly on the watch for good young ballplayers. The major league executives were generally willing to leave such grass-roots scouting to the minor leaguers, contenting themselves with plucking the fruit after it had ripened.

Dunn knew about Morrisette—he later signed him to a Baltimore contract—as he did about most of the good young ballplayers in the area. There was, for instance, a fine young infielder named Gerwig who played for an amateur team in Catonsville, Maryland, in 1913. He was under an Oriole contract the following spring. There was another youngster named Costello who played shortstop for Mount St. Mary's. When Costello made two errors in a game that spring, it was somberly noted in the newspapers that he was a player Jack Dunn had been interested in. A boy named Skinny McCall from the Home, who had played with Ruth on the Red Sox team that won the school championship in 1912, had had a tryout with the Orioles.

Dunn, a gregarious man and a Catholic with many friends among the clergy, certainly knew about Ruth too, although the question of how well he knew him tends to become obscured by the stories that have come down through the years. Take Joe Engel, for example. Engel was from Washington, D.C., and had attended Mount St. Mary's (the college in Emmitsburg) for a while. He was a first-rate pitcher and quit college to sign with the Washington Senators, whom he joined in 1912, when he was only nineteen. His major league career was brief, but he later gained a fair degree of fame as a scout for the Senators and as the operator of the Chattanooga Lookouts in the old Southern Association. Engel was a colorful man, an ingenious promoter (he once arranged for a girl pitcher to strike out Ruth and Lou Gehrig in an exhibition game, a story that still makes the rounds) and a fascinating raconteur. One of the stories he loved to tell concerned the time he went back to Emmitsburg one Sunday to pitch for the alumni in a commencement day game (he had the day off because Sunday baseball was not allowed in Washington then).

There was a preliminary game between the Mount St. Mary's freshmen and an "orphanage" team—St. Mary's of Baltimore. The St. Mary's pitcher caught Engel's eye, partly because of his fastball and partly because of his haircut. Ruth—he was the pitcher, of course—no longer wore his hair cropped short but instead was wearing it in the most mature hair style that he, Engel, had ever seen on a school kid. Clipped on the side, it was "roached" or waved over the forehead, in the mode highly favored by bartenders and other cool cats of the day.

Beyond the haircut, Engel was singularly impressed by the young lefthander's sidearm speed. "He really could wheel that ball in there," he said, "and, remember, I was used to seeing Walter Johnson throw. This kid was a great natural pitcher. He had everything. He must have struck out eighteen or twenty men in that game."

Later that afternoon, as Engel was pitching for the alumni, he spotted Ruth again, still in baseball uniform but now sitting with the school band banging away at a big bass drum. That night, on his way back to join the Senators, Engel ran into Dunn. Dunn was forty, twice Engel's age, but he knew and liked the flip young pitcher. In his book on Ruth, Tom Meany recreated the dialogue between the two:

"Where you been working, Slick?" asked Dunn.

"Aw, just pitching against some college kids."

"That's where you belong. See anybody that looked any good?"

"Yeah. There was some orphan asylum from Baltimore playing in the first game and they had a young lefthanded kid pitching for them who's got real stuff." Engel paused. "He can also beat hell out of a bass drum."

"You don't happen to remember his name, do you?" asked Dunn, reaching inside his coat for a pencil and an old envelope.

"I think they called him Ruth," said Engel.

Whether or not this was Dunn's first report on Ruth is impossible to determine. In any case, it is likely that Dunn came to the big game at St. Mary's in 1913 to see Ruth and Morrisette pitch. Dunn was keenly aware of the high quality of the baseball played at the Home. When, later on, Ruth was playing for Dunn's Orioles, he asked for the afternoon off after pitching and winning the morning game of a holiday doubleheader.

"Sure," said Dunn, "go ahead. What are you going to do?"

"Oh, I thought I'd go out to St. Mary's. Maybe play a little ball. Nothing much. Just an amateur game."

Dunn whooped. "Amateur?" he roared. "Hell, they're all professionals out there."

The story of the Ruth-Morrisette game, or the legend of it, had a splendid melodramatic overlay. For one thing, the boys at the Home had a classic reverse-snobbery contempt for Mount St. Joe's, "the rich school down the road," and they wanted desperately to win. For another, it was a very big event in their colorless lives. It was to be a holiday, and there would be a big crowd. Everybody at St. Mary's—the boys, the brothers, the lay members of the staff— would be there. A large body of students and faculty from Mount St. Joe's was coming, and there would be some specially invited guests, including of course, Dunn, who was a particular celebrity to the boys because of his position as owner and manager of the Orioles. St. Mary's looked forward to the big day as though it were Christmas.

Then one morning a stunning report raced through the dormitories and the classrooms and the shops and the yard. Niggerlips was gone! He had run away. He had climbed through a window during the night and vanished. Why? Who knows why? Perhaps the petty grievances of confinement had simply overwhelmed him—he was nineteen years old, remember—or maybe the opportunity of an open window was too much to resist. At any rate, he was gone.

Ordinarily the boys cheered inwardly whenever they heard that one of their number had run away, but with the big game just ahead the defection of George Ruth was a crushing blow. Classes were canceled as the brothers met to discuss the situation, but even that did not cheer the boys, who moved listlessly around the yard exchanging comments and rumors. The word was that Mr. Hennessy, the school probation officer, and Lefty High, the night watchman, had been sent to downtown Baltimore to nose around the waterfront to see if they could find George. Nothing happened all that long first day as the school waited. Nothing happened the next day or the next, until that evening, when Mr. Hennessy appeared, crossing the yard. The boys clustered around him asking questions. Hennessy nodded his head and told them yes, George was back. He had come back voluntarily, he added. The boys did not buy that, questioning cynically whether anyone who had run away would return on his own, but they were not of a mind to quibble. The big thing was that their pitcher was back. Let it go at that. Besides, Hennessy ordered them not to talk about it.

The next day George appeared in the yard during recreation period. As punishment, he had to stand by himself on the road between the Little Yard and the Big Yard during all his free time. He stood there every day for five days. Then Brother Matthias handed him his glove and a baseball and told him to get in shape for the game.

On the big day there were flags and bunting everywhere. The school buildings and the grounds and the ballfield had been swept and scrubbed and polished. The anticipated crowd was there, and, to the exultation of the boys, Ruth and St. Mary's walloped Morrisette and Mount St. Joe's, 6–0, with Ruth striking out twenty-two batters during his shutout. After the game Dunn and young Ruth went into Brother Paul's office and talked for two hours, and the following February, a couple of weeks before the Orioles were to leave for spring training, Dunn came to St. Mary's again and signed George Ruth to a professional contract.

There are some colorful variations on the theme of Dunn's signing of Ruth, most dealing with Brother Gilbert, who for years received credit in the press for being Ruth's guiding light and for calling him to Dunn's attention. But Brother Gilbert was not even at

St. Mary's (and Ruth's own praise was always for Brother Matthias). Yet Brother Gilbert did know Dunn, and the Baltimore owner may well have first heard of Ruth from him. In later years the Xaverians at St. Mary's, whenever they talked of Ruth, used to relish casting Brother Gilbert in the role of villain. One version held that Gilbert knew Dunn was very high on Morrisette and in a vain attempt to keep his own star pitcher in college and on his team for one more season touted Dunn onto Ruth. Dunn, of course, ended up with both.

A second version says that Gilbert wanted to borrow Ruth for a big game he had coming up (such casual comings and goings of college-level players were far from uncommon) but that Brother Paul of St. Mary's said no. Irritated by the refusal, Gilbert called Dunn's attention to Ruth so that St. Mary's couldn't have him either. A third version says that in the winter of 1914, six months after Dunn had signed Morrisette, he went to Mount St. Joseph's again, this time after another young pitcher, a strong, chunky left-hander named Ford Meadows. Dunn eventually did sign Meadows (and in 1915 sold him to the New York Yankees for $5000), but at the time Brother Gilbert said, "Have a heart, Jack. Leave me one pitcher. If you need a lefthander, why don't you go after that Ruth kid at St. Mary's." Gilbert then brought Dunn to the Home and introduced him to Brother Paul, Brother Matthias and Brother Albin. Dunn knew of Ruth's record, saw the rangy youngster sliding on an ice slick, was impressed with his size and coordination and, after talking at length to the brothers and the boy, signed him to a contract. This seems farfetched, but Roger Pippen, for many years sports editor of the *Baltimore News-Post* and a young sports-writer in 1914, always insisted that Dunn told him he had never seen Ruth play baseball until he went to spring training with the Orioles. Ruth said in an autobiographical sketch written in the 1920s that "Dunn took me out to the Yard and had me pitch to him for half an hour."

The various strings of the legend come together in February 1914, when Dunn went out to St. Mary's on a cold, snowy Saturday, St.

Valentine's Day, just a week after Ruth's twentieth birthday. Even though Ruth's father was alive and running a tavern in Baltimore, the Xaverians had full responsibility for the boy's affairs. Brother Paul, as superintendent of the school, was his legal guardian and would remain so until his twenty-first birthday. It was agreed to "parole" George in Dunn's custody—Dunn was widely respected as a fair and decent man—and let the boy have a chance at professional baseball. If he failed with the Orioles, well, there would be time then to set him to making shirts.

Dunn signed the boy to a contract that would pay $600 for the season, or $100 a month. When he and Ruth came out of Brother Paul's office after the signing, a group of youngsters who had been waiting outside chanted in unison, "There goes our ball club!" The next day the *Baltimore Sun* reported, "The Oriole magnate signed another local player yesterday. The new Bird is George H. Ruth, a pitcher who played with teams out the Frederick Road. Ruth is six feet tall and fanned 22 men in an amateur game last season. He is regarded as a very hard hitter, so Dunn will try him out down south."

Ruth remained at the Home for two more weeks. Then, on Friday, February 27, three days before the Orioles were to leave for the south, the notation was made on Ruth's page in the school ledger: "He is going to join the Balt. Baseball Team," although first George would catch the streetcar on Wilkens Avenue and go downtown to spend the weekend with his father. He said goodbye to his friends and to the brothers, shook hands all around, heard Brother Matthias say quietly, "You'll make it, George," and left.

He was free. After all those years he was finally out of the cage, and nobody was ever going to get him into one again.

CHAPTER 5

First Spring Training:
Home Run in Fayetteville

Jack Dunn was an entrepreneur, an operator. A congenial man who liked people and enjoyed the bits and pieces of life—he kept field dogs and would travel as far as Tennessee for a field trial—he was nonetheless perfectly at home in the jungle world of baseball. He had broken into the major leagues in 1897 as a twenty-five-year-old pitcher for the Brooklyn Trolley Dodgers—Brooklyn had, or seemed to have, more trolley cars than any other town in the world—and he had learned the nuances of running a ball club from two masters of the art, Ned Hanlon and John McGraw.

Ned Hanlon, five years older than Connie Mack and winner of five pennants before Connie ever won one, had become manager of the Baltimore Orioles in 1892, when they were a last-place team in a twelve-team league. He moved them up a few notches in 1893 and then led them to three straight pennants and two strong second-place finishes in the next five years. These were the famous Baltimore Orioles of baseball legend, the "old Orioles" of John McGraw, Wilbert Robinson and Willie Keeler. In 1899 Hanlon left Baltimore for Brooklyn, thoughtfully taking along several of his best players, and won back-to-back pennants in his first two seasons with the Dodgers. His teams became known as the Superbas. (Hanlon's

Superbas were a popular vaudeville act, and baseball writers are quick to pick up things like that.) Dunn, who had been a run-of-the-mill pitcher with the run-of-the-mill Dodgers before Hanlon, blossomed into a 23-game winner with the Superbas in their first pennant-winning season; but the next year, 1900, something hit Jack—age or a sore arm—and he was through as a star. Hanlon traded him to the Philadelphia Phillies in mid-season, and early in 1901 the Phillies let him go.

Dunn then caught on with Baltimore, although this becomes increasingly complex. John McGraw had succeeded Hanlon as manager of the depleted Orioles in 1899. In 1900, as the National League reduced itself from twelve teams to eight, McGraw shifted his Baltimore club into Ban Johnson's newly formed American League, which was challenging the established National. Dunn, finished as a pitcher, had always been a pretty good hitter, and under McGraw he made himself useful playing third base, shortstop, second base and the outfield. In June 1902 McGraw left Baltimore and jumped back to the National League, this time to New York, where he became manager of the Giants. (The moribund Orioles followed him to New York a year later, the franchise becoming the New York Highlanders, who in time were renamed the New York Yankees, who were made famous by Baltimore's Ruth. How beautifully circuitous is history.) With him, McGraw brought several of his Baltimore players, including Dunn, who on the Giants served as utility man and elder statesman. In 1905 Jack left McGraw and the Giants to become playing manager of the Providence Grays in the International League. A manager in those days pretty much ran the entire ball club and was a figure of some importance. A man could make money running a ball club, even in the minors, and Jack Dunn did.

Meanwhile, Hanlon, unhappy that his beloved Baltimore was now entirely without professional baseball less than a decade after his Orioles had been the scourge of the game, bought the International League's Montreal franchise and transferred it to Baltimore. He continued to manage in the major leagues with Brooklyn and later Cincinnati while acting as absentee owner of the minor league Orioles; but his managerial hand had lost its magic touch, and in 1907, after several seasons of increasingly diminished success, he left big league baseball for good. In 1909 he went a step further and sold the Baltimore club to Dunn.

Dunn had five years of relative bliss in Baltimore. Then late in 1913 things changed radically. A group of wealthy men organized a third major league, an "outlaw" operation as far as Organized Baseball was concerned. This was the Federal League, which managed to survive for two full seasons. The newcomers established franchises and began raiding the established major leagues for ballplayers. One of its franchises was placed in Baltimore, where its principal stockholder was Hanlon, now nearly sixty and a highly respected citizen of that city. Dunn and his Orioles were still well liked, but the combination of major league baseball and Hanlon was irresistible. Baltimore fell in love with the Federals. Newspapers were heavy with stories and pictures of the Terrapins, as the team was named, and articles urged Baltimoreans to support their new major league club. When the Terrapins announced that they had persuaded Otto Knabe, a star National League second baseman, to sign on as playing manager, the town was ecstatic and the excitement became contagious. At the Maryland Theatre early in 1914 the acting team of George Moore and Gertrude Vanderbilt was on stage. In mock anger Moore told Miss Vanderbilt to leave. She said coyly, "If I do, I'll go join the Federal League." The audience burst into applause. When it died down, Moore said, "Maybe Otto Knabe won't sign you." At the mention of Knabe's name there was another explosion of applause, and Moore turned to the audience. "Wait till you folks see Knabe around second base," he said. "Take it from me, that boy is some ballplayer." This time there was wild applause, augmented with whistles and the stamping of feet.

The Orioles were still on the sports pages but on a distinctly secondary level. Dunn tried to arouse interest by appealing to Organized Baseball to relieve International League teams of the need to submit to the annual draft of their best players, arguing that this would allow them over the years to develop stronger teams with greater appeal. His proposal was turned down. Dunn then decided he would try to combat the popularity of the Federals by signing the best players he could find, no matter what the expense. Baseball in those days was not a major-league-or-nothing prospect for a ball-player. It was a way of life, an economic endeavor. A man could spend an entire career in the minor leagues, and major league veterans who had seen their best days would come back down and play another half dozen seasons in the high minors. Dunn counted his bankroll and went after these superior fringe players. When it came time to go south for spring training in 1914, his roster was rich in experience. Of the eight men, not including pitchers, in his set lineup (there was no platooning then) five were in their thirties and a sixth was twenty-eight; all six had had major league experience. The two younger men in the lineup had played with the Orioles before, and one was in his fourth minor league season. The two best pitchers had been in the majors too. Thus it was no team of green young kids that George Ruth was joining when he came out of St. Mary's Industrial School. Jack Dunn's Orioles were seasoned pro-fessionals.

George said goodbye at St. Mary's on Friday and spent the week-end at his father's home over the saloon on Conway Street, a block from the harbor. His instructions were to report to Dunn at the Kernan Hotel on Monday afternoon; about a dozen pitchers and catchers would assemble there and leave Monday night from Union Station for the trip to Fayetteville, North Carolina, where the Orioles were going to train. Ben Egan, a big catcher who acted as Dunn's field captain, would be in charge of this advance squad. Dunn would follow a week later with the balance of the team.

The weather that weekend in Baltimore was unpleasant: freezing temperatures, overcast sky, snow scattered here and there. On Sunday it became even colder, the temperature falling into the teens. The wind picked up and it began to snow. By nightfall Baltimore was in the midst of a blizzard, part of a huge storm that struck the entire northeast. In New York winds reached 82 miles an hour, and in Baltimore, where 12 inches of snow fell, the gale blew tin roofs off sheds, shutters off houses and even the steeple off a Methodist church. Windows were shattered, fences were blown down and streets were garnished with bricks and plaster. Earth tremors, an eerie coincidence, were felt in Druid Hill Park in the northern part of the city. The storm, the worst in twenty-five years, raged through the night and did not slacken and stop until Monday morning. Baltimore looked like a war-devastated city, with train and telephone and telegraph service disrupted and snow-filled streets choked with debris.

Through this mess George Ruth made his way to the Hotel Kernan to become a professional ballplayer. Not all the players had been able to reach Baltimore, because of the storm, and Dunn had to alter his plans slightly. Ben Egan, for instance, was snowbound at his home in upstate New York, and Dunn put the squad under the command of Scout Steinmann, an ex-ballplayer who was scout, coach and general handyman around the club. Doc Fewster, the trainer, was in the party too, and so were a couple of young Baltimore newspapermen who had been assigned to cover the Orioles' camp. Of the twelve players in the group, two were catchers and the rest pitchers. Along with Ruth, there were three other young Baltimore boys: Morrisette, Allen Russell and a lefthanded pitcher the reporters took delight in calling Smoke Klingelhoefer. Dunn bustled his men over to Union Station, worrying that the effects of the storm might delay the scheduled departure from Baltimore or the anticipated connection with an Atlantic Coast Line train leaving Washington at nine. Things seemed very uncertain and no one really expected to be in Fayetteville the next morning on schedule.

But railroads did miraculous things in those days—like leaving on time and arriving on time even in the aftermath of a blizzard. The Orioles left Union Station on schedule and arrived at Fayetteville without incident at seven-thirty in the morning. For George Ruth the uneventful train ride was far more exciting than the snowstorm; it was the first time he had ever been on a train. Some of the experienced travelers in the group explained the mysteries of an upper berth to the greenhorn, including the proper use of the odd little undersized hammock that hung over the berth. With profound baseball humor they neglected to tell him it was for his clothes, to keep them from falling out of the berth during the night. "That's for pitchers, George," he was told. "It's to rest your pitching arm in while you sleep." When Ruth went to bed he tried his best to sleep with his left arm suspended in the hammock.

In Fayetteville the players were disappointed to find that it was damp and cold, the temperatures barely above freezing. As they creaked their way to the Lafayette Hotel (Ruth's pitching arm stiff from its night in the hammock) they assumed, with regret, that there would be no baseball that day. But as the morning wore on, the sun came out and the temperature climbed, and after they settled in at the Lafayette and unpacked, Steinmann took them over to the Fair Grounds and had them work out for an hour or so, just lobbing baseballs back and forth. The stiffness soon left Ruth's arm. Fresh from the spartan life of the school, he was in marvelous shape: twenty years old, 180 lean hard pounds beautifully distributed over his six feet two inches. He had exceptionally broad shoulders and long arms, and when he wheeled and threw, the ball whipped across the diamond. He began to show off a little, throwing the ball faster than he should have the first day of practice, and Steinmann told him to let up, to take it easy. In the afternoon the temperature soared to 75 and the outfield, soggy in the morning, dried out sufficiently to let the team shag fly balls. There were still puddles—Klingelhoefer splashed through a big one as he raced after a ball—but the players reveled in the sun. Steinmann had planned to follow Dunn's practice of having the players run around the horse track at the Fair Grounds at the end of the workout, but the track was still thick with mud. So Scout had them jog the mile back to the hotel instead of walking or riding back in carriages.

It was sunny and hot again the next day. Mayor John Underwood of Fayetteville, resplendent in a straw hat (in *March,* the players marveled), came by to say hello. Two more players reported to camp, and a young fellow named John Massena introduced himself to Steinmann and asked for a tryout. Massena had come south on the same train with the Orioles, but it had taken him a full day to work up enough courage to approach anyone on the ball team. He was a pitcher, he said. When he warmed up and threw a few he was not impressive, but Steinmann told him he could work out with the club for a few days. The players took batting practice and hit fungoes to the outfield. The track dried out and everyone ran a lap before heading back to the hotel. Everything was going beautifully. It had been a good two days of work.

But Thursday it rained all day. Steinmann went over to the city hall and arranged with the mayor for the use of the armory, the biggest building in Fayetteville, and the players worked out there as best they could. They were tossing baseballs back and forth when a loud jovial yell filled the place. "It's Egan!" one of the veterans said. Ben Egan, tall, cheerful, fiery, had just arrived from Baltimore, and he lifted them all with his presence. Ruth liked him at once. Egan talked to Steinmann and the newspapermen and watched the players as they worked out. He was impressed with the way Ruth threw the ball, he said.

There wasn't room enough in the armory to do much more than throw. Egan and Steinmann had a few words about that, the catcher telling the coach that somebody was going to get hurt and the coach resenting the diminution of his role, however brief, as team leader. To keep peace and to give everyone some exercise, Steinmann announced they would play handball in the afternoon. He explained the game to those who had not played it before and organized a tournament. Egan and Ensign Cottrell, one of the veteran pitchers, won. It had not been much of a day and they were restless to play baseball, but Egan was there and despite the dispute at command level morale was good. Ruth was enjoying himself.

On Friday it was still wet. Egan took three of the pitchers out back of the hotel to have a catch, but the rain started again and everyone ended up back in the armory. That afternoon some local boys appeared and introduced themselves as the Fayetteville High School varsity basketball team. Would the Orioles care to play them a game of basketball? Girls from the high school had come along too, and it was obvious that the Fayetteville boys, who were apparently adept at the relatively new game, expected to win easily over the inexperienced professionals.

Egan grinned at them. "All right," he said. "We accept the challenge." He had a conference with his team and found that Cottrell, a pitcher named Frank Jarman and a catcher named Gene Lidgate had all played the sport in college. Egan added big Ruth and Allen Russell to the lineup and sent them out on the armory floor. The game was barely a minute old when the Fayetteville boys, to their chagrin, found that the baseball players were pretty good at basketball too. Cottrell, Ruth and Lidgate were outstanding, and Fayetteville had trouble scoring until the second half, when Dave Danforth, another veteran pitcher, persuaded Egan to send him into the game. Danforth's grasp of basketball was rudimentary; he couldn't resist grabbing the high schoolers whenever one got the ball, and most of their points came as the result of his fouls. The Orioles won by the somewhat startling score of 8–6, and the *Baltimore American* solemnly reported that the winning basket came less than a minute before the final whistle. The basketball game was a lot of fun, but when it was over it was still raining, and the Orioles were beginning to wonder if they were ever going to get around to playing baseball. It was obvious that even if the sun came out on Saturday the field would be too soggy to use. And Sunday was an inviolable off-day.

But on Saturday, along with a warm sun, there was a brisk wind that dried the field like blotting paper, and the stage was set for George Ruth's first big day in professional baseball. Egan and Steinmann decided to divide the squad into two teams and play a seven-inning scrub game. Word got around and a couple of hundred townspeople came over to the Fair Grounds to watch. Steinmann called his team the Sparrows. A pitcher named Cranston pitched and a catcher named Potts caught, which seems normal enough, but otherwise the lineup was chaotic. Old Steinmann played first base; Danforth, who was lefthanded, was at second; Lidgate, the catcher, was at shortstop; and Lamotte, a pitcher, was at third base. Caporel, McKinley and Morrisette, all pitchers, were in the outfield. Egan's team, called the Buzzards, had Jarman pitching and Hurney catching, their natural positions; but Egan had himself at first base and Lefty Cottrell was at second. Ruth played shortstop, which gave the Buzzards a lefthanded double-play combination, and Russell played third base. Klingelhoefer was in left field; Pippen, the newspaperman, was in center; and Massena, the aspiring unknown, was in right. These were the dramatis personae of Ruth's first game as a professional.

The Buzzards scored a run in the first inning, and the Sparrows tied it in their half of the first. Egan hit a double with the bases loaded in the second inning that scored three runs, and Cottrell followed with a single, scoring Egan. Then, as Pippen wrote in the story of the game he wired to Baltimore that night, "The next batter made a hit that will live in the memory of all who saw it. That clouter was George Ruth, the southpaw from St. Mary's school. The ball carried so far to right field that he walked around the bases." He crossed home plate before Morrisette, of all people, picked up the ball in the cornfield that grew beyond the ballfield in deepest right.

The Fayetteville fans—those at the game and those who were told about it later—were astounded by Ruth's tremendous drive. For years they had been talking about a home run that Jim Thorpe, the Carlisle Indian, had hit when he played with the Fayetteville team in the Carolina League. Thorpe's home run, they had enjoyed telling the Baltimore players, was by far the longest ever seen at the Fair Grounds. Now, with some awe, they agreed that Ruth's homer had gone 60 feet farther than Thorpe's. The *Baltimore Sun* next day had a headline in its Sunday sports section that anticipated the future: "HOMER BY RUTH FEATURE OF GAME." And the *American,* more picturesque, said, "RUTH MAKES MIGHTY CLOUT." The date was Saturday, March 7, 1914. It was Ruth's fifth day as a professional, his first game, his second time at bat.

After five innings at shortstop Ruth pitched the last two innings, throwing hopping fastballs with an easy, sweeping delivery. The

Buzzards won, 15–9, and the sports pages commented, "This boy is the prize beauty of the rookies in camp." (The man Ruth succeeded on the mound was Massena, who had come in from right field to pitch the fourth and fifth innings. Massena gave up six runs and looked woefully inept. After the game Steinmann told him no, and that night Massena left for the north, his little adventure over but his name forever linked with that of the most flamboyantly successful figure in the history of baseball.)

Dunn came to Fayetteville the following Tuesday with the rest of the thirty-man squad, including his son, Jack, Jr. Dunn was eager to see young Ruth in action, and as he walked over to the Fair Grounds that morning with George Twombly, one of his regular outfielders, he said, "Wait until you see this kid." The players were having batting practice, and as Dunn and Twombly came around the grandstand into sight of the diamond there was the crack of bat against ball, and a long fly sailed over the outfielders' heads and fell safely. It was Ruth. Dunn chuckled happily. "What did I tell you?" he said.

He formed a team of regulars and another of second-stringers for intrasquad games, and the next day Ruth pitched several innings for the Yannigans against the Regulars. George's fastball, which tailed away from righthanded batters, was again impressive, and he struck out four men. Two days later Dunn had him pitch three innings for the Regulars against the Yannigans; he struck out four men again and gave up only two infield hits. He batted safely in both games too, although more modestly than in his debut. After Ruth finished his pitching turn in the second game, a rookie named Alvin Dove, the Yannigans' shortstop, was injured when he smashed the little finger of his left hand trying to catch a line drive and had to leave the lineup. Dunn called Ruth back into the game, this time on the Yannigan side, and had him take Dove's place at short. The next day George started at shortstop for the Yannigans, played the entire game and had three hits. A newspaperman wrote, "This youth swings at a ball in much the same manner as Joe Jackson." Jackson, later banned from baseball after the Black Sox scandal, was a free-swinging power hitter whose batting averages the four previous seasons had been .387, .408, .395 and .373; he was universally acclaimed as a "great natural hitter" and in later years it was accepted in baseball that Ruth had patterned his full, free swing after Jackson's. But at this point, March 1914, the young Ruth had never seen Jackson play.

Dove, the injured shortstop, was one of the brightest prospects in camp, and Dunn expected to keep him with the team. But his injury, a badly broken finger, was misdiagnosed as a dislocation by a doctor who came down from the grandstand to help. Dove went to his hotel room and suffered in silence for two days. Klingelhoefer happened to stop by his room on Sunday morning and found the shortstop in agony; he had a fever and his arm and hand were red and swollen. Klingelhoefer called Billy Wicks, the Orioles' secretary, and Wicks got Dove to a local hospital. Several days later he was sent home to Baltimore, where he was hospitalized for nearly a month with blood poisoning. He played no more ball that season and in midsummer instituted a claim against the Orioles because of his injury. The fact that Dove had to file a claim makes the genial Dunn seem cold and indifferent, but in another personal disaster that struck one of his ballplayers in Fayetteville that weekend he appears just the opposite. On Saturday morning, the day before the extent of Dove's condition became known, the twenty-year-old Russell received word that his mother had died in Baltimore. He had to wait ten unhappy hours before the next train north came through Fayetteville, but when he left, Dunn, who had been in camp only five days, traveled back to Baltimore with him.

Before leaving, Dunn announced the list of players he intended to keep for the regular season (ball clubs made up their minds early then), and Ruth was one of them. Dunn was effusive in his praise for the youngster. "He has all the earmarks of a great ballplayer," he said. "He hits like a fiend and he seems to be at home in any position, even though he's lefthanded. He's the most promising young ballplayer I've ever had."

If Ruth was rapidly coming to maturity as a player, he was still a gauche, overgrown boy off the field. He was continually being amazed by the marvels of the world. He awoke each morning at six—a habit left over from St. Mary's—got up, dressed, left the room, went out through the deserted hotel lobby and walked down to the railroad station to watch the trains go through. He was fascinated by their power. He would hang around the tracks until it was time for the dining room to open for breakfast, then he would hurry back in order to be the first one to sit down. He was astonished to learn that a player could sign the check for his meals and let the ball club pay for it. He ate enormously, and his appetite became a continuing joke with the club. Pippen watched him eat and said, "If I hadn't seen it, I wouldn't have believed it." Pippen and Ruth were roommates, but Ruth could never remember the writer's name. This inability to remember names became another running joke in camp and, indeed, throughout Ruth's career.

The hotel elevator entranced him. He would ride up and down it like a small boy. Dunn advanced him five dollars for pocket money, and Ruth spent most of it bribing the elevator operator to let him run the thing. He would take it to the top of the hotel and back to the bottom, stopping at each floor to open the doors and poke his head out. Once the elevator began to rise with the doors open and Ruth's head sticking out. A player in the hall shouted at him, and George pulled his head back just in time to avoid leaving it in Fayetteville.

The veteran older players were amused by him, as they would have been by any colorful rookie, but they had little to do with him. They were a fairly close-knit group and by and large were a far cry from the crude unlettered roughnecks who supposedly made up the bulk of professional ballplayers in that era. Several had been to college. Danforth later became a dentist and for years ran a successful dental supply house in Baltimore. Claude Derrick became mayor of his home town. Twombly's father was a New England paper goods manufacturer who raised pigeons as a hobby and founded and edited a magazine called *The Pigeon News,* enterprises the son later took over. Except for occasional sophomoric pranks (Twombly once rode a horse into a Fayetteville ice cream parlor, where it fell down), the Orioles were surprisingly sedate citizens. Few of them drank, even beer, and their off-field activities were mild. In Fayetteville the big thing to do at night was to see a silent movie and have an ice cream soda, although one evening several players were drawn like moths to the room of "someone's friend," a stranger passing through who happened to have a roulette wheel. They got burned a little before Dunn discovered and ended the mini-Las Vegas.

Ruth, young, raw, crude, without sophistication or social graces, had almost nothing in common with the older players. Even conversation was difficult, except for badinage that passed for humor. Egan, as Dunn's alter ego, was closer to the youngster than the others, but he was ten years older and there was no real friendship between them. Nor did he give the youngster much advice. As an old man, Egan said, "It would be pleasant to say that I developed Ruth as a pitcher, but that would be hogwash. He knew how to pitch the first day I saw him. I didn't have to tell him anything. He knew how to hold runners on base, and he knew how to work on the hitters. He was a pretty good pitcher on his own." Generally, the veteran players looked on Ruth as something apart, a guileless child. Thus his nickname, Babe, which he had acquired by the end of the second week in camp, soon after the veterans arrived. Dunnie's Babe, they called him, meaning, simply, Dunn's baby. The nickname was a common one in those days for the young and innocent. Twombly's kid brother was called Babe. The Pittsburgh Pirates' baby-faced righthander, Babe Adams, was then in his sixth season in the major leagues. "Babe" fit Dunn's prize; "George" seemed too formal for him. By the middle of the third week of training the Baltimore papers were calling him Babe Ruth, and then the fans were, and soon everybody was.

He really was an overgrown child. If he had no close relationship with any of the Orioles, he made friends easily with the Fayetteville kids who hung around the ballpark. Some of the boys had bicycles that Ruth borrowed and rode around town. One day, barreling around a corner, he missed running head-on into Dunn and Egan only by braking violently and twisting the bike to one side. He smacked into the back of a wagon and ended up on the ground, the bike draped around him, grinning at Dunn with cheerful embarrassment. Dunn looked at him sourly and said, "If you want to go back to the Home, kid, just keep riding those bicycles."

The exhibition game season began before Dunn and Russell returned from their sad journey to Baltimore. The Regulars traveled to Wilmington, North Carolina, to play the Philadelphia Phillies, who had finished second in the National League the previous season, and they upset the Phils, 7–2. The Yannigans, Ruth included, stayed home and met the Donaldson Military Academy. Ruth played shortstop, had a double and a triple and scored four runs in a 24–6 rout of the cadets. The Phils came to Fayetteville, and the Orioles beat them again. Egan, who was running the club in Dunn's absence, let Babe pitch the three middle innings. It was the boy's first full-fledged game as a professional—practice sessions and military academies don't count—and it was against a major league team. Dunn's Babe was shaky. He gave up a single to the first batter to face him, another to the next, and then walked the third to load the bases with no one out. He settled down then and got one man to pop up and the next to hit what looked like a fast double-play ball to the shortstop. But Derrick fumbled the grounder for an instant and was able to get only the force-out at second base. A run scored and a moment later a second one came in on a single. After that there were no more hits off Ruth in the three innings he worked, although he walked two more of the Phils.

Dunn came back from Baltimore the next morning and that afternoon managed the club against the Phillies, who had stayed overnight in Fayetteville. This time, batting against Morrisette and Klingelhoefer, Philadelphia ran up a 6–0 lead. Four of the runs came in the sixth inning before Dunn removed Klingelhoefer and brought Ruth in. There was a man on first and one out. On his first pitch Ruth balked, and the umpire sent the base runner to second. Egan came out to the mound and a redfaced Ruth admitted he had forgotten there was a runner on first base. Seething, he struck out the next two batters to retire the side. The Orioles rallied in the last half of the inning and scored six runs to tie the score; during the rally the three men ahead of Ruth in the batting order hit successive triples, and when Babe came to bat the Fayetteville crowd yelled for him to do the same thing. But this was major league pitching he was facing, with major league curve balls, and he struck out. On the mound, he held the Phillies to two singles and no runs in the last three innings, and when the Orioles scored in the eighth to take the game, 7-6, he was the winning pitcher. Pat Moran, then a coach with the Phils but later to win two National League pennants as a manager, said, "That Ruth is a comer. For a kid just breaking in, he's a marvel. He's a $12,000 beauty."

The rains came again and two more games with the Phils were canceled. The rain turned to snow and sleet, and it was like mid-winter all over again. It had been a miserable spring up and down the coast. The squad was due to break camp to begin a brief barn-storming tour north to Baltimore, and Dunn planned to send the Yannigans directly home from Fayetteville. But Reddy Treulieb, the groundskeeper in Baltimore, wired Dunn that the field there was unusable, so Jack kept the second-stringers with the regulars. They managed to get in two more intrasquad games before leaving camp, and Ruth almost duplicated the enormous home run he hit the first day. But Bert Daniels, playing very deep in right field, ran full tilt into the cornfield and made a diving over-the-shoulder catch of the long drive. The Fayetteville people gave the players a party that night and Mayor Underwood made a speech, and the next day the squad made its farewell appearance at the Fair Grounds. Dunn kept Ruth out of the game, which was marked by a charming bucolic scene. Jack Dunn, Jr., playing left field, turned to shoo away an intruding cow and her calf from the playing field just as Daniels hit a long fly in that direction. By the time young Dunn got back to the ball, Daniels had a home run, assisted.

The Orioles went to Wilmington to play Connie Mack's Phila-delphia Athletics, who were much the best club in baseball. They had won three pennants and three World Series in four years, and they were to win the American League pennant again that year. Dunn picked Ruth to pitch against this formidable team, partly as a test and partly because he wanted to show him off to Connie Mack. After all, Dunn was a salesman, Mack was an important buyer and Ruth was valuable merchandise. Dunn put him on display. To his immense satisfaction, the prize rookie pitched a complete game and beat the Athletics, 6-2. He gave up the remarkable total of 13 hits, but except for the third inning, when the A's scored both their runs, he was totally effective with men on base. In the fifth inning, with the score tied, the bases loaded and two men out, he induced Wally Schang, the powerful catcher, to tap back to the pitcher's box. In the sixth, with two men on and two out, he struck out Eddie Collins, who made more than 3000 hits in his career. Only Frank (Home Run) Baker hit the rookie hard; he had four hits in five at bats, and his one out was a line drive to right field.

Dunn, elated by the youngster's showing, left for Baltimore after the game to ballyhoo a return match between the two clubs the following Saturday at Orioles Park, announcing that Ruth would pitch against the Athletics again that day. The Orioles slowly followed Dunn home, moving on to Virginia, where they played a couple of minor league teams, and then boarded an overnight boat Friday for the trip up Chesapeake Bay to Baltimore. On Saturday morning, March 28, three weeks and five days after George Ruth left town almost totally unknown, Babe Ruth came home to find the newspapers calling him by his nickname, running his picture in the sports pages and urging Baltimoreans to come out and watch him play baseball.

A good-sized crowd did come to the park, although they came to see Home Run Baker as much as they did Ruth. The field was slick, and Ruth was not good. He gave up three straight doubles in the first inning and four runs in the four innings he pitched, and the Athletics won, 12-5. Home Run Baker again had four hits, including a double off Ruth. In two games against Ruth, the lefthanded-hitting Baker had five hits in seven at bats.

The Baltimore newspapermen with the club, trying to help Dunn support his claim that the Orioles were as good as a minor league team could be, solicited and received generally glowing compliments for the Orioles from the Philadelphia players. Only Baker was candid. Asked about Baltimore's pitching, he said, "I haven't seen much of their pitching except Ruth."

The abrupt letdown—the one-sided loss to the Athletics was only their second defeat of the spring—was aggravated by the Baltimore weather, which continued to be wet, cold and miserable. Games with the Athletics, the Phillies and the Yankees were rained out. When the weather cleared, the Orioles played exhibitions against local teams, including Mount St. Joseph's and Ford Meadows, the schoolboy lefthander. Ruth played in none of these games.

Dunn was saving him to pitch against the Brooklyn Dodgers at Back River Park, a racetrack east of downtown Baltimore beyond the city limits, which Dunn used on Sundays because of a city ordinance that prohibited professional ballgames in Baltimore on Sunday. Ruth pitched strongly at Back River, holding the Dodgers hitless for several innings as the Orioles opened up a big lead, and then coasting to a 10–6 victory. On his first time at bat he hit a fly ball deep to right field that was caught after a long run by Casey Stengel, the Dodgers' twenty-three-year-old right fielder. When Ruth came up again, Stengel played deeper, but Ruth hit the ball over his head anyway for a triple. Casey never forgot that.

"We had never heard of him," Casey said more than half a century later, "but that was nothing in those days. He was a good looking kid, big, rugged, had a good arm. He wore his hair parted in the middle and it came down with a couple of little spit curls on each side of his forehead. He had good stuff, a good fast ball, a fine curve—a dipsy-do that made you think a little. When he hit that long fly I was embarrassed. Me, a big leaguer, underplaying him. But no one had ever heard of him—especially as a batter. Wilbert Robinson was managing us, and he was all upset. You know what he told me when I got back to the bench? He said, 'If I was you, Stengel, and I saw a man hit a couple of those baseballs in batting practice, I wouldn't play him with such a short field.' I was burned.

The next time the kid came up, I went back 25 feet. Maybe it was 30 feet or 35 feet, but I was back there. I put my glove up to my mouth and yelled over to our center fielder, 'Hey, do you think Grapefruit'—that's what we called Robby—'do you think Grapefruit thinks I'm back far enough now?' My God, if he doesn't hit one a mile. I was young and I could run. I could fly. Believe me, I could fly. I could go and catch a ball pretty good. But this one—this one was over my head.

"We lost the game. The kid beats us pitching and he beats us batting. That's when I first saw Ruth. I would say I was impressed."

CHAPTER 6

The Young Professional: Winning with the Orioles

There were still two weeks to go before the International League season began, and Dunn kept bringing in major league teams for exhibition games in a vain effort to swing local attention back to his ball club. On the weekend before the Federal League season was to have its grand opening in Baltimore, Dunn scheduled a three-game series with John McGraw's Giants, who had won three straight National League pennants and were a big drawing card everywhere. In the first game of the three the Orioles attracted a good-sized crowd and beat the New Yorkers, 2–1. Ruth's lifelong love affair with the fans really began that afternoon. He was not in the starting lineup, did not come in to pitch, did not bat, but he appeared in the game just long enough to display the crowd-pleasing exuberance that marked so much of what he did. In the last half of the ninth inning Baltimore's first baseman took a hard-hit ground ball in the mouth that split his lip and knocked out a tooth. He had to leave the lineup, and Dunn sent Ruth in to take his place in the field. The tense game ended a few minutes later on a ground ball that was thrown to Ruth at first base for the final out. The boyish Babe, overjoyed by the realization that his team had beaten McGraw's renowned Giants, shouted with pleasure and threw the ball into the bleachers that ran along the left field foul line. The crowd loved it.

It was a wonderful day all around for the Orioles, but the exalted mood did not last long. The Giants won the next day—Ruth struck out pinch-hitting—and beat Ruth the day after that. Losing was not as galling to Dunn as the size of the crowds, particularly at the last game. That was opening day for the Terrapins, whose new ballpark was directly across the street from Dunn's field. It was lonesome that day being an Oriole. The papers were saturated with stories about the Terrapins and the Federal League and the return of big league baseball to Baltimore. The Maryland state house of delegates voted to make the day an official half holiday, and Baltimore's mayor was on hand to throw out the first ball, accompanied by the usual claque of politicians and local celebrities. Dunn knew the Terrapins would draw well, but he hoped those who could not get seats would come across the street to watch young Ruth go against the Giants. He was grievously disappointed. The Terrapins drew nearly 30,000, the Orioles barely 1500.

Dunn sent his team on a quick trip through eastern Pennsylvania to play a string of exhibition games—half were rained out—and then brought it home for a last fling with major league opposition. Ruth pitched three innings against the Braves as a tuneup, and Dunn told everyone that Babe would be the pitcher when the Orioles began their season a couple of days later. On opening day he changed his mind. It was cold and windy, and the manager chose to use the more experienced Danforth. It turned out to be a wise move; Danforth pitched a shutout.

The next day, April 22, was Ruth's day, and the weather finally changed. It was almost too good to believe. The night had been chilly and windy, the temperature still in the 40s at breakfast. But then, suddenly, beautifully, spring rolled into Baltimore. The temperature climbed into the 60s by ten o'clock, to the 70s by noon and to a blissful 83 by three in the afternoon, when the game started.

Despite the benevolent weather, Ruth was nervous and uncertain in his formal debut as a professional when he took the mound against the Buffalo Bisons. The first man to face him grounded out, but the second, Joe McCarthy, who seventeen years later was Ruth's manager with the New York Yankees, walked. Ruth let loose a wild pitch, and McCarthy trotted to second. Babe then retired the third batter, but the fourth was safe on a scratch hit, and McCarthy moved to third. The man on first stole second, and when Ruth hit the next batter the bases were loaded. The sixth man up in the inning, a righthanded batter with the mellifluous name of Roxy Roach, hit a hard ground ball toward right field that seemed certain to go through for a base hit. But Neal Ball, the Orioles' second baseman, who five years earlier with Cleveland had made the first unassisted triple play in major league history, made a superb one-hand stop and threw to first for the third out. Ruth had escaped. He was out of the inning without a run being scored, and after that he was in control all the way. He pitched a six-hitter, the Orioles won, 6–0, for their second successive shutout victory, and Babe had two singles in four at bats.

It was a splendid performance, with only one dismal fly in the ointment. On this beautiful day with their colorful, well-publicized local-boy rookie pitching in his professional debut, the Orioles drew the smallest crowd that had ever attended an International League game in Baltimore. Fewer than 200 people were in the stands. Ten times that number were across the street watching the Terrapins play.

Attendance was almost nonexistent throughout the opening home stand, but Ruth continued to be impressive, both pitching and batting. On the first of May he was absolutely heroic. He went in to pitch in the tenth inning of a tie game with Montreal, held the Canadians hitless for two innings and in the last of the eleventh hit a ball over the left fielder's head to score Egan from first base with the winning run. The next day he beat Toronto and again was overpowering at bat. The Toronto pitcher was an ex-major leaguer named Ellis Johnson. Leading 2–0 in the second inning, Johnson ran into trouble when the first two Orioles reached base. He struck out the next two men, and Ruth, batting ninth, came to bat. To

Johnson, as to Stengel a few weeks earlier, he was only a pitcher, and pitchers are not supposed to be batters you worry about. But Ruth hit the second pitch on a flat, stinging line over the shortstop's head and between the left and center fielders for a triple that drove in both runners and tied the score.

The Babe was beginning to feel like a man. He was no longer merely a promising rookie but a key member of a powerful team. The other young pitchers, including Morrisette and Klingelhoefer, had been dropped, but Ruth belonged. He and Danforth were the big men, the ones Dunn most depended on. And he was being paid now. During spring training he had been housed and fed, but like the other players he received no salary until the regular season began. Ruth's salary of $600 for the season was payable in $50 units twice a month during the six-month season. When Babe received his first pay envelope late in April, the $50 in it was the most money he had ever seen. He went out and bought himself a bicycle. Tooling around Baltimore on it, he felt richer than God.

Early in May, when it was obvious Ruth was a success, Dunn upped his salary to $1200, and in June raised it again to $1800, partly to bring it more in line with the salaries he was paying his veterans but mostly to keep Ruth from being tempted by the inevitable Federal League feelers. Ruth was becoming sophisticated now, after a fashion. He had traveled. He had been south and knew what it was like to find warm weather in winter. He had taken the overnight boat ride on the Chesapeake and the trip through Pennsylvania. He had slept on trains and lived in hotels, and he was getting to be an old hand at ordering meals from a menu.

He was still a kid, of course. There was the bicycle, for instance, and there was the day he asked Dunn for half a dozen passes to the game that afternoon.

"Who are they for?" Dunn, mildly suspicious, wanted to know.

"Some friends of mine," Ruth said airily.

Concerned about the friends (Who were they? Spongers? Gamblers? Federal League agents?), Dunn kept an eye out before the game. When Ruth arrived at the ballpark he had six boys from St.

Mary's with him, little fellows who looked like children next to the tall broad-shouldered pitcher.

"These your friends?" asked Dunn.

Ruth nodded proudly and led them to their seats.

On May 5 the Orioles left on their first road trip, and Ruth's world broadened. The trip was a watershed in his young life. It was a marathon journey that kept the Orioles on the road for twenty-nine days and took them into every one of the seven other cities in the league. It was the longest Ruth had ever been away from Baltimore, even longer than the time spent in spring training. Except for Baltimore and a glimpse of Washington, the only towns he had been in were places like Fayetteville and Scranton, but now he went from big city to big city—from Baltimore to Buffalo to Toronto to Montreal to Rochester to Newark to Providence to Jersey City. Some of these are tired and rundown communities now, but in 1914 they were vigorous metropolises, major stops on the vaudeville circuits, railroad centers back when railroads mattered, big cities with fine hotels and good restaurants. And there were side trips to New York and Boston.

For Babe, things like riding overnight on sleepers, checking in and out of hotels, tipping waiters, became routine. He was a traveler. Never mind the movie theater in Fayetteville and the boat ride on the Chesapeake. Now he saw Niagara Falls, went into Canada, savored the exotic delights of French-speaking Montreal, saw the bright lights of Manhattan. The Orioles stayed in New York when they played in Newark and Jersey City, usually at the Forrest Hotel on West 49th Street, near Broadway. One night George Twombly, the outfielder, came back to the hotel and found Ruth sitting on the curb next to a lamppost.

"What are you doing?" Twombly asked.

The boy, if twenty can be called a boy, is father to the man.

"I'm waiting for a girl."

"What girl?"

"I don't know," Ruth said, looking toward Broadway. "I'm just waiting. The boys at the reform school said if you're in New York and you want a woman, all you have to do is wait for a streetwalker to come along."

Twombly stared, undone by this lecherous innocence.

"You better get in the hotel," he said. "You better not let Dunnie catch you out here waiting for a streetwalker."

Ruth pitched and won in Buffalo, lost, 2–1, in Toronto, lost again in Montreal (where the streetcar taking the Orioles to the ballpark caught fire). He pitched badly in Rochester and was relieved in the third inning but made up for that the next afternoon by pinch-hitting and driving in the winning run. In Rochester one day he played right field and led off, the first time "Ruth, rf" ever appeared in an official box score. He had only one hit, a single in the sixth, but it was the first Oriole hit of the game and the only one they were able to get before the ninth inning. In Newark he won both games of a doubleheader. He had an 8–1 lead in the fourth inning of the first game when he weakened and gave up three runs. Dunn took him out, but the Orioles held on to win, and he received credit for the victory. Then he came back to pitch an eleven-inning 1–0 shutout in the second game.

After the Newark series (they had a day off there and Ruth and some others used it to go see the Yankees play) the team went to Providence, where Ruth gave up only one run in six and two-thirds innings of relief and hit a triple. He took another postman's holiday in Providence and went up to Boston to see the Red Sox play. On Memorial Day he played right field in the second game of a double-header and had two hits, one a triple that drove in the winning run.

His hitting, while spectacular, was inconsistent. He started off well enough with six hits in his first eighteen at bats, but after that his batting average fell off to .200. It was the long hit when it happened, or the threat of a long hit even if it did not happen, that excited those who saw him. He ignored the fashion of the times, which was to protect the plate and punch out singles. He swung from the heels. Good pitchers did not have too much trouble with him except when they were careless. Then the big swing hurt them and sent their outfielders, who played much closer to the infield than they do today, scurrying to the fences after his seeming plethora of triples.

His pitching tailed off too. He had only one complete-game victory in the eight he started between May 11 and June 7. He was knocked out of the box in the second inning in Providence, and the next day in Jersey City blew a 6–1 lead in the eighth. Like the Baltimore club, he was talented, but he had not yet put it all together.

Even so, it was a good road trip for the Orioles. They won 15 and lost eight, an admirable record, and came home a close second. But nobody in Baltimore seemed to care. Only a handful came to watch Ruth pitch the first home game after the trip. The Federal League was the center of attraction, so much so that the city showed interest in the Orioles only when rumors spread that Ruth was going to jump to the Terrapins. A Terrapin official denied the rumor, declaring that no one was trying to sign Ruth and indeed that "We have agreed not to touch any players under contract to Jack Dunn." But Ruth said in his autobiography that he was approached by the Federals and offered a $10,000 bonus and a contract at $10,000 a year. Those were startling figures, but Ruth said he did not sign because he had been warned that those who jumped to the Federals would be banned from Organized Baseball for life.

When the Federal League disbanded after the 1915 season, its players were quickly reinstated by the older major leagues. Ruth claimed that sticking with Dunn and the Orioles thus cost him about $30,000. Ernie Shore, who joined the Orioles in June after he graduated from Guilford College, said he never heard of the offer to Ruth, although he conceded it could have happened. He was approached himself, but the money offered was not enough to tempt him, not anything like $10,000.

Too, Ruth was still the legal responsibility of Brother Paul at St. Mary's, and any contract with the Federals would have required his approval. And the Terrapins, true to their word, never did sign anyone directly from Dunn's team.

After Shore joined the pitching staff, the Orioles began to move. They won three doubleheaders in four days and took over first place. Ruth, who was pitching superbly again, beat Newark, 3–2, in eleven innings in the first game of a doubleheader, and Cottrell won the second game to extend the winning streak to 13 straight. The Orioles were beginning to tear the league apart.

And drawing no one. Dunn, too smart to stay too long with a losing hand, began to look around. A group of men from Richmond, Virginia, discussed a deal in which they would pay $62,500 for a 49 per cent interest in the club—if he would transfer it from Baltimore to Richmond. Dunn let this offer get some ink in the papers and then announced he had not yet decided whether or not to accept it.

"It's up to the fans," he said. "If they want my team to stay here, they'll have to start coming to the games."

Dunn began to talk to his major league friends about some of his ballplayers with an eye to future sales. It was increasingly clear he would have to do something. If he kept losing money he would have to move or begin selling his stars to the highest bidder.

In an effort to forestall the inevitable, he went to New York and talked to Edward G. Barrow, president of the International League. The two then went for help to the National Commission, the three-man group that ran baseball before the days of a single commissioner. The three who composed the commission were Byron Bancroft (Ban) Johnson, the autocratic president of the American League; John K. Tener, the much milder president of the National League; and Garry Herrmann, the genial owner of the Cincinnati Reds. Dunn and Barrow asked the commission to stop the draft of International League players by the majors.

"I dug deep this season," Dunn told the commission, "and I gave Baltimore a team that I believe is as strong as a second-division major league team, if not stronger. I paid men like Cree, Midkiff, Derrick, Daniels, Egan and others major league salaries so that they would be satisfied to play in the International League. To keep them in line, I signed most of them for three years. That makes me personally responsible to them for their salaries for that length of time. I allowed for Federal League sentiment at the beginning of the season, but the novelty has worn off now and Baltimore is still not patronizing the Orioles. Why? Not because the Federals are better, but because the Orioles are in a so-called minor league, and a star player developed there can be taken away by draft and never be seen in Baltimore again. That's what I've been up against. I gave Baltimore a team that won 13 straight games, and on the thirteenth day I played to 150 people. And we were in first place, too."

Dunn thought the commission would eliminate the draft, and he felt it was possible that it would go even further and designate the International a third major league. He stayed in New York, waiting around the hotel where the commission was meeting. There was no decision, no announcement, and Dunn grew pessimistic. Herrmann came bustling down a corridor at one point, and a man with Dunn said, "Here comes your chance."

"Yeah," said Dunn bitterly, "my chance for more watchful waiting."

On Sunday, June 25, Barrow told the press, "There will be a third major league. Its formation will be underway in two weeks." The Baltimore papers greeted the news with headlines, and Dunn, outwardly elated, returned to his ball club. But the National Commission said nothing. In Cleveland Charles W. Somers, president of the Indians, said querulously to inquiring reporters, "I've heard nothing about a third league, and I think I would have if it was to be done. Don't take any stock in that story. It's only talk."

But, the reporters insisted, they said it would be announced in ten days.

"Who said?" asked Somers.

The reporters were not sure, but they guessed Johnson had said as much to Barrow.

Somers laughed. "If he had," he said, "don't you think those of us who have our money invested in baseball would have been consulted on such an important move?"

Two days later Johnson, back home in Chicago, said there would be no third major league in Organized Baseball that season and, he admitted, probably never.

So the third league died a-borning. The situation remained the same as far as the draft was concerned. And now Dunn was suddenly blocked on his first alternative, the move to Richmond. He met with the other International League owners at the end of June to discuss the proposed transfer and learned that because Richmond had a team in the Virginia League that league wanted a $45,000 indemnification fee for giving up the franchise. That did it. Barrow put Dunn's request to move to a vote. The money-conscious owners turned him down.

Dunn returned to Baltimore on Friday, July 3, with only one option left: selling his stars. The Orioles were at top market value. They had had ten victories in 12 games and had opened a five-game lead. Ruth's 4–1 victory in the morning game of the July 4 doubleheader gave them a record of 47 victories and 22 defeats, a .681 percentage. It proved their highwater mark of the season. Danforth lost that afternoon, Shore the next day. Ruth won a game in relief when he retired the side after coming in with the bases full and nobody out, but that was the last gasp. It was also Ruth's last appearance as a Baltimore pitcher. He had won eight games against one loss since the start of the Orioles' winning drive a month earlier, and his record for the season was 14 victories and six defeats.

Everyone was talking about what Dunn might do, of what he had to do. There were reports that the Cincinnati Reds wanted to buy some players, although a Cincinnati official who attended a game at Orioles Park claimed it was just coincidence that he was in town. It was rumored that Birdie Cree, the little center fielder Dunn had acquired from the Yankees, would be sold back to that club. Several major league clubs had expressed interest in Ruth and Shore.

Dunn ducked out of town and went to Washington, where the Boston Red Sox were playing. Joseph J. Lannin, the black-mustached owner of the Boston club, was in Washington too. Ostensibly, he had come down to see his team play the Senators, but he conferred for some time with Dunn in his hotel room. Then the

Orioles' owner went back to Baltimore and talked with the Cincinnati man. He sent a wire to New York and got a wire back.

Things began to break. On Tuesday, Cree was sold to the Yankees. On Wednesday, Twombly, the left fielder, and Derrick, the shortstop, were sold to Cincinnati. On Thursday, Ruth, Shore and Egan were sold to the Red Sox. In three days Dunn sold the heart of his superb ball club—catcher, shortstop, center fielder, left fielder, two of his three best pitchers. A week or so later he sold the third baseman and the right fielder. The Orioles slid downhill and finished the season far behind.

Although no one criticized Dunn's radical action, he was moved to defend himself anyway.

"Against overwhelming odds," he said, "I have tried to do the best I could. Organized Baseball has failed to protect me, and I cannot be expected alone to support the expensive team I brought to Baltimore in the hope of winning the International League flag. It would be nice to hear someone say, 'There's a game fellow,' but what am I going to do when the supply of long green is exhausted? It was a hard blow to me to be forced to wreck the splendid team I had, but nobody is willing to come across if I go broke."

It was unlikely Dunn would go broke now. The six players he sold in the first forty-eight hours brought in almost as much as he would have received if he had sold half his interest in the club to the Richmond group. Cree went for $8000, Twombly and Derrick for $15,000. Boston sources said the Red Sox paid between $25,000 and $30,000 for Ruth, Shore and Egan (one paper called Ruth "the $25,000 Baltimore beauty"). Baltimoreans close to Dunn said it was more like $20,000 for the three, while insisting it could have been twice that if 1914 had not been such a financially precarious year for baseball. Most big league owners were afraid to invest much money in players who might very well jump to the Federal League at the close of the season.

Dunn offered Ruth to Connie Mack before he met with Lannin, but Mack was not in a buying mood and was already making plans to get rid of the stars of his team after the season, which he eventu-

ally did with such thoroughness that the Athletics, who had won four pennants in five years, finished dead last for seven straight seasons. But Dunn failed to contact McGraw, who was definitely interested in Ruth. McGraw was furious with Dunn when he learned that his old friend had sold the colorful youngster to an American League team, which meant McGraw's National League Giants could not even gain a box-office advantage from Ruth. McGraw never forgave Dunn for that, which hurt him more than it did the Baltimore owner. A decade later Jack tried to sell the marvelous Lefty Grove to the Giants, but since McGraw would have nothing to do with Dunn, Jack sent Grove to Mack and the Athletics instead. McGraw won no more pennants; Mack, with Grove, won three in a row.

As for the Red Sox owner, Lannin was new to major league baseball—he had bought the Boston club late in 1913—and he had both the optimism of the newcomer and the freshly earned money of the successful man. Lannin had done very well in the hotel business. An active owner who stayed close to his ball club, he worked in harmony with his manager, Bill Carrigan, who had taken over in mid-season the year before. Carrigan, a playing manager, was a catcher; he understood the value of pitching and was developing a powerful staff. Ruth and Shore were the players Carrigan wanted from Baltimore. Egan was a throw-in. Dunn had asked his veteran righthand man if he wanted another crack at the major leagues and arranged with Lannin to include Egan in the transaction. Boston had three strong catchers already, including Carrigan, and Egan never appeared in a game with the Red Sox; he was traded to Cleveland almost at once. Shore said Dunn put Egan into the deal so that the catcher could keep an eye on the two young pitchers during the trip to Boston and keep them from jumping to the Federal League. Actually, Dunn assigned club secretary Billy Wicks to that task (and promised Wicks a $100 bonus if the players were safely delivered to the Red Sox), but it made it easier all around to have big Egan in the party too.

Although the deal was announced on Thursday, July 10, Ruth

and the other two did not report to Boston until Saturday. Babe played left field for the Orioles Thursday afternoon—Dunn kept him off the mound so that he would be rested and ready to pitch when he reached Boston—and he played left field again Friday afternoon after news of the sale was in all the papers. It was an anticlimax. Ruth had only one single in the two games, and the Orioles lost both of them. Friday night Babe said goodbye to Dunn, boarded a sleeper with Shore, Egan and Wicks and left for Boston and the major leagues.

Before Jack Dunn leaves this story, it should be noted that the following season he did transfer his team from Baltimore to Richmond, but after the Federal League dissolved at the end of 1915 he returned to Baltimore and ran an International League team there until his death in 1927. And did it with a vengeance. Led by fine pitchers, such as Grove and Jack Bentley, his clubs won seven consecutive International League pennants between 1918 and 1924, and Dunn died a wealthy man.

As for the Federal League (which was so directly responsible for the precipitous rise of Ruth to the majors), when it made peace with the established leagues and agreed to fold its tents, satisfactory financial arrangements were made with every owner in the outlaw league except Hanlon, whose Baltimore club was ignored in the settlement. Hanlon and his partners therefore sued Organized Baseball for triple damages under the Sherman Antitrust Act. They lost the case in Federal District Court but won on appeal to Circuit Court. Organized Baseball appealed in its turn and carried the case, known as "Federal Baseball Club of Baltimore Inc. *vs.* National League of Professional Baseball Clubs *et al.*," all the way to the United States Supreme Court. There, in 1922, the Court found for Organized Baseball by a vote of 9 to 0, and Associate Justice Oliver Wendell Holmes wrote the Court's opinion that baseball "is not interstate business in the sense of the Sherman Act." This was the famous Supreme Court decision that served as baseball's bulwark against antitrust suits and attacks on the reserve clause for the next five decades.

CHAPTER 7

Arrival in Boston: Meeting Helen

Ruth was now in the major leagues, the world he was made for. He and the others left the train at Back Bay Station in Boston that Saturday morning, walked over to a hotel to check in and then went to Lander's coffee shop for breakfast. The Babe by now was much more his naturally garrulous and gregarious self than he had been through the early months with the Orioles, and with his deep rich voice ringing out he flirted cheerfully with the pretty waitress who served them that first morning. Her name, it turned out, was Helen Woodford. She was from South Boston and was not only pretty but a nice girl too (the oldtimers who knew her stressed that, recalling perhaps some of the other ladies Ruth met from time to time). She was only sixteen, not much more than a child herself, and the youthful Ruth fell in love with her, courting her each morning thereafter over cups of coffee and platters of bacon and eggs.

Later that first day Ruth, Shore and Egan went to Fenway Park and reported to Carrigan, the Red Sox manager. The three six-footers (Short was six feet four) towered over the five-foot, nine-inch manager, but there was no question of which of the four was in control. Carrigan, a powerfully built catcher in his early thirties, had a pleasantly tough face and with it an indisputable aura of command. He was a decent well-mannered man from a quiet middle-class background, but on the ballfield he was hard and aggressive and in the dugout and clubhouse tremendously sure of himself. Among ballplayers he was known as Rough Carrigan, for the way he played. As a manager he was demanding, but he treated his players with affection and respect. He was profane, as most ball-players are, but unlike John McGraw, the prototype of the harsh, bullying leader, Carrigan never cursed a player or publicly humili-ated one. Apparently he did not have to. Shore, who had played briefly for McGraw and despised him, made a particular point of this. Even the undisciplined Ruth was impressed by his quiet author-ity. In Babe's later years in the major leagues he played under Ed Barrow, Miller Huggins, Joe McCarthy and Bill McKechnie, all of whom were eventually elected to baseball's Hall of Fame, but he always maintained that Carrigan was the best manager he ever played for. Shore went further; he said Carrigan was the best man-ager who ever lived.

Carrigan's record in baseball is unique. He became playing man-ager of the Red Sox in the middle of the 1913 season when they were in fifth place. He finished second with them in 1914, won the pennant and the World Series (in five games) in 1915, did the same thing in 1916, and then at the age of thirty-three retired from base-ball to go into banking and other businesses back home in Lewiston, Maine. A decade later he was persuaded to return to the Red Sox, who had become a miserable team that finished last nine times in eleven seasons. Carrigan managed them for three of those awful seasons, from 1927 through 1929, finished last three straight times and again retired to Maine, this time for keeps. He died there in 1969 at the age of eighty-five.

When Ruth joined Carrigan's Red Sox on July 11, 1914, the team was in sixth place, but it was two games above .500 (40 won, 38 lost) and only five and a half games behind the first-place Philadelphia Athletics. From that day until the end of the season the Red Sox won 51 games and lost only 24 and outclassed every other team in the league—except the Athletics, who did even better: 55 wins, 22 losses. When the season ended, the Athletics were eight and a half games ahead of the Red Sox, who in turn were ten and a half games ahead of the third-place team. In sum, Philadelphia and Boston were much the best teams in the league, and when Connie Mack began to get rid of his star players after that season, the Red Sox more or less automatically took over as the best team in baseball.

It would be pleasant to report that Ruth's presence was the catalyst that transformed Carrigan's sixth-place team into a winner, but the Babe was only a bit player with the Red Sox in 1914. Carrigan wasted no time in trying him out, but after using Babe twice let him sit idly on the bench. Ruth's first test came the very day he arrived in Boston; Carrigan started him that afternoon against the Cleveland Indians. The Indians were mild enough (they were in last place and destined to stay there all season), but their lineup did include Joe Jackson and Nap Lajoie. Ruth's first major league inning was notable. Jack Graney, the leadoff hitter, opened with a single and went to second on a ground-out. Jackson came to bat, the first time Ruth had ever seen him play, and singled sharply to Tris Speaker in center field. As Graney rounded third, Speaker threw toward home plate and Jackson turned first and headed for second. Graney, respecting the center fielder's famous arm (Speaker still holds the major league record for assists by an outfielder), ducked back into third. Ruth deftly cut off Speaker's peg and threw to second base to head off Jackson. Jackson stopped and retreated toward first, and when the ball was thrown there, Graney raced for home again. The first baseman hurriedly threw to Carrigan at the plate and Graney was out, with Jackson holding first. It was a remarkable play. On a solid base hit with a man in scoring position at second base, the Red Sox picked up an out and traded the runner at second for a runner at first. To top it off, Ruth picked Jackson off first base for the third out.

The Red Sox scored in the first inning, but the Indians tied the game, 1–1, in the fourth when Jackson again singled with Graney on second. This time Graney scored without incident. Aside from being the first man ever to bat against Ruth in the major leagues, the first man to get a hit off him and the first to score a run, Graney's career in baseball was otherwise notable for three widely disparate accomplishments. He was once fined $25 by his manager for letting three runs score after he dropped a fly ball with the bases loaded and two out. He was the first major leaguer ever to come to bat wearing an identifying number (in 1916 the Indians experimented briefly with such numbers on their uniform sleeves). And later, with Cleveland, he became one of baseball's pioneer play-by-play radio broadcasters.

The Red Sox scored two more runs to give Ruth a 3-1 lead, which the Babe nursed into the seventh inning. Meanwhile, he had gone to bat twice against Willie Mitchell, a wild lefthanded fastball pitcher who won 13 games for the Indians that year and was their best pitcher (he struck out more men than anyone in the league except Walter Johnson). Mitchell struck out Ruth in the second inning—Babe's first major league at bat—and got him again on a fly ball to Jackson in right field in the fourth.

In the seventh, leading 3-1, Ruth ran into difficulty. Jay Kirke led off with a single. Ray Chapman, the ill-fated Cleveland shortstop who was killed by a pitched ball six years later, followed with another single, and both runners advanced on a sacrifice. Steve O'Neill, the catcher, who batted in only 20 runs all year, hit a single off Ruth to drive in two runs and tie the score, and Mitchell, the pitcher, whose batting average was all of .086, followed with a hard line drive—luckily right to the shortstop, whose throw to first base doubled O'Neill to end the inning.

Carrigan decided that was enough for Ruth, and in Boston's half of the seventh he had Duffy Lewis pinch-hit for him. In retrospect it seems quaint that someone should have batted for the Babe, but Lewis was an established star who was on the bench with a minor injury. The lefthanded Mitchell was still pitching, and Ruth was both a lefthanded batter and a rookie. Lewis was righthanded, a veteran and a proven hitter. Ergo: Duffy. He beat out an infield hit, went to second on a wild throw and scored on Speaker's single to put the Red Sox ahead, 4-3. To protect the lead, Carrigan brought in his best pitcher, a lefthander named Hubert Leonard, variously known as Hub and Dutch. Leonard's record was 11 and three at the time, and in contrast to Ruth he smothered the Indians in the two innings he pitched: four strikeouts, a pop-up and a ground-out. Six up, six down, the game was over, the Red Sox had won, and four and a half months after leaving St. Mary's Industrial School Babe Ruth was credited with his first major league victory. (It should be noted that Ruth's six-foot, two-inch, 190-pound physique was far bigger in the context of the times than it would be today. The other eight men in Boston's starting lineup that day were typical major leaguers in 1914; they averaged five feet, nine and a half inches, and 168 pounds. Only one of them was six feet tall.)

Carrigan tested Shore, his other "$10,000 beauty" (the price tag tended to vary from day to day and from source to source), and Shore responded beautifully, beating Cleveland, 2-1, and allowing only two hits. Ruth was given his second chance against the Detroit Tigers, who were playing without Ty Cobb. Cobb had been in and out of the lineup all season because of an injury he received in a fight with a Detroit butcher with whom Mrs. Cobb had a disagreement; Ty always did enjoy a calm, reasonable discussion of the issues when he found himself at odds with someone. But even without Cobb, the Detroit batting order was formidable. Harry Heilmann, a nineteen-year-old rookie, who later won the American League batting championship four times, played center field and batted third in Cobb's place. Sam Crawford, another Hall of Famer, hit fourth, and Bobby Veach, surely one of the least remembered of the really fine hitters, batted fifth. Ruth gave up only one hit and no runs in the first three innings, but Carrigan was not impressed with his work. In the fourth, Heilmann walked, Crawford doubled, Veach tripled and Carrigan abruptly took Ruth out. The Tigers went on to win the game, and Ruth was charged with the defeat.

After that he stayed on the bench. Shore started again, and again pitched well, far more impressively than Ruth had, and as a right-hander he fit nicely into Carrigan's plans. The team's two best pitchers, Hub Leonard and Ray Collins, were both lefthanders, like

Ruth, whereas the righthanders were suspect. Rube Foster had been hurt, Hugh Bedient was erratic and Joe Wood, who had won 34 games only two seasons earlier, was still hampered by (and never would fully recover from) a sore arm. Shore moved into the starting rotation and stayed there.

Ruth was enjoying life, courting Helen, spending money as fast as he got it, but after that second start on July 16 he did not play at all for several weeks. On July 24 the Red Sox left on a road trip through what baseball then called the west—Cleveland, Chicago, St. Louis and Detroit—and Ruth did not pitch an inning. When Carrigan's starting pitchers faltered, he dug down and used nonentities like Guy Cooper and Fritz Coumbe in relief, but never Ruth. The manager made considerable use of pinch-hitters, but he did not call on Babe's bat at all. Not until August 12, after the Red Sox returned from the west, did Ruth get into a game, and that was an exhibition against the Lawrence club of the New England League. Babe pitched and won, 6–4. Three days later an umpire chased him off the Red Sox bench for excessive bench jockeying. Two days after that he pitched and won another exhibition, this time against Manchester, New Hampshire. At least he felt like part of the club again. Before those exhibition games he had not played an inning in nearly four weeks.

Shore's instant success was obviously one of the reasons for Ruth's inactivity, since he filled Carrigan's immediate need for another starting pitcher. But Ruth's efforts against Cleveland and Detroit were weak only in comparison with Shore's, and Babe's minor league record and reputation were such that it is difficult to understand why Carrigan would not use him. Of course other factors may have had a bearing too. In his autobiography Ruth said he developed a habit of curling his tongue into the corner of his mouth when he threw a curve ball. Carrigan spotted this (another story says it was Harry Hooper, the sagacious right fielder) and warned him to correct the habit. Hitters like Crawford and Veach, for example, could destroy a pitcher if they could tell when a curve ball was coming and when it was not. The story was inflated into nonsense in the grotesque film of Ruth's life; he supposedly became totally ineffective on the mound until he finally managed to stop poking out his tongue. It is probably true that Ruth did display the telltale mannerism and that Carrigan (or Hooper, or someone) told him about it. Many young pitchers telegraph pitches because of habits they are unaware of. One of the most fascinating things in spring training is watching a veteran pitching coach stun a young prospect by calling his pitches, one by one, after just a few minutes of observation. But it is hard to believe that Carrigan would have stopped using Ruth completely because of this, and neither Ruth nor Carrigan was ever quoted to that effect. Moreover, the time-tested veterans in the International League, scrambling to hang on in baseball, would certainly have noticed and taken advantage of the weakness, if it had been that serious an aberration.

The problem may have been one of behavior. Ruth was not enormously popular with the Boston players that summer. His loud, breezy, carefree ways irritated the regulars, many of whom were veterans of Boston's World Championship team of 1912. When he left Baltimore, a writer said, "His coolness under fire . . . and his casual, almost indifferent manner are bound to win the fans." Fans maybe, but teammates maybe not. Decades later, ballplayers called that casual, almost indifferent approach to the game—making plays look terribly easy, maybe even slightly boring—"nonchalanting it." Kids used to call it showing off, and maybe they still do. To major leaguers a showoff is a "hot dog." Ruth was the 1914 equivalent of a hot dog, and the veteran players resented him. He wanted to take batting practice every day, which appalled the regulars. Not only was Ruth a rookie, he was a pitcher! Who did he think he was, trying to take batting practice? They told him to stay away. He persisted and now and then got into the cage for a few swings. They retaliated by sawing off the handles of his bats. He angered Joe Wood, the hero of 1912. One day during practice a ball got away from Wood and rolled toward Ruth. Wood called out, asking Ruth to stop the ball and toss it back. Like the big kid he was, Ruth bowed his legs comically and let the ball roll through them and on.

Wood reacted angrily, Ruth flared up and Carrigan had to quiet things down. Wood was a close friend of Tris Speaker, the outstanding player on the team, and Tris too was cool to the Babe. Speaker and Ruth were in the American League together for fifteen seasons but never really forgot their early differences.

There was a long-range plan to send Ruth down to Providence in the International League, which may have led Carrigan to leave Ruth out of his day-by-day operation. Lannin, the Red Sox owner, bought Providence as a farm team, although his purchase was brought about in part by the Federal League presence. The International League, with a moribund franchise in Baltimore, had another clinker in Buffalo, which, like Baltimore, was being directly challenged by a local Federal League team. A complex deal was arranged in which Lannin agreed to buy Providence from a five-man group headed by Frank Navin, owner of the Detroit Tigers (the syndicate also included Hugh Jennings, the Tiger manager, and Ty Cobb). In turn the Detroit group was supposed to take over Buffalo and keep it afloat. The deal was on the fire the last two weeks of July, and the sale to Lannin was announced on the last day of the month.

The Providence team, officially the Grays and unofficially the Clamdiggers, had played well and was in the fight for the International League pennant. But as part of the July 31 deal with Navin, a star Providence lefthander named Red Oldham, who had been threatening to jump to the Federal League, was to be promoted to the Detroit Tigers as of August 15. At the same time another Providence pitcher named Bill Bailey did jump to the Federals. To placate the Providence fans, Lannin announced on August 1 that he would send a lefthanded pitcher down from the Red Sox to take Oldham's place. Ruth was the pitcher chosen, but before he could be returned to the minor leagues every club in the majors had the right to claim his contract. Lannin routinely asked for waivers on the claims. Cincinnati refused. The Reds, who had bought two players from Jack Dunn earlier, knew all about Ruth and wanted him. Lannin, stymied, tried to get Cincinnati to rally round. On August

13 Ban Johnson, the American League president, wrote to Garry Herrmann, the Reds' owner: "Under no circumstances will Boston release Pitcher Ruth to a major league club. Mr. Lannin paid an extravagant price for this young man and hopes to develop him. He is unable to give him the work at Boston and by sending him to Providence he will have an opportunity to improve the team and possibly make some money." On August 14 Lannin too wrote to Herrmann: "I have been advised by Mr. Johnson's office that you held up Pitcher Ruth. I tried to get waivers on this man in order to send him to the Providence International League club for the balance of the season, thus giving him a little experience and incidentally help out the Providence club. I've no idea of letting Ruth go as he is a very good prospect and the only reason I asked waivers on him is above explained. I have withdrawn Ruth for the present. May ask waivers on him again in a few days as we are short of pitchers at Providence. Oldham returns to the Detroit club and Bill Bailey jumped to the Federals."

Herrmann finally gave in, and Boston was free to dispatch the young pitcher to Providence. Lannin wrote to Herrmann again: "I appreciate your waiving on Pitcher Ruth. I would not consider letting go of Ruth as he is a good prospect. Just wanted to use him for balance of season at Providence in International League in order that he might get some experience and incidentally help out the Providence team, which club I also own. Thanking you for your consideration in this matter, I am yours sincerely, J. J. Lannin."

However, Carrigan said years later, "I've read many times that Ruth was sent down for more seasoning, but that's not true. He was already a finished pitcher, good enough for us or anybody else. But we were out of our pennant race, and Lannin sent Ruth down to help Providence win theirs." This seems to refute the importance of the tongue-and-curve story. On the other hand, if Carrigan felt Ruth was that good, why did he let him pitch only ten innings in six weeks, aside from the two exhibition games?

CHAPTER 8

Retreat to the Minors: Pennant in Providence

Babe was not pleased with the idea of returning to the minor leagues. For one thing, there was Helen in Boston. For another, he considered himself a major leaguer now and he hated to go back down for even a little while. However, he still got his major league salary in Providence, and it was only 40 miles from Boston. He came back frequently to see Helen, usually by train, although sometimes he hired a cab to take him the 40 miles. What the hell, it was only money. He got a chance to pitch regularly again down there too, which was important. And Providence *was* the hottest team in the International League. Baltimore, subsiding steadily since its disemboweling in July, had managed to keep a fingerhold on first place until August 15, but on that day Oldham, pitching his last game for Providence before going up to Detroit, beat the Orioles to drop them out of the lead for good. When Ruth joined the club on August 18, the Grays were second, a half game behind Rochester, setting the stage for a head-to-head confrontation between the two clubs that week in Providence and all the way down the stretch.

The Providence manager was Wild Bill Donovan, another who impressed Ruth deeply in this impressionable first year. Donovan had been an outstanding pitcher (he won 26 games and lost only four for Detroit in 1907), and Ruth used to say he learned much about the art of throwing a baseball from him. Donovan was more than pleased to have Ruth take Oldham's place, because it gave him an even better lefthander to pair with his righthanded pitching ace, the redoubtable Carl Mays. Mays, a twenty-two-year-old from the Pacific Northwest, used an underarm pitching motion, rarely seen in baseball. His style was so extreme that he often scraped the knuckles of his pitching hand on the ground as he threw. Like Ruth, Mays was a strong personality, abrasively tough where Ruth was cheerfully noisy and flamboyant, and the two did not hit it off. They were teammates for ten years on three different teams but never became friends.

When Rochester came into Providence on Thursday, August 20, to begin a four-game showdown for the league lead, Mays was Donovan's starting pitcher. Joe Lannin came from Boston and Ed Barrow from New York to watch Mays beat Rochester, 8–1, and move the Grays into first place. It rained the next day, but a double-header was set for Saturday, and Ruth pitched the first game. It was an extraordinary setting for his debut with the club, and the combination of Ruth and pennant race attracted a great crowd, more than 12,000 people overflowing the tiny park. It was by far the largest crowd ever to see a ballgame in Rhode Island. They came by trolley, "in automobiles by the dozens," in horse-drawn buggies, on bicycles. The hill that rose beyond center field was packed, and trees and electric poles overlooking the diamond dripped with fans. Gate crashers kept drifting over the fences.

The game was as spectacular as the attendance. Ruth pitched well through six innings and hit a triple, but in the seventh he gave up three runs and the Grays were behind, 4–2, when they came to bat in the last of the ninth. With one out, Ruth's catcher, Jack Onslow, who thirty-five years later managed the Chicago White Sox, hit a triple. Ruth came to bat ("lumbered" to bat, the papers said) and the crowd, remembering his earlier three-base hit, roared in anticipation. He responded with a mammoth fly ball that soared over the center fielder's head and came down among the spectators clustered around the flagpole on the hill in deep center field. Because of special ground rules in effect that day, it too was called a triple. Topsy Platt, the Providence right fielder, drove in Ruth with another triple and scored the winning run a moment later when a hard-hit ground ball glanced off the Rochester shortstop's glove. The ecstatic fans poured onto the field, crowded into the dugouts and milled around the entrance to the clubhouse. When Mays, pitching with one day's rest, won the second game to put the Grays two and a half games into the lead, their joy was complete.

Rochester won the last game of the series on Sunday, and that night the Grays left on their last big road trip of the season. In Rochester they lost their first two games to fall into second place, but in another showdown doubleheader Donovan again turned to Mays and Ruth. Mays pitched a 2–0 shutout, Ruth a 2–1 five-hitter, and Providence was in first place again.

The Grays left Rochester on an overnight steamer that took them across Lake Ontario and down the St. Lawrence River to Montreal. For the players the big news on the boat was the incident of Jimmy Duggan's cap. Duggan, a little Irishman, was the Grays' trainer, and in Rochester he had treated himself to a brand-new silk cap that had cost him, he told everyone, an entire dollar. On his way into the dining room of the steamer he hung the cap on a rack near the door. When he came out it was gone and a cheap woolen one was in its place. Duggan took the woolen one and went around the ship looking for whoever had taken his. A big man, presumably an Englishman, stopped him and said, "Ah, fellow, may I ask where you got that cap?" Duggan bristled at the tone of the Englishman's voice. "Sure you can ask," he said truculently. "Someone took my silk cap that cost me a bone and left this cheap imitation of a cap in its place." The Englishman eyed him coldly and said, "That is *my* cap. You stole it from the rack in the dining hall. I should chastise you, but it being the Sabbath, I shall desist." Duggan said, "I didn't *steal* it. Somebody took mine and I thought he left this in its place." The Englishman said he didn't believe him. Duggan exploded. "I don't care if it is the Sabbath," he said. "I'll hand you something if you call me a thief." A deckhand called the first mate, who tried to settle things. Duggan gave the mate the cap, and the mate offered it to the Englishman. The Englishman refused to take it. The mate tried to give it back to Duggan, but Duggan refused it too. The two men glared at each other, turned on their heels and left. When the ballplayers walked down the gangplank at Montreal, they noticed with glee that the deckhand was wearing the woolen cap. Jimmy's one-dollar silk one never did turn up.

In Montreal, as the team waited in front of the hotel for the carriage to take them to the ballpark, Paddy Baumann, the third baseman, climbed into an empty horse-drawn cab. The French-Canadian cabby was a few feet away, talking to another driver. Baumann picked up the reins and pretended he was driving the rig. One of the other players slapped the horse on the rump and shouted, "Gyaaah!" The startled horse bolted and began racing down the street, with Baumann straining at the reins and the cabby, shouting in French, chasing after them. Baumann finally stopped the horse and tried to turn it back toward the hotel, but by that time the cabby and an excited crowd of Canadians had surrounded the hack. Baumann spoke no French and the cabby little English. A policeman appeared, and one of the Providence players ran inside the hotel to get Donovan. The manager, an astute and courteous man, knew the cop from previous visits to the city and was able to explain things. Then he soothed the cabby's feelings with a fifty-cent tip and led Baumann safely away from the mob. The third baseman was contrite, but Donovan said he was going to fine him anyway.

"It will cost you the half dollar and a cigar," he said.

In Montreal the players were very much aware of the outbreak of war in Europe. The guns of August were barely a month old, and while newspapers in the States were heavy with pictures and reports of the fighting, for Americans it was almost like a game that people followed each day. In Montreal it was a reality. Canada was at war, and the people were totally immersed in it. There were men in uniform all over the city, guarding bridges and railroad stations and other vulnerable points. To the carefree ballplayers the hardship of war was most evident in the newspapers. In that day, before the advent of radio and television, newspapers were the source of late news, and baseball fans religiously bought the late afternoon and evening editions to get results of games played that afternoon (night ball was still twenty years into the future). But in Montreal, to the players' dismay, the press of war news kept baseball bulletins out of the evening papers and they had to wait until the morning to get the ball scores. War was indeed hell.

The Grays had a pitcher named Wallace Shultz, known as Toots. He was a Pennsylvanian, but with a name like Shultz he inevitably became a rooter for the German side in the game being played on the other side of the Atlantic, claiming finally that the Germans could beat the whole of Europe singlehanded. The other players began to call him Kaiser. One evening an infielder named Matty McIntyre, who had been reading the paper while Shultz and the others argued, lifted his head and said, "Hey, listen to this. It says here that Kaiser Wilhelm sent a message to the German ambassador in Washington, asking him to raise a force of volunteers. He says he wants either 30,000 Germans or six Irishmen, he doesn't care which." Shultz stared at McIntyre incredulously. "Is that really in the paper?" he said. "Sure," McIntyre said, "and he told the Ambassador if he can't get six Irishmen, three will do." The other players laughed. Shultz got mad and said he'd fight any three Irishmen on the club right now. "Wait until the Germans show a little class," McIntyre said, "and we'll consider your offer."

A day or so later a paper appeared with a big headline that said 75,000 Germans had been killed in France. To the players such morbid figures had no more significance than ball scores. They bought every copy they could find and began sending them to Shultz's room, one by one. They tipped maids, bellhops, porters, anyone they could find, to deliver them. They stuffed copies into Shultz's box at the front desk, and one was under his plate when he sat down to dinner. At the ballpark he found copies in his shoes and in each of his red-and-white baseball stockings. One was even wrapped around his bat.

Shultz saved every copy, tied them around a heavy brick, wrapped the whole thing in brown paper and sent it express collect to McIntyre, who had been expecting a package from home. McIntyre paid a forty-eight-cent charge for the bundle (in a day when an ordinary letter required only a one-cent stamp) and after he opened it cursed out Shultz, the express company and the world in general. "That's one win for the Germans anyway," said the rejuvenated Shultz.

Thus, the world Babe Ruth was part of in the summer of 1914.

The Grays meanwhile went into a slump, and when they left, Montreal was in second place again. Ruth almost singlehandedly kept the club in contention. In Toronto he pitched his best game of the season, a 9–0 shutout in which he gave up only one hit. In the sixth inning of that game—it was played Saturday, September 5—he hit a home run off Toronto pitcher Ellis Johnson, his first since that primeval blow into the cornfield in Fayetteville six months earlier. It was his first official home run as a professional, and it was the only one he ever hit in the minor leagues.

When the Grays returned to Providence, Babe pitched and won four games in eight days, leading the *Providence Journal* to comment, "Babe Ruth seems to have gotten in on the ground floor with the fans as a result of his baffling southpaw pitching and his ability to give the horsehide vigorous punishment with the wagon tongue." Mays wasn't too bad with the wagon tongue either (he batted nearly .300), and as pitchers he and Ruth began to whipsaw the opposition. Babe pitched on a Saturday, Mays pitched both games of a doubleheader on Sunday, Ruth pitched the first game of a doubleheader on Monday and came back with two innings of relief in the second. Mays won again on Thursday, and then Ruth went against his old Baltimore club for the first time and beat them easily. He won twice more in four days during the last week of the season, and Mays clinched the pennant with a 2–0 shutout for his 25th victory.

The season ended with a carefree game against Baltimore which the Grays, leading 22–3 after six innings, won, 23–19. Ruth played right field, batted second, walked twice, had three hits, stole two bases, scored three runs and made a superb catch in the outfield. The next day was Sunday and the Chicago Cubs came to Providence for an exhibition game. There was no Sunday baseball in Boston, New York or Philadelphia, and major league teams used their idle Sunday time to play moneymaking exhibitions. Babe pitched all the way against the Cubs and won. In the third inning he hit a ball over the fence in right field and into the upper reaches of Narragansett Bay; a boy who wanted the ball for a souvenir fell into the water trying to retrieve it. A second bizarre note: In the fifth inning, when a lefthander went in to pitch for the Cubs, the lefthanded Ruth batted righthanded and grounded out.

The American League season still had a week or so to go, and the Red Sox, well out of the pennant race, recalled Ruth. In Boston he pitched against the Yankees and won, 11–5, and had his first major league hit, a double off Leonard (King) Cole. He moved to third base on a sacrifice bunt and came in on a long fly ball to score his first major league run. A few days later against the Washington Senators he pinch-hit against Walter Johnson and struck out. On the last day of the season, in what was described as a fun game, he pitched the middle three innings (he was not involved with the decision), came to bat once and singled.

Thus ended the extraordinary rookie year of George Ruth. Fresh from a boys' school, he won 14 games by July 6 with the Baltimore Orioles and was a key factor in helping them establish a commanding lead in the International League pennant race. At Providence he won nine games and helped his new team capture the pennant he thought his earlier team, Baltimore, had in its pocket back in July. Most record books say he won 22 and lost nine with Baltimore and Providence, but a close check indicates that his International League record was 23 and eight, even though he did not pitch in the league for a seven-week stretch in mid-season. He won one game and lost one with Boston in July and won another in October. He pitched and won two exhibition games with Boston in August and won another for Providence late in September. Therefore, even though he did not pitch at all for twenty-six days between July 17 and August 11—not in the majors or the minors or in exhibitions—he won a grand total of 28 games in 1914 and lost only nine.

His batting, while weaker statistically than his pitching, showed obvious signs of its future brilliance. In 33 games with Baltimore he batted .200 but had four triples and three doubles among his 16 hits. In 12 games with Providence, he batted .300, with five triples and a home run among his 12 hits. His batting average for 45 games in the International League (34 as a pitcher, five as an outfielder and six as a pinch-hitter) was .233, but of his 28 hits, 13 were for extra bases: three doubles, nine triples, one home run. In the American League with the Red Sox he appeared in five games—four as a pitcher and one as a pinch pitcher—and had two hits, one a double, in ten at bats.

With the season over, Babe prepared to go home to Baltimore for the winter, but the thought of leaving Helen, of not seeing her again until the following April, gnawed at him. Helen too was unhappy. In the coffee shop one morning Babe suddenly said, "Hon, how about you and me getting married?" They had known each other less than three months, and much of that time Babe had been away from Boston. But Helen said yes, and a day or so later they left for Baltimore together. For Helen, it must have been an elopement. Her close-knit Catholic South Boston family simply could not have approved of their teenaged daughter casually going off to Maryland with a baseball player to get married. And if she had sought and received their approval, she would almost certainly have been married in Boston.

In Baltimore they stayed with Babe's father, and on Tuesday, October 13, went out to Ellicott City, a small town just west of the city, to get a marriage license. Because he was not yet twenty-one, Ruth got his father to write a note granting his permission. Helen gave her age as eighteen, but she was a year younger (she was seventeen in October). Ruth put down Boston as his address and Helen, for some reason, gave Galveston, Texas, as hers. The following Saturday, October 17, they were married in St. Paul's Catholic Church in Ellicott City by Father Thomas F. Dolan. It was not clear why they chose to marry in Ellicott City instead of a more conveniently located Catholic church in Baltimore. Perhaps Babe was afraid that the brothers at St. Mary's would hear of the proposed wedding and disapprove of it. This would also explain why he asked his father for permission to get married instead of Brother Paul, his legal guardian. It was a small and private ceremony. The witnesses were two St. Paul parish ladies, Maria Dolan and Marguerita Powers (Miss Dolan was probably Father Dolan's sister and perhaps his housekeeper at the rectory). The Ruth family's Protestantism could have had something to do with the selection of an out-of-city site, but the family approved of the wedding. After it they gave the bride and groom a reception at the elder Ruth's flat above the saloon on Conway Street, and the young couple lived there blissfully all winter.

A final note about the 1914 season. That was the year of the Miracle Braves, Boston's other team, the poor relatives. The Braves lost 18 of their first 22 games and were still in last place on July 4. Then they began to win. And win. And win. By September 1 they were in a tie for the lead with the New York Giants, and they went on to win the pennant by 10½ games. Then, in one of the more famous upsets in sports history, they routed the Philadelphia Athletics in four straight games in the World Series, the first time a team had ever swept the Series. It was not an upset to everybody. Before the Series Ed Barrow, hearing that a Philadelphia player had disparaged the Braves for lack of class, said, "As near as I can understand class, it means ability to do things best when under pressure. The foundation of class is consistency, and since the Braves got underway in July the team played better every time it was engaged in a so-called crucial series."

The Braves' triumph, added to past and subsequent victories by the Red Sox, emphasized Boston's paramount position in baseball. New York was the biggest city, the Giants were the most famous team and McGraw had the reputation, but Boston was the home of champions. From 1876 through 1919, Ruth's last year with the Red

Sox, Boston teams won fifteen major league pennants to New York's eight (Brooklyn doesn't count). And Boston teams won the World Series in 1903 (the first time it was played), 1912, 1914, 1915, 1916 and 1918. In the same period New York won the Series only once, in 1905. I stress this to show that Babe Ruth's Boston was an important baseball town, a city that was used to the best. Even the Boston politicians knew how important baseball was to the citizenry. They did more than make perfunctory appearances to throw out the first ball on opening day. When Fred Snodgrass of the Giants made a "derisive" gesture at a Braves pitcher (probably nothing more serious than thumbing his nose) during a tense game in September 1914, James Michael Curley, the colorful mayor of Boston, wrote a well-publicized letter to the president of the National League asking that Snodgrass be punished and that umpires Klem and Emslie be censured for not complying with the mayor's demand, made during the game, that Snodgrass be ordered off the field.

At the World Series a month later ex-Mayor John F. (Honey) Fitzgerald, John F. Kennedy's grandfather and Curley's great rival, wore a green fedora and marched to the ballpark at the head of the Royal Rooters. After the final victory, when the crowd surged around the dugout shouting for their heroes to appear, Mayor Curley regained stature by making a speech from the roof of the dugout and introducing each of the Braves' players as they came out to greet the crowd. After the players had gone back into the clubhouse, Curley stayed on the dugout roof for half an hour, leading the crowd in song. That night he was host at a formal dinner honoring the team. The guest list included the governor of Massachusetts, Cardinal O'Connell of Boston and a diplomat from Peru.

Giants walked the earth in those days. Of course, it was an election year.

CHAPTER 9

The Major Leaguer: Pennant in Boston

In February 1915 Ruth reached his twenty-first birthday. Now the years of apprenticeship were really over. He was legally a man, legally free of the last remnants of parental restraint, free from the tenuous "parole" that St. Mary's had held on him. What a difference a year had made in his life. Twelve months before he had celebrated, if that's the right word, his twentieth birthday behind the walls of the Home, a raw kid in overalls, dirt poor, untraveled, totally unsophisticated. Now, at twenty-one, he was a successful professional athlete, a teammate and friend of national heroes like Tris Speaker and Joe Wood (never mind his differences with them), a Baltimore celebrity whose picture had been in newspapers as far away as Boston. He had been to fifteen states and most of the biggest cities in the United States and Canada. He was rich; his baseball salary for six months' work was more than his father had ever cleared in a year. He was married, the pleasures of the flesh no longer a boy's furtive longings but a sanctioned activity actually approved of by the state and the church. Talk about making it; at twenty-one, before he had played a half dozen major league games, Babe Ruth must have felt that the world was his.

In March he left for spring training with the Red Sox. Carrigan

liked a late camp; most of the other teams had been working out for
a week or two before the manager and owner Lannin and a group
of pitchers and catchers entrained from Boston on Thursday, March
5, for Hot Springs, Arkansas. In Baltimore that afternoon Babe said
goodbye to Helen, his father and stepmother (the elder Ruth had
married again) and his sister Mamie and boarded a sleeper for St.
Louis. There, late Friday afternoon, he joined Carrigan and the
main Red Sox party and went on down to Arkansas. It was the
farthest he had ever been from home—although it is unlikely the
thought entered his mind—and his first major league training camp.
In later years spring training became a rich backdrop for Ruthian
exploits, but in 1915 the Hot Springs camp was wet, cold, isolated
and uneventful. The team played only intrasquad games throughout
March as Carrigan concentrated on his pitchers. Ruth was one of a
lush crop of skilled throwers, and while he pitched well in the camp
games he was distinctly a secondary member of the cast. Shore and
Foster and Leonard and Collins were the pitchers Carrigan was
relying on, although the manager was hoping that Wood, whose
arm still bothered him, would come around to something resem-
bling his 1912 form. Of the rookies, Carrigan paid more attention to
Carl Mays that spring than he did to Ruth. Mays was righthanded,
which was in his favor as it had been for Shore the summer before.
The Red Sox had two superb lefties in Leonard, whose 1.01 earned-
run average in 1914 was the lowest ever for a starting pitcher, and
Collins, who had won 20 games in each of the previous two seasons.
Carrigan did not need another lefthanded starter, and Ruth was
thus somewhat superfluous. Too, the wildness Babe was subject to,
on the mound as well as socially, tempered Carrigan's enthusiasm
for the youngster's obvious talents.

In the first days of April, after three weeks at Hot Springs, the
Red Sox broke camp and went to Memphis, Tennessee, where they
played their first exhibition games of the spring against the local
minor league club. They played minor leaguers again in Louisville,
Kentucky, and it was not until Friday, April 9, when they played
the Reds in Cincinnati, that they faced major league opposition.

After Cincinnati the Red Sox traveled east through the mountains to Richmond, Virginia, where they played Babe's old team, Jack Dunn's transplanted Orioles. The next day they were in Philadelphia for the opening day of the American League season.

Carrigan brought his players into the pennant race after playing only one big league team in spring training, and the lack of competition backfired. Except for Foster, the talented pitching staff was fitful and erratic through the first month or so of the season. Shore did well on opening day, although he lost, but he was hit hard in his next three starts. Leonard was generally ailing and unable to pitch. Collins was sadly ineffective. Wood was still on the sidelines. Mays pitched beautifully in relief in the second game of the season and again for five innings as a starter a few days later, but then he twisted his ankle, had to leave the game and was unable to pitch for almost three weeks.

One man's poison is another man's meat, and Mays's injury proved to be Ruth's opportunity. Carrigan had started Babe against Philadelphia in the third game of the season and he had looked terrible—knocked out of the box in the fourth inning. But with Mays hurt and the staff generally in a bad way, Carrigan turned to Ruth for help as a relief pitcher. Babe pitched impeccably and Carrigan let him start a second time. This time Ruth won, 9–2, in a rain-shortened seven-inning game. Ten days later—it was a rainy spring and five postponements in six days had upset the pitching rotation—he was given another chance to start, in New York against the Yankees. It turned out to be a landmark in his career. He pitched thirteen innings, and although he lost, 4–3, his performance impressed Carrigan so much that after that the manager began to use him regularly. Even so the defeat was a bitter one. Babe held a 3–2 lead into the ninth and then let the tying run score on a hit batsman, a stolen base and a base hit. In the thirteenth he gave up the winning run the same frustrating way: a single, another stolen base and the game-ending hit.

Ruth's victorious opponent was a short, chunky righthander named Jack Warhop, a veteran who had been in the majors since

1908 and who three months later, in August, was to come to the end of a career that without the presence of Babe Ruth would have been totally unmemorable. As it was, Babe came to bat against Warhop for the first time leading off the third inning and lifted a home run into the upper right field stands (the game was played at the old Polo Grounds, which the Yankees shared with their landlords, the New York Giants). It was his first major league homer, and it made quite an impression on the 5000 or so who were there that day—not so much because it was a home run but because of the way Ruth hit it.

Home runs were not common—Home Run Baker and Sam Crawford shared the American League leadership the season before with eight apiece—but even so a home run in itself was not considered a significant event, any more than a triple is today. It was a long hit, that was all. No special daily count was kept of them. The weekly batting statistics in the Sunday sports sections listed sacrifices and stolen bases along with the batting averages, but not home runs. Baker did not earn his indelible nickname because he led the league in homers four years in a row, which he did, nor even because he hit home runs in successive games in the 1911 World Series. It was the circumstances of the two World Series home runs that made Baker a public hero. The first, off Rube Marquard, broke a 1-1 tie and won the game for Philadelphia. The second, off Christy Mathewson, came in the ninth inning, ruined Matty's 1-0 shutout and eventually cost him the game. Those home runs off John McGraw's two best pitchers were electrifying, and they made Home Run Baker famous in a way his consistently superb play in the World Series never did. It was the setting and the timing that mattered, not the home run mystique that came to baseball later on.

As a matter of historical fact, baseball purists in that era were forever frowning on home runs and deploring their increasing prevalence as a sign that the game was degenerating. Henry Chadwick, the English-born sportswriter who invented the box score (and thus is the man responsible for baseball's preoccupation with statistics), looked upon baseball as he would on a slightly froward child he had reared and educated; he wrote a strong attack on the insidious home run as early as 1890. After the 1916 season—still years before Ruth became a fulltime hitter—the National League declared it would attempt to decrease the number of home runs by insisting that outfield fences be a minimum of 270 feet from home plate. This was aimed at two ballparks: the Polo Grounds, with its very short foul lines, and the Philadelphia Phillies' park, later called Baker Bowl, in which the right field wall seemingly rose about ten feet behind the second baseman. Even with the dead ball, 270 feet certainly should have been a minimum distance for a home run, but what was the National League worried about? Its 1916 home run championship was won with 12.

In sum, when Babe Ruth hit his first one, a home run was not an occasion for exploding scoreboards—or even handshakes. After all, do you ever see players shake hands with a teammate who has hit a bases-empty triple in the sixth inning of a one-sided game? But there were signs that sunny May afternoon in the Polo Grounds that the Ruthian home run was going to change things. The upper right field stands were a long way from home plate, the way baseball measured distances then, and the ease with which Ruth hit the ball way up there ("with no apparent effort," one newspaper said) was unforgettable.

A couple of days after that homer the Red Sox went west on their first extended road trip. Ruth started in Detroit and was knocked out of the box, came back with a nice bit of relief pitching in Cleveland, but in Chicago was routed in the second inning of an 11–3 loss. Wood was finally in shape again and pitching strongly, and Mays too was back in action. But despite Ruth's so-so record on the western trip, Carrigan continued to use him, partly on the strength of the thirteen-inning game against the Yankees but mostly because the Boston manager suddenly found himself short of lefthanded starters. Leonard, after a couple of appearances, was on the injured list again, and the twenty-eight-year-old Collins inexplicably continued to be an almost total bust. And the Red Sox, who had been preseason favorites to win the pennant, were still bumbling along.

The low point came in Philadelphia on May 29, when Ruth lost the morning game of a morning-afternoon doubleheader. He pitched splendidly and had a 1-0 one-hit shutout going into the ninth inning. Then he gave up two runs and lost, 2-1. His record was one victory against four defeats, and the club was below .500, far behind the White Sox and Tigers, who were in a day-by-day fight for first place. But Shore won the second game of the doubleheader that afternoon, and the Red Sox took off on a five-game winning streak. Ruth won the fifth game of the streak early in June in New York. Jack Warhop was the pitcher again, and Ruth hit a home run again, this one even longer than the first. He pitched a five-hitter and won, 7-1, and looked very impressive, so much so that an anonymous New York sportswriter was moved to soaring prose: "His name is Babe Ruth. He is built like a bale of cotton and pitches lefthanded for the Boston Red Sox. All lefthanders are peculiar and Babe is no exception, because he can also bat." New York was beginning to be aware of Babe Ruth.

The Red Sox were on a sustained winning surge—for the rest of the season they won 87 and lost only 35, a .713 percentage that was almost exactly equal to that of the 1927 Yankees, who won their pennant by 19 games. Ruth, after his shaky start, won 17 of his last 21 decisions. The Red Sox moved up in the race and by mid-July were in a fight for the pennant with Chicago and Detroit. Ruth was winning steadily, though he had a tendency to tire suddenly in late innings. In one game he blew a 9-1 lead in the eighth inning, and the Red Sox had to struggle to win out, 11-10. In another he had a 2-0 shutout with two outs in the ninth; his opponents rallied to tie the score, and in the tenth, Ruth still pitching, they scored another run to go ahead and would have had more except for an extraordinary diving catch by Speaker in center field. In the last half of the tenth Speaker reclaimed Babe's victory by driving in the winning run. It was hard for Babe to dislike Tris that afternoon.

His batting continued to attract attention, although his propensity for striking out kept Carrigan from looking upon him as a complete hitter. He was taken out for pinch-hitters several times, usually when the opposing pitcher was a lefthander. In turn, Carrigan occasionally used him as a pinch-hitter. The first time he did, early in the season, Babe doubled and was then picked off second, a rare instance of poor base running on his part. Despite the double (and occasional bright spots later on), Ruth was not a good pinch-hitter. In his career he had 13 pinch-hits in sixty-seven at bats, for a puny .193 average. Ty Cobb was as bad; his career totals are almost identical with Ruth's: Sixty-nine pinch at bats, 15 hits, a .217 average.

Nevertheless, Ruth obviously was something special as a hitter. His big flowing swing was exciting to watch. And he hit the ball so hard and so far. Late in June in Boston he hit his third home run into the distant right field bleachers at Fenway Park; only one ball had ever been hit there before. In July in St. Louis he hit his fourth and final home run of the year completely over the right field bleachers, out of the ballpark and across the street that paralleled the right field fence. It was the longest ever in St. Louis. Sid Keener, a St. Louis sportswriter who later became curator of the Baseball Museum at Cooperstown, said the ball broke a plate-glass window on the far side of the street. Ruth also hit two doubles and a single, batted in three of his team's four runs, pitched a complete game and won it, 4-3. He was becoming a phenomenon.

Much later in Ruth's career Ty Cobb argued with considerable logic that Babe's status as a pitcher in these early seasons was a significant help to his development as a home run hitter. "He could experiment at the plate," Cobb said. "He didn't have to get a piece of the ball. He didn't have to protect the plate the way a regular batter was expected to. No one cares much if a pitcher strikes out or looks bad at bat, so Ruth could take that big swing. If he missed, it didn't matter. And when he didn't miss, the ball went a long way. As time went on, he learned more and more about how to control that big swing and put the wood on the ball. By the time he became a fulltime outfielder, he was ready."

Ruth was having a marvelous time. At the very beginning of the season, when the club made its way from Richmond to Philadelphia, he stopped in Baltimore for Helen, and in Boston they set up housekeeping in an apartment hotel, living by themselves as a married couple for the first time. When he was on the road and Helen was back in Boston, he found friends. Washington was a particularly favorite town of his. There was no Sunday baseball in Washington then, and one Saturday after the game he asked Carrigan for permission to go to Baltimore to spend Sunday with his father. Carrigan said he could, as long as he was back with the team on Monday, and Ruth took off. On Monday he reported in plenty of time, and everything would have been fine, except that his father came over from Baltimore to see the game that afternoon. Mr. Ruth had a seat just behind the Boston bench and when he saw Babe warming up with the other Red Sox players before the game he shouted, "You're a fine son, George. Down in this neighborhood and don't even come to see your father." Carrigan, standing there, heard this, but all he did was look at his errant ballplayer. Babe didn't say anything. "There wasn't much for me to say," he admitted later.

Ruth's off-field behavior was a problem for Carrigan. In part it was a result of Babe's natural ebullience, but it was aggravated by his new-found affluence. When Babe signed his first Red Sox contract in July 1914, his salary, which had already been tripled during his half year in Baltimore, was doubled again by Lannin to $3500, not bad for a rookie in that day. In return Ruth agreed to a three-year contract (actually two and a half years, since it would carry from July 1914 through the end of 1916). This pleased Lannin because it meant his prize rookie was less likely to be seduced by the Federals, who were growing wary of lawsuits. They preferred to go after players who had completed a contract and were held to a club only by the infamous reserve clause, the proviso that gave a team an eternal option on a player's future services.

But Babe was happy with the contract too, because now he was rolling in money, and there was no paternalistic Dunn to make him put it in the bank. Carrigan finally had to step in and bring Ruth back to earth. "He had no idea whatsoever of money," the manager said. "You've got to remember his background—that orphan asylum and all—and that this was his first big job. He was getting $3500 and that was all the money in the world. He didn't seem to think it would ever run out. He'd buy anything and everything. So I would draw Babe's pay and give him a little every day to spend. That generally lasted about five minutes. At the end of the season I had to give him the rest of it. I calculated it wouldn't last too long, but that was the best I could do."

Carrigan had to rein in Ruth on his recreational activities too. When Babe first joined Boston, Carrigan took him aside and said, "I hear you like to step out, Babe." Ruth shrugged an embarrassed shoulder. "All right," Carrigan said, "I just want to tell you this. You play fair with me, and I'll play fair with you." Ruth promised but continued to roam. Finally, to keep a closer eye on him, Carrigan arranged for adjoining hotel rooms when they were traveling. Ruth and Heinie Wagner, a veteran infielder who functioned primarily as a coach, shared one of the rooms. Carrigan and Leonard, who was something of a wanderer too, took the other.

"There was no trouble, if that's what you mean," Carrigan protested years later. "He behaved himself." More or less, anyway. Certainly, he had a respect for Carrigan that he did not have for future bosses, but he was still constantly on the move, trying to see and experience everything, eating, drinking, spending all his money, exploring the demimonde that exists on the fringes of major league baseball.

Along with his more carefree companions, Ruth made other new friendships in 1915, one in particular that he treasured the rest of his life. On opening day in Philadelphia the Red Sox were beaten, 2–0, by a slender young lefthanded pitcher named Herb Pennock, who just missed pitching the first opening day no-hit, no-run game in major league history (Bob Feller did it in 1940) when he gave up a single with two out in the ninth inning. Ruth was greatly impressed by the performance, and when Connie Mack sold the twenty-one-year-old Pennock (he was three days younger than Ruth) to the Red Sox in mid-season, the two became close friends. Pennock was quiet, gracious and gentlemanly, but he and the boisterous, often boorish

Ruth for some reason got along together. Pennock was sent down to Providence in August—as Ruth had been a year earlier—but in time he became a key member of the Boston pitching staff. Later he and Ruth were teammates on the Yankees. The Babe was a consistent admirer of his friend's pitching ability (Pennock won 240 games in his career, won five without a defeat in the World Series and was eventually elected to the Hall of Fame), and whenever he picked an All-Star team he would usually name Pennock as the lefthanded pitcher. Ultimately he conceded that Lefty Grove was the best left-handed pitcher he had ever seen, but Pennock, he said, was the smartest.

All in all it was a rich year for him, a fruitful year. He was always a gleeful competitor, and the hectic pennant race he found the team in was the most fun he had ever had. By the end of July the Red Sox were in first place. Chicago fell behind, but the Tigers, led by the ferocious Cobb, matched Boston win for win. When the Red Sox arrived in Detroit late in August for a three-game series, they had won 15 of their last 18 games and the Tigers had won 16 of their last 19. The Tigers, still a game and a half behind despite their sustained good play, hoped to win at least two of the three games, but Shore stopped them in the first one, 1–0. Ruth started the next day and had a 1–0 shutout going into the ninth. The Tigers rallied and tied the score. Leonard replaced Ruth, and the game went into the thirteenth inning before the Red Sox finally won, 2–1. In the last game of the three, the Tigers led, 5–2, after eight innings. In the top of the ninth inning, the Red Sox scored four runs to take a 6–5 lead. The Tigers, facing virtual elimination from the pennant race if they lost this one too, tied the game, 6–6, in the last half of the ninth and won, 7–6, in the twelfth inning.

The two clubs continued to play almost identical winning base-ball. When they met again for the last time in a four-game series in Boston in September, Detroit had won 15 of 21 and had gained only half a game. In Boston a huge weekday crowd was disappointed when the Tigers won the first game, 6–1, and cut the Red Sox lead to one game. The crowd reviled Cobb all afternoon, hissing him, badgering him, throwing hard wads of paper at him. In the eighth inning, with Boston losing, 5-1, Mays, pitching in relief, threw two fastballs close to Cobb's head. After the second one Cobb flung his bat at Mays. The two players went for each other, but the umpires and several policemen, thoughtfully provided for the occasion by the city, prevented a fight. When the shouts and threats subsided, Mays pitched again and hit Ty on the wrist, and the vituperation began all over again. When the game ended, some improper Bostonians came out of the stands and tried to get at Cobb, and the police had to escort him from the field.

Perversely, the crowd the next day cheered Cobb, possibly because Boston had a reputation for having the fairest fans in baseball, possibly because the Red Sox won so easily, 7-2. The defeat put Detroit two games behind again, with the season growing short. Shore pitched against the Tigers' Harry Coveleskie in the third game. It was quite a contest. The score was 0-0 through nine, ten, eleven innings. In the twelfth the Tigers loaded the bases, with no one out, but Shore stopped them and got out of the inning. In their half of the twelfth the Red Sox filled the bases too, with one out, and Carrigan put himself in to pinch-hit against Coveleskie. He hit what should have been a double-play ball to the shortstop, but Hick Cady of the Red Sox slid hard into second base and broke up the double play. The winning run scored and the Tigers were three games behind and dying fast. Ruth finished them off in the final game, 3-2, although Foster had to relieve him with the bases loaded in the eighth. The Red Sox did not clinch the pennant officially for another ten days, but after his victory that afternoon the twenty-one-year-old Ruth knew that in his first full season in the major leagues he was on a pennant winner.

In many ways the 1915 Red Sox remained Ruth's favorite among all his teams. One reason was the manager; Carrigan was the only one of his seven big league managers that Ruth always liked and respected. For another, it was his first big league club, and he had been an integral part of it as it shook off its springtime distress, caught the leaders in the pennant race, fought all summer with

Detroit and eventually won the championship. He was no longer a newcomer, an outsider. This was his team.

It was an odd team, not very powerful at bat but exceptionally capable in pitching and fielding. The outfield was notable. Duffy Lewis in left, Speaker in center and Harry Hooper in right were astonishing fielders. (Lewis used to delight Boston crowds by running up a steep embankment in left field to cut down long fly balls with barehanded catches; the embankment became known as Duffy's Cliff.) Neither Lewis nor Hooper was a high-average hitter, but they were effective run producers—Hooper scored a lot, and Lewis, a legendary clutch hitter, drove them in. Speaker was the star of the club, the best fielder, the best hitter, the best base runner, the best throwing arm. He batted .322 in 1915 and was the only .300 hitter (except for Ruth, whose average was .315 for ninety-two at bats). Nobody on the club was a slugger—except Ruth. Of Babe's 29 hits, 15 were for extra bases. Four were home runs, and no one else on the team had more than two. Indeed, the rest of the team had a combined total of only nine. (The American League leader that season had seven; the highest team total was 31.) The Red Sox depended on singles, sacrifices, steals and the timely run batted in.

The infield was like the outfield: fine fielders, clutch hitters. Dick Hoblitzell, the first baseman, who had come from Cincinnati a year earlier at the same time Ruth and Shore had come up from Baltimore, was a good hitter with men on bases. So was Larry Gardner, unremembered today but a major leaguer for seventeen years and one of the best third baseman in the game's history. Everett Scott, a diminutive 148-pounder, was the shortstop; he had a marvelous arm and although he was a weak hitter he always seemed to be on base in the late innings of close games. Jack Barry, the shortstop of Connie Mack's old "$100,000 infield," came to the Red Sox in mid-season—Mack was continuing to sell off his stars—and solidified the defense. He had been the best shortstop in the league for years, but Carrigan asked him to play second base for Boston, and Barry proved to be superb there too. Hal Janvrin, a local Boston boy who was an adroit fielder, filled in at both second and short. Chet

Thomas and Hick Cady did most of the catching, with Carrigan filling in on occasion.

But pitching was the team's strength. That season there were ten 20-game winners in the majors, and the Red Sox had none of them—but Foster was 19–8, Shore 18–8, Ruth 18–8, Wood 15–5, Leonard 15–7, and Mays was the best relief pitcher in the league. Baseball students say that a man who wins ten games more than he loses in a season is an exceptional pitcher. The Red Sox had four plus-ten pitchers in 1915 and a fifth was plus-eight. Wood, Foster, Shore and Ruth had the four best won-lost percentages in the league. Wood had the best earned-run average; Shore was third. Leonard allowed the fewest hits per nine innings, with Ruth and Wood tied for second. Leonard had the most strikeouts per nine innings. Mays had the best record as a relief pitcher. It was a beautifully balanced staff, one of the best ever seen in the major leagues, and despite the too-short spring training and the early injuries and failures, it was masterfully handled by Carrigan. Early in July the Red Sox had to play five doubleheaders in eight days at a time when the team was still five and a half games behind. Carrigan used eight different starting pitchers in the string of doubleheaders—Mays, who pitched seven scoreless innings in relief in one of the games, could be called a ninth—and won nine of the ten games, to move to within a game of first place. No wonder Ruth, who never had to boast about his hitting, liked to let people know what a good pitcher he had been in his youth.

The team the Red Sox played in the 1915 World Series was an odd one too. The Philadelphia Phillies, the National League champions, won their first pennant that season and in the next half century were to win only once again. They were not a particularly hard-hitting club, but they had Gavvy Cravath, a muscular righthanded batter who led the National League in home runs for the third year in a row with 24, the most anyone had hit since Buck Freeman set the major league record of 25 in 1899. (No one in that neo-Rutherian era had yet dredged up Ed Williamson's fluke home run figures of 1884, which we will touch on later.) Despite the help his home run totals received from the tiny Philadelphia ballpark, Cravath was a legitimate slugger, a dangerous man at the plate. Along with home runs, he led the league in runs scored, runs batted in, total bases, bases on balls and slugging percentage. He was the key to the Phillies' attack. The pitching staff consisted of the incomparable Grover Cleveland Alexander, who won 31 games that season, and several spear carriers.

Carrigan's strategy was to stop the Phils' hitting, meaning Cravath, and hope that his club could squeeze out one win over Alexander, who would start three games and maybe four if the Series went long enough. He decided to throw righthanded pitchers at Cravath (the Phils liked to boast that they could "beat any lefty that walked"), with the exception of Leonard, who when he was in top form could stop anybody. The still somewhat erratic Ruth, despite his impressive won-lost record, did not figure in Carrigan's plans, which became evident at the tail end of the regular season in a doubleheader the Red Sox played only two days before the first game of the Series. Carrigan gave Shore, Leonard, Wood and Mays a tuneup by having them share the pitching in the first game of the doubleheader (the quartet produced a 2–0 shutout), but he let Ruth labor the full nine innings of the second game, which indicated that Babe was going to be a supernumerary in the Series.

Of course, Babe wanted to pitch against the Phils and he kept asking Carrigan when he was going to be used. But the manager stuck to his plans. He had Shore go against Alexander in the first game and lost, 3–1. Cravath did not get a hit, but he did drive in the winning run in the eighth inning. In the ninth a Philadelphia error put a man on base against Alexander, and Carrigan sent Ruth in to pinch-hit for Shore. Babe sent a high bounder to first base for the second out of the inning, and a moment later the game ended. When he got back to the bench Ruth said, "Damn it, I wish I'd have got ahold of that one." Shore, the losing pitcher, said mildly, "So do I."

That was the only action Ruth saw in the 1915 Series. Foster stopped the Phils, 2–1, the next day, and in the third game Leonard got Carrigan his win over Alexander, who was pitching with only two days' rest. The score again was 2–1. Shore came back to win the fourth game by the same 2–1 score, and Foster hung on in the fifth and final game to win, 5–4. Carrigan's strategy worked. Cravath made only two hits in the Series—one a double, the other a triple—although along with batting in the winning run in the first game he scored the only Philadelphia runs in two of their 2–1 defeats. And Alex had been beaten once.

The Red Sox were the World Champions. If the youthful Ruth was disappointed because Carrigan had not let him pitch, he was cheered by the $3780.25 check he received as a member of the winning team. It was more than his annual salary. He took it and Helen back to Baltimore for the off-season and used part of the money to set up his father in a brand-new bar at the corner of Lombard and Eutaw streets, the last place of business his wandering parent would ever have. Babe worked behind the bar that winter too.

CHAPTER 10

The Lefthanded Genius:
Best Pitcher in Baseball

The Federal League died at the end of 1915, and with its death the major league owners reverted to type and began to slash player salaries. During the two-year war, salaries had soared, particularly for star players. Now, with no place to jump to, or threaten to jump to, the players lost their only effective weapon and were more or less helpless. The demise of the Federal League meant there was a horde of ballplayers scrambling for places on the rosters of the legitimate big league teams. It was a buyer's market, and the owners wasted no time in letting the players understand that. The hitherto generous Lannin was no exception.

Ruth was not affected, because he still had a year to go on the three-season contract he signed in the summer of 1914, but Joe Wood, whose 34 victories in 1912 moved him well up in the salary scale even before the Federal League came into being, was cut so drastically that he refused to report to the Hot Springs training camp in 1916. His friend Speaker agreed to report and work out, but he too refused to sign the contract Lannin offered him. In 1914, when the Federals were throwing money like rose petals at the feet of major league stars, Lannin paid Speaker a $5000 bonus to stick with the Red Sox and gave him a two-year contract at $15,000 a year, which was very close to being the highest salary in the majors. Now, in 1916, Speaker accepted the reality that he would have to take a salary cut, which was remarkably understanding when you consider that he was the star of the World Champions, the only .300 hitter in the Boston lineup in both 1914 and 1915 and by all standards the best fielding outfielder in baseball. When he found out what the Red Sox were planning to pay him, Speaker stopped being so understanding. Lannin was offering $9000, a 60 per cent cut. Speaker said he might accept $12,000, but that was the lowest figure he could even consider. All through spring training he and the Red Sox owner sparred. Lannin, adamant, said $9000 was his top price; if Speaker wanted to play with the Red Sox, that is what he would have to sign for. Speaker continued to train but would not sign.

Despite the salary disputes the Red Sox looked very strong that spring. Even though Wood was not there and Ray Collins had gone the way of all failing ballplayers, Carrigan had a wealth of superior starting pitchers. Ruth, the erstwhile erratic rookie, was still clowning around off the field, and his gargantuan appetite had ballooned his weight to 212 pounds, but on the mound he showed every sign of maturity. Mays too looked impressive. And in Shore, Foster and Leonard he had three of the best pitchers in baseball. The rest of the lineup was solid and set. The Lewis-Speaker-Hooper outfield had been playing as a unit since 1910, and all three were in their prime. Hoblitzell at first base and Gardner at third were fixtures. Scott, a rookie at shortstop in 1914, was good enough in 1915 to make the nonpareil Barry shift to second, and behind that pair was the graceful Janvrin. Thomas and Cady were fine catchers. It was a very solid team, a little weak at bat, of course, but nonetheless the class of the league. It was a big favorite to retain the pennant.

The Speaker thing was still unsettled as the Red Sox made their way toward Boston for the opening of the season, but the players— notably Ruth—were bubbling with enthusiasm and optimism. A week before the season began they played Jack Dunn's Orioles in Baltimore, and Ruth appeared before the home folks for the first time as a major leaguer. The next day Lannin announced, almost incidentally, that he had bought an outfielder named Clarence (Tilly) Walker from the Philadelphia Athletics. That was not startling news, since hardly a day went by without someone buying a player from Connie Mack. Walker, who hit the ball hard, had been around the league for five years with Washington and St. Louis and had ended up with Mack that winter as an offshoot of the Federal League settlement. A couple of Federal League owners had been allowed to buy legitimate big league franchises. One of these was Phil Ball of St. Louis, who bought the Browns. Among his Federal League stars was Eddie Plank, who jumped from the Athletics after the 1914 season. It was agreed that Ball could keep Plank with him in St. Louis, but in return he had to give Walker to Philadelphia. Mack, who needed money, decided to sell him. Lannin's decision to buy Walker made sense, everyone agreed, because Duffy Lewis had been slightly injured that spring and it never hurt to have a little insurance. No one thought about the new outfielder as a possible replacement for Speaker—except Lannin, who had been doing some maneuvering behind the scenes.

The day after Walker's purchase the Red Sox lost to Brooklyn, 3-2, in an exhibition game; Speaker, still unsigned but in top form, got Boston its two runs with a pair of homers. Opening day was only five days away, but Bostonians were sure the disagreement between Lannin and his star outfielder would be settled by then. They were right. On the Saturday before the season opened, Lannin stunned players, fans, sportswriters and half the country by announcing he had sold Speaker to the second-division Cleveland Indians. The price was $50,000, the largest amount ever paid for one player up to that time. Two unimportant young Cleveland players also came to Boston in the deal. One of them, Sam Jones, eventually became one of the best pitchers in the American League, but no one knew anything about that in April 1916. It was Speaker for cash, and it was almost unbelievable. It was impossible for Boston to accept the news at first. The Red Sox sell Speaker! He was the big man, the hero of the team. More practically, he was the only really good hitter on a weak offensive club. The Red Sox players walked around shaking their heads. Ruth said he felt as though a rug had been pulled out from under him. What did this do to their pennant chances? Speaker was gone. Wood was gone. (Joe, who held out all season, ultimately was sent to Cleveland, where he rejoined Speaker, gave up pitching and became an outfielder; he hit .366 one season as a part-time player.) Downcast, the players muttered and grumbled.

Carrigan, as hurt as any of them by the deal, which was completely Lannin's idea, reacted the way a leader should. He gathered his team together and chewed them out in his tough no-nonsense way. "All right," he said. "We've lost Speaker. That means we're not going to score as many runs. But we're still a good team. We have the pitching. We have the fielding. And we'll hit well enough. We'll win the pennant again if you guys will just stop your goddamned moaning and get down to business." Fired up, the Red Sox opened the season by winning their first four games and six of their first eight. Ruth, now a major factor in Carrigan's strategy, pitched the opening game and won it, 2–1. In his second start he was sent against Walter Johnson, the best pitcher in American League history. Babe had pitched against Johnson once in 1915 and beat him, 4–3; now he defeated the great Walter again, 5–1.

Babe won his first four starts, the club was in first place and everything seemed to be going swimmingly. But it was not so, not really. The team was not hitting at all. It was shut out in New York and shut out again in Washington; in its first 15 games it was able to score as many as three runs only six times. Inevitably, the defeats began to come. The team slid out of the league lead as April ended, Ruth lost his first game on the first of May and the club began to stumble badly. Carrigan was most disturbed by his unsettled outfield, hitherto the team's pride. Walker was late in reporting and Carrigan put Lewis, who had recovered from his injury, in center and Chick Shorten, a rookie, in left. When Walker was ready, Carrigan put him in left. But Lewis was uncomfortable in center, so Carrigan shifted him back to left and put Shorten, a weak hitter but a capable fielder, in center. Finally he stuck Walker in center and left him there, even though the newcomer was a hitter more than he was a fielder.

For almost two months, through May and most of June, the Red Sox played sluggish .500 ball in a league that had turned upside down because of the infusion of Federal League players. The big teams—the Red Sox, Tigers and White Sox—were far behind, while the perennially weak Yankees, Indians and Senators were taking turns in first place. Speaker, playing like a man possessed, was leading the league in hitting and had lifted drab Cleveland into contention. In May, when the Indians played in Boston for the first time, a delegation of Boston fans gave Speaker a silver loving cup, partly as a gesture to their departed hero, partly as a slap at owner Lannin. The next afternoon, with Tris starring, the Indians walloped Ruth, and the Red Sox fans didn't know whether to cheer or cry. It was an unhappy spring for Boston.

The hitting picked up a little with Walker in the lineup, but then the pitching began to go bad. Something was wrong with Shore. Foster was not right. Mays pitched very little. There were fits and starts of brightness. Leonard's first three starts were shutouts, and Ruth was generally superb. Late in May he pitched a shutout against Detroit. On June 1 he beat Walter Johnson again, this time 1–0. Four days later he pitched another shutout, stopping Cleveland after the Indians had beaten Boston two days running by big scores. Speaker went 0 for 4 against him this time, which made the victory that much more satisfying, and the Babe, who was beginning to hit after a slow start, had two singles and scored a run.

He lost to Detroit a few days later, after holding a 4–1 lead in the eighth inning, but he had a perfect day at bat and even hit a home run, his first since the previous July. Three days later, in St. Louis, Carrigan had him pinch-hit with two men on base and the Red Sox behind 3–0. Ruth hit a three-run homer over the bleachers in right field to tie the score. He pitched against the Browns the next afternoon, won 5–3, had another perfect day at bat and hit another home run, his third in three games, which created a sensation. (Oddly, these three were the only home runs he hit all season.) His batting average jumped to .300, and people were remembering all over again what a powerful batter he was. The Red Sox scored fewer runs than any team in the league except the last-place Athletics, and Carrigan, talking about Ruth's home runs, wondered out loud if he ought not put the Babe in the outfield to fill some of the hitting void that Speaker had left. Carrigan was only speculating. He was essentially conservative when it came to baseball. He always put Ruth in the ninth spot in the batting order, the traditional place for a pitcher, despite Babe's obvious hitting ability, and he was not going to gamble with the man who was now his best pitcher. Indeed, Ruth was not only Boston's best, he was the best pitcher in the league that year, including Walter Johnson.

He was beginning to be something of a character too. Everyone was aware of his amazing appetite and his love of night life (though he really was not much of a drinker yet, except for beer). Now his trait of not remembering names was becoming part of the growing legend. One evening in Philadelphia he was in the hotel lobby after defeating the Athletics that afternoon, when Stuffy McInnis, the Philadelphia first baseman, came in. McInnis was from Massachusetts and he had stopped by to visit some of his old Boston friends. When he saw Ruth he walked over and said, "Babe, that was a hell of a fine game you pitched this afternoon." It was a significant compliment. McInnis had been in the league since 1909, had played on four pennant-winning teams, was, like Barry, a widely publicized member of the famous $100,000 infield and had played against Ruth frequently since Babe's debut against the Athletics in North Carolina in the spring of 1914. Ruth looked at him blandly and said, "Thanks, keed, that's very nice of you. Glad you were able to come out and watch us play." McInnis nodded dumbly and more or less staggered away. "He didn't know me," he would say in awe to people to whom he would tell the story. "He didn't even know I was a ballplayer."

Late in June things began to swing Boston's way. Foster pitched a no-hitter, Ruth and Shore followed with shutouts and Mays and

Leonard won a doubleheader to make it five straight. The beautiful pitching staff was in top form again, and with improved hitting the Red Sox began to move steadily upward. The last three months of the season were much more fun than the first three. There was a lovely fight in Washington one day after a Mays pitch hit George McBride, the Senators' veteran shortstop. McBride threw his bat, à la Cobb, and Sam Agnew, a third-string catcher Boston recently acquired, raged at McBride. Carrigan came off his bench, Clark Griffith, the Washington manager, came off his, Agnew punched Griffith, the police arrested Agnew (he had to pay $50 bail at a police station) and Ban Johnson suspended Carrigan for five days.

Cleveland and the Yankees were still wrestling for first place, but the Red Sox were coming on, winning two games for every one they lost, getting closer and closer to the top. By late July Boston was only half a game off the lead, and after they won three straight in Detroit, including a 6–0 shutout by Ruth, they moved into first place. They fell back again when they lost three games in St. Louis, but in Chicago they took three of four and regained the lead. They were a strong road club, and after this trip they had a commanding lead.

Ruth's pitching sloughed off briefly, but by mid-August he was riding high again. He beat Washington, 2–1, came back three days later to beat Johnson, 1–0, in thirteen innings, beat Cleveland, 2–1, four days after that and shut out Detroit, 3–0, in his next start. The Red Sox lead widened to six and a half games and it seemed as though they would win the pennant easily. But as September began they slumped, and Detroit and Chicago closed in for the long anticipated pennant battle among the three best teams in the league. On September 9 Ruth beat Johnson, 2–1, for his fifth in a row over the Washington star, but Detroit was only one game behind and Chicago two. On September 12 Carrigan sent Ruth against Johnson again, and Walter finally won one, 4–3, in ten innings, although Ruth, who was taken out in the ninth after losing a 2–0 lead, was not charged with the defeat.

That same day, just as the club was about to leave on its last western trip of the season, Lannin revealed that Carrigan was planning to retire at the end of the season. Whether this news upset the players is conjectural, but they lost two of their first three games in the west and fell from first to third place. Then, in that curious way baseball has, the next two days abruptly settled the pennant race. On Sunday, September 17, the Red Sox met the White Sox before more than 40,000 people, the largest crowd in the history of Chicago baseball to that time. Ruth won the game, 6–2, for his 20th victory of the season and lifted the Red Sox past Chicago into second place behind Detroit. The next day Shore defeated the White Sox again and Boston found itself back in the lead, because that afternoon the Tigers suffered an astonishing 2–0 defeat at the hands of the Athletics. To appreciate the impact of Detroit's defeat you must know that the Tigers had won 35 of their previous 50 games, a vigorous .700 pace, and had charged up from the second division into first place. The Athletics, on the other hand, were at the absolute nadir of the worst season any team has had in the modern history of major league baseball. The Mets in their abysmal 1962 season won 40 games and lost 120 for a .250 winning percentage. The 1916 Athletics won 38 games and lost 117 for a .238 percentage, which was bad enough, but on that Monday in September when they beat the Tigers their record was 30 won and 108 lost, a percentage of .217. When the Mets finished last in 1962, they were 18 games behind the next worst team, a staggering margin when you consider that a team is said to have run away with a pennant when it wins by 12 games. But the Athletics —stand back, now—finished 40½ games behind the team next above them in the standings. They had one pitcher who lost 23 games, another who lost 22, a third with a record of one and 19 and a fourth who was one and 16. And yet in the midst of a pennant race this majestically inept team beat Ty Cobb and the Tigers, the hardest-hitting team in baseball, shut them out and knocked them out of first place.

The next day the Red Sox arrived in Detroit for a three-game series, swept all three (Ruth won the final game, 10–2), and that was the end of the season, practically speaking. Boston finished its triumphant road trip by beating Speaker and the Indians three out of four. Ruth shut out Cleveland in the last game there and four days later in Boston blanked the Yankees for his ninth shutout of the season, which a half century later was still the American League record for a lefthanded pitcher. It was also his 23rd and final victory of the season.

It was a year of singular achievement for Ruth—23 wins, nine shutouts, league-leading earned-run average, the three home runs in three games, the 20th victory before the huge crowd in Chicago that started Boston on its final drive to the pennant, the thirteen-inning 1–0 defeat of Walter Johnson—but his biggest moment of the season was still to come.

The 1916 World Series matched the Red Sox with the Brooklyn Dodgers, and Ruth pitched the second game. Carrigan had passed over him for the opener, had used Ernie Shore instead and had won. That first game was played on a Saturday in Boston, and Ruth's game was to be the following Monday, since Sunday was always an off-day in staid Boston. Hugh Fullerton, the old sportswriter, wrote that the players "spent a Boston sabbath, which is considerable sabbath," and things were indeed quiet everywhere in the city except at the Brunswick Hotel, which was World Series headquarters. There, Joe Lannin saw Charlie Ebbets, the Dodgers' owner, and asked him casually if he had arranged for tickets at Ebbets Field for Boston's Royal Rooters, a considerable segment of whom were planning to travel to Brooklyn for the third and fourth games. Ebbets looked at Lannin angrily and said, "No, but I'll do it right now." He picked up a telephone and put in a long distance call to Brooklyn. When he was connected with his Ebbets Field ticket office he said loudly, "I want you to hold out some of the best reserved seats for Tuesday's game. And while you're at it, save 250 of the worst seats in the grandstand for the Boston Rooters." He hung up the phone and glared at Lannin, who stared back in stunned silence for a moment before turning and walking out of the hotel. Ebbets, who was ill (he was suffering from dizzy spells and had disobeyed doctors' orders in order to come to Boston for the Series), was obviously upset. Asked for an explanation of his behavior, he said,

"We received very bad treatment in the first game here. The seats the Brooklyn Boosters got were the worst in the ballpark. I am only retaliating." Ah, the good old days.

Boston's Royal Rooters were much in evidence the next afternoon, sitting in a group, complete with red-coated band, near the Red Sox dugout. Over and over the band played and the Rooters sang a tune called "Tessie," which for some inane reason had become their fight song. "Tessie," they sang, "you make me feel so bahadly. Why don't you turn around? Tessie, you know I love you sadly, babe. My heart weighs about a pound." Tessie might have been popular with the Royal Rooters, but followers of rival teams found her an agonizing bore. "That measly, monotonous melody," one newspaperman called it, but the Rooters, from politicians like James Michael Curley and Honey Fitzgerald down, sang it gleefully, soulfully and repeatedly.

When Ruth took the mound to start what was to become one of the most memorable of all World Series games, dark clouds were hanging low over Boston and rain was threatening. Ruth got rid of the first two Brooklyn batters with dispatch but the third man, Hy Myers, a stocky righthanded-hitting outfielder, hit Babe's second pitch on a line to right center field. Speaker might have caught the ball if he had still been playing center for the Red Sox, but Walker tripped as he started after it and fell. Hooper, coming over from right field, also stumbled, and the ball bounded through for extra bases. Hooper retrieved the ball near the fence and threw it in. The relay was bobbled and Myers, who never stopped running, beat the throw easily with a colorful but totally unnecessary head-first slide into home plate. It was an inside-the-park home run, and it put Brooklyn ahead, 1–0. It was also the only run the Dodgers were to score in the game, which lasted fourteen innings, although they came very close a couple of times.

In the third inning Ruth's rival pitcher, the lefthanded Sherry Smith, hit a clean double down the right field line but was out at third when he tried to stretch it into a triple; if he had stopped at second he most likely would have scored a moment later, because the next batter singled. The Dodgers went out without scoring, but the Red Sox picked up a run in their half of the inning when Ruth grounded out with a man on third. The base runner scored and Babe was credited with batting in a run.

The score was now tied, and it remained tied for eleven more innings, through a succession of melodramatic events. In the fifth, Thomas of the Red Sox hit a double and was tripped by Ivy Olson, the Dodger shortstop, as he tried for third. He was awarded the extra base by the umpires, who then had to break up a fight that erupted between Olson and Heinie Wagner, the Boston third base coach. After all that, Ruth struck out to end the inning.

The Red Sox might have scored in the sixth, except for a diving, rolling catch of a line drive by Myers in center field. In the seventh a Dodger rally was aborted and a furious argument begun when Myers—who seemed to be in the middle of everything—was called out at first base on an obviously bad decision by the umpire. In the eighth the Dodgers should have scored. Mike Mowrey, the third baseman, singled and was sacrificed to second. Otto Miller, the catcher, followed with a clean single to left, but the cautious Mowrey stopped at third. The throw from the outfield to the plate was wide, and Mowrey would have scored easily had he tried. The next batter hit a grounder to Scott at shortstop, and on this one Mowrey started for the plate. Scott threw home. Mowrey stopped halfway, backtracked and was immediately caught in a rundown: catcher to the third baseman to Ruth, who made the tag on the baseline.

When the Red Sox came to bat in the last of the ninth, it was becoming dark, the gloom of the heavy overcast aggravated by the early October dusk. Janvrin opened the inning with a line-drive double off Zach Wheat's glove in left field. Walker tried to sacrifice but hit a little foul ball off to one side of the plate. Carrigan, who wanted the runner moved over to third base, immediately took Walker out of the game and sent a substitute outfielder named Jimmy Walsh to bat in his place. Walsh bunted directly to the pitcher, and Smith pounced on it and threw to Mowrey at third in time to catch Janvrin. The umpire had lifted his arm to call Janvrin out when the ball trickled from Mowrey's glove. The decision was reversed, and there were the Red Sox with men on first and third and no one out in the last half of the ninth inning of a tie ball game. Hoblitzell, the dependable, was up, and sure enough he lifted a fly ball into center field. Janvrin tagged up at third and the crowd began moving toward the exits. But Myers—who else?—took the fly ball on the run, threw perfectly to the plate and Janvrin was out by a foot.

The game went into extra innings. Boston almost scored in the eleventh when Scott singled and went to second on a sacrifice. After Ruth struck out, Hooper hit a ground ball off Mowrey's glove and Scott, moving as the ball was hit, went safely into third. The third baseman chased the ball to his left, picked it up and started to throw to first in an apparently hopeless attempt to get Hooper. It was a fake, but Scott fell for it. He took a couple of strides toward home plate and was tagged out when Mowrey turned and threw to Olson, the shortstop, who had come up behind the base.

Smith was in trouble each inning now, but Ruth, who had difficulty earlier, looked stronger than ever. He had given up six hits and three walks in the first seven innings, but from the eighth inning on he allowed no hits at all and only one walk. Boston was oozing confidence. When the popular Lewis came to bat in the eleventh with a man on first and two out, the Royal Rooters came to life. "Tessie!" they sang, and the band blared its accompaniment. Wilbert Robinson, the rotund Brooklyn manager, came red-faced and fuming off the Dodger bench and complained bitterly to the umpires, who dutifully ordered the Royal Rooters to knock it off. Nothing happened in the twelfth except that Ruth with two outs tried to bunt for a base hit and was thrown out. In the thirteenth Mowrey reached second for the Dodgers on an error and a sacrifice. Smith, a good hitting pitcher, poked a blooper into left field for what seemed a certain hit and an almost certain run. But Lewis came sprinting in and caught the ball off his shoe tops for the third out. You should have heard the Rooters sing "Tessie" then.

In the last of the fourteenth Smith, very tired, opened the inning by walking Hoblitzell for the fourth time. Lewis sacrificed him to second. It was so dark now that it was hard to see the ball. Carrigan therefore put Del Gainor, a righthander, in to bat for the usually dependable Gardner, who hit lefthanded, against the lefthanded Smith. Carrigan felt a righthanded batter would be better able to follow Smith's pitches in the murky light. And using all his weapons, he sent slim young Mike McNally in to run for the heavy-footed Hoblitzell. The wheels of baseball strategy turned even then, but Carrigan's maneuvers paid off. Gainor took a ball and a strike and then hit a liner over the third baseman's head. Most of the spectators could not tell where the ball went, but they could see Wheat, the left fielder, running desperately toward the foul line. McNally was around third and on his way to the plate before Wheat picked up the ball, and he scored easily with the winning run. Pandemonium. More "Tessie." And Babe Ruth, in his World Series debut, unless you count that pinch-hitting effort against Alexander the year before, had a 2–1, fourteen-inning victory in the longest and one of the most exciting World Series games ever played.

Ruth was roaring and shouting and jumping around the club-house afterwards like a high school kid. He grabbed Carrigan and yelled at him, "I told you a year ago I could take care of those National League bums, and you never gave me a chance." Carrigan, easing out of the Ruthian bear hug, laughed and said, "Forget it, Babe. You made monkeys out of them today."

It was Ruth's only appearance in the Series, which the Red Sox won, four games to one. Mays was the only Boston pitcher to lose, dropping the third game to the veteran Jack Coombs, who had previously been a star with the Philadelphia Athletics during their pennant-winning years. Ruth, in his ingenuously boorish way, tried to comfort the bad-tempered Mays by saying, "Well, if we had to lose one I'm glad it was to an old American Leaguer." Mays's reply was not recorded.

CHAPTER 11

Emergence of Temperament:
How to Punch an Umpire

Carrigan retired, going out onto the field after the final game of the Series to wave farewell to the fans, and the bulk of the Red Sox players went to New Haven, Connecticut, the Sunday after the Series ended to play an exhibition game against a semipro team fortified by the presence of Ty Cobb. Ruth pitched the entire game, which ended in a 3–3 tie, and then went off with Helen and several other players and their wives on a hunting and vacation trip to New Hampshire. While they were there the National Commission, baseball's three-man ruling body, raised cain about the New Haven exhibition, saying it was a violation of a baseball rule that barred World Series players from barnstorming tours and exhibition games during the off-season. The Red Sox players claimed they had received permission from Lannin, and perhaps they had. Lannin may well have waved his hand and said, "Go ahead," but since permission was a league matter, Lannin did not have the authority to grant it, and the players were therefore technically guilty. At first the commission implied it would withhold distribution of the World Series checks, but that caused such a furor they decided to forget that idea. Dave Fultz, president of the players' association, protested strongly against any punishment at all, but the National Commission finally decided on a $100 fine for each of the Red Sox players. Then, as though to make sure the fines would be paid, the commission announced it was withholding distribution of World Series emblems to members of the Boston team. These emblems, worth about $100 each, were elaborate jeweled souvenirs, like the massive rings and such that are given today.

Ruth wasn't too worried, either about the fine or the emblem. He and Helen were thoroughly enjoying New Hampshire. Ruth hunted, probably for the first time in his life, and he and Helen relished the fresh country air, watched the logs burn to embers in big fireplaces and marveled at the colors of autumn. When the vacation was over, once again they went south to Baltimore to visit Babe's father. This time the World Series check he took with him came to nearly $4000, again more than his salary for the entire season. It brought his income for 1916 to almost $7500, a lot of money for a twenty-two-year-old kid in a day when a skilled telegrapher, for example, secure in a job that was then vital to the communications system in the country, made less than $25 a week, less than $1300 a year. In short, Ruth was rolling in money, and he began to develop an abiding affection for it.

About this time Joe Lannin found himself fed up with baseball. The vituperation he had been subject to because of the Speaker sale had hurt him, particularly when he recalled the money he had spent on player purchases to strengthen the Boston club. Late in the season he let himself become irrationally angry over an umpire's decision against the Red Sox and accused the American League umpiring staff of being against his club. He had to apologize publicly for that rash remark, and the league talked about issuing a formal censure. Carrigan's retirement disturbed him too. He had hired Bill and— except in the Speaker case—had relied heavily on his judgment. He did not at all like the idea of working with a new man. Then too the incident with Ebbets at the World Series left a bad taste, as had the contretemps over the exhibition game in New Haven. On top of all this he had a bad heart. It was too much. He decided to get out, even though he had owned the Red Sox for only a few months more than three years.

On November 1, 1916, he announced he had sold the club to a three-man group headed by Harry Frazee, a well-known New York theatrical figure (the other two, never prominent in the Red Sox operation, were Hugh Ward and G. M. Anderson). The price was $675,000. "I had intended to sell out," Lannin explained, "and these gentlemen had the cash." How much cash, Lannin did not specify, but it was less than half the total cost of the club. The rest of the payment was in the form of notes from Frazee to Lannin.

Frazee was thirty-six, a plump, dark-haired, smooth-faced man. He was from Peoria, Illinois, where he worked as a bellhop before going on to Chicago, where in time he became the owner of the Cort Theater. He later went to New York and there added the Longacre Theater to his empire. As most theater owners did in that day, Frazee produced his own shows. When he bought the Red Sox the Longacre was housing a smash hit of his called *Nothing But the Truth*, a comedy starring William Collier. A year or two later Frazee put on the successful musical *Leave It to Jane*, with words and music by Guy Bolton and P. G. Wodehouse, and in 1925 he produced his biggest hit, *No, No, Nanette*, which had a triumphant revival on Broadway forty-five years later.

Frazee was charming, convivial, shrewd. He liked to maneuver, to be in the midst of things. He was in on the promotion of the Jack Johnson–Jess Willard fight in Havana in 1915. He was an operator. Irving Caesar, the songwriter who wrote the words to "Tea for Two," the hit song in *No, No, Nanette*, said, "Frazee never drew a sober breath in his life, but he was a hell of a producer. He made more sense drunk than most people do sober."

Frazee is forever indicted in baseball history as the man who destroyed the Boston Red Sox, but during his first years with the club he worked hard to improve it (in 1918 he was even accused of trying to buy a pennant). In his first month as president and principal owner he heard a rumor that the Washington Senators were thinking of selling Walter Johnson and had already received an offer of $50,000 for him. Frazee promptly made a public bid of $60,000. He tried to get Carrigan to come back from retirement and went all the way to Lewiston, Maine—no easy trip from New York then or now—to persuade him. Frazee offered Carrigan a contract that would guarantee him almost $20,000 if he came back to manage, but it turned out that Carrigan had made a total of more than $23,000 in 1916. He had been paid $10,000 to manage, had been given a percentage of the gate receipts that came to about $7000, had picked up a $2500 bonus from Lannin for winning the pennant and had earned another $3900 from his winning World Series share. Frazee talked and wheedled, but Carrigan decided to stay with his new investments in Maine. Frazee conceded defeat and named Jack Barry the new manager.

Frazee had missed with Johnson and Carrigan, but he kept popping up with ideas. Unlike Lannin, who tended to antagonize people, Frazee got along with everybody. He got in touch with Charlie Ebbets, smoothed his feathers, which were still ruffled from his run-in with Lannin in Boston, and suggested that Ebbets shift his spring-training base from Florida to Hot Springs, where the World Series rivals could train side by side, more or less, and meet in a series of exhibition games. Ebbets agreed.

Frazee was also busy signing his ballplayers. Salaries were still being cut that winter as long-term contracts expired, and economy was the war cry of the owners. Ban Johnson said at the American League meeting in Chicago in December that "extravagances, particularly salaries, must be reduced." The National League said it was going to raise ticket prices and cut salaries; payrolls were to be reduced as much as 25 per cent. Frazee was not as harsh in his outlook, but neither was he throwing his money away. He cut some salaries and gave very few raises. One of these was to Ruth, a modest rise of $1500, to $5000 a year, but in the face of the economy drive Babe was content. After all, it was an increase of more than 33 per cent in a year when most players were taking cuts. Dick Hoblitzell, a ten-year man in the majors, signed for $5000 too, but he was taking a $600 cut. So Ruth signed early and amicably and reported to Hot Springs on time for 1917 spring training, accompanied by Helen.

Frazee was at Hot Springs too that spring. He was not much for spartan atmosphere, and he liked the presence of the wives in camp. He tried to keep things cheerful and relaxed and loved to take part in the heavy repartee that is so much a part of baseball practice sessions. When Ruth hit two baseballs over the fence one day, Frazee chuckled happily and said, "That gent is going to cost me a lot of money." He shouted to Barry, the manager, "Hey, Jack, charge those balls to Ruth!" When Babe broke a bat a few minutes later, Frazee yelled, "More expense! The next thing you know he'll be tearing his uniform."

Everybody had fun poking fun at Ruth, who loved it, as he always loved being the center of attention. He was throwing on the sidelines one day to Joe Devine, a new catcher the Red Sox had taken on that spring. (Devine became a New York Yankee scout in later years and was the man who told the Yankees to buy Joe DiMaggio.) Helen Ruth and Chet Thomas' wife were on horseback just outside the park, and Ruth kept watching them, even as he threw the ball. He threw several times to Devine without even glancing at him, and some of the onlookers in the nearby bleachers began to kid him about it. "I'm getting to be a bear on control," Ruth explained, still watching Helen. Devine laughed and said to the fans, "He's getting to be a big boy. He'll be carrying matches in his pockets soon unless we watch him."

There was a standing joke that the livery stable operators were taking out insurance policies on their horses in case the massive Ruth decided he wanted to go riding too. Yet, in truth, the Babe had trimmed down considerably and was fit and hard at 194. He was continually active in Hot Springs, on the field and off. He bowled, both lefthanded and righthanded, and was just about the best in camp with either hand. Barbershop quartets were big things with ballplayers in that era, and Ruth tried to worm his bass voice into a singing group that had got together. The others hooted at him and said he would have to audition first. They made him sing his favorite song, "Molly, My Dear." When he finished, the judges said he was disqualified on the grounds that his voice was still changing.

He sat in on the poker games with a notable lack of success. The caustic Devine said, "He might as well give his money away. Why doesn't he just leave a deposit and go see a movie?"

Heinie Wagner, the coach, was fond of Ruth and loved to ride him. "There was only one lefthander I ever remember meeting who wasn't crazy," he told Babe one day, "and that was Ray Collins."

"He was crazy too," said Ruth, "like a fox."

Despite the carefree atmosphere in the Red Sox camp, there were signs of ominous days ahead. War hysteria had been building for months, and a substantial percentage of the country was strongly in favor of the United States entering the war. "Preparedness" became a byword, and Ban Johnson announced that the teams would do close-order drill during spring training. He said he would put up a $500 prize for the best-drilled team, the competition to take place during the season. The players went along with the idea for a while, but by the middle of March they were fed up with drilling. On March 20 the Dodgers voted overwhelmingly to terminate it on the grounds that they had no time for it. They issued a vote of thanks to the army sergeant who had been working with them, but that was that. The Tigers did the same thing and so did the Indians, but war fever kept rising.

The Red Sox and Dodgers played a couple of exhibitions in Hot Springs, then broke camp at the end of March and traveled across Arkansas, Oklahoma, Kansas, Missouri, Iowa, Illinois and Indiana, playing games every day. Ruth pitched very well, but his hitting generally was subdued. On April 3 they played in Peoria, Frazee's home town. On April 4, when they were in Lafayette, Indiana, the U.S. House of Representatives voted in favor of entering the war. The Senate followed suit the next day, and on April 6, five days before the opening day of the season, President Wilson formally declared war on Germany.

The drill teams were hurriedly reinstated, and when the Red Sox opened their season in New York against the Yankees, the players marched before the game. Baseball was extremely nervous about the status of its players, realizing that a virulent patriotism could turn the country against men playing a children's game while guns were being fired overseas. The proper sentiments were expressed. "It has been indicated," said a baseball official, "that it will be the policy of the War Department to leave undisturbed in their occupations all men who may be subject to service if they are receiving military instruction." The drill teams were considered military instruction. Colleges were closing down sports programs right and left—no one ever explained quite why—but baseball edged warily into the new season.

Ruth won on opening day, 10–0, and the only notable thing about the game, aside from the military drill, was the increasing disaffection Babe was showing toward umpires. The plate umpire was Tommy Connolly, the American League's diminutive senior man. Ruth had a run-in with Connolly in 1916, and now in the first game of 1917 complained continually about the umpire's calls. He showed anger when a Yankee walked in the fourth inning and argued loudly when Connolly ruled that the next batter had been hit by a Ruth pitch. In the seventh inning, when Ruth was called out on strikes, he made a great histrionic show of glaring at the little umpire before returning to the bench. The Babe was becoming a prima donna.

As they had in 1916, both Ruth and the Red Sox started well. Ruth won his first eight games and the club, with 15 victories in its first 20 games, was solidly in first place. Babe beat Walter Johnson again in another 1–0 game. He wasn't hitting much to speak of, but, surprisingly, the club was—it led the league in batting and in runs scored. By the end of May Ruth was a spectacular 10–1 for the season and the Red Sox were still in first place, though only a game and a half ahead of the White Sox.

As June began, most of the talk in the country centered on the "military census," otherwise known as the draft. Ruth and the other ballplayers and the vast majority of adult males in the country registered early in June, only a few days after a college student was arrested in New York for "counseling young men to refuse to register." Eligible single men who drew a low number in the draft lottery were apt to be in uniform before the end of the summer, and Ban Johnson wondered aloud if it would be possible to play the World Series. Babe was not concerned. As a married man he would be exempt from military service.

Despite his pleasant situation vis-à-vis the draft, Ruth's disposition grew increasingly cranky. The blissfulness of his marriage was beginning to erode under the pressure of the fun and girls he sought and found in various towns around the league, and in Boston too. He was well aware of his status as the premier lefthander in the league, and he found it difficult to accept the occasional bad luck that besets all players and umpires' decisions that went against him. His second loss of the season, in June, was particularly galling. Guy Morton of Cleveland pitched a one-hit shutout to beat him, 3–0, but Ruth himself had a one-hitter going into the ninth and it was his own single in the eighth that broke up Morton's no-hitter. Most aggravating was the way Cleveland scored its runs. In the fourth inning Ruth walked Ray Chapman, who stole second while Ruth retired the next two batters. Then Babe struck out Bobby Roth, which should have ended the inning, but the third strike got away from the catcher and Roth was safe at first as Chapman moved to third. The two pulled a double steal, and Chapman slid safely home with the first run of the game. A bad throw on the play let Roth go all the way around to third. Then Roth stole home too, for the fourth stolen base of the inning and the second run. In the sixth inning the lone base hit Ruth allowed drove in a third run. He was pretty sore after losing that game.

His bad temper reached a memorable high later in the month, on June 23. He was the starting pitcher against Washington in a game played at home in Boston. He completed his warm-up pitches and faced the first batter, Ray Morgan, the Senators' second baseman. The plate umpire was Brick Owens, not a notably even-tempered man himself. Owens called Ruth's first pitch a ball, and Babe complained. He pitched again. Ball two. Ruth shouted something, and the umpire angrily motioned for him to desist. Babe threw again. Ball three.

"Open your eyes!" Ruth yelled. "Open your eyes!"

"It's too early for you to kick," the umpire yelled back. "Get in there and pitch!"

Ruth stomped around the mound angrily, wound up and threw again.

"Ball four!" Owens snapped.

Ruth ran in toward the plate. "Why don't you open your goddamned eyes?" he screamed.

"Get back out there and pitch," Owens shouted, "or I'll run you out of the game."

"You run me out of the game, and I'll bust you one on the nose."

Owens stepped across the plate and waved his arm. "Get the hell out of here!" he cried. "You're through."

Ruth rushed him. Chester Thomas, the catcher, got between the angry pitcher and the umpire, but Ruth swung anyway, over the catcher's shoulder. He missed with a right, but a left caught Owens on the back of the neck. Ruth was in a frenzy, and Thomas and Jack Barry, who came running to the plate, had to pull him away from the umpire. A policeman came down from the stands and led the still fuming Ruth off the field.

When things settled down, Barry turned to the bench and waved Ernie Shore into the game. The new pitcher was allowed exactly eight warm-up pitches, the legal limit, and then the game resumed. As Shore threw his first pitch, Morgan, the base runner Ruth had walked, broke for second in a surprise attempt to steal, but Thomas, who had a superb arm, cut him down. One out. Shore got the next two men and went on to retire twenty-six batters in a row, every man he faced in the game. It was a perfect no-hit, no-run game for Shore, the fourth ever to be pitched in the majors. It was so entered in the record books, although purists still quibble about it. If a Washington runner reached first base, they argue, it was not a perfect game; and if it was not a perfect game, how can the pitcher be credited with one? Never mind. As far as Ernie Shore was concerned, it was perfect.

Ruth was in uniform the next day and worked out, but during the game he sat in the stands in civilian clothes because Ban Johnson had suspended him indefinitely. A heavy fine and a long suspension were predicted, but Frazee hurried to smooth-talk Johnson. The league president listened, and after ten days ended the suspension and let Ruth return to action. Johnson explained that he had lifted the suspension because of the closeness of the pennant race. As for the anticipated heavy fine, it was set at $100, the amount Ruth owed to a man named Charley Deal, with whom he was having a dispute over the purchase of an automobile. Frazee sent a check for $100 to Garry Herrmann of the National Commission, but Ruth in the meantime settled the Deal affair himself, and Herrmann returned Frazee's check.

Ruth lost the day he returned and again in his next start, and the overinflated Boston hitting began to find its normal weak level. The White Sox, meantime, won 16 of 17 games to move ahead of the Red Sox. The clubs had met in a four-game series in June that was supposed to be a sort of early-season showdown, but the White Sox easily beat Shore, 8–0, in the first game of the series and Ruth, 7–2, in the second to take a firm grip on the lead. The Red Sox rallied and stayed on Chicago's heels, but it was a long, hard summer. Three or four times in July and for one brief moment in mid-August the Red Sox sneaked into the lead—but never for more than a day or two. The White Sox were too strong. This was the Chicago team that two years later achieved indelible fame as the Black Sox, but whatever its moral fiber it was a unique collection of superb ballplayers, a team that had everything: superior pitching, powerful hitting, impeccable fielding. Ed Barrow called it the best major league team he ever saw, even better than his own 1927 New York Yankees.

The Red Sox did their best, but Shore hurt his arm in August and was out for three weeks and the club fell further and further behind. Ruth was hitting well (he had only one home run—the first ever hit into the center field bleachers at Fenway—but late in August he was batting .348, and only Cobb, Speaker and George Sisler were hitting higher), but the team as a whole was dismal at bat. From August 1 through September 3 it was shut out or held to one run thirteen times. The White Sox pulled away and went on to win the pennant easily.

The war, meanwhile, was everywhere. A second draft was scheduled for September, which prompted several of the single men on the team (among them Barry, Shore and Lewis) to enlist in the naval reserve. In St. Louis a lieutenant colonel supervised a military drill competition between the Browns and the Red Sox. The Browns won and went on to win Ban Johnson's $500 prize as the best drill team in the league.

Ruth won his 20th game on August 31 and added four more victories in September, the first September of his professional career in which he was not involved in a close pennant race. One game in New York that month turned out to be a rich experience for him. Thousands of newly inducted soldiers were marched into the Polo Grounds as military bands played, bugles blew, drums rolled and flags waved. The soldiers, even though most of them were New Yorkers, cheered Ruth, and the Babe reveled in their boisterous adulation. In the fourth, leading 2–0, he gave up a double and a walk to the first two Yankee batters and then bore down to get the next three on a pop-up, an easy fly and a tap back to the mound. Great applause from the stands. In the sixth he brought the soldiers to their feet shouting when he hit a tremendous foul fly over the right field roof, before settling for a single. In the ninth he captured them completely when he hit a legitimate home run—his second and last of the season—into the right field stands. In the last half of the ninth, pitching a two-hitter and leading, 8–0, he gave the soldiers a treat by laying the ball in for the Yankees to hit. The soldiers roared with delight as first one Yankee and then another and then another reached base, moved around and came in to score. Ruth, enjoying himself immensely, grinned at the stands after each hit and laughed out loud when the soldiers begged for more. Finally, with the score 8–3 and a couple of Yankees on base, he turned it on again, retired the side, ended the game and walked off the field waving to the cheering throng.

A week before the season ended, the Red Sox played an exhibition game in Boston against an American League All-Star team (which included one National Leaguer, the Boston Braves' Rabbit Maranville). It was a benefit for the family of Tim Murnane, an ancient Boston sportswriter and former major leaguer who died earlier in the year. Ruth pitched five scoreless innings against a lineup that included Cobb, Speaker, Jackson, Sisler and the other stars of the American League. He was very proud of that, and it proved an apt climax to a season in which he won 24 games, had six shutouts and pitched the startling total of 35 complete games in 38 starts. And he ended the season with a .325 batting average, better than anyone in the league except Cobb, Sisler and Speaker. That made up a little for the unfamiliar emptiness of not being on a pennant-winning team.

After the season Ruth and Helen stayed in Boston for a while before going to Baltimore for their annual visit, and Babe got into trouble again, which he was beginning to be good at. He was in love with cars and had bought and sold several. One October night in Boston, driving a girl (not Helen) from somewhere to somewhere, he suddenly found himself finessed by two trolley cars. He tried to solve the problem by squeezing between them, but the trolleys wouldn't give. He maneuvered brilliantly to avoid a really serious accident, but the car was banged up and the girl was hurt badly enough to be hospitalized. Ruth escaped without injury, except to his feelings, his automobile and his domestic tranquility.

CHAPTER 12

The Beginnings of the Hitter: Switching to the Outfield

The war was getting closer. In Baltimore late in the fall Ruth entertained the troops at Fort George G. Meade. Babe did not do very much beyond doffing his coat and swinging a bat a few times in his shirtsleeves (he was wearing a natty little bow tie), but it gave him and maybe the public the feeling that he was doing his bit, a phrase that had become almost sacred in wartime America. In Boston Jack Barry and the others who had enlisted in the naval reserve were ordered to report for active duty, and for the second time in twelve months Harry Frazee had to scout around for a manager.

While he was at it Frazee decided to look for somebody who might take over some of the executive responsibilities of the club. Harry the producer enjoyed the fun of owning the Red Sox, but he was becoming tired of the day-to-day details. On a trip to Chicago in November he mentioned this to Ban Johnson, who was always quick to help the clubs in his league with personnel matters. Johnson thought he might have just the man Frazee needed in Ed Barrow, the president of the International League. The International was foundering, still licking the wounds it suffered during the Federal League crisis and beset now by the loss of players to the armed forces and the inevitable decline in attendance that the war was causing. Johnson suggested that Barrow might want to switch jobs. Frazee talked to Barrow and found him favorably inclined toward the idea, particularly when Frazee agreed to an arrangement that would let Barrow obtain an interest in the club. A final decision had to wait until after Barrow attended the International League's annual meeting.

When the league met at the Victoria Hotel in New York on the evening of December 12, it was obvious that several of the owners had become openly antagonistic toward Barrow. Jack Dunn had been angry with him for two seasons, ever since Barrow made him pay $15,000 to the league for the right to return from Richmond to Baltimore in 1916. Joe Lannin, the former Red Sox owner who sold Providence and now owned Buffalo—which he wanted to sell too but could not because he was unable to find a buyer willing to take it off his hands—had heard reports that Barrow had been part of a well-publicized plan to create a third major league that would have absorbed some of the International League's cities. The new league was a trial balloon that never got off the ground, but Lannin felt it was evidence of Barrow's disloyalty. One or two of the other owners resented Barrow's imperious way of running league affairs. All of them were worried about 1918 and the chances the league had of surviving another season of war. The meeting was filled with doubt, uncertainty and rancor. When the hitherto routine matter of deciding upon the league president's salary for the coming year arose, Barrow was asked to leave the room during the discussion. When he returned he found that the owners, in a curious halfway step, had voted to reduce his salary from $7500 to $2500. Barrow was furious.

"Gentlemen," he said, "if this is a challenge for me to resign, I accept the challenge. I quit!"

"That's fine," Lannin called out. "Good riddance."

Barrow, a bull of a man who enjoyed using his fists, lunged at Lannin, but a couple of the others grabbed him and held his arms.

"Don't hit him, Ed," one of them said. "He has a bad heart."

Barrow thrust Lannin away and left the room. The sports pages the next morning were filled with stories about the meeting, and all reported that Barrow had resigned. But Barrow, for all his anger, had not submitted a formal resignation, and his contract would not run out until February. After he left the meeting he sent a telegram to Frazee, who was in Chicago, saying, "WIRE IMMEDIATELY IF YOU THINK I SHOULD LEAVE FOR CHICAGO ON CENTURY TOMORROW." He thoughtfully charged the telegram to the International League's account.

Frazee was not an early riser and when Barrow did not hear from him in the next few hours he sat down and wrote a letter as well. He began it "Dear Harry" and then crossed out Harry and made it "Dear Boss." In it he wrote:

> The International League is almost gone, as you will see by the enclosed clippings. We had a very stormy session yesterday.
>
> The newspaper men were all after me last night about the Boston rumor. I denied to everybody that there was any truth to the story. As usual, one or two of these bright young men got the thing balled up, but no very serious damage was done.
>
> Four of my clubs handed me a wallop by voting to cut off two thirds of my salary. I feel quite sure it was a put-up job to make me resign. I did not resign, but I intend to do so when the league meets in February, or perhaps before that time. It was no doubt a rebuke for my supposed activities in forming that new league. No doubt Mr. Lannin had a finger in the pie.
>
> My wife is scared stiff over the league's action yesterday, but I feel more sore than anything else and would like to take a punch at a couple of the ungrateful rats. It was certainly a rotten piece of business. That Boston deal has surely got to go through now.
>
> I wired you this morning asking if you thought I should come to Chicago on the Century tomorrow.

Frazee got in touch with Barrow, heard all about the meeting, including the set-to with Lannin, told Barrow he thought he was wise not to resign at the moment, since it would look bad all around if he left so abruptly, and suggested that he sit tight and let him know if anything else happened when the International League owners resumed their meetings. Barrow wired him again: "NOTHING NEW. FUTURE OF LEAGUE VERY UNCERTAIN. POSTPONED FINAL ACTION UNTIL FEBRUARY TWELFTH. PLEASE DO NOT MENTION LANNIN TROUBLE TO ANYONE."

It was fairly evident that Barrow was through with the International League and apparent too that he would join Frazee and the Red Sox. Indeed, he may have given Frazee counsel and advice on club matters through these winter months, although Jack Barry was stationed in Boston and he and Frazee met and discussed things from time to time. A fancy of Barry's that he might be able to work some sort of extended leave from the navy that would let him manage anyway in 1918 was dashed, and it was obvious that Frazee had to have a new man. There were rumors in January that he was trying again to persuade Bill Carrigan to come out of retirement, and in Maine Carrigan announced he would be "willing to help out the Red Sox in the emergency." But Frazee said only that the managerial question was still undecided.

In the meantime he was charging ahead in his efforts to improve his team, which like others in the major leagues was losing players right and left to the armed services. Barry was gone, of course, and so were Lewis, Shore, Pennock, Shorten, Gainor, McNally, Janvrin and Thomas. Hoblitzell was expecting a commission and Leonard was talking about enlisting. To fill some of the gaps Frazee gave Connie Mack $60,000 and three second-line players in exchange for Joe Bush, Wally Schang and Amos Strunk. Bush was a pitcher of considerable talent, Schang a powerfully built catcher and a strong, dangerous hitter, and Strunk a superior outfielder who usually batted in the neighborhood of .300. They had all been with the Athletics in the pennant-winning years and were among the handful of legitimate major leaguers Mack still had. Their sale to the Red Sox aroused criticism—this was when Frazee was accused of trying to buy a pennant—and surprise. Baseball could understand why Mack, fearful of whatever economic crises 1918 would bring, was bailing out, trying to get full value for players who still had high market value. If not admirable, it was at least understandable. But owners who were standing pat until the war was over, making do with second-line players while their regulars were in service, were astonished at the way Frazee was pouring money into an operation that might be moribund in a few months. Frazee paid no attention. He went to Mack again and this time came away with Stuffy McInnis, whom he felt he would need to take over first base when Hoblitzell received his commission. Frazee again gave Mack a substantial sum of money and three players, though this time the trio included two Boston regulars, Larry Gardner and Tilly Walker.

It was easy to do business with Mack, who was fairly desperate that winter. The saintly old devil had even proposed to his ballplayers that they accept a profit-sharing system in 1918 instead of taking straight salaries. Since it was odds-on that during a war year the last-place Athletics would not make a profit you could see with a magnifying glass, the players failed to rally round. They wanted salaries, guaranteed by contracts, and some of them wanted a little more salary than Mack was willing to give. One of these was the colorful outfielder Ping Bodie, who had led the Athletics in runs batted in in 1917. In the course of his dispute with Mack, Bodie was moved to comment, "I ain't bragging about myself or anything like that, but I got to admit I'm the only real ballplayer Connie's got. I and the Liberty Bell are the only attractions left in Philadelphia." Soon it was only the Liberty Bell, for Mack sold the unsigned Ping to the Yankees.

Frazee too was busy with salary matters. He was eager to sign Ruth, who said he wanted a big raise. Frazee was worried because holdouts were popping up all over. In St. Louis, Rogers Hornsby was asking for $10,000. Grover Alexander, recently traded to the Cubs, wanted $12,000. Most of the unsigned players were simply resisting salary reductions, because the owners were being even more stringent than in 1917. The owners expressed shock at the "regiment of holdouts," having assumed "that during these war times the ballplayers would graciously accept a cut in salary. But again the players have disappointed the clubowners, for many of them have made it plain that they do not intend to accept any cuts."

And some, like Bodie and Ruth, were insisting on raises. Ruth wanted his salary doubled, to $10,000. Frazee, jollying him, expressed horror at such a salary. "I've never paid an actor that much," he said. He suggested $7000, with the promise that if the Babe had another good year the $10,000 would be his in 1919. A $7000 salary meant a $2000 raise—a 40 per cent increase—and Ruth finally accepted it. On January 14 he became the first Red Sox player to sign a 1918 contract. A few days later the newly purchased McInnis followed suit, and Frazee did not have too much trouble with the rest of the team.

He still did not have a manager, at least publicly. Then in February the International League met again. There had been indications that the owners were having second thoughts and would restore Barrow's pay cut and ask him to stay on. But Barrow, after meticulously fulfilling his duties as president by conducting the meeting, announced that his resignation would take effect the following morning. That afternoon the news broke that he would join the Red Sox, not in the front office, as had been surmised on the sports pages, but as field manager, sitting on the bench.

It was surprising news. Barrow's major league managing experience had been confined to a season and a half with the Detroit Tigers nearly fifteen years earlier. But he had managed in the minor leagues too, and he had been in organized baseball in one role or another—except as a player—since 1894. Born just after the Civil War, he had grown up on the prairies of Nebraska and Iowa and had gone to work at the age of sixteen. He worked for the business side of newspapers, sold soap and became a hotel clerk, although he was the antithesis of the Franklin Pangborn fussbudget. He was powerfully built and as pugnacious as he was powerful. When as a young man he was put in charge of circulation on a Des Moines newspaper it was because he could beat up all the newspaper boys. He was tough.

He had played baseball as a boy, but as he grew into his twenties he became a manager and a small-time promoter, putting town teams together and challenging teams from other towns. He traveled about and eventually found himself in Pittsburgh, where he went into the hotel business. As interested in boxing as he was in baseball, he began to meet the leading sporting types of the city and in time became a close friend of Harry Stevens, the scorecard and hot dog man. This led him in the 1890s into semipro and minor league baseball as a promoter, clubowner and league president. During these days he discovered and signed Honus Wagner, whom in 1897 he sold to Louisville, then in the National League; Wagner later was transferred to Pittsburgh, where he became the finest player in the league's history.

In 1903 Barrow became manager of the Tigers, but after a series of disagreements with Frank Navin, then business manager of the team, he quit halfway through the 1904 season. He went back to the minors, managed there for a while, ran a hotel in Toronto for a year or two and finally was made president of the International League. Now, in 1918, only three months short of his fiftieth birthday, he was a major league manager again. His experience in tactical baseball was meager, but Barrow had no doubt whatever of his ability to handle the job. He was always a supremely confident man.

Curiously, he said late in his life that his first meeting with Ruth was in regard to Babe's 1918 contract. He said he called Ruth and McInnis in together to discuss things and signed them both at the same time. A photograph of Ruth and McInnis in overcoats (Ruth holding a cigar in his left hand but looking very boyish) standing behind Frazee and Barrow, who are seated at a desk, hung in Barrow's home at the time of his death in 1953. Barrow said it had been taken the day Ruth and McInnis signed their contracts, and he liked to add that it was the only time Ruth had ever been photographed signing a contract at the same time as another player. But Ruth and McInnis signed in mid-January, Barrow did not become Boston's manager until mid-February and a calendar in the photograph shows that the picture was taken in March, probably just before the Red Sox left Boston to go to Arkansas for spring training. The memories of old men are, unhappily, imprecise. And sadly, as Ronald Blythe wrote in *Akenfield,* "The old people have gone and have taken a lot of the truth out of the world with them."

Barrow told another story of the day the photograph was taken that rings a bit truer. He said he gave five dollars to Larry Graver, the club secretary, and told him to take Ruth and McInnis to lunch. The five dollars might be considered roughly equivalent to $30 or $40 today. When Graver returned he told Barrow, "You owe me $2.85." Barrow, who had assumed that Graver would take the players to a simple everyday restaurant, was startled. "Where did you go?" he demanded. Graver said, "It wasn't the restaurant, Ed. Did you ever see that big guy eat? He had a whole custard pie for dessert."

Whether or not he had anything to do with signing Ruth, there was no question that Barrow, who functioned as both field manager and general manager, had taken over the operation of the ball club. The day after he assumed office he signed Joe Bush, who had been holding out since his purchase from Philadelphia in December, and two days later he hired the fiery Johnny Evers, the famous old Chicago Cubs second baseman, to act as coach and righthand man, his baseball brains. Barrow wanted someone with him on the bench who could handle moment-to-moment tactics, and he assumed that Evers, who in the twilight of his career in 1914 had helped the Boston Braves win their miracle pennant, would be a natural. It did not work out. Evers, tense, thin, driving, was so frenetic during spring training that he drove the ballplayers half crazy. He wanted to go all out to win every exhibition game—never mind giving a pitcher the work he needed or showing patience with a questionable rookie—and his methods so upset the morale of the team that before the regular season began Barrow had to fire him. He relied for a time on Dan Howley, another new coach who a decade later became a manager himself, but ultimately he turned to Harry Hooper. The quiet, intelligent Hooper suggested the strategic moves, player shifts, pitching changes, and Barrow issued the orders. The arrangement worked pretty well. Hooper knew the team and the league, and Barrow respected him.

Despite the gadfly presence of Evers during spring training, Ruth had a splendid time. He had become an amateur of the running horse, and Hot Springs had Oaklawn Park. Hot Springs also had more formal types of gambling, and Ruth's night prowling led him frequently to the casinos. He was eating on a prodigious scale again, and the 1917 dip to 194 proved to be fleeting. He was up around 215 and climbing.

The sybaritic existence did not seem to affect his ballplaying at all, and an argument could be advanced that the uninhibited life he led off the field contributed to his exuberant success on it. He hit well that spring. Although he was still a pitcher, Barrow let him play first base and bat fifth when the Red Sox opened their exhibition season against the Dodgers. Ruth had a perfect day at bat, with two walks and two home runs. The clubs met again several days later at Camp Pike, an army camp near Little Rock. The game was rained out but the storm held off long enough for the players to take batting practice before a huge crowd of soldiers. Ruth put on a spectacular show by hitting five balls over the right field fence. People did not hit like that in those days, and he was uproariously cheered as each succeeding ball disappeared beyond the fence. The soldiers wanted more, but Barrow finally called a halt, protesting that baseballs were too expensive to be used up at such an extravagant rate. In his next game, at Hot Springs, Ruth played right field and hit a homer with the bases full. When the clubs played again a few days later and he had only one hit, a single, a newspaper reported plaintively, "Babe Ruth was not able to make any home runs." The magic was spreading.

Just before the Red Sox and Dodgers left Hot Springs to begin their long homeward trek, they played one more game at Camp Pike. Ruth was not in the lineup, because Barrow had begun to develop his starting rotation, and it was not Ruth's turn to pitch. But the soldiers clamored for him, and in the fifth inning Barrow sent him into the game. In the eighth he delighted his military audience by hitting a long home run to right field, and in the ninth, with the score tied, he hit a ball over the center fielder's head to drive in the winning run. The soldiers wrote home about that day.

On the barnstorming trip, which led down through Texas and back through Alabama and Tennessee before heading north and east to Boston, Ruth pitched in his regular turn but otherwise did not play. When the Red Sox opened their season he was the starting pitcher, and for the third straight year he won on opening day. Barrow had the pitching staff in perfect condition, and his four starters—Ruth, Mays, Leonard and Bush—appeared like clockwork. Through the first five weeks of the season they pitched in that same order, day after day, none of them missing a turn, no other pitcher squeezing into the rotation. Ruth pinch-hit once or twice and was hitting well, but he was strictly a pitcher in these early weeks of 1918 and batted ninth in the order.

In his fifth start he hit a home run over the roof in the Polo Grounds, his first home run of the year. That was on a Saturday. The Red Sox were to play the Yankees again on Monday—there had been considerable agitation for Sunday baseball in New York, but it was not yet legal and would not be for another year—and on Sunday they went out to Princeton, New Jersey, for an exhibition game with a team called the Silk Sox. Ruth played first base. This was partly to draw spectators, since the Babe's reputation was growing enormously, but it was also an experiment. Hooper had been arguing with Barrow about playing Ruth every day. God knows the Red Sox needed his power. No one else on the team batted as high as .290 that year, and only five of them were able to hit homers—one each for the year. Barrow had brought up a thirty-five-year-old minor leaguer named George Whiteman to take the departed Duffy Lewis' place in left field, but now Whiteman was on the bench with an injury. Hooper suggested that Ruth take Whiteman's place. Barrow decided against it and put Wally Schang, the catcher, in left field. He had the old-line baseball man's respect for pitching. He told Hooper, "I'd be the laughingstock of baseball if I changed the best lefthander in the game into an outfielder."

Hooper frequently heard Barrow say he had a $50,000 investment in the club, and he reminded the manager that when Ruth played there were always bigger crowds—and these extra fans came to see him hit, not pitch. Barrow rubbed his big chin and looked at Hooper from under the soft straw hat he usually wore on the bench (he preferred to manage in civilian clothes and seldom put on a baseball uniform). There were other problems with the team, and Ruth's bat might solve them. Hoblitzell, the first baseman and for four years the team's cleanup hitter, had been in a dreadful slump ever since opening day. He was still waiting for the officer's commission he had applied for, and perhaps his mind was not fully on baseball. Whatever the cause, he had only four singles in his first fifty at bats and was batting .080. Barrow dropped him from fourth to sixth in the batting order, a significant move in an era when managers seldom changed a lineup once they had settled on it. You batted third or seventh or second the way you played right field or shortstop; that was your position, and you stayed in it.

Hoblitzell's slump continued, but he remained in the lineup. He was playing with a slightly injured hand, and Barrow, listening to Hooper, decided to use the injury as an excuse to have Hoblitzell sit out a few games. Ordinarily, Stuffy McInnis would have taken over at first base, but McInnis had been playing third base all spring and had been doing so well there that Barrow disliked moving him. After watching Ruth show to advantage in the exhibition at Princeton, he gave in and decided to let him play first base and bat sixth in Hoblitzell's place the next day against the Yankees.

Thus, on Monday, May 6, 1918, precisely three years to the day after he hit his first major league home run in the same ballpark, Babe Ruth appeared in a major league game for the first time at a position other than pitcher and (except for pinch-hitting) in a spot other than ninth in the batting order. He came through majestically, hitting his second home run in two games and playing well in the field. Frazee was at the game and so was Jacob Ruppert, president of the Yankees, who, like Frazee, was bucking the tide of owner conservatism by continually trying to strengthen his club despite the uncertainties of wartime baseball. Ruppert was acutely aware of Ruth's ability—five of Babe's first 11 major league home runs had been hit in the Polo Grounds—and his growing appeal to New Yorkers. He offered to buy him, but Frazee laughed and shook his head. He was still on the upgrade, or buying phase, of his baseball venture. But he remembered the offer.

The Red Sox were in Washington the next afternoon and Ruth played first base again, although Barrow now moved him up to the cleanup position. For the third straight game he hit a home run, this one an immense poke over the right field wall into a "war" garden, where it frightened a dog. It was the first home run anybody had hit in Washington that season. The next day he hit a double. The day after that it was his turn to pitch, which he did, and he not only worked ten innings (he lost, 4–3) but had a perfect day at bat with a single, three doubles and a triple. His batting average rose to .484, and he was the sensation of baseball.

Paradoxically, during his explosive debut as a fulltime player the Red Sox were in a losing streak. When they left Boston a week earlier for this brief six-game road trip to New York and Washington, they had a 12–3 record for the season and a firm hold on first place. They lost all six games on the road—Mays, Leonard and Bush gave up an astonishingly atypical total of 31 runs in Ruth's first three games as a fulltime batter—and returned to Boston in second place. Barrow put Hoblitzell at first base when Ruth pitched in Washington, and when the club returned to Boston he kept Dick there and put Ruth in left field, the first time Ruth played the outfield in the majors. He went hitless, breaking a ten-game batting streak ("He didn't hit a thing, not even an umpire," a newspaper said), and complained afterward, "Gee, it's lonesome in the outfield. It's hard to keep awake with nothing to do."

Barrow put Ruth back at first base the next afternoon before a big Saturday crowd. Apparently comforted by his more populous surroundings, Ruth made three hits and fielded spectacularly, although on one desperate attempt to catch a pop-up bunt he fell flat on his face. The fans loved it. Whenever he came to bat they applauded vigorously, and when rival outfielders retreated toward the fences they hooted and cheered.

Barrow was pleased with the crowd's favorable reaction to Ruth, but he was uneasy about the effect playing every day might have on his pitching. The big fellow developed a cold and a sore throat, and before he pitched again Barrow had him sit out a game to rest. When he used him next as a pitcher he batted him ninth. The next afternoon he had him batting fourth again and playing left field. Left field became Ruth's regular nonpitching position. Barrow gave up completely on Hoblitzell, who in any case would be leaving for the army soon, and decided to go fulltime at first base with McInnis, who, after all, had been for years the best in the league at that position.

Babe was still bothered by his cold, and his hitting slackened considerably. His throat was sore, and he did not feel well. With no game scheduled on Sunday, May 19, he should have stayed home and rested, but he and Helen packed a picnic basket, got in the car and drove out to a beach near Boston. Babe ate a good part of the basket, drank some beer, swam, played ball on the sand and that night was burning with fever. His temperature rose to 104. In the morning he felt terrible but insisted on going to Fenway Park. He was supposed to pitch that day and he did not intend to miss his turn.

At the ballpark it was obvious he was too ill to play, and he was told to go home and go to bed. The team trainer went with him and on the way they stopped off at a drugstore, where the trainer swabbed his throat with an overliberal dose of silver nitrate, a torture regularly prescribed in that day for sore throats. Ruth's throat was raw anyway and the pain of the swabbing was excruciating. He gagged, choked and collapsed and was hurriedly taken to Massachusetts General Hospital, where his ailment was described as acute edema (swelling) of the larynx and his condition as serious. He could not speak and he was having trouble breathing, and rumors scurried around Boston that he was dying. But by nightfall the hospital reported he was out of danger.

He remained in the hospital all week, Helen sitting with him most of the time. Hoblitzell, as captain of the team, sent him a basket of flowers, and so did Bill Carrigan from Maine. It was the first time Ruth had ever received flowers from anyone, and he was greatly impressed. He still was not able to talk, but when visitors came in he would proudly point to the flowers. By the end of the week he was greatly improved, and on Sunday afternoon he was discharged from the hospital. On Monday he appeared at the ballpark in civilian clothes and received an ovation from the crowd. In another day or two he was in uniform, and on Thursday, May 30, Decoration Day, he pinch-hit. The big holiday crowd cheered him, but he made an out.

The club left for its first western trip of the season, and Ruth went with it. Barrow kept him on the bench in Detroit on Saturday because, in the inexorable clockwork of the Red Sox starting rotation, Ruth was scheduled to pitch on Sunday. It was the first time since his illness that he appeared in the starting lineup, and while he lost the game he hit a home run. The next day he played center field in place of Amos Strunk, who had a slight injury, and hit another home run. He played center again the next day and hit another home run. And the next day he hit another, his fourth in four games. It was almost unbelievable. Here he was just back from the hospital and he had hit four home runs in four straight games.

He was supposed to pitch again, but for the first time all season, except when he was ill, he missed his turn. He told Barrow he did not want to pitch, that pitching and playing the outfield at the same time were too much. Pitching had become a chore. He had not done well in his last four starts and had lost three of them. It was no fun any more. Hitting was what he liked to do and what he wanted to do. Barrow said he wanted him to pitch. Ruth grew stubborn about it, and he and Barrow were soon at swords' points.

Fortunately, during Ruth's illness Barrow had discovered another capable pitcher. He was Sam Jones, who came to Boston in 1916 as a throw-in in the Speaker deal and who pitched only forty-three innings in two seasons with the Red Sox. Barrow had used him out of desperation, and Jones had pitched well. Now, with Ruth refusing to go to the mound, Barrow turned to Jones again and Sam pitched his second successive shutout.

All right, then, thought Barrow. If Ruth wants to give up pitching, let him, just as long as Jones holds up.

CHAPTER 13

The Impact of War: Baseball in World War I

Jones held up splendidly—he went on to win 230 games in his career—but barely two weeks later Barrow was faced with another pitching crisis, and this one led to a major clash between the manager and Ruth. The war—or war hysteria—was closing in on baseball. The game had lost many men to the draft and enlistments, but for the body politic that was no longer sufficient. The moral feeling of the country (war tends to breed extremes of license and puritanism) was that everybody ought to be engaged in the war effort. There was no notable shortage of labor in essential industry, but Secretary of War Newton Baker, reflecting the mood of the times, decided to issue a "work or fight" order. Draft-age men engaged in nonproductive work were liable to be drafted, even if they had been deferred previously. In theory, the order was designed to keep factories, steel mills, shipyards, munitions plants and the like well supplied with the workers they might need. In practice, it was to prevent able-bodied men of soldierly age from engaging in frivolous pursuits while their contemporaries were fighting and dying in France—or working behind a desk at the Brooklyn Navy Yard.

The responsibility of executing the work-or-fight rule lay with the

Provost Marshal of the army, General Enoch Crowder, who was in charge of the draft. Anyone born after 1900 would be hard pressed to identify Crowder today, but the men who played baseball during World War I remembered him beyond Pershing, Foch, Joffre, Von Hindenburg or any of the other history-book generals. As the man in charge of the draft, he was the one the ballplayers were aware of. A decade later when a fine righthanded pitcher named Alvin Crowder came into the American League he was instantly nicknamed General.

When the work-or-fight order was pronounced in the spring of 1918, local draft boards moved quickly to demonstrate their patriotism, and ballplayers who had thought themselves immune from service were advised that they were now subject to being called to military duty. A New Jersey board dropped the black spot on Joe Finneran, a pitcher with the Yankees who had previously been deferred because he was married and a father. Finneran appealed, saying he had been a professional athlete for almost a decade and that no other occupation for which he was qualified could give him an income comparable to what he could earn in baseball. Since baseball was his chosen field he asked permission to stay in it. This was to be Organized Baseball's argument: Its players were not seeking special exemption, but those still active in the game who had been deferred on valid individual grounds should be allowed to continue in their work. Finneran's draft board accepted that reasoning and granted his appeal. Draft boards elsewhere, however, found differently, and one after another players were ordered to leave baseball and find productive jobs.

There were plenty of farm boys in the major leagues, and because farming was deemed productive they began to leave for home and the plow. Others looked for jobs in factories. Some went to work at steel mills and shipyards, particularly mills and shipyards that happened to have fast semipro baseball teams. Indeed, some mills and shipyards actively proselytized major league players. Baseball began to panic at the prospect of a mad rush from dugout to farm and industry. If the work-or-fight order was carried out *in toto,* there would be only a handful of players—those under twenty-one or over thirty-one—left to carry on. Crowds, already declining, would disappear completely and the owners would go broke.

Treading on eggshells in its effort to avoid appearing unpatriotic while at the same time doing all it could to keep the game alive, baseball cautiously approached Secretary of War Baker and General Crowder. Actors had been exempted from the work-or-fight order on the grounds that public entertainment was necessary. Was not baseball public entertainment? In response, General Crowder late in June announced that while baseball was presently regarded as nonproductive, no blanket ruling on the status of individual players would be sent to local draft boards until a case then in the hands of the Secretary of War was decided. This was the matter of Eddie Ainsmith, a twenty-eight-year-old catcher who had been with the Washington Senators for nine seasons. He had been deferred in the draft earlier but now had been told he was to be called up because of the work-or-fight order. Ainsmith, backed by the Washington club, had appealed the draft board's decision and had carried his appeal all the way to Secretary Baker.

Baseball had to wait nearly a month, until the middle of July, for Baker's decision. While it waited, the defection of its players continued. One of those who left was Dutch Leonard, the Red Sox lefthander, and his departure hurt. Leonard had been at a peak of accomplishment. He had pitched a no-hit, no-run game on June 3, followed that with another shutout on June 9 and pitched a third straight shutout on June 13. He lost, 2–1, on June 16 and after starting one more game on June 20 jumped the club to take a job with the Fore River Shipyards in Quincy, Massachusetts, just outside Boston. No one knew for sure what Leonard's everyday job was at the shipyard, but everyone was aware that he was also pitching for the Fore River baseball team.

With Leonard gone, Barrow again found himself short a starting pitcher, and this time he was unable to find another Sam Jones hidden in the back reaches of the dugout. The Red Sox, who had not been playing well anyway, slipped out of first place, and Barrow turned to Ruth for pitching help. Babe's hitting had been ordinary after that home run binge early in June—he had hit only one more since and his extravagant batting average had declined slowly but steadily into the low .300s—and Barrow felt he would be of greater value to the team on the mound than in the outfield. Ruth resisted the suggestion. He did not want to pitch. He had come to think of himself as an outfielder. He would really have preferred to play first base, but McInnis was obviously his superior at that position and Babe had become content in the outfield. Pitching was part of his past, as far as he was concerned. Hitting was what he lived for now, at least on the baseball field.

Barrow pressed him. Ruth said no. He said he couldn't pitch, that his arm bothered him. What was wrong with it? Well, it didn't feel right. The wrist hurt. He began to wear a leather strap around his left wrist as proof. This went on for several days until Barrow lost his patience and told Ruth flatly he would be starting against the Yankees in New York the following Monday. On Saturday Ruth slid into second base in a game against Philadelphia and got up grimacing and holding his wrist. Barrow ignored the purported injury. He told the press that Babe would be pitching against New York.

But in New York on Monday Ruth insisted his wrist did hurt, and Joe Bush started the game in his place. Ruth sat on the bench. Barrow intended to keep him there, but Strunk twisted his bad ankle again and on Tuesday Barrow had to use Ruth in Strunk's place in center field. As if in reaction to Barrow's pressure on him to pitch, Ruth's hitting immediately picked up. He hit a home run, his ninth of the year (and was referred to in print for the first time as the Home Run King), and the next afternoon hit a towering double that just missed being a homer when it glanced off the right field fence in the Polo Grounds. But he still would not pitch, and Barrow had to turn to a thirty-year-old righthander named Loren Bader, who had spent most of his career in the minors. In Bader's debut, which he lost, Ruth hit his tenth homer of the year; it was the only hit the Red Sox made in the game. A couple of days later, on June

30, he hit a game-winning homer off Walter Johnson in the tenth inning to put the Red Sox back in the league lead. Now he had 11 home runs, a fairly staggering total. In fifteen previous seasons only three American Leaguers had hit as many in a full season, and each had ended the year with 12. And here was Ruth with 11 before the season was half over. His fame was spreading. A naval officer noted that the wireless report that went out from Arlington every night at eleven included a quick rundown of the day's baseball scores. Just the bare results were given, except for Boston's games. Here the operator would interrupt the report to advise whether Ruth had hit a home run or not.

Barrow was not that impressed. He still wanted Ruth to pitch. The relationship between manager and star became more and more strained. There was continual bickering. Barrow intimated that Ruth was dogging it in refusing to take his turn on the mound. Ruth told Barrow to stop pestering him and added, "I'm tired." Barrow snapped, "If you'd get to bed on time once in a while you wouldn't be so damned tired."

On July 1 the Red Sox slid from the lead again, and the next afternoon in Washington the situation between the two men exploded. In the sixth inning Barrow bawled Ruth out for swinging at the first pitch when the manager wanted him to wait the pitcher out. "That was a bum play," Barrow said. Ruth flared up. "Don't call me a bum," he yelled, "not unless you want to get a punch in the nose." Barrow, furious but still occupied with the game at hand, snapped, "That'll cost you $500." Ruth shouted, "The hell it will. I quit!" and stomped off to the clubhouse. He dressed, left the ballpark, checked out of the hotel and went home to his father's place in Baltimore. When the Red Sox left Washington that evening for Philadelphia, it was glaringly obvious that Ruth was not with the team.

That night in Baltimore—this was Tuesday, July 2—Ruth sent a wire to Frank Miller, manager of the baseball team that played for the Chester Shipyards in Chester, Pennsylvania, just south of Philadelphia, asking what he would be paid if he left the Red Sox and joined the shipyard's team. Miller immediately sent a representative to Baltimore to talk to Ruth, and they worked out terms for Babe to appear with the shipyard team when it played on the Fourth of July, two days later.

Barrow knew nothing of this. In Philadelphia Wednesday morning he denied that Ruth had quit the team, telling reporters that Ruth's going off to Baltimore was only a momentary aberration on Babe's part, a sort of boys-will-be-boys willfulness. Later, during batting practice, Barrow was sitting in the back of the grandstand with Frazee, who had come down from New York to watch the Red Sox play, when a reporter came over to them and said, "We've just heard that Ruth has signed to play with the Chester Shipyards."

"I don't believe it," Barrow said, but Frazee, instantly alert, asked "Where is this shipyard? Who's in charge of the team? I've got a contract with Ruth and they have no right to use him." Frazee said he would go into court if he had to. "Ruth can't get away with this," he added.

That afternoon the headlines shouted, "RUTH JUMPS RED SOX. WILL PLAY IN DELAWARE RIVER SHIPBUILDING LEAGUE." In Baltimore reporters found Babe in his father's flat and pumped him with questions. He was surprisingly quiet and subdued, even contrite. He talked about the fuss with Barrow and admitted that his temper had got away from him. "I guess I said a lot of things I shouldn't have said," he conceded. He added that he thought it would all blow over, although he made it clear that he would not pay the $500 fine. He said he would probably rejoin the Red Sox in a few days. "I'm all right," he said. "I'm ready to go back to playing. I just don't want to be fighting and being fought with all the time."

One of the reporters told him that some people thought he was jumping to Chester because of the work-or-fight order, that he was trying to avoid the draft. "No," said Ruth. "That's not it at all. I've been deferred because I'm married, but we've all signed up anyway [he and several other players had joined a reserve unit in Boston] to do our bit after the season is over. Any time they want me, all they have to do is call me and I'll go." What about the deal with Chester? "Oh," said Ruth. "Well, I'll play with them tomorrow. I thought it would be fun to play somewhere tomorrow."

Frazee felt rather differently about it. He said he would seek an injunction to prevent Ruth from playing with Chester on July 4 and that if Babe did play he would sue the shipyard for damages. Miller, the Chester manager, was unimpressed by Frazee's threats and declared that he fully expected Babe to play, but Ruth, apparently unnerved by the vigor of Frazee's language, sent the Red Sox owner a wire in which he said he had not jumped the club. He neglected to add anything about when he was coming back or whether or not he would be playing with Chester.

That evening the amiable Heinie Wagner, who had been Ruth's keeper under Carrigan and who was still serving as a player-coach under Barrow, took a train from Philadelphia to Baltimore and went to see the runaway. Babe was glad to see him. He had always liked Heinie and it took very little persuasion from Wagner before Babe agreed to return to the ball club with him. They reached Philadelphia at two in the morning and went to sleep.

The Red Sox and the Athletics had a morning-afternoon double-header the next day, the Fourth of July. Ruth reported to the clubhouse in the morning and put on his uniform, but Barrow ignored him and did not put him in the lineup. Ruth had returned in an expansive, conciliatory mood, feeling like the prodigal son. Now he was hurt, and when Barrow still refused to speak to him after the morning game, Babe blew up again. He took off his uniform and said that was it, now he was quitting for good.

Wagner and Hooper and several other players gathered around him, soothed him, calmed him down. Hooper or Wagner, or possibly Frazee himself, talked to Barrow and got him to retreat from his stubborn position. This may have been when Frazee nicknamed his manager Simon Legree. In any case, a truce was effected. Amos Strunk was still on the sidelines with his bad ankle, and Barrow put Ruth into center field for the afternoon game. Babe made one hit but he also struck out twice and popped up, which greatly pleased the Philadelphia fans who, no gentler then than they are now, rode him unmercifully and hooted when he struck out.

After the game Barrow and Ruth worked out the details of their peace. The fine was rescinded, but in return Babe agreed to pitch the next afternoon, the first time he had started a game in nearly five weeks. He won it too, 4–3, in ten innings. And with the pennant race so tight, he apparently agreed to go along with Barrow's wish that he remain solely a pitcher for the time being. At any rate when the Red Sox returned to Boston on Saturday, July 6, to open a series with the Cleveland Indians, who were in first place, Ruth was on the bench and a rookie named Walter Barbare was in left field. In the sixth inning, when Barbare came to bat with two men on and the Red Sox behind, 4–2, Barrow could not resist the temptation. He sent Ruth in to pinch-hit. Babe hit a triple that drove in the tying runs and when the throw to third base went awry came across himself with the winning run.

That victory moved the Red Sox past Cleveland into the lead, and Barrow gave up. The next day Ruth was in left field, batting fourth, and he stayed there. The Red Sox beat Cleveland four out of five, Chicago three out of four, St. Louis three out of four and Detroit four straight. Ruth hit ferociously. He hit no home runs, but he had five triples in seven games, including one with a man on first base in the last half of the tenth inning of a 0–0 game that actually went into the right field bleachers on the fly. Under today's scoring rules it would be a home run, but in that day the game ended as soon as the winning run crossed the plate, and Ruth's blow was officially designated a triple.

Against the White Sox he was particularly overwhelming. A theory had been advanced that because Ruth was such a pronounced pull hitter, he could be stopped if he were given nothing but low outside pitches. Chicago's Eddie Cicotte tested the theory and Ruth pushed three successive doubles to the opposite field. The next day he hit another double and two triples. End of theory. His hitting simply amazed baseball people. Everyone marveled at the force with which he swung, and how when he missed the ball his body would be twisted around in a complete circle by the violence of his effort. Newspapers ran detailed charts analyzing his accomplishments. One article noted that 40 of his 65 hits (to that date) had been for extra bases, and it compared his "extra bases"—that is, the number of bases beyond first to which his hits had carried him—with those of other outstanding American League hitters. Ruth had 75 such bases from his 65 hits, whereas Home Run Baker had only 38 from 108 hits and Ty Cobb 35 from 105. Ruth was, the papers wrote, "The Mightiest Slugger of Them All," and a Boston sportswriter named Burt Whitman said, "The more I see of Babe, the more he seems a figure out of mythology."

During Boston's winning surge Babe played left field in every game but one. On July 17 the Red Sox had a doubleheader with St. Louis. Mays, Bush and Jones had been doing nearly all the pitching, and Barrow asked Ruth if he would help out by starting one of the games in the doubleheader. Ruth said sure, came in from the outfield after the first game and turned in a rain-shortened 4–0 shutout (the game ended after the fifth inning). The manager was pleased, and for the moment, as far as Babe was concerned, everything was sweetness and light.

It was not sweetness and light for baseball, however. On July 19 Secretary of War Baker finally announced his decision on Eddie Ainsmith. Baseball, he declared ominously, was not an essential occupation under the work-or-fight order. Therefore, Ainsmith faced induction into the army unless he left baseball and got a productive job. The ruling was not unexpected, but it nonetheless shocked baseball. It meant that the game would very soon lose almost all its players. In Chicago, Ban Johnson impulsively declared that the American League season would end two days later, after the games of Sunday, July 21. James Dunn, owner of the Cleveland Indians and a faithful follower of Johnson, dutifully said he would close and lock his park on Sunday night.

The other owners were not so ready to comply. Johnson's dictatorial authority—he had singlehandedly founded the American League and always assumed the right to rule it without question—

was on the wane, and on Saturday, after the league president's Götterdämmerung statement had been printed in newspapers all across the country, Jacob Ruppert, an unflappable individual, said quietly that he saw no reason for ending the season so abruptly. The Yankees had only one nondraft-age player, the venerable Home Run Baker, but Ruppert said that, even so, he was in favor of continuing with the schedule for the time being. Frazee, who got along well with Ruppert, agreed, pointing out that baseball had at least a little time before the draft boards would act. He suggested cutting the season from its regular 154-game schedule to 100 games (his Red Sox up to that day had played 86) and holding the World Series in August. As for Johnson's declaration that the season would end the next day, Frazee said, "My answer to that is: I will not give my consent, and it requires the unanimous consent of the owners to end the season."

Ruppert, Frazee and one or two others managed to stem Johnson's initial panic, and the next day Ban reversed his field and said the league was going ahead. The National League had already decided to continue. After a hasty conference the National Commission wired General Crowder and asked if it might discuss the situation with him. The General agreed to the request and said he would meet with them in Washington on Wednesday, July 24. He would delay application of the work-or-fight order to baseball, he said, until after the meeting.

Frazee was a member of a twelve-man group that went to see Crowder. They stressed the seasonal aspect of baseball and asked if the order could be held off until October 15, after the World Series. If that was impossible, they asked at the very least for enough time to let baseball make orderly preparations for a suspension of activity. Crowder said he would take up the matter with Secretary Baker. On Friday, July 26, Baker announced that baseball could have until the weekend of September 1. This cut a month and about 30 games from the original schedule, but baseball was happy to be getting that much time. Garry Herrmann, the president of the National Commission, immediately declared that the season would end on Labor

Day, September 2, and suggested that a brief World Series would probably follow, although John Tener, the National League president, said gloomily, "I don't think a Series will be played this year."

Johnson, who did not like to be upstaged by Herrmann, a National Leaguer, announced a day or so later that he had asked the American League owners for permission (he had learned a lesson there) to end the season on August 20, but again his wishes were ignored. The American Leaguers went along with their National League counterparts and set Labor Day as the terminal date. Then, not content with one cookie, baseball went back to the War Department and asked if it would be all right for two teams, the two pennant winners, to continue on into September long enough to put on the World Series, and the War Department eventually okayed this proposal too (although not until August 22, just two weeks before the Series began).

This, then, was the "green light" baseball received in World War I. The Red Sox were in Chicago on July 26 when the news of it broke, and Barrow promptly approached Ruth again about pitching. It was an amicable discussion this time. The manager remarked that the season had little more than a month to go. He wondered if Babe could handle the extra effort of coming in from the outfield every fourth day to pitch during that fairly brief stretch. The Red Sox had a fair lead (it was four and a half games at that point) and an excellent chance to win the pennant, if the pitching held up. But the staff was showing signs of wear. Bader had not come through, and Mays, Bush and Jones were starting all the games now. Mays had been superb (he won his 17th game on July 22) but he was exhausted. Bush and Jones were beginning to flag too. Barrow—and the Red Sox—desperately needed a fourth starter. Otherwise the pitching was apt to collapse completely and with it the team's chances of winning the pennant.

Barrow asked, instead of ordering, and Ruth agreed. After playing left field and batting fourth in Chicago on Thursday, Friday, Saturday and Sunday, he went to the mound in St. Louis on Monday, July 29. He had pitched only twice in nearly two months, a total of only fourteen innings, yet he immediately became the top man on the staff, starting and winning more games than anyone else from then to the end of the season. He completed eight of his nine starts (in 1917 and 1918 he started 57 games and completed 53 of them). He batted fourth when he pitched against the Browns and won, 3–2. The next afternoon he was in left field and was in the outfield again on Wednesday. On Thursday, still batting fourth, he pitched against St. Louis again and won, 2–1. Friday and Saturday he played left field in Cleveland. On Sunday he pitched against the Indians in the first game of a doubleheader and won, 2–1, and in the second game played left field.

It went on that way for the rest of the season, and he won seven games in little more than a month while leading the team in hitting. There was one hiatus in his strenuous schedule. On Saturday, August 24, he beat the Browns, 3–1, in Boston (and even stole home on the front end of a double steal). That victory left the Red Sox four games ahead with only nine games left in the abbreviated season, which meant that another pennant, Boston's third in four years, was assured. The team had Sunday off, and Babe and Helen planned to go out to the beach. But word came Sunday morning that Babe's father was dead. On Saturday night in Baltimore a family quarrel had ruptured into tragedy. Babe's father and his second wife had taken her sister in to live with them. The sister's husband had been arrested a few weeks earlier on charges of statutory rape with a sixteen-year-old girl. He was now out on bail and, as a matter of fact, was downstairs in the bar that very evening. A brother of the two women, a Baltimore fireman, stopped by Saturday night to see if the sister needed money and became angry when she told him of the ways her husband had mistreated her. The fireman went downstairs to the bar, accosted his brother-in-law and began a harangue about his various inadequacies. An argument followed and Ruth senior, angry at all the noise in his tavern, came over to stop the dispute. He and the fireman had a few sharp words, and when the man left, Ruth followed him outside. They got into a fight, in the course of which Ruth fell and hit the back of his head.

He was carried into the bar and then was taken to University Hospital, where he died.

Babe and Helen took a train to Baltimore for the wake and the funeral and did not return to Boston until late in the week. He missed three games, the first time since his illness in May that he had gone more than one day without playing. It was his last extended visit to Baltimore, which he never again thought of as home. His father and mother were dead, his only sister was eighteen, a grown woman, and his stepmother had the bar. He was Babe Ruth of Boston now.

He pitched his last game of the season the following Saturday, August 31, beating Philadelphia, 6-1, to clinch the pennant for the Red Sox. It was his 13th victory against seven defeats, and his ninth in his last 11 starts. His .650 winning percentage was second best in the league. He had also played 59 games in the outfield and 13 at first base. He batted an even .300. He did not hit a home run after June 30, and he had been tied for the league championship at 11 by Tilly Walker, his ex-teammate now with Philadelphia, but more than half his 95 hits were for extra bases.

If they had been selecting a Most Valuable Player that year, he would have won the honor in a breeze, the Chester Shipyard caper notwithstanding.

CHAPTER 14

The 1918 World Series: The Abortive Strike

The World Series between the Red Sox and the Cubs began in Chicago on Thursday, September 5, the earliest a Series game has ever been played and the first time one was held before the beginning of October. Frazee protested the scheduling, which provided for the first three games to be in Chicago and the remaining ones—either one, two, three or four, as needed—in Boston. Frazee felt this was unfair, since Boston could be certain of only one playing date at home in the best four games of seven series. He assumed that Ban Johnson, bitter toward him because Ruppert and he had led the resistance to Johnson's plans for ending the season early, had connived with the two National Leaguers on the National Commission to job Boston out of a fair share of playing dates. But Garry Herrmann, the commission president, always courteous, patiently explained to Frazee that wartime travel restrictions had dictated the pattern of the schedule and a flip of the coin had decided which city would get the first three games. Frazee gave in, and the Red Sox went to Chicago.

Ruth, of course, was expected to dominate the Series, possibly as a pitcher, certainly as a hitter. Chicago geared its entire strategy to Ruth's bat. The Cubs had three fine pitchers in Jim Vaughn, Lefty

Tyler and Claude Hendrix, but because Hendrix was a righthander and the lefthanded Ruth was murderous against righties, the Cubs used only the lefthanded Vaughn and Tyler in the Series. The two alternated starts and between them pitched all but two innings for the Cubs in the six-game affair.

Everybody wondered whether Barrow would have Ruth pitch the first game, although Mays, who won 21 games, was probably the more logical choice. Mays had been pitching poorly for almost five weeks, but a few days before the season ended, Barrow had him start both games of a doubleheader and Mays won both, 12-0 and 4-1. He was ready. Bush too was pitching strongly, and young Sam Jones won his last five starts to finish with a 15-5 record, especially impressive since he had not pitched at all to speak of in the first month of the season. Even so, Ruth was the best Boston pitcher down the stretch.

The day before the Series began, Barrow said Ruth would be in left field and probably would not pitch at all. Either Mays or Bush would open the Series, he said. Ruth emphasized his role as the prospective hitting hero of the Series by hitting the first ball pitched to him in batting practice before the first game into the seats.

All this was a ruse. When the teams finished batting practice, Bush went out to warm up. Then, to the confusion of the Cubs, Ruth joined Bush and began to warm up next to him. When the Boston lineup was handed to the umpires at game time, Ruth was the starting pitcher. Moreover, he batted ninth against the left-handed Vaughn, and old George Whiteman, the righthanded-hitting left fielder, batted fourth.

The strategy worked perfectly. Ruth defeated Vaughn, 1-0, and Whiteman had two of Boston's five hits, one of which set up the winning run. Ruth, cheered by the Chicago crowd each time he came to bat, flied to center and struck out twice (which brought louder cheers from the Chicago crowd). He also "took care" of Leslie Mann for Barrow. Mann was the Chicago left fielder, a right-handed hitter who hit lefthanders well.

"Watch out for this fellow Mann," Barrow warned Ruth before

the game. "Don't let up on him. Don't ever let him dig in at the plate."

"Don't worry," Ruth said. "I'll get him."

Mann, who had hit a home run off Ruth in the spring of 1914 when Babe was a rookie with Baltimore, was short and stocky. Max Flack, the Cubs' rightfielder, was short too, although not nearly as chunky as Mann. And Flack batted lefthanded, not righthanded. But Ruth studied Max closely when he came to bat in the first inning, brushed him back from the plate twice and struck him out with a fastball on the outside corner. The Cubs filled the bases after that—for all Barrow's warnings, Ruth let Les Mann hit a single—and Babe had to struggle to get out of the inning. If he had intended to say anything about either the Flack strikeout or the Mann single when he came to the bench he had forgotten about it by the time he got there. In the third inning Flack singled sharply, and when he came to bat again in the fifth Ruth hit him on top of the head with a fastball. Fortunately, Flack was not hurt and he trotted on down to first base, but when Ruth came to the bench after the inning was over he sat down next to Barrow and said, "Well, I guess I took care of that guy Mann for you." He had been throwing at the wrong player all afternoon.

A long-standing baseball tradition had its origin in that game. When the hometown fans stood up for their customary seventh-inning stretch, the band unexpectedly began to play "The Star-Spangled Banner." The players stood at attention and turned to face the flag flying from a pole in center field and one of them, on leave from the Great Lakes Naval Training Station, saluted. The crowd began to sing the song—it was not yet the national anthem—and when it was over there was a great burst of applause. The incident was entirely spontaneous, but it was repeated in the following two games in Chicago, and when the teams moved to Boston, Frazee, the showman, had his band play "The Star-Spangled Banner" to open the festivities. Thereafter it was usually played on opening day and at World Series games and other special occasions that warranted the presence of a band. The coincidence twenty-five years later of electronic public-address systems and World War II brought about the current practice of playing the anthem before every baseball game (and, by extension, before practically every major sports event). It is estimated that a twenty-year veteran like Willie Mays heard "The Star-Spangled Banner" played 3000 times. Usually badly.

The war made its presence felt in other ways. During the eighth inning six warplanes (not jets but World War I biplanes) flew over the field in formation as the crowd watched in wonder. And, because of the war, it was not much of a crowd. Ticket prices had been cut in half, but attendance was a disappointing 19,000, not much more than half of what it was a year earlier when the Giants and White Sox opened their Series in the same park. It was almost as bad on Friday, when the Cubs beat Joe Bush, but it rose to 27,000 on Saturday, when Mays, in top form, gave Vaughn his second defeat, 2–1. Ruth did not play in either of these games.

With attendance bad, the low ticket prices made gate receipts even worse than bad, which was a matter of concern to the players. They were on the edge of a financial desert, what with the work-or-fight order presumably wiping out the 1919 season (no one in September 1918 knew that the war would be over in two months), and the shortening of the season had hit them in the pocketbook already, since they were paid biweekly and their salary checks ended when the regular season did. The Red Sox players confronted Frazee on that, demanding that their salaries be continued through September 15. At first Frazee refused, but when the players said in that case they would not play in the Series, he gave in.

Now the players had to worry about their Series shares too. The World Series was traditionally the great plum of baseball, but every time they looked up, the plum was shrinking more and more rapidly into a prune. The complex formula for dividing gate receipts equitably gave the players 60 per cent of the money taken in at the first four games; they did not share in receipts from later games, in order to avoid suspicion that they might deliberately extend the Series in order to achieve a greater financial return. But now for the first time the two Series teams had to split the pot with players on the second-, third- and fourth-place teams in each league, a system that subsequently became standard baseball practice.

This new system had been decreed by the National Commission the previous January, partly because of an uneasiness about possible wartime reaction to World Series players hauling down vast sums of money for a few days' work and partly because baseball brass was increasingly unhappy at the windfalls the Series players were getting—especially since a wave of new, larger ballparks greatly increased attendance and receipts. Individual shares for members of winning and losing teams were substantial, often equaling or surpassing a player's annual salary—and in the case of high-salaried players being equivalent to a 25 or 50 per cent bonus. At this point in the game's history only a handful of players made as much as $10,000 a year, and only two or three—Cobb, Wagner, Speaker—had gone beyond $15,000.

The commission therefore established flat figures of $2000 for each winning share and $1500 for each losing one. The balance of the money would be spread around among the other first-division ballplayers. One baseball executive said gleefully, "The heyday of players reaping a harvest from World Series spoils has come to an end." The players made no objection to the new system, probably because most of them thought more in terms of picking up a little extra cash for finishing second, third and fourth than in picking up a bundle for finishing first. After all, almost 90 per cent of the players each year did not make the Series. And $2000 was still a lot of money; even $1500 wasn't bad.

In Chicago, however, the low receipts gave the players pause, especially when they remembered then that they had to give 10 per cent off the top to war charities (baseball promised a 10 per cent donation from World Series revenue when it asked the War Department for permission to put the Series on). It began to appear that even if no money at all was passed on to the other first-division teams, there still would not be enough money in the players' pool to come close to the projected $2000 and $1500 shares. The National

Commission conceded that the actual amounts would be more like $1200 and $800.

The players became restive. The two clubs left Chicago for Boston Saturday night on the same train, and during the long journey—the train did not reach Boston until late Sunday—players from both teams met and discussed the matter. Something had to be done, they agreed, and representatives were dispatched to speak to one or another or all three members of the National Commission: Ban Johnson, Garry Herrmann or John Heydler (who a month earlier had been elected president of the National League to succeed John Tener). The commissioners put them off. The players persisted. They declared they would not play in Boston on Monday unless a satisfactory settlement of their grievance was reached. The commissioners relented slightly and said they would meet with a players' committee Tuesday morning before the fifth game of the Series. The players accepted this and agreed to play Monday's game without question.

Ruth went along with all this, although he was not an active participant. He was more interested in straw hats on the train ride. Hard straw hats were a favored summer style, but now it was September—Labor Day was past—and connoisseurs of style on the train decreed that with summer over the straw hat should go too. Ruth chose to enforce this fashion dictate and with a few boisterous teammates went whooping and hollering through the cars confiscating every flat straw skimmer in sight and punching a hole through the bottom of each. One of his companions in the guerrilla operation was a big lefthander from Texas named Walt Kinney. Kinney wasn't much of a pitcher—he had appeared in only fifteen innings that year—but he was as tall as Ruth and rangy and strong, and the two of them liked to wrestle and spar and generally clout each other around—like very large tiger cubs at play. Late Sunday afternoon when the train was halfway across Massachusetts, only an hour or so from Boston, the straw hat supply gave out and Ruth and Kinney fell back on horseplay to while away the time. Ruth took a left-handed swing at the Texan, Kinney ducked, the train lurched, and

Ruth's pitching hand smacked against the hard steel side of the car. He yelped in pain and sucked the middle knuckle of his left hand. The knuckle became red and swollen, and his middle finger began to ache.

Ruth tried to keep Barrow from learning of the injury, but the manager found out, looked at the hand and growled, "You damn fool. You know you're supposed to pitch tomorrow, and you go fooling around like this."

"I'll be okay," Ruth said. "I'll be able to pitch."

And he did, and surprisingly well too, although for only the second time that year he was not able to complete a game. He went into it with a string of twenty-two consecutive scoreless innings in World Series competition: the last thirteen innings of his memorable win over Brooklyn in 1916 and his nine-inning shutout of the Cubs four days earlier. He struggled—he gave up seven hits and six walks before he was relieved in the ninth—but the Red Sox made three double plays and the hapless Max Flack was twice picked off base (once by the catcher and once by Ruth, who nipped him off second). The Cubs were not able to score until the eighth, which gave Ruth seven more scoreless innings, or twenty-nine in all, breaking the famous World Series record of twenty-eight set by Christy Mathewson in 1905. Ruth's record lasted for forty-two years, and of all his accomplishments in baseball it was the one of which he was most proud.

Barrow had moved him up from ninth in the batting order to seventh—the only time in his career that he hit seventh—and when he came to bat for the first time in the second inning he was roaringly acclaimed by the Boston crowd, which was far more interested in his hitting than in his shutout pitching. Disappointment. No one was on base, and he grounded out to second. When he came to bat again in the fourth inning the score was still 0–0, and this time runners were on first and second. The crowd was bouncing with anticipation. If first base had been open, Lefty Tyler would have given Ruth an intentional base on balls, but now he had to pitch to him. He threw three consecutive curves low and away, and the count went to three and nothing. He threw two more curves that caught the plate, and it was three and two. Ruth cocked his bat. Tyler stood nervously on the mound. He turned toward right field and signaled Max Flack to play deeper. Flack backed up a step or two. Tyler waved again, but Flack stayed where he was. Tyler turned and pitched. Ruth swung and hit a long fly to right. Flack, momentarily misjudging it, took a step in and then turned and raced back. The ball went over his head and rolled all the way to the fence, and by the time Max got to it and threw it in, Ruth was on third base with a triple, the Red Sox were leading, 2–0, and the crowd was making more noise than any Boston crowd had since the Colonials took two from the British at Concord and Lexington.

The score stayed 2–0 until the eighth inning, when Ruth, laboring, gave up a walk and a single. An infield out brought in one run, ending the scoreless streak, and a second Chicago hit tied the score. The Red Sox scored again in the last of the eighth to go ahead, 3–2, and Ruth went out to pitch the ninth. The first batter singled and the second walked, which meant the Cubs had the tying and winning runs on base with no one out. Barrow called time and brought Joe Bush in to pitch, but instead of taking Ruth out of the game he sent him to left field. A force-out at third base on an attempted sacrifice and a quick double play, and that was the ballgame: Ruth's third World Series pitching victory, and his third by a one-run margin (2–1, 1–0, 3–2).

The Red Sox now had a 3–1 lead in games, and Boston's fans were talking optimistically about wrapping it up the next day. The players, on the other hand, were talking pessimistically about the attendance that afternoon. Only 22,000 had come to the game and rough arithmetic indicated that receipts from the first four games would yield a winning share of only $900 a man and a losing share of $500. The players moaned.

The next morning their four-man committee (Hooper and Dave Shean of the Red Sox, Mann and Bill Killefer of the Cubs) met as scheduled with the National Commission at the ballpark. That is, they met with Herrmann and Heydler. Johnson had stopped off at the bar of the Copley Plaza Hotel in downtown Boston to have a few drinks with a friend. The players reminded Herrmann and Heydler that right up to the beginning of the Series they had been assured that they would receive shares of $2000 and $1500 and that these figures had been accepted without protest, even though they were drastically smaller than in previous years. Herrmann mentioned the meager crowds. Hooper, who acted as spokesman for the players, said they were aware that attendance had been disappointing. They knew ticket prices had been sharply reduced. They realized receipts were small. They were therefore willing to accept a further reduction—but only to $1500 for each winning share and $1000 for each losing one. Herrmann said it was impossible, there wasn't enough money. The players' shares had to come from the players' portion of the gate receipts. It was a shame that portion wasn't larger, but that's the way it was. Everyone was losing money in the Series, the clubs, the leagues, the commission. The only ones who would make anything beyond expenses were the players themselves.

Hooper said he understood all that, but he suggested that because of the scarcity of receipts this year the new system of bringing the second-, third- and fourth-place teams in each league into the pot be postponed until normal conditions returned after the war. That would be only fair, he claimed.

Herrmann disliked arguments and disputes. He wished Johnson were there. Heydler, young and inexperienced, said nothing at all. Herrmann shook his head sadly at Hooper and the other players and said he could do nothing about it right now. After the game perhaps a decision could be made—by which he meant after he and Heydler had had a chance to talk to Johnson.

Hooper said no. Make the decision now. Herrmann repeated that it was impossible. Hooper said, "Then we will not play today."

By two-thirty, which was the scheduled time for the game to start, only one player had appeared on the field (Stuffy McInnis wandered out to take a look at things). No explanation for the delay was given the spectators, but stories on the threatened strike had appeared in the papers, and the people in the stands had a pretty good idea of what was going on. Honey Fitzgerald, who had come to the park with the Royal Rooters, listened to the murmuring in the grandstand and, fearing a riot if the game was called off, sent for police reinforcements. Fitzgerald was only an ex-mayor at the time, but he was still a potent political force. Several wagonloads of police were sent at once to Fenway Park, and four mounted policemen came in through an outfield gate to take up positions in front of the unruly bleachers.

Meanwhile, Johnson arrived at the ballpark, feeling absolutely splendid after his session at the Copley Plaza bar. The players' committee and the commission renewed the discussion. Johnson, in an expansive mood, took over the meeting. He told Hooper for the last time that nothing could be done. There was not enough money, and the commission was not going to change its plans to include the other first-division clubs in the split. Hooper said again that the players on both clubs would strike; they would not play.

"If you don't want to play, don't," Johnson said, "but, Harry, you fellows are putting yourselves in a very bad light with the fans. There are going to be wounded soldiers and sailors at the game again today. With a war going on, and fellows fighting in France, what do you think the public will think of you ballplayers striking for more money?"

Hooper sagged. He realized they were beaten. He and the other members of the players' committee talked briefly and then Hooper turned to the commission and said they would play. They would finish the Series. But on two conditions. The first was that they be allowed to make a public statement before the game began. The commission agreed and Honey Fitzgerald, who had come into the room, said he would read it to the crowd. The second was that no punitive action be taken against anyone on either team. Johnson waved his hand grandly and said, "Go out and play, Harry. Everything will be okay." Neither Herrmann nor Heydler said anything. Three months later, just before Christmas, each player received a letter signed by Heydler saying that because of their "disgusting conduct" during the strike none would receive a World Series emblem. More than fifty years later Hooper, by then a member of baseball's Hall of Fame, still burned with resentment at the commission's action.

After capitulating, the committee returned to the locker rooms, broke the news to the other players and began to dress for the game. Out in the arena the band had been playing "Tessie" and "Keep the Home Fires Burning" and other songs. At one point there was a hush and the crowd grew very still as a few dozen wounded servicemen, some of them on crutches, were escorted down to front-row seats that had been reserved for them. The crowd rose and applauded and the band softly played "The Star-Spangled Banner." Into this atmosphere strode Honey Fitzgerald carrying a megaphone. He walked up to home plate, stood there for a moment in dramatic silence and then, lifting the megaphone to his mouth and twisting and turning as he spoke so that his words could be heard in every part of the ballpark, he read the statement Hooper had hurriedly prepared. It said in part, "We will play not because we think we are getting a fair deal, because we are not. But we will play for the sake of the public, which has always given us its loyal support, and for the wounded soldiers and sailors who are in the grandstand waiting for us."

There was applause for that, but when the players took the field the cheers were well sprinkled with boos. Ban Johnson had been right about the public's reaction.

The Red Sox lost that afternoon but won the next day to take the Series four games to two. (Ruth got into the final game as a fielding replacement for Whiteman, who hurt his neck diving for a ball in the outfield in the seventh inning.) A few days later the official figures on the winning and losing shares were officially announced. They were slightly higher than the players had anticipated, but they were still minuscule. Ruth and the other Red Sox regulars each received $1102, the smallest winning share in World Series history (a year later a *losing* share was worth $3254). Each of the losing Cubs got $671. The Boston players noted that the 10 per cent earmarked for charity had already been deducted and in a sardonic gesture of their confidence in the National Commission (Harry Frazee called it the National Omission) instructed Hooper to get the money from baseball's governing body and distribute it himself among Boston's war charities.

CHAPTER 15

The Big Fight: Ruth vs. Barrow

Two months after the war-ruined 1918 World Series the war itself was over. The war had relatively small impact on Babe Ruth, and to him its ending meant little more than that baseball would be played in 1919 after all, despite the threats to the contrary. And that meant money. Ruth was well aware of his commercial appeal—a Boston cigar manufacturer had taken him in as a "partner" for the right to capitalize on his name—and he made it clear to Barrow and Frazee that he wanted a substantial raise in 1919. Aside from the esthetic appreciation of his own worth, Ruth needed more money because he was spending more and more of it—on clothes, on automobiles, on girls, on partying. And, yes, on Helen.

Even though she had been married for four years, Helen was barely twenty-one and she found herself increasingly unable to comprehend her husband's exuberant ways. She felt less and less a part of his life. In 1916 they bought an 80-acre "farm" out in the country in Sudbury, 20 miles west of Boston, and the two quondam waifs played at being happy together back on the land. But it was Helen who was more often on the land, alone, while Babe was on the road with the team or on the town with his night people. Only rarely was she able to bring home to him her loneliness and distress, and he assumed that his generosity with money and gifts made up for that. In truth, he was never greatly concerned. He was primarily interested in himself, and his young wife's unhappiness rarely penetrated his restless questing after fun and games.

He was very much a celebrity now as the country turned away from war and toward peace. On the Red Sox ball club he was the king, the unquestioned star of the best team in baseball, winners of the World Series three times in four years. He was only twenty-four, but except for Harry Hooper and Deacon Scott he was senior man on the club in point of service and far and away the best-paid.

Wherever he happened to be he was the focus of attention. During the 1918 season he drew louder and more sustained applause than anyone else. The other players, teammates and opponents both, liked him, or at least enjoyed being around him. He was such an outspoken, engaging extrovert they could not help being amused and entertained by him. And they were in genuine awe of the way he could hit, the way he could play baseball. Nonetheless, they rode him constantly, his teammates relatively gently but his opponents often viciously. They mocked him, jeered him, made pointed insults about his round, flat-nosed, heavily tanned face. They called him monkey, baboon, ape, gorilla. The terms were not used with rough affection; they were insults, harsh comments on his homeliness, his ignorance, his crudity. When he was still relatively new to the major leagues, someone noticed in the clubhouse that he had the distressing habit after taking a shower of putting back on the same sweaty underwear he had taken off after the game, and of wearing the same underwear day after day. Baseball wit is seldom subtle, and the ignorant boy from the Home took a cruel barrage of heavy-handed comment for this singular lack of personal fastidiousness. He reacted by abandoning underwear completely and for years thereafter wore nothing at all under his expensive suits and silk shirts.

Loud, profane, outspoken, supremely confident in most things, he returned insult for insult, although he sometimes was not sure whether he had been insulted or not. He was frequently called Tarzan, after Edgar Rice Burroughs' recently published best seller.

Ruth rather liked being called Tarzan, sensing that it had something to do with his nearly superhuman feats on the ballfield, but he did not know what it meant. He asked a teammate, "Hey, what's this Tarzan stuff? Why do you guys keep calling me Tarzan?"

"You know, Babe," the teammate answered in some surprise. "It's from that book."

"What book?"

"The Tarzan book. *Tarzan of the Apes.*"

"*Apes?*" snapped Ruth. "You're calling me an *ape?*" He was suddenly furious. It took fast talk and adroit dissembling to calm him down.

Beyond the simian insults were rougher epithets built around the word nigger. He was called nigger, nigger this, nigger that, all the vituperative changes on the theme that Jackie Robinson was to endure thirty years later. Ruth was called nigger so often that many people assumed he was indeed partly black and that at some point in time he, or an immediate ancestor, had managed to cross the color line. Even players in the Negro baseball leagues that flourished then believed this and generally wished the Babe, whom they considered a secret brother, well in his conquest of white baseball. Ruth, from southern-oriented Baltimore, found the allusion an insufferable calumny, the worst insult of all, although his personal relationship with blacks over the years was amiable. His occasional evidences of bigotry were for the most part casual and unthinking reflections of the age. A New York judge noticed one day that Ruth was a spectator in his court and when the case at hand was over spoke to him from the bench and invited him to give his reactions. "It was interesting," Babe boomed from the back of the court, "but I thought that little kike over there should have won the case."

As he made and spent money he tried to pick up social graces, sometimes with hilarious results, particularly later on after he joined the Yankees and began to live in New York, where he was inevitably drawn into the social whirl. He met society hostesses and one day, inevitably probably, referred to the husband of one of the ladies as the hoster. Mrs. Adler, of *The New York Times* Adlers, asked a

Times baseball writer if he could possibly get Ruth to appear at a benefit she was running. The sportswriter said he would try, but he warned that he could not guarantee Ruth's appearance. He asked Babe, who said sure but added, "Listen, I have to go out to New Jersey first. What time do you want me there?" At the appointed time Ruth drove up in his big car, was introduced to the elegant Mrs. Adler, beamed on the monied throngs who gently pressed around him, and helped make the affair a smashing success. When it was over Mrs. Adler thanked him profusely for his time and effort. The Babe waved his hand. "Oh, shit, lady, I'd do it for anybody," he said.

Another time, he accompanied Ford Frick to a formal dinner party. Frick said that Babe would always move slowly at first when he was at affairs of this sort, watching, noting, finding out how you did things before doing them himself. A rather splendid asparagus salad was served. Babe's eyes sidled around until he saw which fork was to be used. He casually lifted the fork, poked at the salad and then without touching it put the fork down and pushed the plate an inch or so away in dismissal.

"Don't you care for the salad, Mr. Ruth?" his hostess asked.

"Oh, it's not that," he replied, his voice elegant and unctuous. "It's just that asparagus makes my urine smell."

It was toward this world of wealth and social activity that Ruth began to move in 1919. He had acquired an agent of sorts, a Boston friend named Johnny Igoe, and he told Frazee he wanted his salary raised from $7000 to $15,000. Only Ty Cobb, then in his fifteenth season, was being paid more than that. Ruth also said he wanted a two-year contract at that exalted figure. In other words, a $30,000 deal, astronomical in a day when a six-room house rented for sixty dollars and a full-time "hired girl" received room and board and a few dollars a month.

Frazee said no, absolutely no, and for the first time in his career Ruth became a holdout. For Frazee it was not just a matter of his will and personality against Ruth's. It was a major battle in his struggle for economic survival. Frazee knew he needed Ruth, both for his play on the field and his draw at the box office. But Harry had overextended himself in 1918 and had lost a great deal of money. Attendance at Red Sox games had fallen off badly in 1917; and in 1918, even though Boston won the pennant, it dropped another 35 per cent. The dismal World Series receipts that so upset the players had been a financial disaster for Frazee. And his theatrical ventures were not going well. He was desperately in need of cash, so much so that during the winter he shifted from his earlier policy of buying ballplayers and began to sell them instead. Ernie Shore and Duffy Lewis had been released from service, and Dutch Leonard was back from his war job. Frazee sent all three to the Yankees in deals that netted him $50,000.

He resisted Ruth's demands. They met briefly in Boston one day, but otherwise the only contact between the two was through the press. Babe said he might quit baseball and devote all his time to improving his farm, which now had twenty head of cattle, a couple of dozen pigs, three horses, fifty hens and a collie named Dixie. He made a production of chopping wood lefthanded and wandering through the woods of the farm in a big fur coat. Frazee grinned and said, "Can you imagine him not playing baseball?"

But Ruth was adamant. He said he had been promised $2000 when he returned to the club after jumping it the July before, but that the contract he received from Frazee did not show even this. Through Igoe he issued a statement saying he did not think he was unreasonable in asking $15,000 and hoped that the fans understood that all he was doing was trying to get what he was worth. He said now he wanted either $15,000 for 1919 or a three-year contract at $10,000 a year. Frazee offered him $8500. Ruth also said he did not want to both pitch and play left field any more. Barrow, asked to comment on this, said, "If Ruth plays for the Red Sox in 1919, he will probably pitch and pinch-hit." Ruth answered by saying that he wanted to play left field only and that he felt he would hit better if he was in the lineup every day. "I'll win more games playing every day in the outfield than I will pitching every fourth day," he said.

Because of postwar turmoil the season was beginning late that year (the schedule called for only 140 games instead of the then-standard 154), and the Red Sox did not leave for spring training until the middle of March. Late in February Babe said he was thinking of becoming a professional boxer. He claimed a Boston promoter had offered him $5000 to fight Gunboat Smith, a prominent heavyweight, and he came in from Sudbury to work out in a Boston gym, supposedly for the fight.

The other Red Sox players signed one by one and in March assembled in New York, where they were to board a coastal steamer for the trip south to Florida. Frazee had shifted the Red Sox training site from Hot Springs to Tampa, Florida, at the suggestion of John McGraw. McGraw, still angry because Jack Dunn had failed to sell him Ruth, was not so angry as to ignore the Babe's moneymaking possibilities. He suggested to Frazee that the Red Sox and the perennially popular Giants meet in Florida and barnstorm north together, and Frazee quickly agreed.

But, obviously, Ruth was the key to the tour, and when the Red Sox party, led by Barrow, steamed out of New York without him, Frazee realized something had to be done. That was a Wednesday, March 19. On Thursday Frazee got in touch with Ruth and asked him to come to New York to see if they couldn't reach an agreement. The Babe, restive now that the team had gone south without him, which made him a genuine holdout, took the midnight train down from Boston and met with Frazee Friday morning. After a surprisingly short discussion the two came to terms and Ruth got his three-year contract at $10,000 a year. In retrospect it seems foolish for a rising young player to have tied himself to such a long-term deal, but it must be remembered that the major leagues had gone through three consecutive seasons of uncertainty and falling salaries, what with the death of the Federal League and the onslaught of war. Abrupt salary cuts were common practice. Too, for all his headlines, Ruth at this point in his career had hit only 20 major league home runs. Pitching had been his forte, and he was in the uncertain position of trying to give up pitching for hitting. He had not yet established himself as a fulltime batter. Under the circumstances a three-year contract at $10,000 a year, one of the top salaries in the game, was a marvelous plum for a young man.

After the signing a beaming Ruth told reporters he felt fine and was in good shape. "I've been exercising by doing hard work on my farm all winter," he said, and in a dig at the absent Barrow added that he hoped he would be kept at one position all season instead of being switched back and forth.

Frazee, eager to get Ruth south to training camp, wanted him to leave at once for Florida. Ruth had come to New York without luggage. He phoned Boston, asked Helen to pack his things and had a friend bring them to New York. That night he left for Tampa on the midnight train, and Frazee wired Barrow that Tarzan had signed and was on his way.

In Florida Barrow acceded to Ruth's wishes and used him only as an outfielder. When, after a couple of weeks of practice, the Red Sox met McGraw and the Giants in Tampa on Friday, April 4, in the first exhibition game of the spring, Babe was in left field, batting fourth. The game, a historic one, was played at the Tampa fairgrounds on a diamond laid out in the huge infield of a racetrack. The Giants' pitcher was a tall, thin righthander from Connecticut named George Smith. Smith had attended Columbia University and was called Columbia George by the sportswriters. Columbia George had a modest career in the major leagues—he won only 39 games in eight seasons—but he is indelibly remembered in baseball lore for one pitch he threw that Friday afternoon in Tampa. Ruth, in his first time at bat, leading off the second inning, timed one of Smith's fastballs perfectly and hit an astonishing drive deep to right center field. Ross Youngs, the Giants' rightfielder and a superb athlete, looked like a little boy chasing the ball, which ultimately cleared the low rail fence and rolled across the racetrack.

No one had ever seen a baseball hit anywhere near as far before. A couple of sportswriters talked to Youngs afterwards and got him to show them the precise spot where the ball had ended up. They paced off the distance back to home plate and found themselves disbelieving the result. They scrounged around and found a tape measure and they measured the length of the homer with that. Unhappily, how far the ball carried on the fly and how far it rolled after it landed are obscured by time and conflicting stories. The most modest account said the ball carried "more than 500 feet," the most extravagant said "more than 600 feet." Barrow, who was there that day, said it was 579 feet. Whatever the precise distance, all who saw it agreed it was the longest home run Ruth or anybody else ever hit.

He had another base hit that afternoon and two more the next day, and drove in seven runs in the two games. He was off and running. The clubs broke camp and began moving north, publicity ahead of them, crowds with them, oohs and aahs following them. Attendance was huge everywhere, with Ruth the continuing center of attention. The New York sportswriters discussed the Babe as endlessly as the Boston writers did, speculating on how many home runs he might hit during the season if Barrow continued to let him play every day. But McGraw, a staunch proponent of the bunt and the hit-and-run, the traditional "inside" baseball that played for a run at a time, disparaged Ruth.

"If he plays every day," McGraw said loudly, "the bum will hit into a hundred double plays before the season is over."

Ruth was aware of McGraw's comment, and whenever he made a particularly impressive hit off a Giant pitcher he would hoot at the Giant bench, "How's that for a double-play ball, Mac?"

The jockeying got rougher, and so did the games. The casual springtime exhibitions began to turn into all-out battles, as though the teams were fighting for a pennant. Joe Bush ruined his arm for the year during the feud. One day Art Fletcher, the Giant shortstop, deliberately stuck his hip in the way of a slow Bush pitch. It was an obvious attempt to be hit by the ball, and the umpire refused to let Fletcher take first base. Bush threw the next pitch directly at the batter, yelling, "Stick your head out on this one!" The ball barely missed Fletcher's jaw. On the next pitch Bush threw as hard as he could and struck Fletcher out, but as he threw he felt something go in his shoulder. The next day he was unable to lift his arm or even hold a ball in his hand.

Things came to a head when Larry Doyle of the Giants slid roughly, his spikes high, into Mike McNally at second base. There were angry words and after the game the angry Red Sox held a meeting and decided to retaliate. They picked out individual Giants for personal vengeance. That night Barrow sought out McGraw and told him what his players intended to do. After some discussion the two managers agreed things had gone far enough. Each agreed to restrain his players, and from then on the games were played at a more casual pace.

Ruth continued to be the man the crowds wanted to see. Winston-Salem even declared a half holiday so that folks could go out to the ballpark. Everything he did was sensational. In Charleston he swung so hard striking out that as he spun around, his spikes caught in the hard clay of the batter's box and he wrenched an ankle. He was carried off the field writhing with pain. No one in Carolina could recall seeing a man swing so hard he hurt himself when he missed. How badly hurt he was was another matter. Despite doleful headlines he was back in action the next day, as he so often was after being "seriously injured."

The triumphal tour reached a climax in Baltimore, after the Red Sox had parted ways with the Giants in order to play Jack Dunn's Orioles. It was the first time Ruth had appeared before the home folks in his new role as slugger, and he outdid himself. In six at bats he walked twice and hit four home runs. Everyone in Baltimore was talking about him, and it became an article of faith that while Dunn had undoubtedly developed Ruth into the fine pitcher he was, hitting was something Babe had achieved for himself. The ingenuous Ruth agreed with this analysis, telling a group of reporters after the game that no one could teach a man to hit the way he could. "It's a gift," he admitted modestly. Then he added, "I was afraid a few of my old Baltimore neighbors didn't believe all that they've read in the papers about my hitting. Today was my chance to show them what I could do. So I did."

When the season began a few days later the Red Sox were favored to win the pennant again. Even without Shore and Leonard, and with Ruth in the outfield, Barrow had what seemed to be an impressive pitching staff with Mays, Pennock, Jones, Bush and Ray Caldwell, who had come from the Yankees. On opening day in New York the Red Sox made the odds look good when they crushed the Yankees, 10–0, behind Mays. The Mauler, as Ruth was now being called, batted fourth and had two hits, including a home run. Rain canceled the rest of the Yankee series, but when the Red Sox moved on to Washington they won two more games, with Ruth contributing a double, two triples and five runs scored.

Everything seemed serene, but it wasn't. With the Red Sox on the road in New York and Washington, Babe had been living it up. He had not been home to Boston since leaving for spring training and had not seen Helen for weeks. In Washington, always his favorite playground, he spent almost no time at all in the room in the Raleigh Hotel he shared with coach Dan Howley. Howley was supposed to be Ruth's keeper and he had told Barrow, "I'll take care of that guy if I have to put a ring through his nose." But Barrow was well aware that Ruth's ample nose was not easy to ring. He knew Babe was staying out to all hours of the night, and despite Ruth's fine hitting and the club's impressive start he was determined to do something about it. On Monday night, April 28, after the Red Sox had won their third straight game of the young season, he sat up in the hotel lobby until well after midnight waiting for his errant star. At four in the morning he gave up and went to bed.

The next afternoon Ruth went hitless and the Red Sox lost. After the game the Babe dressed quickly and hurried off. At the hotel that evening an angry Barrow, raging at his inability to control his youthful star's off-field behavior, sought out the night porter, who would be around the lobby all night long, and asked him if he knew Babe Ruth, the big fellow. The porter nodded.

"All right," Barrow said. He gave the porter a couple of dollars, a substantial tip. "Here. When he comes in tonight, you come to my room and tell me. Wake me up. I don't care what time it is. Wake me up and tell me."

When the knock finally came it was six in the morning. Barrow climbed out of bed and opened the door.

"That fellow just came in," the porter said.

Barrow nodded grimly and put on his robe and slippers. Ruth and Howley were in a room on the same floor. When Barrow got to their door he saw a crack of light and heard voices. He knocked. The voices stopped and a moment later the light went out. Barrow rattled the knob angrily and the door, unlocked, opened. He walked into the room and turned on the light.

Ruth was in bed, awake, the covers up to his chin. One hand peeking out from under the covers held a lighted pipe. Howley's rumpled bed was empty. The keeper had fled to the bathroom. Barrow, his great black eyebrows beetling, glared at Ruth.

"You always smoke a pipe this time of night?"

"Sure," Ruth said. "It relaxes me. It helps me get back to sleep."

Barrow stalked to the bed and whipped off the covers. Ruth was fully dressed, even to his shoes.

"You're a fine citizen, Babe," Barrow said. "I must say, you're a fine citizen."

He turned and walked out, pausing at the door to say, "I'll see you at the ballpark."

Ruth, trapped and embarrassed, began to fume, and during the morning his anger grew. By the time he reached the ballpark that afternoon he was brimming with resentment. He had just begun to put on his uniform when Barrow entered the locker room. Ruth stood up and called out, "If you ever come into my room like that again, you son of a bitch, I'll punch you right in the nose."

The clubhouse went dead silent. The massive Barrow turned toward Ruth. "Call me that again," he said.

Ruth, suddenly abashed, stood there saying nothing.

Barrow turned to the other players. "You fellows finish dressing and get out of here. All except Ruth." He looked at Babe again. "You stay here. No one can call me that and get away with it. We'll lock the door. I'll give you a chance to see if you can punch me in the nose."

Barrow, at fifty, was more than twice Ruth's age. Harry Hooper and Dave Shean came over to him.

"You can't fight him, Ed," Hooper said. "That won't do anybody any good."

Barrow shrugged them off. "It's time I had it out with that young man," he said.

He waited, watching, as the players dressed. In the silence pervading the room Ruth put on his uniform along with the other players. As they began to sidle out the door toward the field, he glanced once at Barrow. Then he went out with the others.

He was shagging flies in the outfield when Barrow came out and sat in the Red Sox dugout. After a while Babe trotted in and came to the bench. Barrow pointedly ignored him.

Finally Ruth spoke to him. "Am I playing today?"

"No," Barrow said. "No, you're not playing. And go inside and take off your uniform. You're suspended until further notice."

Ruth obeyed without argument. After the game he went quietly along to Union Station, where the team caught a sleeper home to Boston. The Red Sox defeated the Senators easily that afternoon, 6–1, even without Ruth, and Barrow was in a slightly better mood. He was in his compartment with Larry Graver, the club secretary, when there was a knock on the door.

"Who is it?" Barrow called out.

"It's me—Babe. Will you talk to me?"

Barrow motioned for Graver to leave.

"All right, come in." The door opened. Graver nodded at Ruth and ducked past him into the corridor. Ruth shut the door.

"Sit down," Barrow said.

Ruth sat. After a moment he said, "I'm awfully sorry about what happened today."

"You ought to be."

Ruth hung his head. Then he muttered, thinking almost certainly of the argument in Baltimore that had caused his father's death eight months earlier, "Ed, someday somebody is going to kill me."

Despite his anger, Barrow smiled. "Nobody's going to kill you, Babe. But don't you know you can't go around calling people names like that? What kind of bringing up did you have?"

Ruth hesitated, started to say something, and Barrow interrupted him. "I'm sorry, Babe, I forgot. I know you had it tough as a kid. But don't you think it's time you straightened out and started leading a decent life now? You can't go on the way you've been going."

The contrite Ruth agreed. He asked Barrow if he would lift the suspension and let him play. The manager asked him if he would stop his all-night partying. Ruth said he would but added that he did not want a keeper following him. He did not want people checking on him all the time.

"Listen," he suggested. "Suppose I do this. If I promise to leave a note in your box when I come back to the hotel at night, if I put down the exact time I get back, will you lift the suspension? Will you let me play?"

"You mean you'll tell me the exact time you get in?"

Ruth nodded.

"Can I take your word on that?"

"You bet you can," Ruth said fervently. Barrow said all right, and they shook hands on it. For the rest of the season, whenever the Red Sox were on the road, Babe would leave notes for Barrow every night. "Dear Eddie," he would write (no one else ever called the majestic Barrow Eddie), or "Dear Manager," and then, "I got back at 11:30" or "Back at two minutes before midnight." What he wrote when he came back somewhat later than that was never revealed, but the system seemed to work, and he and Barrow had no more trouble in Boston. In later years Barrow said he never knew whether Ruth lied to him in the notes. "I never checked up on him again," he said. "I took his word."

CHAPTER 16

The First Home Run Record: Magic 29

Despite the peace treaty between Barrow and Ruth—the Babe was back in the lineup the next day—the season was a catastrophe for the Red Sox. They had a good start (four victories and only one defeat the night Barrow and Ruth talked on the train), but after that it was one long decline. The splendid pitching staff sputtered and stalled. Bush's arm injury persisted and he started only two games all year. Pennock pitched once during the first six weeks of the season. Jones was out for almost three weeks. Caldwell pitched a couple of fine games and then several bad ones and finally was released. Only Mays was dependable, but the cheerless righthander became increasingly surly as he lost game after game by scores such as 1–0, 2–1, 2–0, 3–2. The Red Sox were shut out three straight times in games Mays pitched, and in seven games that he started during June they scored a total of eight runs. The team fell into the second division by mid-May and stayed there the rest of the year, finishing a depressing sixth.

Ruth too went into a precipitous slump after his vigorous start and a month into the season was batting .180. He had hit only one home run since opening day, although it was with the bases full, the first time he ever hit a grand slam homer. It also gave him a pitching victory, since Barrow, despite his promise in spring training, asked Ruth to help out on the mound again. Babe filled in for Pennock early in May and won, and in another game he relieved Bush when that sore-armed pitcher had to give up in the second inning. Ruth allowed 11 hits in eleven innings of relief but won, 6–5. Barrow put him in the regular pitching rotation again, and during the next six weeks Ruth started in turn. He played left field most of the time when he did not pitch, although once in a while the manager would keep him on the bench if a particularly tough lefthander was going for the other team.

By June 20 he had won five games and lost two, but he was not pitching well. When Washington routed him, 8–3, on June 25, Barrow let him go back to being a fulltime outfielder. For one thing, Babe's batting had picked up sensationally. His average soared from .180 to .325 in less than a month, and he was beginning to hit home runs again. For another, it was obvious even to the competitive Barrow that the Red Sox were irrevocably out of the pennant race. Since Ruth was the only gate attraction the Red Sox had, he might as well concentrate on hitting.

Along with his homers, Ruth made headlines early in June when he twisted his knee sliding into third base and was carried off the field. Again he was back in the lineup in a day or so. And again he hit a home run the day he returned, which brought more headlines. The fans began to dote on his idiosyncrasies, such as the way he would hold up his bat and look at it in wonder when he missed or did no more than tip a foul back to the screen. One day after striking out he banged his bat on the ground so hard that he cracked the handle. It was a favorite bat, so he kept it and meticulously repaired it with tape and small nails, which was technically against the rules. Later, when he was in a slump, he gave it to Harry Hooper. His strikeouts were almost as interesting as his homers. "When Ruth misses a swipe at the ball," a newspaperman wrote, "the stands quiver." And, of a dull game, "Waiting for Ruth to come to bat was about all the interest the crowd worked up in the first eight innings."

The sportswriters picked up the title of a popular love song called "Along Came Ruth" and used the title phrase freely in their copy, particularly in descriptions of dramatic situations when the Babe came to bat. One such moment occurred in June in a game against the Yankees in New York. The Red Sox were behind, 4–1, in the eighth inning, but they put two men on base—and along came Ruth. A home run would mean three runs and a tie score, so the Yankees brought in Bob Shawkey, their best pitcher. When Shawkey struck Ruth out, the big Saturday afternoon crowd cheered ecstatically, tossed hats in the air and threw programs on the field. A couple of days later Ruth faced Shawkey again, this time with the bases full, and this time he hit his second grand slam of the year.

On July 5 he hit two home runs in one game for the first time in his career and a week later hit homers in successive games to bring his total for the year to 11, equaling his 1918 mark. He stopped there in 1918, but now he kept going. On July 18 against Cleveland he again hit two in one game, and the second was typically melodramatic. It came in the ninth inning with the bases loaded and the Red Sox behind, 7–4; it gave Boston an 8–7 victory and angered Cleveland owner James Dunn so much he fired manager Leo Fohl and replaced him with Ruth's old antagonist, Speaker. Three days later Babe hit the longest homer ever seen in Detroit, and three days after that a two-run homer in Boston that gave the Red Sox a 4–3 win. On July 29 he hit yet another, his ninth of the month and 16th of the season, which tied the American League record set in 1902 by Ralph "Socks" Seybold.

During this sensational streak Ruth returned to pitching on a regular basis for the last time in his career. Again it was to help out in an emergency, this one caused by the defection of Carl Mays. Mays had become increasingly bitter about the poor batting support he was receiving. One day he petulantly threw a ball at a jeering spectator and was fined $100 by the league president Ban Johnson. When he lost, 3–0, in St. Louis on July 9, his record for the season fell to five wins and 11 defeats, even though his earned-run average was fourth best in the league. His last appearance with the Red Sox came four days later in Chicago. In the second inning catcher Wally Schang tried to cut down a man stealing second, but his throw was too low and as it passed the pitcher's box it glanced off Mays's head. When the inning ended, Carl stalked angrily into the clubhouse. Barrow thought the pitcher had gone inside to have the trainer look at his scalp. But when the Red Sox finished their turn at bat and went onto the field, Mays did not reappear. Barrow sent Sam Jones in after him. Jones came out, slightly bewildered, and reported that Mays said he was through, that he was not going to pitch any more. Barrow hurriedly put in a substitute pitcher.

After the game Barrow learned that Mays meant not only that he was not going to pitch any more that day but that he was not going to pitch any more for the Red Sox. He left Chicago, went to Boston, picked up his belongings and left town. The stubborn pitcher had jumped the club, and Barrow and Frazee had a hasty telephone conference. The Red Sox should have suspended Mays at once, but if he was suspended he could not be sold or traded, which was what Frazee had in mind.

"Don't do anything," he warned Barrow. "I might be able to work out something with Ruppert."

Unsuspended, Mays became the focus of attention. Here was a superb player, dissatisfied with a club whose owner needed money. Alert to the situation, Ban Johnson warned the seven other American League clubs not to deal with the Red Sox for the pitcher. But Ruppert, his partner Colonel Tillinghast L'Hommedieu Huston and his business manager Harry Sparrow went from New York to Boston and met with Frazee and Barrow when the Red Sox returned from the western road trip. A week later it was announced that Mays had been sent to the Yankees for Allen Russell, Ruth's old Baltimore teammate, a second player of little value, and $40,000 in cash. It was one of the biggest cash transactions baseball had ever had. It also came very near to destroying the American League, and it was a major factor leading to the election of Kenesaw Mountain Landis as High Commissioner of baseball.

Johnson refused to approve the trade, saying that the Boston club should have suspended the player. He declared Mays suspended by league order for the rest of the season. Ruppert and Huston immediately went into court in New York and obtained an injunction against Johnson. This freed Mays to pitch for the Yankees, and from August 9 to the end of the season he won nine games for them (and 26 the next year, and 27 the year after that). Nonetheless, the hassle went on. Chicago joined New York and Boston in challenging Johnson's authority, while five clubs supported him. Ruppert continued to attack the league president, who was under severe criticism for arbitrary decisions he had made, for the putative strike at the World Series the year before and for reports, later confirmed, that he had invested $58,000 of his own money in the Cleveland Indians.

"Johnson will be put out of baseball," Ruppert promised. Most baseball men were dissatisfied with the unwieldy three-man National Commission, which Johnson tried to dominate. There had been a movement for some years to name an impartial nonbaseball man as permanent chairman and executive head of the commission (Judge Landis was the most frequently mentioned candidate). Johnson fought this proposal, but the rift that appeared in his league after the Mays affair brought about his downfall. Before the year was out the three rebel clubs joined with the eight National League teams and threatened to form a new league. Faced with the destruction of the American League, Johnson was forced to back down, and an agreement was reached that led to the dissolution of the old three-man commission and the appointment a little more than a year later (just after news broke about the Black Sox scandal) of Landis as the supreme ruler of baseball.

In July 1919 all that Babe Ruth knew or cared about all this was that Mays was gone and he had to take his place, while continuing to play in the outfield on the days he did not pitch. His ordeal lasted only a couple of weeks this time (he started three games and lost two of them), for on July 31 the nineteen-year-old Waite Hoyt joined the Red Sox. He took Ruth's place in the starting rotation and won his first game, 2–1, in twelve innings. Ruth, as though in gratitude for being relieved of his burden, helped the young pitcher with four hits in six at bats. For the rest of the season Hoyt was a regular starter, and Ruth, except for scattered pitching appearances for publicity reasons, was finally and irrevocably an outfielder for good.

Curiously, Ruth's home run hitting slacked off when Hoyt joined the club. After tying Seybold's record on July 29, Babe went more than two weeks without hitting another. This was frustrating to reporters and fans waiting for the record-breaking 17th, for Ruth's home run quest was now being followed in minuscule detail in the sports pages. Some papers ran detailed boxes listing the date of each homer, the opposing team and the opposing pitcher. Records were not kept in the profusion they are today, but researchers came up with various marks for Ruth to aim at. First, of course, was Seybold's American League record of 16, which Ruth had tied. Then there was the modern major league record of 24, set by Gavvy Cravath of the Phillies in 1915. The pre-1900 record was 25, set by Buck Freeman of the Washington Senators in 1899. This was considered the ultimate goal until someone, rooting about in old files, found that a long-dead player named Edward Nagle Williamson had hit 27 for the Chicago Colts in 1884. In time Ruth passed them all, but it is ironic that Williamson's was the final barrier. Seybold, Cravath and Freeman were solid power hitters, their home run performances added evidence of their consistent strength at the plate. But Williamson's record was a fluke. The year before he had hit only two, the year after only three. What happened in 1884? Simple enough. The Colts that year played in the Congress Street grounds, where right field was a ridiculous 215 feet from home plate. A year earlier the entire Chicago team hit a total of only 13 home runs. In 1884 they hit 142. When Williamson hit 27 (25 of them at home), he was closely followed by teammate Fred Pfeffer with 25, Abner Dalrymple with 22 and Cap Anson with 21. A season earlier the four of them had a combined total of five.

Nonetheless, Williamson had hit 27, and in mid-August, after a two-week drought, Ruth began his move toward it. He hit number

17 on August 14 to set a new American League record. Two days later before a big Saturday crowd in Chicago he hit another of those "longest evers," and the next day in St. Louis before another huge crowd he hit number 19. Three homers in four games. The fans began buzzing again, but the pursuit almost ended abruptly the following Friday in Cleveland when Ruth's old umpiring antagonist, Brick Owens, called a strike on the Babe. Ruth, objecting strenuously, backed out of the batter's box and cursed the umpire. Owens tossed him out of the game, and Ruth threatened to punch him in the nose. Players from both teams grabbed him and pulled him away. Despite the outburst, he was neither fined nor suspended and the next day in Detroit hit his 20th home run of the year, his fourth with the bases full. No one had ever done that before, and four bases-filled home runs in one season remained the American League record for forty years.

Ruth was hot. He followed his Saturday grand slam with two homers on Sunday and another on Monday afternoon. How the fans bubbled now. Four in three games! Seven in twelve days! Twenty-three for the season! Babe was bigger than the pennant race. Crowds poured out to see him. Fans in Boston who came to watch him play after the explosion of power in Detroit saw no home runs but went home laughing about a tremendous pop fly he hit to short center field. It went so high that the Athletics' center fielder lost the ball, it fell safely and Ruth was on third base with a triple.

His total stayed at 23 for a week. In Boston the Red Sox announced that as an added attraction Ruth would pitch the first game of the Labor Day doubleheader. Babe won, 2–1, driving in one Boston run with a triple and scoring the other himself a moment later. In the second game he hit his 24th homer to tie Cravath's modern major league record. Later in the week he tied Freeman's more antique mark with his 25th and missed another when his line drive hit a couple of feet below the top of the right field fence. A few days later he hit number 26, and now only Williamson's 27 lay ahead.

Inevitably, considering Ruth's innate flair for milking a situation, he went into another dry spell. For eleven days baseball waited and for eleven days Ruth did nothing but hit singles and doubles and pop-ups. On Saturday, September 20, Boston had a doubleheader scheduled with the Chicago White Sox, who were about to clinch the American League pennant. The Red Sox announced it would be Babe Ruth day, a day on which the fans could honor him for his marvelous hitting. In turn, the Babe would once again pitch the first game of the doubleheader. Fenway Park was absolutely jammed for the occasion. The Pere Marquette Council of the Knights of Columbus presented Ruth with $600 in U.S. Treasury Savings Certificates, and he received other gifts, including a diamond ring he wore for years. After the game a reporter, thinking of the crowds Ruth had drawn all season, asked what Frazee had given him. "A cigar," Babe said.

On the field Ruth was, well, heroic. He did not pitch too well, lasting only into the sixth inning before shifting to left field. But in the ninth inning he hit a spectacular home run to left field off Lefty Claud Williams. It won the game, tied Williamson's record, utterly delighted the crowd and awed other players. It was unheard of then for a lefthanded batter to hit a ball that hard to left field off a lefthanded pitcher, particularly a pitcher of Williams' exceptional skills. Between games, the famous White Sox third baseman, Buck Weaver, stopped by the Red Sox bench to comment, "That was the most unbelievable poke I ever saw."

Ruth broke Williamson's record a few days later in New York with another landmark drive, this one over a distant section of the Polo Grounds roof—yes, the longest ever hit at the Polo Grounds, according to reports of the game. It was dramatic, of course. The Red Sox were losing, 1–0, in the ninth when he hit it, and it tied the score. (Boston eventually lost, 2–1, in the thirteenth.)

The Red Sox went to Washington for the last weekend of the season, and there Ruth hit the 29th and last home run of his triumphant year. It was the first he hit in Washington in 1919, and it gave him the distinction of having hit at least one homer in every city in the league. No one had ever done that before either.

After his 1919 season, before he had played one game for the New York Yankees, Ruth was acclaimed the greatest home run hitter baseball had ever seen, even though he had only 49 for his entire career to that point. Roger Connor held the record for most lifetime homers with 136. When Ruth passed Connor in 1921, his third season as a fulltime player, he became the most prolific home run hitter of all time. Each of the nearly 600 runs he hit after that only extended his own record.

The home run belonged to him. During the years that followed, different players—Rogers Hornsby, Ken and Cy Williams, Lou Gehrig, Hack Wilson, Jimmie Foxx—challenged him from time to time, but Ruth's consistency was overwhelming. The 29 home runs made him a national sensation, but he almost doubled that in 1920, when he hit 54. Others followed his lead, and 29 quickly became a modest figure. By the end of 1924, 30 home runs or more had been hit nine times—but five times by Ruth himself. By the end of 1928, 40 or more had been hit ten times, seven by Ruth. He did not merely break through, he made the breakthrough and kept going, leading the way. From 1918 through 1934 he led the league in home runs twelve times and hit 699 homers, an average of more than 40 a year for seventeen straight seasons. From 1926 through 1931 he averaged 50.3 a year.

He hit his 700th home run in 1934. When he hit it, only two others had hit more than 300. When he retired with 714, he had more than twice as many as the second man on the list. The home run was his.

CHAPTER 17

Departure from Boston: Sold down the River

Johnny Igoe arranged a postseason tour for Ruth that took him through the west and eventually to Los Angeles, where he appeared in exhibition games with other major leaguers, played golf with Buck Weaver and reportedly hit a drive 340 yards. He was also supposed to make a series of movie shorts with such gripping titles as *Home Sweet Home, Touch All Bases, The Dough Kiss, The Bacon* and even *Oliver Twist.* Frazee posed for a publicity picture, doling out porridge with a spoon while Ruth supposedly said, "Please, sir." The films were postponed but money was pouring in, and, prompted by Igoe, Ruth began to complain that his three-year contract with Frazee at $10,000 a year was grossly inadequate. He wanted $20,000 a year, he said, or he might not play at all in 1920. Since 1919 had been the best year baseball had ever had in terms of crowds and revenues, Babe had a pretty good argument. But Frazee was in a financial bind with Joe Lannin, from whom he had bought the Red Sox after the 1916 season and who still held Frazee's notes for a substantial portion of the purchase price. Lannin was calling for payment, and Frazee was having difficulty complying with his demands. His credit in Boston was becoming shaky.

Frazee and Colonel Huston, Ruppert's partner, were both convivial party types and got along well. Huston was a self-made man, an engineer who had grown up in Ohio and made a fortune in construction in Cuba after the Spanish-American War. He was a big heavy man, a careless dresser, open and friendly, who considered the ballplayers and sportswriters his friends. In contrast, Ruppert was a New York aristocrat whose father had been a millionaire brewer. Ruppert owned horses, was a member of the Jockey Club, exhibited show dogs, dressed meticulously, had a valet, collected *objets d'art* and moved easily in New York society. He served four terms in Congress from Manhattan's Silk Stocking District and, while a ladies' man, was discreet. He never married, but his will provided generously for a "friend." Ruppert, who carried on the family business of brewing beer, had a faint trace of a German accent (our hero was always Babe Root to Ruppert) and never called anyone by his first name.

He and Huston had nothing in common but money, a keen interest in the Yankees and the appellation "Colonel." Ruppert got his at twenty-two when he was made an honorary colonel on the personal staff of Governor Hill of New York. Huston, who was a captain of engineers in the Spanish-American war (his nickname was Cap), served overseas in World War I and became a colonel. The two had become acquainted because of their rooting interest in the New York Giants. John McGraw learned that the Yankees were for sale and suggested that Ruppert and Huston get together and buy the club. The pair put up $460,000, and in 1915 the Yankees, then a chronic second-division team, became theirs.

Despite his fastidiousness and the dilettante impression he gave, Ruppert was a hard, practical businessman. Huston was much more sentimental and impulsive. Huston liked Wild Bill Donovan, whom they had hired as manager, but Ruppert was impatient with the slow progress toward respectability the team was making. When Huston went to France, Ruppert decided it was time to hire a new manager. He asked Ban Johnson, with whom he was still on good terms, if he could suggest a replacement.

"Get Miller Huggins," Johnson said. Huggins was a tiny man—

five feet six and a half inches tall, barely 140 pounds in weight—who had been managing the St. Louis Cardinals for five years without spectacular success, but Johnson was always a shrewd judge of talent. "He's a fine manager, and we'll take a good man away from the National League."

Ruppert wired Huston about the proposed change and Huston instantly replied negatively. He did not want the unimpressive little Huggins. He suggested instead that Ruppert hire the Dodger manager, big fat Wilbert Robinson, a jolly crony of Huston's. As a courtesy to his partner, Ruppert interviewed Robinson, but his mind was already made up. Impressed with Huggins, he hired him and told Huston about it after it was a *fait accompli*. Huston was furious, and the relationship between the two colonels, never close, was always uneasy after that.

Still, on some things they worked together well, and when Frazee indicated that Ruth was available, Huston was quick to discuss with Ruppert the possibility of getting him. The Yankees had been acquiring ballplayers aggressively during 1918 and 1919, and Ruppert was heartily in favor of obtaining an obvious star and drawing card in Ruth. The only drawback was money. Ruppert had ample wealth, but he was a practical man. Prohibition was about to go into effect, and Ruppert knew it was going to cause a precipitous decline in the revenue of his Manhattan brewery. Too, he was aware that McGraw and the Giants might at any time terminate the arrangement that permitted the Yankees to play in the Polo Grounds (and particularly so if Ruth joined the club). The vague plans he and Huston had tossed around about building their own ballpark might have to be implemented, and great quantities of cash would be needed for that. So a lump cash payment for Ruth was out. Nonetheless, the colonels met with Frazee and worked out a deal satisfactory to both sides.

The Yankees agreed to buy Ruth for $100,000, which was double the largest amount ever paid for a ballplayer before that. No other players were involved—it was a straight purchase—but the financial arrangements were complex. According to the contract of sale

signed on Friday, December 26, 1919, Ruppert and Huston gave
Frazee $25,000 in cash and three promissory notes for $25,000 each,
one payable November 1, 1920, the second November 1, 1921, the
third November 1, 1922. The notes were at 6 per cent, so the total
amount the Yankees paid was nearer to $110,000. The cash-hungry
Frazee moved at once to sell (discount) the notes, and the amiable
Huston acted as an agent for him, writing to the Royal Bank of
Canada on December 30 on Frazee's behalf. He sent a letter to
Ruppert that day (local mail service was much faster and more
efficient a half century ago than it is today) asking him to endorse
the note to facilitate discounting. "As you will remember," Huston
wrote Ruppert, "I told Mr. Frazee that I would try to get him a
short-time loan at my bank, with one of the notes we gave the
Boston Club as collateral."

Two months later, in February 1920, Huston again sent a message
to Ruppert, this time saying, "Mr. Harry Frazee is asking us to aid
him in getting three $25,000 notes discounted. He says events with
Mr. Lannin made it impossible to follow his original intention of
having the notes discounted in Boston. As you will remember, I had
one of his notes of $25,000 discounted at my bank in New York. Al-
though I only asked for a temporary accommodation of 90 days,
which was all that Mr. Frazee wanted at that time, I can possibly
have the note renewed . . . However, the balance I carry with my
bank hardly places me in a position to ask for a larger accommodation, and, frankly, I must keep my credit absolutely green there, so
as to utilize same in case we are called upon to build new grounds.
. . . I don't know whether or not you are in a position to further
Mr. Frazee's desires, but he feels we should help him out some way,
as he could have sold the fellow for cash."

For along with the $100,000 for Ruth, Frazee wanted a substantial
loan. This was the crux of the deal, and Ruth came to the Yankees
because Ruppert agreed to it. He gave Frazee a letter on December
26 that said, "I hereby offer to loan or cause to be loaned to you
$300,000 . . . to be secured by a first mortgage [upon the] land
now used as a baseball playing field by the Boston American League

Baseball Club." In other words, Ruppert, co-owner of the New York Yankees, would hold a mortgage on Fenway Park, the Boston team's home field. Ruppert's letter said the loan offer would expire if it were not acted upon in ninety days. Frazee's continuing financial difficulties were evident in a letter he sent to Ruppert in April 1920:

> Dear Colonel,
>
> You remember that I phoned you about ten days before the expiration of your agreement to make a loan of $300,000 on Fenway Park and asked you to extend the time, which you advised me you would tell Mr. Grant to do. However, I have received no word from Mr. Grant. I telephoned Col. Huston today, as I could not reach you on the phone, asking the Colonel to see you and advise that I have cleaned up all matters upon the Preferred Stock which your Attorney wanted before making the loan and I am now ready to accept it on May 15.
>
> You can understand how important this is to me as my plans have all been based on my ability to secure this loan. Therefore, will you please send me signed agreement, copy of which Mr. Grant has, stating that you will advance the $300,000 . . . and if possible make the date May 20th. . . . I need this agreement signed by you here very badly to complete the balance of my negotiations.

Frazee sent a copy of the letter to Huston, who was much more accessible than Ruppert, with a scribbled note saying, "Dear Col, This is copy of letter just mailed to Col Ruppert after my phone to you. Wire or phone me quick."

The loan was made and relations between the two clubs continued to be cordial, with Frazee sending player after player to the Yankees over the next few seasons for more and more cash. The Red Sox soon became a baseball disaster area, finishing dead last nine times in eleven seasons, but Frazee survived, eventually sold the Boston team and in 1925 hit the jackpot financially in New York with the enormously successful *No, No, Nanette.*

In all, then, counting the initial payment, notes, interest and loan, the Yankees put up more than $400,000 in cash and credit to obtain

Ruth. They knew what they were getting, in more ways than one. The contract of sale clearly reveals that Ruppert and Huston were well aware of Ruth's discontent with his $10,000-a-year contract with Frazee and the likelihood that he would demand a substantial increase when he learned of his transfer to New York. The second clause in the agreement said if Ruth did not report before July 1, the deal was off and Frazee would return the cash and the notes. The third clause said if Ruth demanded an increase in salary and the Yankees "deem it necessary to increase the salary in order to retain the services of said player," the Yankees would pay the increase as long as it did not raise Ruth's salary beyond $15,000. If they had to go beyond $15,000, the Red Sox would be obliged to pay "such excess up to the sum of Twenty-five Hundred ($2,500) for each of the years 1920 and 1921." The fourth clause said if Ruth did not ask for a salary increase but did demand a bonus for agreeing to play with the Yankees, the New York club would spring for the first $10,000 of the bonus, but the Red Sox would have to pay anything over that up to $15,000.

In brief, the Yankees anticipated trouble with Ruth. To allay it, they hurriedly dispatched the diminutive Huggins to California to find him and discuss things. Announcement of the deal was to be delayed until Huggins met with the Babe.

Meanwhile, a day or so after signing the contract of sale, Frazee phoned Barrow, who lived on Riverside Drive in New York City.

"I want to talk to you," he said. "Meet me at the Knickerbocker Hotel."

When Barrow arrived at the Knickerbocker, Frazee was having a drink with an actor. After perfunctory hellos, he wasted no time.

"I'm going to make you mad as hell with what I have to tell you. I'm going to sell Ruth to the Yankees."

"I thought as much," Barrow said. "I felt it in my bones. You're making a mistake, Harry. You know that, don't you?"

"Maybe I am, but I can't help it. Lannin is after me to make good on my notes. My shows aren't going so good. Ruppert and Huston will give me $100,000 for him, and Ruppert has agreed to loan me $300,000. I can't turn that down."

In California Huggins had some trouble tracking down the restless Ruth but eventually found him playing golf in Griffith Park. When Ruth came off the course, Huggins introduced himself. "I'm Miller Huggins of the Yankees, Babe. I'd like to talk to you."

"Sure," Babe said, shaking hands. I've been traded to the Yankees, he said to himself.

They found a quiet place and made small talk for a few minutes. Then the manager said, "Babe, how would you like to play for the Yankees?"

"Have I been traded?"

Huggins hesitated. "Well, the deal hasn't been made yet. I'd like to find out a few things. I want to know if you'll behave yourself if you come to New York."

"I'm happy with the Red Sox," Ruth said, bridling a bit. "I like Boston. But if Frazee sends me to the Yankees, I'll play as hard for them as I did for him."

"Babe, you've been a pretty wild boy in Boston. In New York you'll have to behave. You'll have to be strictly business."

Ruth became irritated. "I already told you I'll play the best I can. Let's get down to business. How much are you going to pay me?"

Huggins mentioned the two years left on Ruth's $10,000 contract.

"I want a lot more dough than that," said Babe.

"All right," Huggins said. "If you promise to behave yourself, Colonel Ruppert will give you a new contract."

"For how much?"

Huggins mentioned $15,000 a year and then $17,500. Ruth said no. He repeated what he had told Frazee during the autumn. He wanted his salary doubled to $20,000. He also wanted a piece of the money the Red Sox would be getting for him. Huggins shook his head. He would have to get in touch with New York. They shook hands and parted. When they met again there was more haggling, but they came to terms and Ruth signed an agreement. Technically, he would continue under his old contract—$10,000 a year for 1920 and 1921—but he would also receive an immediate bonus of $1000 and then $20,000 more over the next two years, to be paid in $2500 lumps at regular intervals during each season. The Yankees could do nothing about giving him a percentage of the money they were paying Frazee.

In sum, then, Ruth received $41,000 from the Yankees for the 1920 and 1921 seasons. Huggins wired Ruppert, and in New York the press was called in and told the startling news that the Red Sox had sold Babe Ruth to the Yankees. It was Monday, January 5, 1920.

In Boston the story created consternation. A cartoon appeared in one of the newspapers showing Faneuil Hall and the Boston Public Library decked with For Sale signs. Frazee faced the criticism coolly and blandly blamed Ruth for Boston's sixth-place finish in 1919. "It would be impossible to start next season with Ruth and have a smooth-working machine," he said. "Ruth had become simply impossible, and the Boston club could no longer put up with his eccentricities. I think the Yankees are taking a gamble. While Ruth is undoubtedly the greatest hitter the game has ever seen, he is likewise one of the most selfish and inconsiderate men ever to put on a baseball uniform."

Sportswriters dutifully echoed that theme, arguing that the sale of Ruth would benefit the Red Sox. One school of thought held that Ruth would never again be the player he was in 1919.

Fans generally were more realistic. "For the love of Mike," one said in disgust, "I give up." Another prescient follower of Boston baseball said succinctly, "I figure the Red Sox is ruined." A policeman commented, "From what I can see, there no longer is any sentiment in baseball."

During the season that followed, Frazee had posters put up in Fenway Park advertising a show of his called *My Lady Friends*. A disgusted fan jerked his thumb at the poster and said, "Those are the only friends that son of a bitch has."

In California Ruth was a bit taken aback by Frazee's comments and the sensation the news of the sale created. For some reason, perhaps sentiment, perhaps with the idea of strengthening his hand with Ruppert and Huston, perhaps with an eye on cigar sales, he sent a wire to Boston saying, "WILL NOT PLAY ANYWHERE ELSE. MY HEART IS IN BOSTON." A cynic said, "He means that's where his cigar factory is."

New York felt a lot better about the whole thing, although *The New York Times* ran an editorial called "The High Price of Home Runs," comparing the money that was paid for Ruth to the salary being paid a visiting professor at a city university. In New Jersey, where he was working in a shipyard, Ping Bodie, the incumbent Yankee left fielder, said, "I suppose this means I'll be sent to China."

Ruth stayed in California another month before returning to Boston. Late in February he said goodbye to Helen and left for New York to join his new club on its trip south to spring training. The Yankee dynasty was about to begin.

In 1912 at St. Mary's, Ruth *(left, top row)* was the lefthanded catcher and star of the Red Sox, the school champions. (Photograph courtesy of National Baseball Hall of Fame and Museum, Inc.)

Brother Matthias, prefect of discipline at St. Mary's, was 6½ feet tall and weighed 250 pounds. Ruth admired and respected him above all other men. (Photograph courtesy of National Baseball Hall of Fame and Museum, Inc.)

In 1919 Ruth was in his physical
prime. He had not yet acquired the
bulbous torso that became his
trademark. (Wide World Photos)

Miller Huggins, the scrawny but
supremely tough little manager of the
Yankees. (*N. Y. Daily News* Photo)

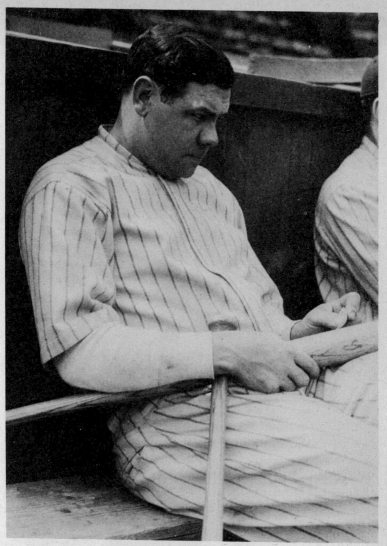

A gloomy Ruth sits in the Yankees'
dugout in 1922. He was suspended
five times during the season.
(*N. Y. Daily News* Photo)

Ruth and Lou Gehrig in the 1927 World Series. Gehrig, nine years
younger than Babe, became a Yankee regular in 1926, and the two sluggers
were called home-run twins. In 1927, Ruth hit his historic 60 home runs
and Gehrig had 47, more than anyone other than Babe had ever hit.
(United Press International Photo)

Ruth knocks out his historic 60th home run on September 30, 1927, in
Yankee Stadium. (United Press International Photo)

Photographers loved Babe Ruth because he was so cooperative. The boxing picture was taken after a long winter of hard work at Artie McGovern's gymnasium. (*N. Y. Daily News* Photos)

Babe and his new wife, Claire Merritt
Hodgson, in Florida in the winter of
1930. As practical as she was
attractive, Claire exerted a restraining
influence on the high-flying home-
run king. (United Press
International Photo)

Despite his weight and age, Ruth remained an exciting, aggressive ball
player. Here he slides home for yet another score against Detroit in 1934.
(United Press International Photo)

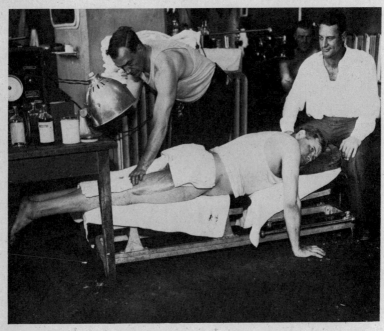

More and more frequently, Ruth required the attention of the team's
trainer. (*N. Y. Daily News* Photo)

At an old timers' affair at Yankee Stadium, photographers assembled what many think were the three best outfielders of all time: Ty Cobb, Ruth, and Tris Speaker. (Wide World Photos)

During World War II, Babe, almost
fifty, appeared in an exhibition game
against Walter Johnson and showed
his swing had the same vigor.
(United Press International Photo)

Sadly ravaged by cancer, an
uncharacteristically frail Ruth was
visited in the hospital by Mayor
William O'Dwyer of New York City.
(Wide World Photos)

Babe's farewell to Yankee Stadium
in June 1948, eight weeks before his
death on August 16.
(Wide World Photos)

PART TWO

1920-1948

CHAPTER 18

Revolution in Baseball: Ruth Reaches New York

America was in social revolution as the 1920s began—Prohibition went into effect on January 16, eleven days after the announcement of Ruth's sale to the Yankees—and baseball turned around as radically as the country did. The game changed more between 1917 and 1921 than it did in the next forty years. Despite the high-profile presence of such outstanding batters as Cobb, Wagner, Lajoie, Speaker, Jackson and a few others, during the first two decades of the century hitting was a lesser art in a game that honored pitching and low scores. The term "inside" baseball was almost sacred, and John McGraw was its high priest. It meant playing for a run, a single run. You bunted safely, stole second, went to third on a sacrifice and scored on a fly ball to win 1–0. An exaggeration, of course, but that was the ideal. Even after the cork-center ball was introduced in 1910, tight baseball continued to dominate.

All this changed after the war, after Ruth's breakthrough in 1919. It was not a gradual evolution but sudden and cataclysmic. Baseball statistics give dramatic evidence of this. For fifteen seasons before 1919, major league batters as a group averaged around .250. By 1921 that figure had jumped above .285, and it remained steadily in the .280s throughout the 1920s. With this increase in hitting came an increase in scoring. Before 1920 it was a rare year when more than two or three men in both leagues batted in 100 runs; but in 1921 fifteen players did it, and the average for the 1920s was fourteen a year. Earned-run averages, the measure of a pitcher's run-suppressing ability, shot upward. Before 1919 the average annual ERA was about 2.85. In 1921 it was over 4.00, and it stayed in that generous neighborhood through the decade.

What caused the explosion? The end of the war, Ruth, money and the lively ball. Attendance in 1919 rose for every one of the sixteen major league teams, in some instances doubling and even tripling. The release from war was largely responsible for the first burst of interest, and then Ruth's home run hitting came into focus. Babe was the most exciting aspect of the 1919 season, even more than the pennant races. New fans bubbling into the ballparks could not begin to appreciate the austere beauty of a well-pitched game, but they thrilled vicariously to the surging erectile power of the Ruthian home run. They wanted more. They wanted hits and they wanted runs, lots of hits and lots of runs. They wanted homers. The owners, delighted by the windfall at the ticket windows, were happy to give them what they wanted. They instituted legislation against the myriad trick pitches, like the spitball, that tended to befuddle batters, and they pepped up the ball. No hard irrefutable facts exist to verify this—indeed, a laboratory test in August 1920 "proved" the ball had not been changed—but the data cited in the preceding paragraph seem overwhelming circumstantial evidence.

Too, Ruth's full free swing was being copied more and more, and so was his type of bat, thinner in the handle and whippier, in principle something like a golf club. (Early in his career Ruth used a massive 52-ounce bat, but this slimmed down as Ruth himself ballooned.) Strategy and tactics changed. A strikeout heretofore had been something of a disgrace—reread "Casey at the Bat." A batter was supposed to protect the plate, get a piece of the ball, as in the cognate game of cricket. In Ruth's case, however, a strikeout was only a momentary, if melodramatic, setback. Protecting the plate declined in importance, along with the sacrifice and the steal (the number of stolen bases in 1921 was half the prewar average). The big hit, the big inning blossomed.

With them, so did attendance. It had been a good year in 1919, but 1920 was marvelous. Attendance went up again in every city in the majors except Detroit (the Tigers fell to seventh place that year) and Boston, where bitterness had replaced the Royal Rooters. Seven clubs established new all-time attendance highs in 1920, and the Yankees set a new major league record. The old record was 910,000, by the 1908 New York Giants. No other club had ever drawn as high as 700,000, and for most of them yearly attendance was usually well under 500,000. In 1919 the Yankees had been like John the Baptist, preparing the way for the Lord. They were a powerful team, and their pre-Ruth batting order of Home Run Baker, Wally Pipp, Duffy Lewis, Ping Bodie, Roger Peckinpaugh, Del Pratt et al. was dubbed Murderers' Row by a newspaper cartoonist. The name seemed justified when the Yanks led the major leagues in home runs, with 45—only 16 more than Ruth hit by himself for Boston. They were in the race for the pennant a good part of the season, finished a respectable third and drew 619,000, more than 20 per cent above their previous high. But in 1920, with Ruth, they were in the pennant race all season long, finished a much closer third, hit 115 home runs (Babe had 54 of them) and drew phenomenally. The Polo Grounds had a seating capacity then of 38,000, and capacity was reached and surpassed time and again. The Yankees passed the Giants' old record in mid-summer, became the first major league team ever to draw a million people, and ended the season with 1,289,422, almost 380,000 better than the previous high. The Giants drew well too, surpassing their 1908 mark themselves, and the two clubs together drew 2,219,031 to the Polo Grounds, almost a million more than ever before.

Ruth was made for New York. It has been said that where youth sees discovery, age sees coincidence, and perhaps the retrospect of years makes Ruth's arrival in Manhattan in 1920 seem only a fortuitous juxtaposition of man and place in time. Nonetheless, Ruth in that place at that time was discovery. And adventure. And excite-

ment. And all the concomitant titillations. One of his famous nicknames, the Bambino, came about because New York's polyglot
immigrants, and their children, found themselves strangely excited
by Ruth and baseball. Many of those riding the subways and ele-
vated trains and streetcars up to the thin northern neck of Manhattan where the Polo Grounds was, or who talked about Ruth on
street corners and in the neighborhood stores, were Italian. The
rhythm and alliteration and connotative impact of the Italian word
for babe, *bambino,* made the nickname a natural. In time, headlines
would say simply, "BAM HITS ONE."

Ruth did not come to New York as a Yankee until the day the
club left for Jacksonville and spring training. He had dawdled in
California, occasionally sounding off about getting more money
from the deal, and sidestepped New York on the way back. In
Boston he tried to wangle a percentage of the sale price from Frazee.
He smoked cigars in a show window to promote the cigar factory,
even smoking three cigars at the same time. He basked in the sad
adulation of Red Sox fans at a testimonial dinner given in his honor
at the Hotel Brunswick by the David J. Walsh Collegiate Club.

Finally, on February 28, he took a train for New York to join the
rest of the Yankee contingent at Pennsylvania Station, where the
team was to catch the 6:20 sleeper to Florida. He did not appear
in the station until ten past six, but when he did a mob of fans
crowded around him trying to touch him or shake hands. Autograph hounds happily were still a rarity in those days. Ruth, hulking
over the people around him, beamed, shook hands, exchanged
greetings and obviously enjoyed the stir he was creating. He was
wearing a heavy leather coat and was clinging to a new set of golf
clubs he had bought in California.

The affable Ping Bodie took him around and made a great show
of introducing him formally to each of the Yankee players, even
though Babe knew most of them already. When a club official
parceled out five dollars in expense money to each player, Bodie said
it would add up to just about enough for one fair-sized pot. Ruth
grinned and said, "Let's get a game going." On the train he passed

around Babe Ruth cigars and smoked some himself, as well as pulling at a handsome meerschaum pipe he said had cost him $12. He chewed gum incessantly ("He always had something in his mouth," Lee Allen wrote) and talked freely about his switch from the Red Sox to the Yankees. He cursed Frazee. When someone asked if he had managed to get part of the sale price from the Boston owner, he roared, "The son of a bitch wouldn't even see me."

In Jacksonville, whose chamber of commerce had advertised Ruth and the Yankees throughout Florida like a circus, he played golf with Bob Shawkey and Del Pratt and on one hole mis-hit the ball so badly he broke the head off his club. In early practice sessions at the ballpark he worked out at third base and surprised the other players with his lefthanded agility. His winter of golf and baseball in California had left him in pretty good shape. His weight was just about 200. He quickly became an accepted member of the team and enjoyed himself hugely clowning about in practice. One day when the chunky five-foot, eight-inch, 195-pound Bodie cut in front of him to take a grounder away, Ruth yelled in mock anger, grabbed Bodie, turned him upside down, dropped him on the grass and sat on him. He and Bodie got along well. They were roommates and often ate together. Bodie had been considered the biggest eater on the club before Ruth came along, but now he admitted defeat. "Anybody who eats three pounds of steak and a bottle of chili sauce for a starter has got me," he said. Not everything was jovial. Ruth got fed up with the biting jibes of a spectator one afternoon and went into the stands after him. The man stood his ground and pulled a knife. Ernie Shore, then with the Yankees, pulled Ruth away, and the fan left quietly.

Off the field, except for an occasional round of golf with other players, Babe was gone most of the time. Lee Allen described Ruth years later as "a large man in a camel's hair coat and camel's hair cap, standing in front of a hotel, his broad nostrils sniffing at the promise of the night." The essence of that vivid picture suited him in spring training in 1920. There was an outsize complement of reporters from New York's dozen or more newspapers in camp, most of them there because of Ruth, and they had trouble catching up to him off the field.

He was never around. When the team would come into a town on its way north, the players' luggage would be delivered to the hotel and left in the lobby. Each player would pick up his own bag and take it to his room. But Ruth would go from the train directly into town, looking for a girl he knew, or knew of, or hoped to know. In the hotel the good-natured Bodie would pick up his bag and the Babe's and carry both up to their room. Ruth might look into the room for a change of clothing during his visit, but he was gone most of the time, and more often than not Bodie would dutifully bring Babe's luggage back downstairs when it was time to leave. An enterprising reporter, scraping around for some sort of new angle on the Babe, approached Bodie one day and asked him to talk about Ruth.

"I don't know anything about him," Bodie said.

"You room with him. What's he like when you're alone with him?"

"I don't room with him," Bodie said, in a remark that entered baseball legend. "I room with his suitcase."

One trip from Jacksonville down to Miami proved so riotous—Ruth, still hazy one morning, ran into a palm tree chasing a fly ball—that Ruppert never again let the Yankees play a spring-training game in that city. In any case, Ruth started slowly and did not hit his first home run until April 1. Happily, Ruppert was there and was delighted by the homer, which was especially Ruthian. The fence was 429 feet from the plate and ten feet high, and the ball cleared it by 50 feet. Ruth hit more homers and lifted his batting average above .300 before the season began, but even so it was not a particularly good spring for the Yankees. Bodie, beset by personal problems, jumped the club in March and did not return until the season was well under way. Another outfielder, the colorful Chick Fewster, was hit in the head by a pitched ball and was so badly hurt he was unable to speak for nearly a month. He was eventually sent north to Baltimore for surgery to remove a blood clot and was out almost all season. Before he was hurt, Fewster had inspired a choice bit of sports-page doggerel:

> Said slim Chick Fewster to big Babe Ruth,
> I haven't had a hit since Hector was a youth.
> Said big Babe Ruth to slim Chick Fewster,
> You don't hit the ball as hard as you uster.

With Bodie and Fewster gone, Ruth asked Huggins if he could play center field. He said he did not want to play left or right because he might run into the short outfield walls in the Polo Grounds. "I'll get myself all smashed up going after a fly ball," he said. Huggins acceded to the request, and Ruth made his regular season debut with the Yankees as a center fielder, although it was not an auspicious debut. The Yankees opened in Philadelphia against the Athletics, and Ruth gave the last-place A's the game-winning runs when he dropped a fly ball in the eighth inning with two men on base and two out. At bat all he could produce were two meek singles.

Joe Dugan, the Philadelphia third baseman (known as Jumping Joe for his practice of jumping the ball club at irregular intervals), hit the fly ball Ruth dropped, which pleased Dugan, who liked a laugh. He felt Ruth's muff could not be ignored. After the game he scraped around and found a brown derby, in those days a symbol of ineptitude (Al Smith had not yet made it nationally famous as a political trademark). He had it wrapped up and the next afternoon a messenger brought it onto the field when Ruth came to bat in the first inning. Such presentations were not uncommon, and the umpire dutifully called time. The other players gathered around and Ruth opened the package. When he lifted out the brown derby, the crowd and the players and even the umpires howled with laughter. Huggins tensed, waiting for Ruth's famous temper to explode. But after staring at the derby in stunned surprise for a moment, Ruth grinned, put it on and waved to the crowd.

His graceful acceptance of the joke did not help him at bat. He struck out three times and did not get a hit. The Yankees went on to Boston for three games before returning to New York for their home opener, and before his old fans Ruth's slump continued. And the Yankees lost three straight to the Red Sox.

When the club began its home season in New York a big crowd was on hand to see the hero's debut. Again there was disappointment. Ruth pulled a muscle in his rib cage in batting practice, hurt it again striking out in the first inning, and to the chagrin of the crowd left the game.

"How do you like that?" complained a fan. "I come all the way from Red Hook and they take him out five minutes after the game starts."

Babe was out for several days, disappointing big crowds on the first weekend of the season, and when he did get back he struck out twice in one game and made another error. Then the Red Sox came to town and in the opener of a five-game series beat the Yankees for the fourth straight time in the young season. New York was becoming uneasy. The Ruthless Red Sox, as they were being called, were leading the league with a 10–2 record, while the Yankees were in the second division. The Babe had not hit a single homer. Maybe Frazee was right. After all, Boston had finished sixth with Ruth the year before.

On Saturday, May 1, a skeptical crowd came to see the second game of the series with the Red Sox. And that was the day Babe started. With Huggins, coaching at third, shrilling, "Come on, big boy!" Ruth hit his first home run of the year, a truly amazing drive far over the Polo Grounds roof, even farther than the one he had hit there the September before for his record-breaking 28th home run. The Yankees shut out Boston, 6–0, won two of the remaining three games, and were on their way. The Red Sox balloon went pffft. Frazee's depleted team slipped and slipped and eventually finished fifth with a 72–81 record, while Ruth and the Yankees began their climb to glory.

Babe's home runs came with exciting regularity—he had 12 before the end of May, far more than anyone had ever hit in one month before—and the crowds followed. On Sunday, May 16, a record 38,600 jammed the Polo Grounds, and 15,000 others had to be herded away by police when the ticket windows were shut down well before game time. Ruth hit another dozen homers in June, and his batting average climbed as sensationally as his home run total. On June 20 it was .345; on June 28, .359; on July 1, .372. It was up to .385 by July 11—he hit safely in 26 straight games—and peaked at .391 on August 4. After that the fires banked somewhat, and he finished the season at .376, fourth in the league behind Sisler (.407), Speaker (.388) and Jackson (.382).

All around the league, fans jammed the ballparks to see him, and they booed their own pitchers whenever Ruth was given a base on balls, which happened often (he had 148 walks in the 142 games he played that season). Because he was walked so often, Huggins moved him up from fourth to third in the batting order and put Bob Meusel, a good cleanup hitter, in the fourth spot. Most of the bases on balls Ruth received were intentional, or all but intentional, and with good reason, for it seemed almost impossible to get him out. Typical was a game in June when the Yankees were losing, 5–3, to Boston in the eighth inning. The Yanks had men on first and third with one out, Ruth up. The Red Sox wanted to walk him, but a walk would fill the bases, put the winning run on first and move the tying runs to scoring position at second and third. So they pitched to him, and Ruth tripled against the exit gate in deep right center to drive in both runners. Meusel doubled Ruth home, Pratt singled Meusel home, and the Yankees won, 7–5.

As the season wore on, the bases on balls became more frequent. On July 11 Ruth went to bat four times against Howard Ehmke of Detroit and took his bat from his shoulder only twice. In the first inning, with men on second and third and no one out, he walked on four straight pitches. In the third, with the bases empty, he swung and missed at the first pitch and hit a home run on the second. In the fifth and seventh innings, both times with the bases empty, he walked on four straight pitches. The crowd booed the walks.

He still had occasional bad days. He extended his hitting streak to 26 straight games in the first half of a doubleheader (before a capacity crowd on a Tuesday afternoon) but ended the streak when he walked twice and struck out twice in the second game. When he struck out on his last time at bat, which meant the streak was all over, he smashed his bat on the ground so hard that it broke. Such failures, which seemed rare, inspired one more bit of Ruthian verse:

> *There was a man in our town*
> *Who was a baseball fan;*
> *And who was always in his seat*
> *Before the game began;*
> *And every time the Yanks were here,*
> *And Ruth came up to bat*
> *And failed to bust the ball, he rose*
> *And yelled and waved his hat.*

He tied his own record of 29 homers on July 15. He hit his record-breaking 30th (the first time anyone ever hit that many in a season) on July 19 in the second game of a doubleheader, hit another in the same game and the next afternoon hit another. In those two games he made out only once; the rest of the time he either hit a home run or received a base on balls.

By the end of July he had 37. Maintaining that pace would have carried him past 60, but he slowed drastically and hit only seven during the next five weeks. In September he came alive again and hit ten in his last 24 games to finish with 54. Second to him was Sisler, with 19. The National League champion had 15.

His performance in 1920 is a baseball landmark. He batted .376, hit 54 home runs, nine triples, 36 doubles, scored 158 runs, batted in 137, stole 14 bases. His slugging average was .847, still the major league record. Sports researcher George Russell Weaver, quoted by David Willoughby in his book *The Super Athletes,* said it was the best single season any major league hitter has ever had. Weaver based his opinion on a comparison of Ruth's home run performance with that of the league as a whole. As an example, Weaver noted that Bill Terry's oft-cited batting average of .401 in 1930 was achieved in a season when the league as a whole batted .303; Terry's performance was therefore nowhere near as impressive as Honus Wagner's .354 in 1908, when the league as a whole batted only .239. Only five men batted over .300 in 1908, whereas more than fifty batted over .300 in 1930. When Ruth hit his 54 home runs in 1920, Weaver noted, only one other team in the league hit more than 44.

CHAPTER 19

The Amazing Season: Nothing Like It Ever Before

Thus Ruth came to New York and in his first year there gave the fans the best season a ballplayer ever had. The city was crazy about him, and Babe felt completely at home. After he brought Helen down from Boston, the two began living in a suite in the elegant Ansonia Hotel on Broadway at 73rd Street. It was a lavish, exuberant time, establishing the tone for all his years in New York. Babe, often without Helen, began moving with the night people, and the legend began to grow, the stories running together, until the adventures of one year become indistinguishable from those of another.

"Where were you last night, Babe?" a teammate asked.

"I was at a party with those movie people."

"What movie people?"

"Oh, you know—what the hell are their names?"

Their names, it turned out, were Douglas Fairbanks and Mary Pickford, rather like saying half a century later that he had spent the evening with Richard Something and Elizabeth What's-her-name.

Women were available and he found them with no trouble. He seldom boasted of his sexual exploits, but neither was he shy about them. More sort of admiring. "You should have seen this dame I was with last night," he told a teammate. "What a body. Not a blemish on it."

He bought a succession of splendid automobiles, in which he got into trouble regularly. He ignored traffic signals and speed limits when he drove from the Ansonia to the ballpark and was often stopped by policemen. More often than not the cop, impressed with his catch, would chat for a few moments, issue a jovial warning and send Ruth on his way. Sometimes the cop, not so jovial, would issue a ticket and Ruth would pay a fine. On June 8, 1921, Ruth was racing along Riverside Drive in his maroon sports car when he was stopped by a policeman. It was the second time in less than a month that he had been arrested for speeding. This time the cop took him directly into traffic court. Ruth did not protest, except when the policeman, obviously not a baseball fan, said he did not believe he was really Babe Ruth. In court the magistrate fined him $100, which Babe paid by whipping a hundred off the top of the roll in his pocket. The magistrate also sentenced him to a day in jail. The court attendants, finding this all very amusing, escorted Ruth to a jail in downtown Manhattan. They explained that the Babe would not have to serve twenty-four hours. A "day" ended at four P.M., and one-day prisoners brought in during the morning were released at that hour in the afternoon. Since the ballgame did not start until three-fifteen, it meant Ruth would be able to make part of it. He phoned the ballpark and had his uniform brought down to the jail. He put it on in his cell and put his street suit, an impressive dove-colored cutaway, on over it. His car was parked at the jail's exit. He told a cellmate, "I'm going to have to go like hell to get to the game. Keeping you late like this makes you into a speeder."

The cops basked in the glow of their famous visitor's presence, and the word spread around. Hundreds of people gathered outside, and a photographer on a fire escape across the street tried to get Ruth's picture behind bars, without success. At four o'clock the crowds of people were pushed back and a phalanx of police led Babe through the basement and out to his car. A motorcycle escort led him uptown. The trip from downtown Manhattan to the Polo Grounds, nine miles through New York traffic, was made in eighteen minutes. Babe reached the Polo Grounds, stripped off his suit in the car and came through the gate in center field in uniform to a huge ovation. The Yankees were losing, 3–2, when he arrived, and while Ruth did nothing at bat himself, the club rallied to win, 4–3.

The vulgar humor of dugout and clubhouse pleased him even when he was the butt of it. As the ultimate riposte in some broad horseplay his old friend Mike McNally, another of those who came from the Red Sox to the Yankees, put manure in a hard straw hat belonging to Ruth, and when the Babe breezily donned the hat the manure spilled down over his head and shoulders. Half furious, half laughing at the indignity, Ruth cleaned himself off, mopped his clothes and hurried off to a New York courthouse where he was involved in a minor lawsuit. People usually crowded around him, but now he noticed they were sidling away. Suddenly, his big nostrils sniffed, and his face reddened. Abruptly he settled the case, grabbed Helen and said, "Let's get the hell out of here." Oldtimers say he never wore a hard straw hat or anything but a cap after that.

In July 1920 Ruth took his auto, a big four-door touring sedan, on a Yankee road trip to Philadelphia and Washington. When the games in Washington were over, Ruth started driving back to New York with Helen, a rookie outfielder named Frank Gleich, a second-string catcher named Fred Hofmann, and Charley O'Leary, an old infielder who was now a coach under Huggins. Such company was typical of Ruth, whose varying friends over the years were often rookies or fringe members of the roster.

Ruth was particularly fond of O'Leary, a short, stocky man who was wearing a brand-new straw hat. The trip was a jolly one, with songs, much laughter and occasional stops for sips of bootleg liquor. Babe was driving, which he did with élan and exuberance and not too much attention to minor vagaries of the road. The narrow highway weaved and curved its way into Pennsylvania. It was night, perhaps two in the morning. Ruth was singing at the wheel. He was always unduly impressed by the musical quality of his rich bass voice, and he was really letting it all out in the soft summer night. Just outside the hamlet of Wawa, near Philadelphia, the road curved sharply. Babe was driving much too fast and could not make the curve. He hit the brakes, the car skidded, spun off the road and turned over. O'Leary and Helen were thrown from the car, Helen onto relatively soft dirt at the side of the road, O'Leary onto its hard surface.

Ruth squirmed out of the wreckage. Gleich and Hofmann were okay. Helen was bruised, her stockings almost torn off, but she was not otherwise hurt. O'Leary, lying on his back in the middle of the road, appeared to be unconscious, possibly dead.

Ruth, stricken with fear and remorse, ran to him and fell on his knees. "Oh, my God," he cried. "Oh, my God. Oh, God, bring Charley back. Don't take him. I didn't mean it."

He lifted O'Leary's head, and Charley's eyes opened.

Ruth's face brightened. "Speak to me, Charley. Speak to me."

O'Leary looked around. "What the hell happened?" he growled. "Where's my hat?"

Except for a headache, he was all right and so were the others, although Ruth had banged his knee and was limping. The five of them walked half a mile down the road to a farmhouse, where they were able to spend the night. Next day a mechanic came out and they all went back to look at the car. It was a mess.

"Sell it," Ruth said. "Take whatever you can get for it. I'm through with it."

They made their way into Philadelphia and were startled to discover a newspaper headline saying "RUTH REPORTED KILLED IN CAR CRASH." Other papers, less impulsive, were more accurate, but it was not until the bedraggled party reached New York that evening that Ruppert and Huston could be sure their expensive acquisition was alive and well.

And he was well, despite the banged knee and accompanying limp. He was able to play next day and run at top speed. He hit another memorable pop fly that afternoon, an immense towering thing that drifted toward the short left field corner of the Polo Grounds and eventually fell safely among third baseman, shortstop and left fielder. Ruth, sprinting all the way, got a triple out.

That year, 1920, he was repeatedly on the sick list. There was the pulled rib muscle in April. In May he strained his leg and then came down with a bad cold (they called it the flu) and missed a few games. In June he was leading off first base in a game against the White Sox when Meusel hit a ground ball through the middle to Buck Weaver at shortstop. Weaver fielded the ball, stepped on second for the force-out and threw on to first in an attempt to complete the double play. His throw hit Ruth flush on the forehead, and the Babe fell like a dead tree. He was carried off the field, but he was back in the lineup the next day.

In July there was the banged knee from the auto accident. Later in the month he jammed his wrist sliding. In August he twisted his knee sliding and again was carried off the field. And again he was back in the lineup the next day. Toward the end of August he spent a lot of time driving back and forth to Haverstraw, New York, to make a motion picture called *The Babe Comes Home*. In Haverstraw something stung him on the right forearm and the sting became infected. The wound had to be lanced and Ruth missed several games at the beginning of September.

Through it all, the fans adored him. July 9 was Babe Ruth Day in the Polo Grounds and a chapter of the Knights of Columbus presented him with a diamond-studded watch fob. Ruth responded by hitting a home run and dedicating it to the K of C group by tipping his hat to the section where members of the council were sitting. In June in an exhibition game in Columbus, Ohio, he batted six balls out of the park in batting practice, hit a legitimate homer during the game and pitched the last inning. He enjoyed giving the fans a show, and he appreciated their reaction. When he inadvertently left the watch fob in a Detroit hotel room he sent frantic wires to the hotel and sent the maid who found it a $100 tip.

His instincts were crowd-pleasing. In New York he posed for a boy who came down from the stands with a camera (cameras were not all that common). After the boy snapped his picture, Ruth took the camera from him and gave it to Del Pratt. Then he posed with his arm around the boy's shoulders while Pratt took a picture of them both. The watching crowd cheered.

The fans noticed everything he did. In the Polo Grounds there was a clock high on top of the clubhouse in deep center field. When Ruth stepped into the batter's box, he would glance briefly at the clock before setting himself to face the pitcher. "See that?" one man would say to another, nudging him. "He always does that."

In St. Louis a delegation of admirers gave him a bouquet of flowers. In St. Louis too the spectators in the right field bleachers booed him lustily one afternoon when he came out to his position after making an out. Babe paid no attention, and the boos and hoots and catcalls grew louder until there was a tumult of noise. Finally Ruth turned, grinned, tipped his hat and bowed, and the boos turned to applause. In Chicago, when he came homerless to bat in the ninth inning, the fans yelled, "Hit one! Hit one!" and booed their own beloved Dickie Kerr when the tiny pitcher walked Ruth intentionally.

It was a great life, and the sour notes in it seemed to pass him by. He paid little attention to Helen's complaints, even though his lonely young wife was becoming noticeably discontent. In August 1920 he was in the outfield when Carl Mays hit Ray Chapman of the Indians with a fatal pitch, but even that did not affect him unduly. He never much liked Mays, his teammate for years, and there is no record of him either criticizing or supporting Carl after the incident. The Yankees were in second place at the time, only half a game behind the Indians. They had just swept four straight from the Indians in Cleveland, and after that series the two clubs moved directly to New York for another showdown. It was in the first game at New York, on August 16, that Mays hit Chapman, the sound of the ball as it struck the player's left temple clearly audible in the stands. Chapman crumpled to the ground but was revived and helped to his feet. Aided by two teammates, he began to walk toward the clubhouse in center field. As he reached the outfield grass he collapsed again and had to be carried the rest of the way. He was taken to a hospital, was operated on that night and died early the next morning.

The reaction against Mays was venomous. In Boston, where he was particularly unpopular for jumping the Red Sox the year before, his old teammates talked about going on strike if he was allowed to pitch again. The Senators said much the same thing and so did the Tigers, although Cobb, who had been quoted in the papers as calling for Mays's banishment, denied ever saying anything at all along those lines. Ban Johnson, impulsive as always, said he did not think Mays would ever play again, but Connie Mack defended Mays and so did Frazee, who called Johnson's statement irresponsible and unfair to the player.

Mays was a cold man and a hard competitor who had no compunctions about throwing close to a batter, but Chapman's style was to stand very close to the plate, crouching slightly, so that his head was almost over the plate. Too, as many at the game noticed and Muddy Ruel, Mays's catcher, affirmed, Chapman made no attempt to get out of the way of the pitch. He apparently "lost" the ball, which sometimes happens to a batter. Mays, who went to the hospital to ask about Chapman after the game and to a police station for questioning after Chapman's death, said he had not tried to hit him and had not thrown a "trick pitch." Because baseball was in the process of outlawing the spitter and other erratic deliveries, it was very sensitive about them. Later Mays told Waite Hoyt, "Hell, I threw him a curve ball. You don't throw a curve when you're trying to hit somebody."

It rained the afternoon of Chapman's death, and the Yankee-Indian game was postponed. They did play the next afternoon, but Mays was not in uniform nor was he the day after that. Despite the accident, the Indians held off the Yankees and left New York still in first place. Then they faltered, and the White Sox, who were the subject of a grand jury inquiry into reports that the 1919 World Series had been fixed, took the lead. Mays pitched exactly a week after Chapman's beaning, and after receiving a welcoming round of applause from the New York crowd he shut out Detroit, 10–0. That made anti-Mays feeling rise again, and the Indians asked the league to take action against him. But Kid Gleason, manager of the White Sox, supported Mays and so, finally, did Ban Johnson. Feeling against the pitcher subsided and he worked regularly for the rest of the season, ending with an impressive record of 26 victories against 11 defeats.

The Yankees challenged for the lead again in September, when Ruth's home run production picked up. But in an exhibition game in Pittsburgh at the beginning of their last western trip (it was the first time Pittsburgh had seen the Babe; he came through with a long homer), Ping Bodie broke his leg and was lost for the season. Even so, the Yankees won five of six games in Cleveland and Detroit and edged into first place. Perhaps they were inspired. They were accompanied on the trip by Brother Mathias and the boys' band from St. Mary's. The school had suffered a serious fire the winter before, and the boys were on tour trying to raise funds to rebuild. Ruth had arranged for them to accompany the team, but whatever inspiration they may have engendered faded in Chicago, where the Yankees lost three straight and fell out of the race for good.

The Indians moved past the White Sox to take the lead again and were a game and a half in front when, on Tuesday, September 28, a few days before the end of the season, the stunning news came that eight Chicago players had been indicted for their part in the 1919 affair. The White Sox were not scheduled to play again until Friday; when they did, they put a makeshift team on the field and lost. Next day, the day before the season ended, Cleveland clinched the pennant. The White Sox were second and the Yankees third, three games behind.

While the Black Sox scandal was breaking and the pennant was being settled, New York fans were waiting for Ruth to hit his 50th homer, which was a long time coming. (Babe was the first man ever to hit 30, the first to hit 40, the first to hit 50 and the first to hit 60. The Yankees in their great years were always power hitters, and Yankee Stadium was famous for home runs. Yet only four Yankees other than Ruth ever hit as many as 40 home runs in one season. Lou Gehrig did it five times, Mickey Mantle four. Joe DiMaggio did it once and Roger Maris once, when he hit his 61. Ruth hit 40 or more eleven times, 50 or more four times.)

When Babe finally reached 50 in 1920, in the first game of a doubleheader a week before the season ended, he donated the bat he hit it with to the Near East Fund to auction off for money to be used for the starving Armenians in Turkey. Then he hit his 51st in the second game, added two more a couple of days later and had his 54th and last in the final game of the year.

The season over, he played in several exhibitions at a reported $1500 per game and was offered $2500 for another appearance that he could not fit into his schedule. Then, taking Helen, he joined a party of players from the Giants and sailed to Cuba for a series of exhibitions. Ruth commanded extravagant fees in Cuba and made nearly $40,000 in the several weeks he was there. He lost most of it betting on horse races in Havana, including $25,000 on a race that was supposedly fixed. He told Bob Considine about losing the money betting when the two were working on his autobiography, but cautioned, "You better leave that out. It wouldn't be good for the kids." He spent and lost so much money in Cuba that when it came time to buy boat tickets for home he found himself short and had to borrow some money that Helen had tucked away. From Cuba he wrote Huggins a letter in which he sounded remarkably like Ring Lardner's Alibi Ike, saying that 54 homers were a lot, but he would have hit more if he hadn't been hurt so much. In 1921, he promised, he was going to play every inning.

He had a lively time in Cuba, so much so that when he came back to New York he weighed a jarring 240 pounds, his heaviest yet. He began to work out in gymnasiums and got involved in a basketball game in Passaic, New Jersey. The deftness he had displayed years before in Fayetteville was gone; he missed nine straight shots and when he playfully grabbed an opponent to keep him from shooting, the crowd booed.

CHAPTER 20

Encore:
Topping the Amazing Season

The 1921 season was exhilarating from spring training all the way to the World Series. The Shreveport training camp was even livelier than Jacksonville had been the year before, and the boisterous Yankees, breezy and optimistic after a season of Ruth and the recent acquisition of Waite Hoyt and Wally Schang from the Red Sox, roared into that Louisiana city like cowboys coming to town on Saturday night. Shreveport was in the optimistic throes of an oil boom, and there was money and action everywhere. In a presentation at the ballpark Ruth was given an Essex car that was his and his alone for the four weeks he would be in town. It didn't even have a license plate, its only identification big lettering on the spare tire cover that read "Babe Ruth's Essex." He drove it everywhere, and the other players were able to keep track of the Babe's amorous adventures by noticing in which otherwise placid neighborhood his car happened to be parked. One day they were stumped, because the car was found empty and seemingly abandoned in the middle of a main street. Someone drove it back to the hotel and put it in its regular parking spot, and not until later did the players learn what had happened. A well-to-do local widow pulled her car up next to Ruth's and said hello. A bit of banter passed back and forth, one thing led to another, and the Babe, never one to put things off, got into her car and drove off, leaving his behind.

He found a roadhouse out in the country where he could eat fried chicken, drink Prohibition liquor and listen to jazz (later, in New York, he used to drink occasionally with Bix Beiderbecke, the near legendary jazz cornetist). According to Hoyt, one night when Ruth and some of the other players were whooping it up at the roadhouse a local man took exception to the noise they were making and he and Babe squared off to fight. Things were calmed down and the local man left. After a while Ruth abruptly decided to leave too, a not uncommon practice of his. He got into his car and sped off. Harry Harper, a lefthanded pitcher who later became sheriff of Bergen County in New Jersey, was watching from a window, and he saw a second car start up and follow Ruth.

"Come on," he said to the others, "there's going to be trouble."

They ran out to Harper's car and took off after the other two. After a mile or so they saw Ruth's car by the side of the road with Babe standing alongside it with his hands up. The other car had cut him off, and the man he had quarreled with was pointing a gun at him. Ruth, his face solemn, was saying nothing. Harper honked and drove directly at the man, who hurriedly jumped to one side. Ruth grabbed him, and Harper scrambled out of his car and took the gun away. Except for angry words and vague threats, the players did nothing to the man and eventually let him go, though without his gun. What they really were afraid of was Huggins, if he were to find out what had happened.

When the 1921 season opened, Ruth began hitting immediately and kept it up all season. He had five homers by the end of April, and never fewer than ten a month for the rest of the year. His 25th homer, on July 15, was the 138th of his career, which made him the most prolific home run hitter of all time. His batting average was above .400 in the early weeks and stayed at or near .380 the rest of the year. As for the optimistic Yankees, they began slowly but after a few weeks moved up sharply on the World Champion Indians and began a two-club duel (the third-place team was nowhere) that went on for more than four months before it reached its crisis late in September. On September 15, when Ruth hit his 55th home run to break his year-old record, the Yankees held the lead. On the 16th the Indians regained it. On the 17th it was the Yankees again. On the 18th the Indians. On the 20th the Yankees. When Cleveland came into New York on Friday, September 23, for a four-game show-down, the Yankees led by two percentage points.

The Yankee-Indian games roused great attention in New York, partly because the Giants had already more or less clinched the National League pennant, which meant an all–New York World Series if the Yankees could beat off Cleveland and win the flag. It would be a subway series, the old established Giants against the upstart Yankees, inside-baseball McGraw vs. free-swinger Ruth.

The Yankees beat the Indians, 4–2, in the first game as Ruth hit three doubles and scored three runs, but the next day they were smothered, 9–0, by Cleveland. The third game was played on Sunday before a capacity crowd. Ruth was a minor factor, but four other members of Murderers' Row—Meusel, Pipp, Peckinpaugh and Carl Mays, always a good hitting pitcher—had three hits each, and the Yankees opened a 15–0 lead before Mays allowed a run. They then coasted to an astonishing 21–7 victory. The Indians had to win the fourth game to stay in the race, but the Yankees defeated them, 8–7, in a wild affair. Ruth had two home runs, his 57th and 58th of the year, a double, a base on balls, scored or batted in five of his team's eight runs and was by all odds the hero of the day—and the season. He hit his 59th before the year ended to complete a batting record that was even more remarkable than 1920. He improved in everything. He batted .378. He had 119 extra base hits (59 homers, 16 triples, 44 doubles). He scored 177 runs and batted in 170. His slugging average, .846, was one point lower than the record he set in 1920 (and which still stands), but he had 457 total bases, far beyond his 1920 figure. He had 204 hits and 144 walks, and it was a better than even money bet he would reach base each time he came to bat.

The Yankees clinched the pennant a few days later in the first game of a doubleheader, and during the second game Ruth bullied Huggins into letting him pitch a few innings. Earlier in the year he started a game, went five shaky innings and won. In 1920 he had had a similar shaky winning effort. Now he went to the mound in the eighth inning, with the Yankees ahead 6–0, and was pounded for six runs, which tied the score. Perhaps mischievously, Huggins let Ruth stay in, and he pitched shutout ball through the ninth, tenth and eleventh innings before the Yankees won the game in the bottom of the eleventh, 7–6. Ruth got credit for the win, so that he was 3–0 as a pitcher with the Yankees in 1920 and 1921. But that was the end. He pitched only twice more in his career: in 1930 and in 1933, each time to hypo attendance at the very end of the season. And he won each time.

Ruth never lost his affection for pitching or respect for his own ability. He seldom bothered to boast about his hitting—he knew everyone was aware of it—but he often reminded people how good a pitcher he had been. Late in his career he scoffed when someone said Cleveland's huge Municipal Stadium was a good park to pitch in. This was before an arbitrary fence was built across the vast outfield to encourage home runs. "Hell, that's not pitching," Ruth said. "That's just throwing. Now the Polo Grounds, with those short foul lines, that's pitching. I remember what it was like there. You couldn't just throw the ball and let them hit flies. You had to think, you had to work the corners." When George Earnshaw of the Athletics was compared to Christy Mathewson after pitching twenty-two consecutive scoreless innings in the 1930 World Series (Matty had pitched twenty-seven scoreless innings in 1905), Babe grumbled, "How about Ruth, who pitched twenty-nine consecutive innings? Did they forget the old Babe used to pitch pretty good ball in the World Series?"

The Yankees went into the 1921 World Series with the Giants bursting with confidence, and that seemed more than justified when they won the first two games by identical 3–0 scores. Ruth swung at the first pitch thrown to him in the first inning of the first game and lined a single that drove in the first run. But he also struck out twice and walked once. The Giants were pitching carefully to him. He walked three straight times in the second game, which was as frustrating to the fans as it was to him. After the third of these, almost as though he simply could not stand the inaction any longer, he bolted for second and stole the base standing up. That shook the Giants and pleased the crowd. And then he stole third, which really shook the place.

In the third game of the Series the Yankees took a quick 4–0 lead, and it seemed like an unseemly rout of McGraw and his team. But after twenty scoreless innings the Giants rallied, tied the score in the third inning, scored eight more runs in the seventh and won easily, 13–5. It was a best-five-out-of-nine Series that year, and there was still a long way to go. And it was learned then that Ruth was hurt. The day before, he had scraped his elbow badly on the scrabbly infield when he slid into third with the second of his colorful stolen bases, and the elbow had become infected. He played in the 13–5 game—drove in two runs, as a matter of fact—but scraped the elbow again sliding into base and left the game in the eighth inning. The infection had to be lanced, and the Yankees dolefully announced that he would be out for the rest of the Series.

Babe was in uniform for the next game, but he sat on the bench throughout batting practice. No one expected him to play, but when the Yankees ran out to their positions to start the game, Babe popped from the dugout and jogged to left field. An exultant yell went up from the crowd. His arm was bandaged and when he ran he held it out stiffly at an angle to his body. He touched it continually. Despite the pain, Ruth had a single early in the game and a home run in the ninth, his first World Series homer. But the Giants won.

He played again the next day, his arm still bandaged, a tube draining the wound; and one of his legs was strapped because of a muscle tear he suffered a week or two before the season ended. As he limped to bat in the top of the first—it was a marvelous moment for an injured hypochondriac who was also a ham—the crowd cheered almost as much as it had when he ran out to the outfield the day before. He struck out, swinging hard. When he batted again in the fourth inning, with the score tied 1-1, he stunned the Giants by dropping a bunt down the third base line and beating it out for a hit. Meusel followed with a double and Ruth scored all the way from first with the eventual winning run in a 3-1 Yankee victory. He slid across the plate, got to his feet, stumbled to the Yankee dugout and collapsed. When the inning was over and the Yanks took the field, Ruth slowly followed—again to tumultuous applause.

But in that day's *New York Sun,* columnist Joe Vila, writing of Ruth's melodramatic appearance on the field the day before, said, "Ruth possibly enjoyed the trick he played on the fans by going into the game after the report had been spread that he had been forced out of the series by an operation on his 'infected elbow.' On numerous occasions during the pennant race the public was informed that Ruth had been disabled and couldn't play, yet the Home Run King invariably bobbed up to battle for the Yankees. According to official information on Saturday, the Babe had been seriously injured and the Hugmen would have to worry along without him. But Ruth, with a bandage around his elbow, surprised everybody in the stands by taking his place in left field and by hammering the ball for a single and a four-bagger. Further reports of the Bambino's indispositions will be taken with plenty of salt."

But Ruth's arm *was* swollen and infected. Pus was draining from the incision and he was warned by the team physician not to play any more in the Series. Lurid stories of blood poisoning and possible amputation circulated. Ruth spent a restless night at the Ansonia and showed up at the ballpark the next afternoon with his arm in a sling. He did not go on the field but sat in a box seat with Helen. Someone showed him Vila's column from the day before—Babe seldom bothered to read anything on his own—and he went over to the ground-level press section and shouted at Vila. Other sportswriters prevented a fight, but the angry Ruth shoved his left elbow forward and yelled, "Why don't you take a picture of this and put it in your paper?"

The next afternoon Vila wrote, "Peeved over something that had appeared in print, Ruth tried to pick a fight with a newspaper writer. . . . Ruth, it seems, is no different from other baseball stars who consider praise and flattery belongs to them as a matter of course but are unable to stand criticism without showing their true colors."

Ruth was out of uniform for two games, and the Yankees lost both, to fall behind the Giants, four games to three. He dressed for the eighth game, but did not play. It was a tight, closely played game, and the Giants led, 1–0, in the ninth. Huggins sent Ruth in to pinch-hit. The bases were empty, but a home run would tie the score and a base hit or even a walk would give the Yankees a chance. But Ruth grounded out, and soon after that the game and the Series were over.

CHAPTER 21

The Second Big Fight:
Ruth vs. Landis

Ruth's arm healed quickly, and with the Series out of the way he prepared to go off on another postseason exhibition tour. He and a team called The Babe Ruth All Stars were to play in various cities in Pennsylvania and upstate New York and then shift west to Oklahoma. These off-season affairs made a great deal of money for Babe, and on this one he expected to earn $25,000. But this time there was a hitch.

In the early years of the century players from World Series teams would go on barnstorming tours and replay the Series in backwater towns. Sometimes the touring players were truly representative of the pennant-winning teams; more often they had only two or three top players and a bunch of supernumeraries. In either case they were billed as World Series heroes and tickets were sold on that basis. The baseball establishment, fearing that the special impact of the World Series was being devalued by these ersatz reruns, and worried too that such barnstorming was detracting from their own exhibition games in the spring, passed a rule in 1911 forbidding players on World Series teams from appearing in exhibition games after the Series. It was this rule that Ruth and other Red Sox players violated in 1916 when they played an exhibition in New England after the World Series.

Ruth was aware of the rule, but because barnstorming was such a big part of his income—he earned double his salary in exhibitions after the 1919 and 1920 seasons—he had asked Cap Huston late in the season for permission to go on the tour. Huston told him it was okay as far as the Yankees were concerned, but that permission could not come from the ball club. He would have to get permission from the league or, possibly, Judge Kenesaw Landis.

Landis was just completing his first season as High Commissioner and was still consolidating his position. In his authoritative way he assumed complete charge of the World Series, deciding that while the pennant races were primarily league affairs, the Series was above the leagues and therefore his to run. He more or less ignored Ban Johnson and John Heydler, the league presidents. "I'm about as important around here as the office boy," the unhappy Johnson complained, and Landis publicly disagreed with Heydler on the question of the length of the Series. Landis thought the best-five-games-of-nine formula too long. Heydler was strongly in favor of it. In 1922 the Series went back to four-games-of-seven, as Landis wanted. So much for Heydler.

When the matter of Ruth and the postseason tour came up, Landis decided it was a matter for him to settle. Ruth blithely ignored repeated warnings that the judge had heard about the trip and was against it and went ahead with his plans. He and Meusel, Mays and Schang were the All Stars; they would be supplemented by Bill Piercy and Tom Sheehan, two young Yankee pitchers, and half a dozen semipro ballplayers from New York. The trip was discussed freely the last few days of the Series, and, partly inspired by doubts like Vila's, the question inevitably arose: How could Ruth play exhibition games if he couldn't play in the Series? "I heal quick," Babe said. "I always heal quick." Which was true.

The subject came up for some spirited discussion at a party Ruppert and Huston threw for the ball club at the Commodore

Hotel the night after the series ended. Ruth was still insistent about going on the trip, and Meusel almost always did what Ruth did. But Mays and Schang were worried, and the next morning they went to see Landis in his suite at the Commodore. Afterwards, they told Ruth they were backing out, and they added that Landis wanted to talk to him too. Others told Ruth that Landis wanted to see him, and after some delay Ruth phoned the Commissioner. Landis was annoyed that Ruth had not called earlier, and he told him to come to the suite at once to discuss the matter of the tour.

Ruth said he couldn't, he had to see a party. This annoyed Landis even more and the conversation became sharper. Ruth told him he was leaving that night for Buffalo and would play the first game of the barnstorming tour the next afternoon.

"Oh, you are, are you?" snapped Landis. "If you do, it will be the sorriest thing you've ever done in baseball." He slammed down the phone. "Who does that big monkey think he is?" he said, pacing around his room. "It seems I'll have to show somebody who's running this game."

Fred Lieb, the sportswriter, who was in Landis' suite when Ruth phoned, hurried over to Huston's apartment at the Martinique Hotel. Huston had been partying with Frazee, and the two of them were sprawled out fast asleep. Lieb shook Huston into wakefulness and told him of Landis' anger. "You've got to stop Babe from going to Buffalo," he said. "Landis will throw the book at him. He may throw him out of baseball."

Huston shakily dragged himself up and went to see Ruth, but the Babe was angry too. As always, he reacted defiantly to direct acts of authority. "Aw, tell the old guy to go jump in a lake," he said. He and Meusel were still going. So were Piercy and Sheehan, who figured they didn't have much to lose anyway. At midnight the quartet left for Buffalo.

When Landis heard this the next morning he said, "If Ruth breaks the rule against World Series players engaging in such contests, then it will resolve itself into an issue between the player and myself. Whether or not the rule is fair or unfair is not the question.

It was in the code before I came into baseball. My duty concerns its enforcement or penalizing for its violation."

Everyone assumed that Ruth would be fined, possibly his entire World Series share. Landis' office handled all World Series details, including sending checks to the players for their winning or losing shares, so he had a firm hold on that purse string. However, a losing share in 1921 was $3362, and since Ruth would earn that much in a couple of exhibitions it did not look like too severe a punishment. But Landis said, "I have warned Ruth that he need expect no light penalty if he appears in any further games this season."

He left for his home in Chicago (riding in the engineer's cab of the Twentieth Century Limited as far as Albany, New York) and on his arrival next morning was told that the Babe had crossed the Rubicon. He and the others had played in Buffalo. New York was buzzing over the act of defiance and wondered what Landis would do. Would he be content merely to fine Ruth? After all, players from other teams in the league were barnstorming, and the rule seemed patently unfair to Ruth and other Series players. Or, as persistent rumors said, would Landis throw the book at him and suspend him, possibly for the entire 1922 season?

The judge, a consummate politician, knew how to wait. He said, "I have a mass of papers to read over before deciding the Ruth case. I'll make my decision in due time. But I warned Ruth two weeks ago that the rule prohibited this sort of thing." Again he pointed out that he had not made the rule, but that it was part of the agreement the American League and National League had signed in January 1921, when the judge formally accepted the office of Commissioner. As Commissioner he was obliged to enforce the rule, and, he added, "Law-abiding baseball men need have no fear that the laws of the game will not be enforced. The law of gravitation is still in force and what goes up must come down."

One of the things Landis was waiting for was support, both in and out of baseball. An immediate decision against Ruth, the favorite of the crowd, the wounded hero of the Series, might backfire. But in time, as the glow of his exploits paled and the usual reaction against a hero set in, Landis would be in a better position. He decided to wait and see how Ruth was received on the tour, perhaps wait until it was over, and let the press and the owners react to Ruth's behavior first. That reaction was not long in coming. Huston, after his fruitless talk with Babe, consulted with Ruppert and the two issued a statement leaving Ruth on his own. "It is regrettable that the rule of baseball . . . has been violated so defiantly," their statement read, "that Judge Landis has no alternative but to meet the situation firmly. The rule appears to be unjust in many respects, but as long as it exists it should be obeyed. The players made the mistake of not petitioning for a modification of the rule."

A newspaper opinion, after repeating that the rule was unfair, said, "Nevertheless, the ethical must disappear before the legal, and Judge Landis is absolutely correct in his attitude. Baseball made Ruth, and not Ruth baseball, and the slugger is just as amenable to the code of rules as the veriest tyro just up from the bushes. He will not gain friends, neither among fans or elsewhere, by an attitude of defiance towards the commissioner, who has taken upon himself the task of ridding baseball of abuses and keeping it free from them. Baseball needs a Landis much more than it does a Ruth."

Ruth and his troupe moved from Buffalo to Elmira, New York, where he and Meusel each hit two home runs before a disappointing crowd of 1500. Ruth, talking on the bench between innings, said, "We're going to play exhibitions until November first, and Judge Landis isn't going to stop us. I'm not in any fight to see who's the greatest man in baseball. I'm out to earn an honest dollar, and at the same time give baseball fans in these towns a chance to see the big players in action. I think we're doing something good for baseball. Why are we picked on when players from second- and third-place teams can play postseason games?"

From Elmira they went to Jamestown, New York, where Ruth played first base and hit two doubles but no home runs, which disappointed another disappointing crowd. The tour was neither an artistic nor a financial success, but Ruth remained stubborn. "I don't care if my case comes up before Landis tomorrow," he said. "I'm not worrying." Ruppert and Huston were. They were very much afraid of what Landis might do. Their statement of support had been an attempt to placate him, to keep the punishment mild. Each day that Ruth continued his defiance, the greater the chance that Landis would suspend him—and for a full season, if not longer.

Huston told friends he was leaving for a vacation at Dover Hall, his hunting lodge in Georgia, but instead he went to Scranton, Pennsylvania, and met Ruth there. The Babe was glum. The weather had been bad, the publicity bad, the crowds bad, the receipts bad. The troupe was thinking of abandoning the eastern schedule, but they were still planning to go west to Oklahoma City and other towns in that area.

Huston argued with Ruth, asking him to end the barnstorming trip right there in Scranton. Ruth said he wouldn't. He didn't care what happened to him, he said, but he would not give in to Landis. Huston cleverly suggested that Ruth would not be hurt as much as the Yankees would. If he and Meusel were suspended for a year, where would the team be? This patriotic argument appealed to the altruistic side of Babe's nature. "I didn't think of that," he said. "Maybe you're right." He agreed to pack it in, and the ill-fated exhibition tour folded in Scranton. Huston helped further by writing a few checks to pay off local promoters who had put up guarantees, and then he and Ruth returned to New York.

An elated Huston told everyone that Babe would be going to Chicago to talk personally to Landis about his case, which strengthened the picture of a penitent Ruth going barefoot to the Pope at Canossa. But a day or so later Babe left instead on a hunting trip with Herb Pennock. In Chicago, Landis said he had seen nothing but newspaper reports about Ruth's proposed visit and apology. In any case, he said pettishly, an apology would have no bearing on his decision. It was obvious now that Ruth was going to be suspended.

The Yankees hurriedly sent an emissary to talk to Landis. They chose Ed Barrow, Ruth's old antagonist, who had become the Yankees' business manager a year earlier. Harry Sparrow, the old business manager, died suddenly in May 1920, and Huston mentioned to his old drinking buddy Frazee that they were looking for someone to replace him. Frazee recommended Barrow, who was unhappy managing the ravaged Red Sox. Barrow finished the 1920 season as Red Sox manager and then switched to the Yankee front office in October. Almost at once he arranged a deal with Frazee that brought Hoyt and Schang to New York, but generally he had little to do with Ruth, which was fine with Babe.

Now he went to see Landis, whom he had known for several years.

"Well, what do *you* want?" Landis snapped as Barrow came into his office.

"I guess you know what I want."

"Yes, I guess I do." Landis pivoted in his chair. The Yankees had been leaders in the revolt against Johnson that resulted in Landis being named Commissioner, and he did not want to alienate his prime supporters. He looked out his window. "I suppose everybody out on the street is saying, 'That's where that white-haired son of a bitch works who's going to throw Babe Ruth out of baseball.'"

Barrow grinned.

"Ed," Landis said, "what would you do if you were in my place?"

"I'd suspend him too," Barrow said and went back to New York.

But his visit probably helped. Landis knew now that he had won. He was going to subdue Ruth publicly with the support of Ruth's own club and thus dramatically strengthen his position as the absolute boss of baseball—the Czar, as he came to be known. There was no need to go too far and hurt Ruppert or Huston or Barrow.

He held off his decision for a while and had Leslie O'Connor, his assistant, send a questionnaire to each of the errant players. Ruth, back from his hunting trip, held a press conference on the stage of the Palace Theater in New York to announce details of a vaudeville tour he was going to make on the Keith circuit with Wellington

Cross, a well-known entertainer. The tour would run for sixteen weeks, and he would make $3000 a week. Then Babe went off to Pittsburgh, for some reason, to rehearse. The act opened Thursday, November 3, in a sort of off-Broadway tryout at Proctor's Theater in Mount Vernon, New York. The critics were gentle. The act consisted mostly of comic patter, with Cross handling the straight lines. Babe also sang. ("Despite a cold," one critic said, "the slugger unblanketed a not unpleasant baritone voice.") The high point of the act came when Babe received a stage telegram.

"Who's it from?" asked Cross.

"Judge Landis."

"Judge Landis! Is it serious?"

"I should say it is. Seventy-five cents collect."

They opened in Boston on November 7 and were in the Palace in New York on November 14, before going on to other cities. They were in Washington on December 5, when Landis finally announced his decision. Ruth, Meusel and Piercy were fined their World Series shares ($3362 each) and were suspended for the first six weeks of the 1922 season. Sheehan was not punished at all because he had not been eligible for the Series and was thus not affected by the rule.

A reporter found Ruth in his Washington hotel suite, stretched out on a pink chaise longue, wearing a lavish multicolored silk shirt. A waiter was taking his order for lunch, and Ruth was reminding him to "put a few lamb chops around that steak. And lots of potatoes." The reporter asked how he felt about the Landis decision.

"I'm not going to say anything about it," Ruth replied. "I've told about ten reporters already that I don't even know if it's authentic. Anyway, I'm not going to talk about it."

A hanger-on in the suite—Ruth was always surrounded by a court—said, "We'll just leave the whole matter to the public for judgment."

Ruth nodded. "We'll just wait and see what happens," he said. "We don't know what the situation will be next spring. Maybe the public and the managers will have something to say. I may cut loose myself in about a month and say something, and if I do all the world will know about it.

"In the meantime, I'm going to wait until I get formal notice. I'm not worrying. Leave Judge Landis make the next move. I'm going to leave it lie."

CHAPTER 22

The Fall of the Hero:
Ruth in Disgrace

Despite his Washington proclamation that he might say something in about a month, Ruth kept his mouth shut about Landis and the suspension. As for Ruppert and Huston, the two colonels were visibly relieved by the Commissioner's decision. It had taken him an unbearably long time, and the suspension could have been worse.

Babe's vaudeville tour ended in February in Milwaukee, and he went directly to Hot Springs, Arkansas, ostensibly to take the baths and get in shape, but actually to play golf, gamble in the casinos, play the horses and generally relax for a week or two before going on to the Yankee training camp in New Orleans. His holdover contract from the Red Sox had expired, and Huston and Huggins came down to Hot Springs to talk about a new one. Ruth was no intellectual, but he understood two things well: baseball and his own worth. He was a sharp, smart ballplayer, and he knew that he was the prime reason why two and a half million people had paid between 55¢ and $2.20 to get into the Polo Grounds in 1920 and 1921. He may not have sat down with a pencil and paper and figured out precisely what the Yankees made—they probably netted more than $1,000,000 a year after expenses in Ruth's first two seasons—but he wanted more of it than he had been getting, a lot more.

Rumors said Babe would be upped to $30,000, with bonus clauses to give him an extra $20,000. If that offer was made, Ruth rejected it out of hand. Huston did propose $40,000 on a straight salary, but Babe turned that down too. Huston eventually came up to $50,000 on a five-year contract, a quarter-of-a-million-dollar package.

Ruth's big black eyes stared at Huston. "Make it fifty-two thousand and it's a deal."

"Fifty-two thousand?" Now it was Huston's turn to stare. "All right, agreed. But why fifty-*two* thousand?"

"Well," said Ruth, "there are fifty-two weeks in the year, and I've always wanted to make a grand a week."

The impact of $52,000 a year on America at that time can be better understood if it is compared with other players' salaries. The Yankees were wallowing in prosperity, a pennant-winning team with huge attendances and the prospects of more. They were not a bunch of rookies and young players just coming into their own, but a team of established stars; most had made their reputations on other clubs, notably Boston. The Yankees were paying top salaries. Yet Home Run Baker, one of the really famous names in the game and a man so stubborn in contract talks that he twice sat out an entire season, was making only $16,000, and that was much the highest salary on the club after Ruth. Wally Schang, one of the two or three best catchers in the game, a member of four championship teams, was making $10,000. Bob Shawkey, a 20-game winner three times who would win 20 again that year, was at $8500. Wally Pipp, the first baseman, going into his ninth big league season, a proved hitter who twice led the league in home runs, was making $6500; Whitey Witt, who came from Philadelphia in the spring of 1922 to become the regular center fielder, $4000; and Fred Hofmann, the reserve catcher, $3000. A man could live in a big frame house, own an automobile, raise a family and live comfortably on $75 or $80 a week. Even more than a decade later, after Ruth's retirement, the top player salary in baseball was Lou Gehrig's $30,000. Dizzy Dean was raised to $19,500 the year after he won 30 games. In 1957, after inflation had come in the wake of World War II, T. Coleman Andrews, the Director of Internal Revenue during the Eisenhower administration, said that Ted Williams, then baseball's highest paid player, would have to make a million dollars to equal the true value of Ruth's top salary.

In brief, Ruth's pay was enormous, and it fed the flames of criticism that were beginning to rise around him. Ruth said, "It isn't right to call me or any ballplayer an ingrate because we ask for more money. Sure I want more, all I'm entitled to. The time of a ballplayer is short. He must get his money in a few years or lose out. Listen, a man who works for another man is not going to be paid any more than he's worth. You can bet on that. A man ought to get all he can earn. A man who knows he's making money for other people ought to get some of the profit he brings in. Don't make any difference if it's baseball or a bank or a vaudeville show. It's business, I tell you. There ain't no sentiment to it. Forget that stuff."

With the big salary, Ruth also was appointed captain of the team to replace Peckinpaugh, who had been traded. Being named captain was a signal honor in those days, and Ruth was genuinely pleased. In New Orleans he and Meusel were full members of the team, working out with the others, playing exhibition games, everything. But they were told that when the season began they would be allowed to practice with the club only in the morning and would have to be out of uniform by the time the gates opened, although they could take part in the exhibitions that big league teams played in almost every off-day. The extent of the punishment began to sink in, and when Landis came to New Orleans on his tour of spring training camps, Ruth and Meusel called on him at his hotel to ask for commutation of their sentences. They visited for a couple of hours and listened while the Commissioner lectured them on baseball, authority, discipline, the past, the future and sundry other topics that happened along. He did not change his mind about the suspensions, as Ruth conceded after the interview. "He sure can talk," Babe said wistfully.

Even without their two big sluggers, the Yankees got off well. Barrow had swung another deal with Frazee during the winter that brought Joe Bush, Sam Jones and Everett Scott to the club, three outstanding players. Jones won 23 games for Boston the year before. Bush, despite a cut on his hand that kept him out most of the first month, was to win 26 and lose seven for the Yankees that season. Scott, an impeccable shortstop who had the gift of pulling a team together, was in the process of playing 1307 consecutive games (a record Lou Gehrig eventually broke). The Yankees were in first place most of April and May, which gave rise to the obvious remark: Who needs Ruth? Babe, meanwhile, played in an exhibition or two, did some practicing (but missed more morning sessions than he made), went into St. Vincent's Hospital to have his tonsils and adenoids removed (he was a chronic victim of bad colds) and spent a lot of time at the Jamaica racetrack betting wads of money with the bookies, who were then legal.

Despite the occasional critical remark, excitement heightened as the time grew near for Ruth's return. The suspension was up on Saturday, May 20, when the second-place St. Louis Browns would be in town. Because Ruth and Meusel had to observe the technicality of applying for reinstatement and because such application could not be made before May 20, rumors arose that Landis might not reinstate them in any case. But even though there was no guarantee Ruth would play, long lines of fans filed into the Yankee office on 42nd Street to buy tickets to the weekend games. A girl arriving late was told by a doorman, "They're all sold out. You know, Babe Ruth is going to play."

At the Ansonia on the eve of his return, Ruth was excited too. "It's going to be a big day tomorrow," he said. "I hope it don't rain." Helen had been in St. Vincent's too, for an operation described as "slightly more serious" than Babe's tonsillectomy. (She had several previous operations, none described; it is possible they were miscarriages or complications arising from miscarriages.) She had come home only the day before and would not be able to go to the game.

"It's kind of a holiday for both of us," she said. "I wish I could be there to see him."

"Six weeks is a long time to be away from your life's work," said the Babe. "I'm lonesome for it. I'm not predicting I'm going to slug one, but here's hoping."

On Saturday the applications for reinstatement were made by telegraph, and Landis immediately wired back affirmation. In the afternoon there was an overflow crowd of 40,000 at the Polo Grounds. Babe arrived at the ballpark in a limousine and was given a great welcoming cheer by the thousands milling around outside the gates. Just before the game he was presented with an award by the National Vaudeville Association, which helped remind some of the restless fans that Ruth had made nearly $50,000 on his vaudeville tour, a fact noted in the stands with increasing sarcasm when the Babe, using a vivid green bat, proved to be a bust at the plate. He struck out, popped up twice and grounded out, and there were hoots and boos each time. A writer of the day noted, "If there is one thing that pleases the American public more than cheering a hero when he is elevated, it is jeering him when he fails." A half century later the Olympic star Mark Spitz, commenting on the adverse publicity he received during the year after he won seven gold medals, said, "American people love heroes, and they love to tear them down, and then build them up again." Ruth was in the process of being torn down.

The next day, before another overflow crowd, he was booed again; he had only one hit, a double, in five appearances at the plate. On Monday he listened to more boos as he popped up, flied out, walked. When he caught a simple fly ball in the seventh inning, the crowd applauded derisively. Ruth tipped his hat in reply. The same thing happened in the eighth inning: easy fly ball, derisive cheering, another sarcastic tip of the cap. Then in the last of the eighth he hit a home run, his first of the year, and the crowd went berserk. Ruth trotted around the bases with his eyes on the ground, refusing to smile, tip his cap or acknowledge the applause in any way.

Despite the homer Ruth continued in a slump. He switched from the green bat to a pale yellow one but struck out, popped up and grounded out in his next game, all to a steady razzing. He got to first base on a walk but was out trying to steal second, and the boos were tumultuous. It was getting to him. The worst seemed to come in his fifth day back in the lineup, when he went zero for five. He came to bat in the seventh inning with the bases loaded and the Yankees behind by two runs and grounded out to end the inning. In the ninth, the Yanks still behind by two, he came to bat again with the bases loaded and made out to end the game. He was batting .093.

But that was not the worst. That came the next day, Thursday, May 25, a hot, humid, muggy, overcast, bad-tempered day. In the third inning he singled sharply to center; when the center fielder juggled the ball, Ruth tried to stretch the hit into a double and was thrown out. When he heard the decision he jumped to his feet and angrily flung a handful of dust in the face of the umpire, George Hildebrand. Hildebrand threw him out of the game, the first time Ruth had been put out of a game as a Yankee. As he walked grumpily across the infield toward the bench, the crowd hissed and hooted. Fifteen feet from the dugout Ruth stopped, took off his hat and made a deep mocking bow. A tall man in the seats behind the dugout cupped his hands to his mouth and shouted, "You god-damned big bum, why don't you play ball?" The crowd was small, less than 10,000, and Ruth had no trouble seeing this particular heckler. He jumped onto the roof of the dugout and plunged into the stands after him. The heckler scrambled away, climbing over the seats as fast as he could, and other people in the crowd slowed Ruth down, trying to placate him. A fan shouted to them, "Hit the big stiff!" Ruth shook his fist at the first heckler, now safely at the rear of the grandstand, and climbed back on the dugout roof. Hatless, his hair tangled, his face an angry dark red, he shouted at the crowd, "Come on down and fight! Anyone who wants to fight, come down on the field! Ah, you're all alike, you're all yellow!" He jumped down on the field, picked up his cap and glove and made the long walk across the Polo Grounds to the center field clubhouse. He was drenched in boos and catcalls. As he neared the clubhouse he shook a warning finger at someone in the bleachers.

It was a sorry exit. After the game Ruth said bitterly, "I didn't mean to hit the umpire with the dirt, but I did mean to hit that bastard in the stands. If I make a home run every time I bat, they'd think I'm all right. If I don't, they think they can call me anything they like. I don't know what they're going to do to me for this. I'll probably be fined or suspended, but I don't see why I should get any punishment at all. I was only kicking the decision. I'll go into the stands again if I have to."

That night Ban Johnson, as president of the league, announced that Ruth would be suspended pending an investigation. The Yankees left the next morning for a series with Washington, whose owner, Clark Griffith, was in near panic. Griffith ran a shoestring operation, and he had ballyhooed Ruth's first visit of the season all over the south. People were coming from as far away as North Carolina. He got in touch with his old friend Johnson and literally begged him to lift the suspension. And Johnson did, after the Friday game, which Ruth sat out. But he fined Ruth $200. "Dust on umpires happens in the heat of the moment," Johnson said, "but we cannot condone anyone going into the stands." He also ordered Ruth divested of his captaincy. This meant that the Babe's active career as captain of the Yankees had lasted exactly six games. Scott, a logical choice, was named to succeed him.

Relieved that his punishment was no worse, Ruth said in Washington, "I'm sorry it happened, but I stood as much as I could. I had to break loose."

Ruth was batting .100 when the Yankees returned to New York, but then he began to hit. In the Memorial Day doubleheader he drove in the winning run in the first game and a two-run homer in the second. The crowd cheered the homer lustily, and this time the Babe tipped his hat and smiled. When the bleachers cheered him as he returned to the outfield after the inning, he tipped it again.

Everything seemed fine.

CHAPTER 23

The Jinx and the Baby: The Weird Season Ends

The Yankees left on a long, long road trip that took them out through the west and back home via Washington and Boston. They won for a while and then sank into a sorry losing streak. The players, a rowdy, independent group of drinkers, gamblers and wenchers—most of them, anyway—raised hell every night. Poker games went on until dawn. Empty bottles of bootleg liquor piled up in the halls. Some players were never in their own rooms all night. Huggins looked littler than ever trying to control his willful troupe. He had troubles with his players all year. He fined Mays in spring training, and he and the pitcher had a loud shouting argument about that in the streets of Norfolk, Virginia. In May the hotheaded Hoyt, resenting Huggins' directions on how to pitch to a certain batter, blew up, lost a tight ballgame and got into a scrap with Huggins on the bench. Reports said Hoyt punched Huggins, but the pitcher said all he did was grab the manager's shoulder to turn him around. Huggins did not fine Hoyt, but in any case discipline was lacking.

In Cleveland on June 19 the Yankees were winning, 2–1, in the eighth when the Indians' Les Nunamaker, a heavy-footed catcher, hit a double, barely beating Meusel's throw into second base. The

Yankees were convinced that he was out and argued with Bill Dinneen, the umpire. Ruth came running all the way in from left field to join the argument and in the course of it used a particularly choice bit of obscenity. Precisely what he said is lost in time, but Dinneen threw Ruth out of the game. A triple and a single followed Nunamaker's double, and the Indians won, 3–2, to give the Yankees their eighth straight loss. After the game Dinneen made a telephone report of the incident to Ban Johnson, and that night Johnson announced that Ruth was suspended again, this time for three days. Asked if that wasn't a bit severe, Johnson airily replied, "They've lost eight straight games. Maybe with Ruth out they'll turn around and win a few. My report shows that Ruth used vulgar and vicious language, calling Umpire Dinneen one of the vilest names known. I will not stand for action of that type from any player."

Ruth was given the news during batting practice the next day. He exploded. He saw Dinneen in the Cleveland dugout and went over to him shouting, "If you ever put me out of a game again, you son of a bitch, I'll fix you so you'll never umpire a game again. I don't care if they put me out of baseball for life." Dinneen, a big man in his late forties, replied angrily, and Ruth yelled, "You're yellow!"

"Nobody calls me yellow!"

"If you don't like it come under the stands," Ruth said. Bristling with fury, he moved toward Dinneen, but the two were held apart by three Cleveland players. One of them persuaded Ruth to go back to the Yankee clubhouse. Dinneen made another report, and that night Johnson suspended Ruth for an extra two days, making it five days in all and the fourth suspension for the Yankee star in the still young season. He was not fined, but, as the newspapers were quick to point out, he was losing about $300 a day in pay for the days he was suspended, which meant $1500 for the five days on the bench.

Ruth's temper subsided quickly. Before the game the next afternoon he walked into the umpires' little dressing room and said quietly to Dinneen, "Bill, do you think I'm getting a square deal?"

"I don't have anything to do with the suspension," Dinneen said. "All I do is make a report."

Placated, Ruth sat against a table and chatted amiably with the umpire and his partner, Dick Nallin. "When a fellow's down and out," Babe said, "it seems to be a case of holding him down. I don't mind being out because of the money it's costing me. I don't need the money. But I love to play, and it hurts when I can't get into the game. The criticism hurts too. They're saying I wanted the suspension because it would give me an alibi if I don't equal my home run record. Hell, that's ridiculous. I can't equal it anyway this year. And they're saying I've got a swelled head. Well, my friends know different. But I'll tell you one thing. You can bet this is the last time I'll be suspended for wrangling with an umpire. Especially if it involves another player."

When he returned to the lineup on June 26 he not only hit a home run but ostentatiously sat on the outfield grass when the Yankees got in another argument with Dinneen and waited quietly there until it was over. He was still being booed, however, and when the Yankees played an exhibition in Baltimore on June 30 it was noted that the roar of welcome he received was the first warm cheer for him since the Yankees left the Polo Grounds more than three weeks before.

Meanwhile, reports of the riotous goings on during the trip had come back to New York. "All in all," wrote one reporter, "the stories of the road trip are calculated to make a New Yorker admit that this town is an angel village compared to some in the west." At one point Huston hired a private detective, a man named Kelly, who met the team on the road and passed himself off as one of those congenial people who enjoy the company of athletes and have money enough to travel around with them. He seemed to pop up in every city, and he proved a congenial companion. In Chicago he took several players, among them Ruth, Meusel, Witt and an unsuccessful young pitcher named Lefty O'Doul, to a party at an illicit brewery in Joliet. Everybody had a fine time, even though it was a stag affair, and when a photographer happened to appear—at that point nobody would have been surprised if the Mormon Tabernacle Choir had materialized—Kelly suggested a group picture as a momento of the evening. They posed dutifully, all in shirtsleeves in the hot midwestern night, and the next day Kelly disappeared. Back in New York he gave the incriminating photograph and a report to Huston, who passed both on to Barrow with instructions to tell Huggins to use them as a weapon against the misbehaving players. Barrow told Huggins, but he kept the photograph and eventually had it framed and hung on the wall of his office.

Ruppert and Huston joined the club as it traveled from Washington to Boston near the end of the trip, and they told Huggins to clamp down, to plaster fines on the players. "Bookmakers and bootleggers are around wherever they go," they told the manager. There were reports that a pitcher was boasting about beating the races for thousands of dollars each year and that he seldom let a day go by without betting a few hundred here and there. And Ruth, of course, was a heavy bettor.

Landis was aware of the situation and now appeared in Boston, where he called both the Red Sox and Yankees together in the Boston clubhouse. He was disturbed about the betting prevalent among all teams in the majors and had been going from team to team delivering lectures. Now he again warned them about betting on horse races, saying that some players were getting an unsavory reputation. He reminded them about the Black Sox scandal, and the easy access that betting people had had to members of that ball club. He bawled them out about the unremitting night life. "Sunrise is a wonderful sight," he said, "but it is far better for a man to get up in the morning to see it than to wait up for it. You can't stay up all night and be worrying about a big bet and still play your best." He also cautioned them about their carefree sexual habits and the scandal that could arise from that.

Not noticeably chastened, the Yankees continued to fight, carouse and—at last—play excellent baseball. Ruth, in top form, hit five home runs in three days. He hit his 14th on July 6, his first grand slam home run with the Yankees, but he was still well behind Ken Williams, the St. Louis slugger who was having an outstanding year. The Browns, with Williams and Sisler and Baby Doll Jacobson and Marty McManus, all of whom batted in more than 100 runs, were a powerful hitting team and kept pace with the Yankees all season. Late in July Barrow pulled another coup by buying Joe Dugan, the best third baseman in the league, from Boston. (By the World Series of 1923, eleven of the twenty-four Yankees eligible to play had come from the Red Sox.)

Still, the intramural squabbling continued. The players carped at Huggins, who did his best to control them. Al DeVormer, an oddball catcher (he jumped into Lake Michigan in his street clothes to win a $25 bet), had a fight one day with Mays and the next day with Hofmann. On July 26 in St. Louis Meusel and Schang tangled on the bench, and later in the same game Ruth and Pipp fought. Ruth had been riding Pipp about his fielding, which had fallen off slightly. In the last of the fifth Pipp bobbled a ball at first base. When he came in to the bench he said to Shawkey, "If that ape says one word, I'm going to belt him." Ruth trotted in from left field, came down the steps of the dugout and said, "For God's sake, Pipp," and Pipp belted him. Wally was a big man, tall and rangy, and he had quick hands. He popped Ruth several times in the face with fast open-handed slaps as Ruth flailed wildly in return. They were pulled apart (Huggins, in the first base coaching box, called over plain-tively, "Now stop that"), and Ruth said, "We'll settle this after the game."

"That's all right with me," Pipp said.

But things happened to distract Babe. With the score tied 1–1 in the seventh, he hit a home run to put the Yankees ahead, and then runs started to pour across the plate for both sides. The Browns scored five in the last of the seventh to take a 6–3 lead, but in the eighth Ruth drove in one run to close it to 6–4, and Schang tripled home two and scored himself to put the Yankees ahead. In the ninth inning Ruth hit a second home run to make the final score 11–6.

He came roaring and yelling into the clubhouse after the last out, and there was Pipp waiting for him. "I'm ready," Pipp said. Ruth looked at him in utter surprise, as if wondering what *this* was all about. Remembering, he waved his hand and said, "Oh, Christ, forget it."

The serene season moved on. On August 30 in New York Babe hit a home run in his first time at bat but was called out on strikes the second time up. He objected loudly and obscenely, and plate umpire Tom Connolly threw him out of the game. Ruth played again the next day, but on September 1 Ban Johnson notified him that he was suspended again, this time for three days for abusing the umpire. Five suspensions in one year—surely that's one Babe Ruth record nobody is ever going to break.

The Browns and the Yankees were still scrambling for the pennant. They played a succession of exciting games with each other during the season, with the climax coming in September in St. Louis. The Yankees came to town leading by half a game. Sportsmans Park was filled, and the Yankees were jeered from the moment they stepped on the field. "Yellow, yellow, yellow!" the fans shouted at Ruth, whose batting average was up to .321 and his homers to 32. The Yankees won, 2-1, but in the ninth inning, when Witt and Meusel were converging on a fly ball, a bottle came flying out of the crowd and hit Witt in the forehead. Bleeding, he fell unconscious, and three players carried him to the bench. As Meusel looked up at the silenced stands, a raucous voice shouted, "We'll get you too, Meusel."

The bottle was a fragile one, fortunately, and though his forehead was cut Witt was not seriously hurt. He played again next afternoon, with a bandage across his forehead, and ran into the overflow crowd in right center to make a courageous catch of a long fly ball. This time the St. Louis crowd cheered him. A $1000 reward for information on the bottle thrower was offered by Ban Johnson and the American League. Word leaked out that the miscreant was a ten-year-old boy, but he was never identified. A more popular version of the accident was offered by an earnest spectator who insisted that the bottle had not been thrown at all, at least not at the time Witt was hit. It had been tossed on the field earlier, and when Witt was chasing the fly he stepped on it; the bottle flipped up in the air and hit him in the forehead. Everybody in St. Louis felt that the man who made up that story deserved the $1000.

The Browns won the second game of the series, 5–1, as Sisler batted safely in his 41st consecutive game, a record that stood until Joe DiMaggio broke it in 1941. The winning St. Louis pitcher was Hub Pruett, a young lefthander who is also an integral part of Ruth's legend. The legend says Pruett struck Ruth out every time they met, and while that is not so, the truth is almost as impressive. Pruett, only twenty-one years old, faced Ruth for the first time in May, when Babe had just come off the Landis suspension. Pitching in relief, he struck Ruth out once and walked him once. When the teams met again in June, Pruett again came in as a relief pitcher and again struck Ruth out. Two days later he was the starting and winning pitcher; he struck Ruth out three times and walked him once. In July Ruth was again helpless; he tapped weakly to the pitcher's box in the first inning (the first time he had hit a fair ball off Pruett) and then struck out three straight times, the last with the bases loaded. Pruett was out with a sore arm when the teams met again later in July, and the arm still bothered him when they played in August. But when Ruth came to bat with the bases loaded and nobody out, the Browns called Pruett in to pitch—and Ruth struck out. At this point Ruth had batted twelve times against Pruett and had struck out nine times, walked twice and hit one measly little tap to the mound.

Now in September he faced him again. He walked in the first inning, but to the hilarious, almost hysterical, delight of the crowd he struck out in the third (ten strikeouts in fourteen at bats). In the fifth inning he finally got his bat squarely on one of Pruett's pitches and lifted a home run into the seats. The silence of the crowd was deafening. When Babe crossed home plate, somebody threw a hard straw hat at him; he picked it up, put it on and wore it jauntily into the dugout. And he had another hit, a single, in the eighth to lift his batting average against the rookie to .158.

Pruett won the game, even if Ruth did break the spell, and the teams were knotted together again. Young Hub was the hero of St. Louis for a day, but in the third and final game he was the losing pitcher. He came in to relieve in the ninth inning with the Browns leading, 2-1. A victory would give them first place, but Pruett gave up a hit and a walk to load the bases. Then he was taken out, and Whitey Witt, bandage and all, hit a single to drive in two runs to win the game for the Yankees. They left town with a game-and-a-half lead and, as far as they were concerned, the pennant. They celebrated all the way across Illinois and Indiana on their way to Detroit. They knew they were the champions, and they were right. The Browns slumped, the Yankees swept the Tigers, and that was that.

As for Pruett, he made a stab at continuing his jinx on Ruth the following season, but the magic was disappearing. Ruth struck out three times in his first five trips to the plate against Hub in 1923, but he had a walk and another home run mixed in with the strikeouts. And he struck out only once more that year against Pruett. Still, for the record, in his first twenty-one trips to the plate against the young pitcher he struck out thirteen times, which is a good enough launching pad for any legend.

Pruett and Ruth never spoke to each other on the ballfield, although now and then the Babe would wink at the youngster as he passed him. It was not until a quarter century later that they met formally, not long before Ruth's death. Pruett was a doctor in St. Louis then. He put himself through medical school with his earnings from baseball. He lasted as a professional for ten seasons, in no small part because of the reputation he earned against Ruth. "I want to thank you for putting me through med school," Pruett told Babe. "If it wasn't for you, no one would have heard of me." Ruth smiled and said, "If I helped you get through medical school, I'm glad of it."

Still another odd thing happened in that zany season. On September 23, when the Yankees were in Cleveland, it was revealed in New York that Helen Ruth had a baby. Not a little baby, but a sixteen-month-old girl she had been pushing in a carriage in and out of the

Ansonia. People around the hotel said they had seen the Ruths with the baby for a month or so, and that Babe seemed very fond of it. When reporters questioned Helen, she said the baby, named Dorothy, had been born at St. Vincent's on June 7, 1921. Asked if she adopted it, she said indignantly, "No, it's my own baby." Well, came the awkward question, where has it been? She replied that the birth had been kept secret because the baby weighed only two and a half pounds when it was born and Babe was afraid he would be kidded about its size. It had been with a nurse, she said. Someone recalled Helen saying in 1920 that she had had four babies, all of whom had died.

In Cleveland, reporters asked Babe about the baby. "Oh, you found out about that," he said calmly. He said it had been born February 2, 1921, at Presbyterian Hospital. It had been very small, he said. When Mrs. Ruth was told this in New York and was asked about the discrepancy, she laughed. "Oh, he's got it mixed up with his own birthday," she said. But no record of the birth was found at either St. Vincent's or Presbyterian, and in later years the little girl was always referred to as Babe and Helen's adopted daughter. When, years later, Helen's will was probated, it referred to Dorothy as her adopted daughter and said she had also been known as Marie Harrington. It was always a bit of a mystery.

When the season ended, Ruth had a .315 batting average and 35 home runs, third in the league to Williams' 39 and Tilly Walker's 37. Babe scored 94 runs and batted in 96, but it was a bad season for him, a dismal season, and his performance in the World Series against the Giants continued the pattern. McGraw ordered his pitchers to throw Ruth nothing but curves, most of them out of the strike zone, so that he would chase them and swing wildly. The strategy worked. Ruth had one single and one double in seventeen at bats, scored only one run, batted only one in, and the Giants swept the Series, four games to none. One of the games, the second, was a 3–3 tie and provoked a major controversy. It was called after the tenth inning by umpire Hildebrand, supposedly because of darkness, although the sun was still shining on the farther reaches of the

outfield. The crowd was furious, and baseball was accused of foster-
ing the tie to recoup some of the revenue lost when Landis returned
the Series to a four-out-of-seven format. The judge had to announce
that all receipts from the game would go to charity to soften the
angry criticism.

The Giants jockeyed Ruth unmercifully throughout the Series.
His worst tormentor was Johnny Rawlings, an infielder who had
been a regular the year before but was now on the bench. Undoubtedly fed lines by McGraw, who was determined to keep Ruth off
balance and ineffective at bat, Rawlings sounded off, his penetrating
voice sending out fouler and fouler epithets. After the third game, in
which the Yankees were shut out, 3–0, and the Babe had gone hitless, Ruth decided enough was enough, and Meusel agreed. When
they were dressed they went over to the Giant clubhouse and barged
in.

"Where's Rawlings?" Ruth demanded.

"Right here," said the infielder, who was six inches shorter and
sixty pounds lighter.

"You little bastard," Ruth said, "if you ever call me that again I'll
choke you to death."

Rawlings, still sitting by his locker, grinned at him. "Can't you
take it?"

"I can take plenty, but I can't take that."

Jess Barnes, a Giant pitcher, said, "You got a hell of a nerve
complaining after some of the things you called me yesterday."

"I didn't call you anything."

"You're a goddamned liar!"

Ruth went for Barnes, but other players got between the two. Earl
Smith, one of the Giants' catchers, who was called Oil and was said
to be the toughest man in baseball, had been in the bullpen during
the game and missed the bench jockeying. Mildly he asked, "What
did he call you, Babe?"

"He called me a nigger."

"That's nothing," Smith said. He turned away.

Ruth was calming down rapidly, and when one of McGraw's

coaches told him he'd better leave he said, "All right. I know I shouldn't have come in here, but I wanted to get things straight. Listen, I'm sorry, fellows. Tomorrow, let's cut out the rough stuff and just play baseball."

Heinie Groh, the Giants' third baseman, hooted. The day before, Ruth had slid into Groh like a fullback hitting the line. "Baseball?" said Groh. "Look who's talking. Yesterday I thought we were playing football."

Everybody laughed. Ruth and Meusel started to go, but at the door Babe turned back for a moment. "Don't get me wrong, fellows," he said seriously. "I don't mind being called a prick or a cocksucker or things like that. I expect that. But lay off the personal stuff."

Then he left.

CHAPTER 24

The First Reformation:
How to Bat .393

Ruth began to be besieged by commercial opportunists in 1919 in Boston when he was setting his first home run record; and after he moved to New York and performed so sensationally in 1920 and 1921, the business proposals multiplied. At first he accepted practically everything that came his way, but as the tide of offers grew into a flood he ignored most of them and tried to pick and choose among the few that seemed particularly inviting. Sometimes he and Helen would spread the offers out on a table and try to decide which were best.

People wrote to him, phoned him, waylaid him outside his hotel, all trying to interest him in one deal or another. He was inundated. Ordinarily a friendly man, he now refused to chat with strangers and instead cut people off abruptly. It was difficult to talk to him, which was particularly galling to an ambitious, quick-thinking man named Christopher Walsh. Christy Walsh was a sports cartoonist turned ghostwriter who had done a series of articles with Eddie Rickenbacker, America's most famous flying hero of World War I. He was trying to put together a stable of syndicated ghost-aided columnists, and he wanted Ruth as his star attraction. He had met Babe briefly in 1919 but now simply could not get his ear. Ruth would not speak to him on the phone, would not come to the door of the apartment to see what he wanted, would brush by him if Walsh chanced to meet him at one of the several entrances to the Ansonia.

Then Christy discovered that Ruth, who always liked plenty of beer around, had been ordering his bootleg brew from a neighboring delicatessen. Walsh was in the store one day in the winter of 1921 when he heard the proprietor complaining, "Where is that boy? Babe Ruth wants his beer and that damned boy is never here to deliver it." Walsh quickly offered to help and a few minutes later was delivering the beer to Ruth's apartment. He was admitted without question and told where to put the bottles. Ruth paid him and peeled off a generous tip. Instead of accepting the tip, Walsh said, "What did you get for those newspaper stories of yours?" The United Press had distributed a little feature under Ruth's name the year before each time he hit a home run. Ruth would telephone UP in New York or send a wire, giving the details of each homer. He was a faithful reporter at first, but as the homers piled up his messages became shorter. One from St. Louis said only, "UNIPRESS NY LOW OUTSIDE BABE."

"How much did you get?"

"Five bucks each," Ruth said. "What's it to you?"

"Five bucks a story, and you had 54 home runs. That means you made $270 all season. I can get you $500 for anything you write. More than that."

"Who the hell are you?"

Walsh explained quickly, detailing his experience, his contacts, his knowledge, his belief that Ruth was innocently losing thousands of dollars he could be making. Babe seemed interested.

"I've been trying to get you to listen to me for weeks," Walsh said.

"Yeah, I remember your face now."

Walsh soon convinced Babe that he was honest and bright and that Babe needed him, all of which was true. He told Babe he would guarantee him $1000 within sixty days of opening day. Ruth signed a contract and went off to spring training. On opening day, Walsh gave him a check for $1000, sixty days earlier than promised, and Ruth was greatly pleased. Walsh did not bother to tell Ruth that he had borrowed the money in order to make a good impression on his prized new client.

For fifteen years Walsh placed articles by Ruth in newspapers and magazines, utilizing the ghostly talents of several sportswriters, among them Ford Frick and William J. Slocum. (Ruth once said of Slocum, "Bill writes more like I do than anyone I know.") Stories on the World Series were particularly lucrative, and Ruth, aided by his current ghost, covered every Series from 1921 through 1936, whether he was playing or not. He earned $2000 during the 1921 Series, but thereafter his take was never less than $5000 and sometimes went as high as $7000, depending on the number of papers that used his stories. He also produced a feature each year on "Babe Ruth's Annual All-Star Team."

Beyond syndication, Walsh became Ruth's friend, financial adviser and business representative, and the association was of lasting value to the Babe. Before Walsh, Ruth saved little or no money and he spent it lavishly and impulsively. He tipped extravagantly, and to counteract rumors that he and Helen were on the verge of separating, which was almost the case in 1922, he bought her a $5000 mink coat. He sometimes found himself broke during spring training—his regular salary checks did not begin until the season started—and he borrowed from Dugan and Hoyt and a few others. He would ask them to let him have $1000 or $1500 until the first payday, and then he would pay them back with full interest, as though he had borrowed the money for an entire year.

In 1924 Walsh persuaded him to invest some of his huge earnings, comparatively little of which was taken by the modest income tax of the era, in annuities that would pay off after Ruth retired from baseball. Babe bought one of these through Harry Heilmann, the Detroit outfielder, who was a favorite drinking and racetrack companion of the Babe's and dabbled in insurance during the off-season. In subsequent years Walsh convinced the sometimes reluctant Ruth to buy more annuities, with the result that for all his carefree spending he was not greatly affected by the stock market crash in 1929 and was financially comfortable until the day he died.

One of the policies cost Ruth $35,000 out of hand, and the insurance company was so pleased with the transaction that it put on a little ceremony when the deal was formally closed. The president of the company made an ornate speech in which he complimented Ruth profusely for his sagacity in buying the annuity. He ended by saying, "Babe, you are to be congratulated. You are a lucky man." A not noticeably elated Ruth replied, "Yes, I guess so. There's no doubt I'm lucky. There is also no doubt that you have my $35,000."

Mostly because of Walsh, Babe became involved in quite a few off-field ventures. Most of these were lucrative, but a few were resounding flops. A haberdashery on Broadway called Babe Ruth's for Men opened in a flourish of publicity one autumn and died quietly six months later. When Babe endorsed a new product called Babe Ruth's Home Run Candy, the Curtiss Candy Corporation appealed to the Patent Office. Curtiss had been making a candy bar called Baby Ruth, ostensibly named for President Grover Cleveland's daughter Ruth, who was born in the White House. Curtiss claimed that the new Ruth candy bar would be impinging on the Baby Ruth bar. The Patent Office agreed and Ruth was abruptly out of the candy business.

Walsh worked hard for Ruth, and the succession of disasters in 1922 worried him. He was afraid of what bad publicity might do to Babe's income. A month after the World Series of 1922, when Babe came back to New York after another financially disappointing barnstorming trip (the major leagues, at Landis' urging, had modified the no-barnstorming rule), Walsh suggested he do a little fence mending. Christy set up a dinner party at an Elks Club in Manhattan to which he invited newspapermen and various well-known people around town, among them James J. Walker, not yet mayor of New York but a rising politician with a keen interest in sports and other lively arts.

At the dinner everyone was to let his hair down and ask Ruth anything at all. Babe was to answer honestly and completely. The back and forth was blunt and direct, and Ruth came in for a great deal of rather sharp criticism. The final touch came when Jimmy Walker, a superb speaker, got through any defenses the Babe had left by touching on his weakness for children. Pulling out all the stops, Walker spoke about the "dirty-faced kids" who idolized the Babe and ended by asking, "Are you going to keep on letting those little kids down?"

It was a virtuoso performance, and it got to Ruth, who made a speech of his own. "I know as well as anybody else," he said, "just what mistakes I made last season. There's no use in me trying to get away from them. But let me tell you something. I want the New York sportswriters and fans to know that I've had my last drink until next October. I mean it. Tomorrow I'm going to my farm. I'm going to work my head off—and maybe part of my stomach." He paused as his listeners laughed and then, always honest, added, "Oh, maybe now and then I'll come down to New York to see the old town, but it won't be too often. I'm serious about this. I'm going to work hard. And then you just watch me break that home run record next year." Great applause.

True to his word, he left a day or so later for Sudbury, where he had recently remodeled the farmhouse, adding two wings and modernizing the interior. He worked hard to get in shape that winter, and while he may not have observed the strict letter of his promise not to drink for a year, he observed the spirit of it. He was reformed.

Ruth reformed was as impressive as Ruth rebellious. Still a heavy man at 215, his belly not quite flat, he nonetheless was fit and ready on opening day 1923, and he played beautifully all season long. He got into no noticeable trouble, led the Yankees to a runaway victory in the pennant race and was a unanimous choice for Most Valuable Player in the American League. He batted .393, highest of his career (although it was second in the league to Heilmann's .403), led in home runs (a relatively modest 41, but still a dozen better than Ken Williams, and more than double the third man's total) and in runs scored, runs batted in, total bases, slugging average and bases on balls. He had 205 hits, and 99 of them were for extra bases. He was walked the startling total of 170 times, more than half of them intentional or almost so. Once he was walked purposely with the bases loaded. His on-base percentage was .542. He stole seventeen bases. He more than earned his $52,000 salary.

By happy coincidence, that was the year Yankee Stadium opened. After the 1920 season, when the Yankees outdrew the Giants by 350,000 in the Polo Grounds, McGraw told the Yankees they would have to leave. No hurry, just get out as soon as possible. Ruppert and Huston had already been talking about building their own park, and in May 1921 they paid $600,000 to the Astor estate for a plot of land in the Bronx, directly across the Harlem River from the Polo Grounds. Bids were asked the following fall and construction began in the spring of 1922. A year later the house that Ruth built was ready. Some thought it should be named Ruth Field, but Ruppert insisted it be called Yankee Stadium. After Ruppert's death two decades later, it was suggested the place be renamed Ruppert Stadium, but Ed Barrow rejected the proposal. "The Colonel wanted it called Yankee Stadium, and that's what we'll continue to call it," he said. The only area in the ballpark named after Ruth was the right field bleachers, where most of his home runs landed. It was commonly known as Ruthville.

Yankee Stadium cost $2,500,000, an extravagant figure for the day, but with Huston, a professional engineer, keeping a close eye on things, it turned out to be a bargain: a big, beautiful, modern stage for Ruth and the Yankees. It also turned out to be the last joint effort of the two colonels as partners.

Their differences, always considerable, became too much after the 1922 Series. In the eighth inning of the last game, with the score tied and Giants on second and third, Huggins ordered Joe Bush to walk the next batter to fill the bases. Bush objected, but Huggins insisted and Bush walked the batter. When the next man singled to drive in the winning runs, Bush yelled angrily at Huggins from the mound.

After the game Huston was outspokenly critical of Huggins and told everyone that Miller had managed his last game for the Yankees. Ruppert overruled Huston and insisted that Huggins stay. And the little manager had a surprise ally in Barrow, whom Huston had hired a year earlier. When Barrow joined the club, Huggins had been uneasy. Here was Huston, openly contemptuous of him; there was Ruppert, who despite his support had little to do with him. And now he was faced with Barrow, Huston's man. But Barrow had gone to Huggins and told him, "You're the manager. You'll get no interference from me. Your job is to win on the field. My job is to get you the players you need." He did something else to help Huggins. As proud owners, the two colonels liked to drop into the Yankee clubhouse now and then to chat with the players, which inevitably diminished the manager's already shaky hold on his troops. Barrow suggested they stop the visits. "That's the manager's territory," he told them. "You should stay out of it." He himself observed the protocol, and now he agreed with Ruppert that Huggins should continue running the team on the field.

Huston, feeling himself alone and without any real power on the club, decided to get out. He agreed to stay until the Stadium was completed and then, in May 1923, he sold his half of the club to Ruppert for $1,500,000, six times what he paid for it slightly more than eight years earlier. Ruppert, in turn, sold Barrow a small percentage, so that the general manager became in a minor but profitable way a part owner.

The first game at the new Stadium was a rousing success, what with the Yankees winning, Ruth hitting the first home run and the attendance a rousing 74,217. Or, at least, 74,217 was the attendance Barrow announced to the press. A month or so later, when figures relating to a Milk Fund benefit at the ballpark were being checked, it was discovered that the Stadium had only 62,000 seats at that time. Reporters confronted Barrow with this, and he admitted that the park did indeed have only 62,000 seats. But, he added, there had been a lot of standees in the crowd on opening day. Twelve *thousand* standees? the reporters asked. Well, no, Barrow conceded, there probably had not been that many. Then where did the 74,217 figure come from?

"It was an estimate," Barrow said lamely. But, as so often happens, the fabrication survived the truth, and for years it was widely assumed that Yankee Stadium's capacity was more than 70,000.

Ruth's resurgence on the field carried into the World Series, which the Yankees won from the Giants (the third straight year the two teams met) to give them the first of their many World Championships. McGraw's pitchers tried hard to stifle Ruth again, but except for one memorable moment, when Rosy Ryan struck Ruth out with the bases full on a low curve down around his ankles, they failed. He batted .368, hit three home runs, two in one game, had a triple, a double, three singles and a walk and scored eight runs in the six games. The Giants won only two of the games, both in Yankee Stadium on home runs by Casey Stengel, who thus beat Ruth to the honor of hitting the first World Series home run there. When he was rounding the bases with his second homer, Stengel merrily thumbed his nose at the Yankee bench. The fastidious Ruppert complained to Landis, demanding that Stengel be punished. Landis shrugged it off, and when someone asked Ruth how he felt about Casey getting away with it, Babe answered, "I don't mind. Casey's a lot of fun."

The Babe had another marvelous season in 1924, even though the Yankees faltered after winning three straight pennants and finished second behind Washington. He hit .378 to win the batting championship by almost 20 points, had 46 home runs, 19 more than the next man, and was second in runs batted in. It was Ruth's only batting title. He never won baseball's triple crown (first in batting average, home runs and runs batted in the same year), but he amassed an impressive number of "almost" triple crowns: in 1921, third in batting, first in homers, first in RBI's; in 1923, second in batting, first in homers, first in RBI's; in 1924, first in batting, first in homers, second in RBI's; in 1926, second in batting, first in homers, first in RBI's; in 1931, second in batting, first in homers, second in RBI's. He led in both home runs and runs batted in in six different seasons, and was first, second or third in batting six times.

But around Ruth, the team was beginning to fray. Schang, the catcher, was not the superb player he had been. Scott, who by now had appeared in more than 1200 consecutive games, was showing signs of wearing out at shortstop. Ward, the second baseman, no longer seemed able to do the job, and Witt, the center fielder, was beginning to dissatisfy Huggins. The pitching was not as dependable, except for Pennock, the last of the Red Sox refugees, who came down from Boston in 1923 to establish himself as the ace of the staff. Mays was sold to Cincinnati. Bush was suddenly washed up. Hoyt and Shawkey won only a few games more than they lost.

Huggins was worried. The team was not playing well, and the disciplinary problem, while not as bad as it had been in 1922, was by no means solved. Players barked and yapped at him, and Ruth, who called Huggins the Flea, was obvious in his disdain. Babe, his reform movement safely behind him, paid scant attention to the little manager's rules and was again carousing and drinking almost every night. So far, his wild behavior had not affected his play, and Huggins took no action against him, although he thought about it and even went so far as to tell an old friend, Bob Connery, a Yankee scout, that he was going to punish Ruth.

"I know he wasn't in his room last night," Huggins told Connery one morning. "He wasn't in it at all. He can't keep on behaving like this. I'm going to fine him and suspend him."

That afternoon Ruth hit two home runs and the Yankees won. At dinner that night Connery asked Huggins, "Did you do what you said with Ruth?"

"What do you mean?"

"You said you were going to fine and suspend him."

"Hell, no," Huggins said wearily. "How can I fine and suspend him the way he played today?"

But Huggins still talked about doing something about Ruth. He resented his contemptuous attitude in the clubhouse and his uproarious behavior away from the ballpark, which he felt was having a bad influence on the other players. "I'm going to speak to him," he told Mark Roth, the traveling secretary. "I'm going to sit him down and give him a good talking to." That day Ruth was late getting to the clubhouse. Inside, Huggins sat watching the door, waiting. Ruth arrived, barreling in, noisily exchanging greetings and insults, lifting the whole room with his presence. He came toward Huggins as he made his grand progress toward his locker.

"You going to speak to him?" Roth asked.

Huggins, smiling at some loud remark Ruth had made, said, "Sure." As Babe passed, Huggins leaned forward. "Hiya, Babe," he said.

"Hiya, keed," Ruth rumbled as he breezed by.

Mark Roth looked at Huggins.

"I spoke to him, didn't I?" Huggins said.

CHAPTER 25

The Disaster:
The Bellyache Heard
Round the World

Nonetheless, Huggins was not on good terms with his star, nor his star with him. Friction was always in the air, even on innocent occasions. Once Joe Dugan brought a couple of youngsters who had cut his lawn into the clubhouse as a treat. They were wandering around, properly impressed, when Huggins came out of his office.

"Who are those kids?" he snapped. "What are they doing in here?"

Dugan was somewhere else, in the trainer's room perhaps, and the youngsters froze with fear and embarrassment. But Ruth walked over, put his arm around one and said coldly, "They're my guests." Huggins, half angry, half apologetic, muttered something and went back into his office.

The situation was distinctly worse in 1925. Ruth's behavior was as flagrant as ever, and his marriage was disintegrating. Helen was no longer able to cope with him. As Dugan said, "She was just a kid when she got married, and now Babe was bigger than the President." She was less able to ignore her husband's sexual adventures, which she could not help but hear about, and which upset her terribly. The worst was when a Long Island girl named Dolores Dixon filed a $50,000 paternity suit against him. The charges were dropped, but Helen was hurt anyway. And he was restless around her. She liked to go to spring training with him, but once in New Orleans he had turned on her and said, "Why don't you blow out of here? You cramp my style." They had angry quarrels and they separated. A Catholic priest, Father Edward Quinn, effected a reconciliation, but it was only a surface peace.

For Babe had met, among all the women he had known, the Other Woman. Her name was Claire Merritt Hodgson, Mrs. Claire Hodgson. She was beautiful: dark hair, snapping dark eyes, pert face, red lips, small, trim, a superb figure. She came from Athens, Georgia, where at fourteen she had run off and married Frank Hodgson, who was more than twice her age. The marriage did not work and a few years later, at the end of World War I, she came to New York with her baby daughter. Hodgson died, and Claire became the epitome of early twentieth-century glamour: a beautiful young widow.

In New York she lived at first with her baby and a southern maid, but a few years later, about the time she met Ruth, her mother and her brothers Eugene and Hubert came to live with her too. She worked for a while as a model for illustrators, including Howard Chandler Christy and Harrison Fisher. She appeared on stage (in a show called *Tangerine* and, for a time, *The Ziegfeld Follies*) and she had bit parts in silent movies. She was not a chorus girl, nor a singer, nor a dancer, nor even an actress; she was simply a striking-looking girl who wore clothes well and knew the right people.

She was young and bright and great-looking, and she had been around. When Ruth met her she was no youthful teenager overwhelmed by the glamour of a big league baseball player. She had known Ty Cobb, and in New York her circle of acquaintances included other members of the Yankees before she knew Ruth. She first met Babe in May 1923 at a ballgame in Washington, where she was on tour with a show that starred James Barton, who later scored a smash hit in *Tobacco Road*. She and a girl friend were taken to a Senators-Yankees game by Barton, and when Ruth came over to their box to say hello to Barton they were introduced. He was impressed, as he often was by a pretty girl, and later sent a note to the theater asking her to dinner. He suggested his hotel suite, and she reacted coldly.

"I can't go out to a restaurant," he explained. "I always get mobbed."

She said she would come if she could bring her roommate, and Babe agreed. She asked him to come see the show and he did, bringing along two or three teammates. She was slightly miffed because she had to pay for the tickets. Dugan was one of those with Babe. "See that black-haired girl on the end?" he said. "She's coming to the hotel for dinner later. I want you guys to meet her." They went up to his suite and met her and then Ruth said, briskly, "All right, get the hell out," and they left. "God, she was a pretty girl," Dugan said.

After the Yankees left Washington, Babe kept in touch with her by phone, and in New York they met again. This was different from the usual Ruth fling, the fast date, the quick lay. Women often phoned him in the Yankee clubhouse and asked him to come see them. He would not agree to dates until they made it clear that they were willing to go to bed with him. He did not want to waste his time. Sex was a constant part of his life. But Claire was different. She was something beyond sex.

Babe fell in love with her, and they were seen together in public. He had a fight over her with another Yankee player in the clubhouse, the two of them grappling naked before they were pulled apart by teammates. His big Packard was seen parked near 219 West 80th Street, where she lived. One day someone stole the ornamental radiator cap from the car, and after that Ruth parked it in the Apthorp Garage across the street. One day a private detective came nosing around the garage asking questions, such as did the car stay there all night when Babe came to visit? Helen was hearing stories and was getting suspicious.

She had good reason to worry, because Babe wanted Claire. She wanted him too. The subject of marriage came up, closely attended by the subject of divorce. "I can't get a divorce," Babe said. "I'm a

Catholic and she's a Catholic. We can't get divorced." He and Helen stayed married, and he and Claire stayed friends.

Early in 1925 he left New York for Hot Springs for his traditional prespring-training trip. He was fat. In January he weighed 256. In Hot Springs he played a little golf, jogged a little, took hot steam baths. But he also drank and ran around town with women and stayed up all night and ate like a hog. He was always on the go. He would take a steam bath, the hotter the better, and then without waiting for the cooling shower after the bath, would dress and rush off to a date. For the third straight year he caught a terrible cold, sometimes called flu, sometimes called pneumonia and, feeling terrible, left for St. Petersburg, where the Yankees were training.

He was bundled in a sweatshirt the first day he reported for practice.

"Babe, you look sick," Huggins said.

"Sick? You're goddamned right I'm sick. I've got a temperature of one hundred and five and eight-fifths."

Helen had come down to St. Petersburg, and Babe behaved reasonably well while she was there. He shook his cold and looked pretty good on the field. When the team broke camp to start the annual barnstorming trip north with the Dodgers, Helen went directly to New York. Without Helen around, Babe broke loose. He charged off the train in every town looking for what he wanted. He ate at odd hours. He drank a great deal. And he always found women. "He was going day and night, broads and booze," said Dugan. One night in Savannah, Georgia, he and Steve O'Neill, the old Cleveland catcher who was now with the Yankees, went out on the town and were late getting to the railroad station where the Yankee car was waiting. Huggins was pacing the platform when their taxi arrived, and he angrily castigated Ruth. More than a little drunk, Ruth got mad and lunged for Huggins, but O'Neill stopped him and got him aboard the train.

An oft-repeated story says that sometime that year Ruth picked Huggins up and held him off the back of a moving train, threatening to drop him. There are variations, one saying he did it as a joke, another that it was in anger, a third that he went so far as to dangle Huggins by the heels. Hoyt said, "I was on the train when that was supposed to have happened, but I never heard about it." Dugan knew nothing of it. Shawkey said, "Once we were coming from somewhere, I think it was from Boston after clinching a pennant, and Colonel Ruppert was on board. He was sitting with Huggins in his compartment. Ruth and Meusel were a little tight and raising hell and they banged on the door. Well, it was locked, of course. Babe banged on the door and said open up. He kept banging and he said come on and open up or he'd throw Huggins off the damned train. Well, they didn't open it, and he and Meusel went away. They were just having fun. Nobody took it seriously."

"Did he ever hold Huggins off the end of a train?"

"No, of course not."

Nonetheless, he was a continuing source of aggravation and frustration to Huggins as the Yankees wandered back and forth across the south playing exhibitions. For, despite his carousing, Ruth was superb on the field—while he lasted. In Birmingham one Tuesday he had two home runs, a double and a single, and the next day in Nashville he hit a triple and a double. On Thursday he was not feeling well and had only a single, and on Friday in Atlanta he had to leave the game after striking out in the first inning. He was running a fever and feeling rocky, and Huggins sent him back to the hotel. The Yankees stayed overnight in Atlanta, which gave Ruth a night's rest in bed, and he insisted on playing the next day, even though it was raining on and off. He hit a triple. That night in Atlanta he had chills and fever and a violent pain in his belly. The hotel doctor was called in the middle of the night, and Sunday morning, when the Yankees were about to leave for Chattanooga, Huggins told Ruth to stay behind and catch up with the team later. But when the Yankees arrived at the train station, Ruth was with them.

"Sure I'm going," he said. "Don't we play today?" He slept most of the way to Chattanooga and that afternoon hit two home runs. The team moved on to Knoxville, and on Monday, Ruth was in the lineup again, although he was still running a temperature. He grounded out and struck out, and there were jeers from the crowd. On his third time up he hit a line-drive home run over the left field fence that knocked a branch off a dead tree and scared several boys sitting in the tree to the ground.

The Yankees had not looked good as a team, but Ruth was batting .447, the highest on the club. That night he felt worse. Stomach cramps were bothering him again, and his face was hot with fever. The train ride in the morning through the mountains from Knoxville to Asheville, North Carolina, the track winding and twisting and bumpy, was torture for the Babe. "I'm burning up," Babe told Doc Woods, the trainer. "I want to go home." The train reached Asheville at noon Tuesday, April 7, and Ruth, in a bad way, got off with Steve O'Neill and a big rookie named John Levi. "I'm going home," he muttered. "I'm going home even if I have to take an airplane. I don't give a damn if the thing falls." As he walked slowly along the platform he faltered and collapsed. O'Neill and Levi grabbed him before he hit the ground and with a couple of others dragged his huge bulk, which must have weighed close to 270 by then, to a taxi and took him to the Battery Park Hotel, where the Yankees were staying. A local doctor named Charles Jordan examined him and said he had a severe intestinal attack and symptoms of flu and needed complete rest.

In the hotel Ruth complained, "Every bone in my body aches," but he felt a little better. Huggins phoned Barrow in New York, and they decided it would be best if Ruth returned directly to New York. Paul Krichell, the Yankee scout, would accompany him. Dr. Jordan objected, saying Ruth needed rest and should not be moved, but the Babe overruled him, saying "I'm going home." It was agreed he would stay in bed Tuesday and Wednesday and leave for New York Wednesday night. Ruth usually slept in the nude, but the doctor said he had to be kept warm, so Krichell scouted around Asheville and bought him a pair of pajamas. He tried to find a size 48, Ruth's size, but had to settle for a 42, in pink. Krichell slit the back of the pajama shirt so it would fit over Babe's big torso, but he could not use the pants.

The Yankees moved on to Greenville, North Carolina, from Asheville, and Krichell was pretty much on his own with Ruth. He helped Babe dress Wednesday evening and got him to the station, where they caught an eight P.M. train to New York.

Ruth's collapse was news, but not sensational news. He had been sick and injured and suspended so often that it seemed like nothing more than just another bead on a colorful string. On the train Ruth felt distinctly better, and he and Krichell played pinochle. The section they were riding in missed connections at Salisbury, North Carolina, and had to hook up to a later train. When the earlier northbound train reached Washington with no Ruth, a rumor sprang up that he was dead. It spread with fantastic speed, and in London, where Ruth's exploits and fabulous salary were well known, one paper ran a banner headline announcing his death, and others ran the story with his photograph. Now it was big news.

When they did arrive in Washington, Krichell squelched the rumor, and the two continued on to New York. They ate breakfast on the train; Ruth had orange juice, toast, eggs, coffee and some fried potatoes on the side. When all that reached his battered intestines, he almost passed out with pain and began to vomit. When the train neared New York, Krichell helped Ruth to the men's room to wash up. Babe fainted again in the washroom and cracked his head against the basin as he fell.

Krichell and a train detective somehow got the unconscious Ruth to his berth, and when the train reached Penn Station Babe stayed there while Krichell phoned Barrow. Helen had come to the station with Christy Walsh and chatted idly with reporters who were also waiting for Babe. When the minutes went by and he failed to appear, Helen grew increasingly nervous and finally ran through the gates and onto the train. An ambulance was ordered from St.

Vincent's Hospital, but it broke down and a second was summoned from New York Hospital. Meanwhile, a rolling stretcher was brought down to the train platform and, an hour after he reached the station, Ruth was lifted through a window and placed on it. He was unconscious, wrapped in blankets. Another half hour passed as they waited for the second ambulance. Babe opened his eyes, saw his wife, said, "I feel rotten, Helen," and passed out again. He grew delirious and swung his arms and kicked out with his legs. He had to be held down by those around him, among them Ed Barrow, who had come to the station as soon as Krichell phoned. As the Babe quieted down, Barrow patted his cheek.

A few minutes later Ruth thrashed about again, and was given a sedative. The ambulance arrived, but when they started to lift him Babe fought to get off the stretcher. He was given another injection and a few minutes later was loaded onto the ambulance. Helen, sobbing, sat up front with Walsh as the ambulance sped down Seventh Avenue to St. Vincent's. It sped silently because its alarm was broken, but the police cleared the traffic away. Ruth had two more convulsive attacks in the ambulance, and at St. Vincent's as he was being wheeled inside he again began to move about violently. Six attendants held him down.

By the time he reached his room he was calm, and he was examined by Dr. Edward King, his own physician. King said he was in no serious danger and that the injury to his head when he fell was minor. But he was badly run down, King said, had a touch of the flu and was suffering from an intestinal attack. Babe regained consciousness during the afternoon and spoke to Helen and Barrow, and by suppertime was laughing and chatting. Dr. King put him on a bland diet and kept him under observation, and it seemed likely that he would be in uniform by the following Tuesday, opening day of the season, and might even play. However, he continued to run a temperature and on opening day he was still in bed. The fever went higher. On Thursday, a week after the dramatic return to New York, Dr. King announced that Ruth had an intestinal abscess and would have to undergo surgery. At eight-thirty Friday morning, April 17, he was operated on by Dr. George Stewart. The incision was several inches long, but the operation took only twenty minutes and was a complete success.

Dr. King said Ruth's condition had been caused by his own carelessness in taking care of himself, particularly in not being careful of what and how much he ate and drank. The popular story that he had gorged himself on hot dogs just before he collapsed was the invention of a colorful writer named W. O. McGeehan, and his illness was called "the bellyache heard round the world." Several newspapermen of the era whispered that he had gonorrhea, and one of his old teammates, gesturing toward his own genitals, said, "It was the whole thing," meaning gonorrhea, syphilis, everything. That seems a bit extreme, although it would not have been surprising for a person as promiscuous as Ruth to contract a "dose of clap." Still, abdominal surgery is not standard procedure for correction of venereal disease, and there is no question that Ruth bore a long vivid scar on the left side of his abdomen, beginning just under his rib cage, when he returned to the team.

Whatever the truth, he was a sick man. He was in St. Vincent's from April 9 until May 26, although for a week before his discharge he left the hospital every day and was driven to the Stadium, where he worked out, at first slowly and gingerly, later more forcefully. He was quite weak—he had lost thirty pounds in the hospital—and his legs bothered him.

On Tuesday, May 26, he rejoined the Yankees and took batting practice. Barrow and Ruppert suggested he take more time to recuperate fully, possibly even the rest of the season, but Ruth said no. He was desperately eager to get back in the lineup. Baseball, the actual playing of the game, was as important to the physically oriented Ruth as sex or eating or drinking, and the thought of not being able to play for another year was impossible for him to accept. He worked out for two more days, stayed behind in New York while the team went to Philadelphia for a brief series, and was in the starting lineup on Monday, June 1, when the Yankees returned to New York. He came back too soon. Dugan said, "It made you sick watching him slide into third with that wound in his belly."

The club, meanwhile, had been having a terrible year and was in seventh place. The infield had fallen apart. Dugan had a bad knee and played only 96 games all season. Scott's consecutive-game streak ended early in May, and so did his career with the Yankees. An inconsequential rookie named Pee Wee Wanninger took his place and is remembered today only because Gehrig began his consecutive-game streak by batting for Wanninger on June 1, the day Ruth returned to the lineup. Gehrig was not yet a regular, but Pipp, who had been hit on the head with a pitched ball, was being phased out, and Gehrig replaced him as the regular first baseman on June 2. Even so, Gehrig was still an untried rookie, and his .295 average in 1925 was no more impressive than .255 would be in the 1970s. Ward, who was hitting .236, was about through at second base. A couple of antique utility men, thirty-seven-year-old Ernie Johnson and thirty-five-year-old Howard Shanks, filled in a good part of the time, and some days Meusel came in from the outfield to play third base. Schang was supplanted by Benny Bengough, a delightful man and a fine receiver but really no more than a second-string catcher. Ruth, of course, had been out sick, and except for Pennock, who had one of the best earned-run averages in the league, the pitching was ordinary. The only bright spots were Earle Combs, a handsome, prematurely gray Kentuckian, who became the center fielder, and Meusel, still a hard hitter.

The team was bad and Ruth was not much help when he returned. Physically he was under par, and psychologically he was a mess. His personal life was badly confused. Helen and Dorothy, now four, had been for a while the only visitors he was allowed at St. Vincent's, and he chafed under the monotony. Helen was so upset by his attitude that she had a nervous breakdown and was put to bed in the hospital, while Dorothy was sent back to Sudbury in the care of friends. Helen was not well enough to accompany Babe on his outings to the Stadium during his last week in the hospital, and she remained a patient there after his discharge. He wanted to see Claire, who had moved to a seven-room apartment on West 79th Street, a block from her old place. In Boston, early in the summer, he and Helen had another angry quarrel in a hotel, and after it she packed her bags and left for the farm at Sudbury, telling the wife of another player, "I'm through." She phoned a lawyer and vaguely discussed a legal separation, but nothing came of it and later in the summer she was back in New York, living at the Concourse Plaza Hotel, close to Yankee Stadium.

Babe was eating too much again, and even before he began playing he had regained eight of the thirty pounds he lost during his illness. And he was still weak. Through June and July he batted only .250 and hit only a handful of home runs. He looked terrible. He was thirty-one years old, and a lot of people felt he was finished as a ballplayer. Fred Lieb, astute observer of the game, did not agree, but he did write on August 1, "It is doubtful that Ruth again will be the superstar he was from 1919 through 1924. Next year Ruth will be 32, and at 32 the Babe will be older than Eddie Collins, Walter Johnson and Ty Cobb at that age. Babe has lived a much more strenuous life. Nevertheless, we see no reason why Ruth should not be a good dependable hitter for several years more, a .325 hitter with some 30-odd home runs. Still, he may surprise the baseball world next year with one of his better seasons."

Ruth looked so bad at bat that one day Huggins sent Bobby Veach, the old Tiger star now in his last year in the majors and trying to hang on with the Yanks as a pinch-hitter, up to bat for him. Huggins said later it was only because Ruth had wrenched his back slightly, but it was more than that. Huggins was becoming impatient with Ruth's ineptitude, particularly since the Babe was behaving almost as badly off the field as he had been before his collapse in spring training. Once Huggins slapped a $1000 fine on him for being out of the hotel all night on a road trip, but he rescinded the fine a few days later when tempers cooled off.

CHAPTER 26

The Third Big Fight: Ruth vs. Huggins

In August the Yankees left on another road trip, and Ruth finally began to hit. He had a home run in Washington, three in three games in Cleveland, and he looked good in Detroit. But he was still moving at top speed off the field too, and he angered Huggins by staying away from the hotel all night in Cleveland. In Chicago his hitting stopped, although his partying did not, and he and Huggins came on collision course when Ruth twice disobeyed orders from the manager during a game. In St. Louis Ruth again stayed out past the one A.M. curfew Huggins had set. He was contemptuously defiant, and Huggins decided it was time to stop him. He phoned New York and got approval ahead of time from Barrow and Ruppert.

On Saturday afternoon, August 29, in St. Louis, Ruth was late getting to the ballpark. Most of the players were already on the field when he came sauntering into the locker room, took off his jacket as he walked across the room and briskly hung it up in his locker. Huggins was sitting on a bench smoking a pipe. He turned around on the bench and said, "Don't bother getting dressed, Babe. You're not playing today."

Ruth stopped, stared at him, reached in the locker for his jacket and put it back on.

"I'm suspending you," Huggins said, "and I'm fining you $5000. You're to go back to New York on the five o'clock train. Mark Roth has your tickets."

"Five thousand dollars?" Ruth said. "Five thousand dollars? Fuck you, you little son of a bitch. Who the hell do you think you are?" He poured obscenities on the manager and ended by shouting, "If you were even half my size, I'd punch the shit out of you."

Huggins, standing, said, "If I were half your size, I'd have punched you." Six inches shorter, a hundred pounds lighter, fifteen years older, he poked a finger against Ruth's chest. "And I'll tell you something else, mister. Before you get back in uniform, you're going to apologize for what you've said, and apologize plenty. Now go on. Get out of here."

He turned and went out onto the field. Ruth slammed his way from the clubhouse, checked out of the hotel, canceled his railroad booking to New York and spent the night at a favorite St. Louis bordello, an elaborate place, complete with restaurant, that catered to big spenders like Ruth. The next day he took a noon train, not to New York but to Chicago. Before he left St. Louis he said he was going to see Judge Landis, who appeared to represent ultimate justice to him. He wanted the judge to know the truth about his alleged transgressions and he wanted to know what the judge thought about the $5000 fine. He criticized Huggins. "I come in an hour and a half late and he fines me $5000. I was with friends until midnight, and then we took an auto ride because it was so hot. I was back at the hotel by two-thirty, and we were supposed to be back by one. If Huggins says I was drinking, he's a damn liar and you can make that as strong as you like. I never trained so hard in my life as I did this year. I'm in condition to play. Huggins only suspended me because he wants the publicity. It's a grandstand play for the public, so he can shift the blame on me for the team being seventh.

"People have been asking me all year what the trouble with the team is. I haven't wanted to say it before, but I will now. The trouble with the team is Huggins. Last year we lost the pennant to Washington when we should have won by 15 games. That was

Huggins' fault. He didn't get the most out of the players. I think we have the best team in the league this year, and look where we are."

He was asked about reports that he disobeyed Huggins' orders in a game in Chicago.

"I'll tell you about that. I came up in the first inning with two men on, one run in, nobody out. Huggins ordered me to swing away, to try to get a hit. But I sacrificed instead, because I thought that was the proper play. The man up after me went out, but the second one singled and drove in both base runners. So we got three runs that inning instead of one, because I might not have hit safely. Now, in the ninth inning of that same game, we were a run behind with men on first and second, and no one out. This time he ordered me to sacrifice. Instead, I hit away, because a single would have tied the score and an extra-base hit would have won the game. I hit a hard liner that the first baseman turned into a double play, but I still say I was right both times.

"I wouldn't have gone into this at all," he added, "except it was made public, and I wanted to explain my position. The truth is, Huggins is incompetent."

When he reached Chicago Sunday afternoon, he was greeted by another horde of newspapermen. The story of the suspension and the $5000 fine made front pages all over the country. There were stories too about his involvement with Claire Hodgson, with pictures of both Claire and Helen on the same page and reports that Helen was planning to sue him for $100,000 and separate maintenance. In New York Helen denied she was going to sue but admitted, "Yes, I'm going to discuss these reports about other women with Mr. Ruth the minute he gets here."

Babe told the reporters in Chicago that he was going to see Landis Monday morning. He said, "I want to tell him the truth about all this. I want him to hear my side."

"What about the Yankees?"

"I'm through with them. I won't be playing with them next year if Huggins is still there. Either he quits or I quit, because I'll never play for him again."

Still spouting defiance, he went out into the Chicago night. Landis was at his summer place on Burt Lake in Michigan, and when he heard that Ruth was in Chicago he stayed at Burt Lake. By telephone he said, "Under baseball rules, I have no jurisdiction in the case until ten days after the suspension begins. I don't know what Ruth wants to see me for, but if he wants to come to Burt Lake, he's welcome. I'll be here another two or three days. If he comes here, I'll be glad to see him."

Ruth left word at the hotel that he did not want to be disturbed before ten o'clock Monday morning and at that hour reporters gathered outside his door. When one of them knocked, the door opened a few inches and a suit was shoved out. "Here," said Ruth's voice. "Have this pressed, and be sure it's back in an hour." Peering after the suit, he saw the reporters and said, "Holy Jesus. I didn't know it was you fellows. I'm sorry. Come on in." So many reporters piled into the room that Ruth had to phone the desk and arrange for a larger place in which to hold the impromptu press conference.

Babe was more relaxed and amiable than he had been the night before. The morning papers reported that Ruppert said he was backing Huggins in the dispute with Ruth, and Babe made no more threats about quitting the Yankees. He said again he was going to see Landis that morning. The reporters told him the Commissioner was in Michigan. Ruth seemed surprised that Landis was out of town, but pleased with what he said.

"That was nice of the judge, inviting me up there," said Ruth, "but I don't think I'll go. I'll send him a wire instead. When he reads my side of the story, he'll do the right thing."

"Are you going to come back and see him after the ten days are up, and he has jurisdiction?"

"I don't know. I might. I'm not sure."

"Why do you want to see Landis anyway?"

"I just want him to understand things," Ruth said plaintively. Then, truculent again, "I'll go to New York and see Jake. Huggins has Jake buffaloed, but when Jake hears my story everything will be all right. Huggins is trying to make me the goat for the way the

Yankees have played, but I'm going to fight for my rights. It's all up to Jake."

In New York Ruppert repeated, "I'm behind Huggins to the limit. There will be no remission of the fine, and the suspension will last as long as Huggins wants it to last. I understand Ruth says he will not play for the Yankees as long as Huggins is manager. Well, the situation is this: Huggins will be manager as long as he wants to be manager. So you can see where we stand and where Ruth stands."

When Babe arrived in New York Tuesday morning, he was much quieter. A vast mob was in Grand Central to get a glimpse of him, and reporters crowded around. Father Quinn got to him first and guided him past the reporters to a taxi.

"Leave him alone for now, please," said the priest. "He wants to see his wife first. She's been ill, as you know."

"Come up to the hotel later, boys," Ruth said in a subdued voice. "Maybe I'll have something to say then."

The reporters followed him to the cab. One asked, "Are you really going to quit the Yanks?" Ruth shook his head.

"Are you going to patch it up with Huggins? Will you meet him halfway?" Ruth nodded.

"What about Mrs. Hodgson? Are you going to see her?" Ruth pretended not to hear and got into the cab with Father Quinn.

In a fleet of taxis the reporters followed him to the Concourse Plaza, where Helen was. Ruth admitted reporters and photographers to the suite and talked to them freely. He was more feisty than he had been in Grand Central. He said he was willing to make peace with Huggins, but on an equal basis. He was retreating, but slowly.

"I know I said in Chicago I wouldn't play for Huggins again. I guess I was a little too rash. What I really meant was that I couldn't do my best playing for him until we straightened things out between us. I don't want to be traded. New York is my city.

"I think Huggins realizes now that he didn't treat me exactly right. Imagine fining a baseball player $5000! If they slapped a fine like that on some of the boys, they'd be working all season for nothing. Hell, people murder people and get away with it, and I get fined $5000 for staying out until two in the morning."

He went on, not saying anything directly critical about Huggins, but attacking him anyway. "If I had kept on hitting, this never would have happened. When I was going strong, Hug never bothered me about where I'd been or what I was doing. He never complained that staying out late was interfering with my hitting. But now that I'm down a little and the club is seventh, it's a different story."

He waved a hand in disgust.

"Aagh, maybe we're both wrong. I know I came back to the team in June with an incision in my belly six inches long. I was a damn fool. It didn't heal until this last trip. I should have taken more time, but I wanted to get back in the game. In all sincerity, I wanted to help Hug and the club."

The photographers asked if they could get some pictures of Babe with Helen. "Sure," Babe said. "But first I want to say something. What really gets me sore is those stories about me and women, and the pictures. I can take the baseball stories, but can't you lay off the women stuff?"

"What about Mrs. Hodgson?"

"There's nothing wrong in my friendship with Mrs. Hodgson or any other woman. I told Mrs. Ruth that just now and she said how much she appreciated my saying it. Those stories and those pictures are what put her in her sick bed. So I'd be very much obliged if you boys stuck to my baseball troubles and left my marital affairs alone."

They went into Helen's bedroom for photographs. A nurse was with her. Helen was again suffering from a nervous breakdown, and she also had a badly infected finger. It was the ring finger of her left hand, and her engagement and wedding rings had to be cut off, a distressingly symbolic note for poor Helen. "She couldn't cope," Shawkey said. "She couldn't stand the talk of Babe and all those women." Some of them had even telephoned her, which made Helen's condition even worse.

The photographers took some shots of Babe standing and then sitting by the bed. A photographer suggested a more intimate pose and Babe dutifully leaned his head against Helen's chest. She threw her arms around his neck and began to cry. He began to cry too, and he straightened up in the chair and put his face in his hands. He stood up and looked out the window for a minute or two before turning again to the photographers.

When they returned to the living room, someone asked, "What do you do now?"

"Well," Babe said briskly, his little bout of emotion past. "First, I'm going down to see Jake. He told some friends of mine he was ready to see me this morning and talk things over. Then I'm going back up to the Stadium to get into my uniform and take some practice. Even if I'm suspended, I'm not going to lay around and get out of shape."

He took a taxi to Ruppert's brewery at 90th Street and Second Avenue, and again the reporters trailed along. They waited in an anteroom while Babe was in Ruppert's private office. After a long time the two came out, Ruppert calm and poised, Ruth solemn.

"What happened, Babe?" a reporter asked. "Are you reinstated?"

Ruth said nothing, and the imperturbable Ruppert answered the question.

"No, he is not reinstated. The fine and the suspension stand. I told Ruth, as I tell you now in front of him, that he went too far. I told him Miller Huggins is in absolute command of the ball club, and that I stand behind Huggins to the very limit. I told him it is up to him to see Huggins, admit his errors and apologize for his hotheadedness. It is up to him to reinstate himself."

Turning to Ruth, Ruppert said, "We have treated you very liberally in the past. We have several times accepted your regrets and your promises to turn over a new leaf. Now you have got to stop short. I appreciate that you begged to return to the lineup even though we urged you to remain out another month. Your heart is in the right place. But your head has run away from you. You must look forward to the day when you are no longer able to play ball.

You must guard your name and your reputation for the time when they may be the only assets you have.

"I think you are big enough to go to Huggins and admit your error. We want you in New York and we need you, because we must regain the championship next season. We are ready, able and willing to pay you your big salary, but the fan who pays his dollar at the ballpark expects a full measure from you. Think it over. Then go see Huggins. I will do nothing for you. The matter lies in his hands."

"What about it, Babe?" a reporter asked.

"Colonel Ruppert has been very nice to me," he said in a low voice, "and he's given me a new view on things. I know I said a lot of things I shouldn't have."

"Are you going to see Huggins?"

"Yes, of course. Maybe we can get this settled."

Basking in his new humility, Ruth shook hands with Ruppert and left for the Stadium. In the clubhouse he greeted a couple of friends and then sought out Huggins.

He began to say something, but Huggins cut him off. "Look, Ruth, when I want to talk to you I'll let you know."

Ruth persisted. "Can't I play today?"

"No, sir."

"Can I practice?"

"No, sir."

Huggins turned away from the now thoroughly disorganized Ruth. Babe did not mind apologizing; he had done it a thousand times. But this was different. Huggins would not let him apologize. Word came for him to go to Ruppert's box in the mezzanine, and he watched the game sitting next to the colonel. Several times he had to stand up and wave in response to calls from the crowd. He signed many autographs. He was still immensely popular, but the Yankees, who lost 12 of 16 games on the cataclysmic road trip, won, 2-1, which did not hurt Huggins' position at all.

Huggins said after the game, "I'm not impressed with his apologies and his promises to be good. I've heard them before, and I'm tired of them. He seems penitent and apologetic now, but he can have a few more days to think things over."

Ruth went to the Stadium again on Wednesday. Huggins was in his office, and Babe rapped gently on the door. The manager, pipe in hand, opened the door.

"Can I talk to you?"

"Not yet."

"Can I practice?"

"Not today." Taking the pipe from his mouth, Huggins said, "Call me Friday afternoon," and went back into his office.

Ruth turned away, and the reporters gathered around.

"I'm ready to play," Babe complained, "but Huggins won't let me. I told them all I'm sorry for what I did. All I want now is to go out there and prove I'm as good as I ever was." There were more questions, but Ruth shook his head. "No, I don't want to do any more talking. It only gets me in bad. I did too much of it with those reporters in St. Louis and Chicago."

He sat down at a table with Dugan and mechanically began to play pinochle. "I'm licked," he said, "and I know it." After a while Huggins and the players, including Dugan, went out to the field, and the reporters followed. Ruth sat alone for a while turning the cards. Then he left the ballpark.

The Yankees won again that afternoon. They had Thursday and Friday off before playing a two-game set with Philadelphia in the Stadium on Saturday and Sunday. On Monday, Labor Day, they would go to Boston for a doubleheader. Huggins said Ruth might not be reinstated until Sunday or possibly Monday. In his extremity, Ruth went to Barrow and asked him to intercede. Barrow said he would not.

"At least ask him to let me take batting practice."

"It's up to Huggins."

Ruth left, muttering, "Jesus, I'll go stale."

He phoned Huggins on Friday, but the manager put him off, telling him to see him Saturday. "I'm in no hurry," Huggins told a friend. "A few more days of thinking things over will do him a world of good. I may let him play Sunday, or maybe Monday in Boston. I'm not sure. One thing we don't want to do is let people think we're trying to capitalize on the suspension in order to draw a crowd. This is more important than that. We've been through this with Babe before. This time it simply must mean something."

Ruth tried again on Saturday. Huggins said, "Come on in," and they went into his office and talked. Ruth was properly contrite, but Huggins, unrelenting, said he wanted Babe to apologize to him before the entire team in the clubhouse before the game on Sunday. Babe said he would. At that point he would have crawled through broken glass on his hands and knees to get back on the field. He made the apology on Sunday ("I'm hotheaded," he kept saying) and on Monday in Boston, after nine days in purgatory, he was in the lineup.

And so the great rebellion ended. While Ruth in time renewed his abiding affection for food, drink and willing women, he never again challenged Huggins' authority. Despite his big belly, which waned and waxed through the years like the moon, he was never again seriously out of shape. To the critics who said he was through, and to Fred Lieb, who thought that from now on he might be nothing more than a good steady hitter, Babe could have smiled and said, "You ain't seen nothin' yet." From 1926 through 1931, as he aged from thirty-two to thirty-seven, Ruth put on the finest sustained display of hitting that baseball has ever seen. During those six seasons, he averaged 50 home runs a year, 155 runs batted in and 147 runs scored; he batted .354. He hit his 300th home run the day after Huggins reinstated him, but there were more than 400 yet to come. He had been a dominant figure in six World Series, but the best of his World Series were still ahead of him, too. From the ashes of 1925, Babe Ruth rose like a rocket.

CHAPTER 27

The Real Reformation:
The Superb Seasons

Babe and Helen separated again, and in 1926 she was back in Boston, this time for good. There was no reconciliation. The farm at Sudbury was sold, and they never again lived together as man and wife. He spent much of his time with Claire when he was in New York, often quiet evenings of mild domesticity with Claire and her mother and her brothers and her daughter Julia, now almost ten.

He was still avidly chasing women. His escapades were so well known that he was unmercifully roasted at the New York baseball writers' dinner the following winter, at which sportswriter Rud Rennie, in the role of Miller Huggins, sang a parody written by Bill Slocum:

> *I wonder where my Babe Ruth is tonight?*
> *He grabbed his hat and coat and ducked from sight.*
> > *I wonder where he'll be*
> > *At half past two or three?*
> *He may be at a dance or in a fight.*
> *He may be at some cozy roadside inn.*
> *He may be drinking tea or maybe—gin.*
> > *I know he's with a dame,*

I wonder what's her name?
I wonder where my Babe Ruth is tonight?

But as evidence of the sincerity of his latest reform, Ruth turned down a proposed exhibition tour of Canada in the fall that would have earned him $25,000. And during the winter he worked out regularly and strenuously at Artie McGovern's gymnasium. When he reported to Huggins at St. Petersburg in the spring of 1926, he weighed 212 and was in the best shape he had been in since his early years with the Red Sox.

The Yankees seemed ragged early in training as Huggins tried to fit the new parts of his machine together, but the seeds of the coming renaissance were evident, as they had been during the last month of the 1925 season. Even though the 1925 club did not rise above seventh place after Ruth's return (the only time between 1918 and 1965, with the exception of the war year of 1945, that the Yankees finished lower than third), it played better than .500 ball those last few weeks. And Ruth, who had been at .267 with only 15 home runs when he came back to the lineup on September 7, hit ten homers in the 29 games remaining and batted .343 in those games. Gehrig hit 20 homers in 1925, fifth best in the league, and appeared to be a genuine slugger. One day in September he and Ruth and Meusel hit home runs in succession, the first time that had been done in the majors since 1902. Huggins and Barrow scoured the minor leagues for infielders and came up with three outstanding shortstops who cost Ruppert $115,000 in all: $60,000 to Salt Lake City of the Pacific Coast League for Tony Lazzeri; $35,000 to St. Paul of the American Association for Mark Koenig; $20,000 to Hartford of the Eastern League for Leo Durocher. Koenig reported to the club the day after Ruth returned to the lineup and immediately established himself as the regular shortstop. Huggins, satisfied with Koenig, noted that Lazzeri, who did not join the Yankees until the spring of 1926, had also played second base, and he earmarked the Salt Lake City star for that position. Durocher was with the team briefly at the tail end of 1925; he was a superlative fielder but a woeful hitter and was sent back to the minors for a couple more years.

And there was Meusel, who led the league in runs batted in in 1925, even though the Yankees were seventh in batting and seventh in runs scored. And Combs, who fielded beautifully and hit .344. And Dugan, whose knee seemed stronger after his operation. The pitching was sharper at St. Petersburg, and Ruth was Ruth, looking fine. Everything slowly fulfilled its promise, and spring training of 1926 was the most satisfying of Huggins' managerial career.

By the middle of March the club was functioning well and won four exhibition games in a row before breaking camp to join the Dodgers for the long trip north. Ruppert was pleased and said he would not be surprised if the club finished in the first division. Ruth, more optimistic, said first place, and Ruppert, smiling, "Maybe the Babe is right."

The Yankees beat the Dodgers in Waycross, beat them in Montgomery, beat them in Birmingham. Coming back from the ballpark in a taxi with Hoyt and Dugan, Ruth said, "If we keep on beating these guys, we're going to win the pennant." Hopping from town to town through Georgia, Tennessee, North Carolina and Virginia, the Yankees kept winning, and by resounding scores. They beat the Dodgers in every game they played, 12 in all, finishing their exhibition season with 16 straight victories. They won the last four by scores of 14–4, 11–1, 4–1, and 14–7, and went into the season the popular favorites for the pennant, even though the sportswriters were not as sanguine about their chances.

And they won the pennant, rising from seventh place to first in one season. They opened a ten-game lead by the middle of June, held it through the summer, lost most of it late in the season but held on to win by three games. Ruth was superb. He batted .372, second in the league. He hit 47 home runs (the second man had 19) and drove in 155 runs (second had 114). He led the league in walks, runs scored, total bases, slugging percentage. He played practically every game. Strangely, he was not voted Most Valuable Player. The selectors in their wisdom named George Burns of second-place

Cleveland instead. In fact, Ruth in his career was named Most Valuable Player only once, a curious injustice. No selections were made from 1915 through 1921; if they had been, Ruth would have been a strong candidate in 1916, a sure winner in 1918, a sure winner again in 1921. He was certainly the player of the year, if not the most valuable, in 1919 and 1920. He did win the award in 1923, and he should have won it in 1926.

One reason why his accomplishments were obscured in 1926 was the play of Lazzeri. The rookie second baseman teamed perfectly with Koenig, the rookie shortstop, and turned out to be a powerful batter. He hit 18 home runs, two more than Gehrig, and drove in 114 runs, seven more than Gehrig, to tie Most Valuable Player Burns for second place behind Ruth. The Yankee batting order was becoming awesome—Ruth, Meusel, Gehrig and Lazzeri in succession were a terrifying prospect for any pitcher.

The Yankees went into the 1926 World Series a big favorite over the St. Louis Cardinals, who had won their pennant with a record low winning percentage. But Ruth had only two singles in his first ten at bats, and the Cardinals won two of the first three games. In the fourth game, in St. Louis, Ruth exploded. He hit the first pitch to him in the first inning for a home run. He hit the first pitch to him in the third inning for a home run. He went to three balls and two strikes in the sixth inning and then hit the ball high into the center field bleachers, where it bounced over the wall and out of the park, the longest home run ever in St. Louis. It was the first time Babe had hit three home runs in one game, and the first time anyone had ever hit three in a World Series game.

The Yankees won that day and the next, but the Cardinals tied the Series at three games each to set the stage for one of the most memorable games in baseball history. Grover Cleveland Alexander, the oldtime star of the Philadelphia Phils, who won 30 or more games in a season three times, had come to the Cardinals in midseason. He was thirty-nine, an epileptic and a drunk, but his ancient skills won nine games for the Cardinals and helped them win their pennant. He beat the Yankees, 6–2, in the second game to tie the

Series at one game each, and he beat them again, 10–2, in the sixth game to tie it at three games each. Alex had a few drinks to celebrate that night, and during the seventh game sat quietly in the bullpen recovering. Ruth hit a home run in the third inning, but the Cardinals rallied to take a 3–1 lead. The Yankees scored again in the sixth to make it 3–2, and in the seventh inning filled the bases with two out and Lazzeri, the extraordinary rookie, coming to bat. Rogers Hornsby, the St. Louis manager, came out of his dugout and motioned to the bullpen. He wanted Alexander, hangover or no hangover.

Bases loaded, two out, tying run on third, winning run on second, seventh inning of the seventh game of the World Series, twenty-three-year-old rookie at bat, thirty-nine-year-old veteran on the mound. It was one of those classic moments that baseball does so well. Alexander pitched a ball and a called strike. He threw again, and Lazzeri hit a long drive high into the stands in left field that went foul by a few feet. Alexander threw again—and Lazzeri struck out.

The crisis was over. Alex breezed through the eighth inning, one-two-three, and got the first two men in the ninth. Now Ruth was up, the first time he had batted against Alexander since the 1915 World Series. Alex walked him. Ruth, on first base, was the tying run. Meusel was at bat, Gehrig was on deck, Lazzeri was after him. Alexander pitched to Meusel, and suddenly there was Ruth racing for second, trying to steal. The catcher threw the ball to the bag and Ruth was out, the Series abruptly and stunningly over.

Ruth's decision to steal was discussed for years. It was generally considered a bad play, a dumb play, but some baseball men defended it. There were two outs, not much chance left to develop a rally. A man on second base could score on a single, and the way Alexander was pitching, a single was about all you could hope for. A successful steal at such a startling moment might upset the pitcher, even the veteran Alexander.

But it did not work, and despite his four home runs, a new World Series record, Babe was considered a bit of a goat. He didn't seem to mind. It was a hell of a try, he thought. Strikeouts never embarrassed him, and neither did this.

The following year the Ruthian Yankees reached their peak. The lineup that had coalesced a year earlier around the new men through the middle—Combs, Lazzeri, Koenig—was much stronger in 1927. Gehrig's batting average jumped from .313 to .373. Lazzeri hit .309, Combs .356, Meusel .337, Ruth .356. More important were the runs pouring across the plate. Gehrig batted in 175 runs, Ruth 164, Meusel 103, Lazzeri 102. The pitching was sharply improved. Earned-run averages went up that season, but they were lower for every important Yankee pitcher. Hoyt had the best ERA in the league, and Urban Shocker, who had come from the Browns in 1925, was second. Hoyt's won-and-lost record was 22–7, Pennock's 19–8, Shocker's 18–6. Jones and Shawkey had faded out of the picture, but Huggins replaced them with two new acquisitions, the veteran Dutch Ruether and the rookie George Pipgras, who between them won 23 and lost 9.

The most striking addition to the staff—and to the team, for that matter—was a tall, strong thirty-year-old Oklahoma farmer named Wilcy Moore, whom Barrow had bought sight unseen from the Piedmont League after reading at one point during the previous season that Moore's record stood at 20–1. "He's too old," a scout told Barrow, "and anybody can win 20 games in a league like that." Barrow said, "Anyone who has a 20–1 record anywhere is worth taking a look at," and bought him. Moore started some games, but his real forte was relief pitching. He was 13–3 in relief and his overall record was 19–9. Laconic, shrewd, witty, he became a favorite of Ruth, who loved to mock Moore's hitting. Wilcy batted .080 in 1927, and his career average in the majors was .102. Moore looked so awful at bat during spring training that Ruth bet him $300 to $100 that he would not make more than three hits all season. Moore took the bet, got six hits in seventy-five at bats and won the bet. He told Ruth later that he bought two mules for his farm with the money and named one Babe and the other Ruth.

The Yankees opened the 1927 season at home before a capacity crowd, probably near the 70,000 it was reported to be, and in a short time were taking the league apart. Batting .307 as a team, setting a new major league home run record, they won 110 games and lost only 44. The second-place Philadelphia Athletics finished with precisely the same record the 1926 Yankees had in winning the pennant (91 victories and 63 defeats) and ended up a frustrating 19 games behind.

Gehrig, coming into full maturity, matched Ruth homer for homer from April to the middle of August and was, in fact, three home runs ahead of the Babe on August 10, with 38 to Ruth's 35. It was the first time anyone had directly challenged Ruth's preeminence (when he lost the home run championship in 1922 and 1925, he had missed the first six or seven weeks of the season each time) and it more than made up for the lack of excitement in the pennant race. But after August 10 Gehrig hit only nine home runs while Ruth hit 25, his pace becoming faster and faster as the season neared its end. When he hit his 50th he talked of breaking his record, but it seemed all but impossible: There were only 17 games left to play. He hit three in the next eight games, which is very close to a 60-homer pace, but that was not fast enough. At 53 homers, he still needed seven more, and there were only nine games left. He hit three in the next three games. On number 56 he carried his bat around the bases with him to frustrate souvenir seekers. As he passed third base a boy came out of the stands, pounded him joyfully on the back and grabbed the bat. Babe dragged boy and bat all the way across home plate.

He hit no home runs in the next game or the game after that. Only four games left now and four homers still to go. He hit his 57th, a grand slam, in the first of these four games. In the second he hit his 58th, hit a triple off the right field fence, hit his 59th (another grand-slammer) and hit a long fly that the right fielder caught at the fence. On September 30, in the next to last game of the season, he hit his 60th. It was hit down the right field line, just fair, and Tom

Zachary, the opposing pitcher, yelled, "Foul ball! Foul ball!" and argued with the umpire. In 1947 Zachary shook hands with Ruth in Yankee Stadium, and the Babe, his voice a croak from the cancer that was killing him, said, "You crooked-arm son of a bitch, are you still claiming that ball was foul?" In 1927 he whooped it up in the clubhouse, shouting, "Sixty, count 'em, sixty! Let's see some other son of a bitch match that!"

He played again on the last day of the season but had no hits in three at bats.

The 60th homer meant a great deal to Ruth. In the early years he had bettered his home run total each season—11 in 1918, 29 in 1919, 54 in 1920, 59 in 1921—but he had been trying futilely since to break the record again. Now at last he had done it, and he had demonstrated to young Gehrig (who, deservedly, won the Most Valuable Player award) that Ruth was still the king. Yet, while the 60 home runs were a shining peak of accomplishment, 1927 was not his best season, as a comparison of his performances in 1921 and 1927 clearly shows:

Year	Games	AB	R	H	2B	3B	HR	BB	RBI	TB	Pct	Slugging Average
1921	152	540	177	204	44	16	59	144	170	457	.378	.846
1927	151	540	158	192	29	8	60	138	164	417	.356	.772

Except for home runs, he was better in every way in 1921.

The Yankees went off to Pittsburgh to meet the Pirates in the World Series and made a profound impression on their rivals in a practice session the day before the Series began. They powered ball after ball toward the distant fences in spacious Forbes Field while the Pirates, who were sitting in the grandstand near home plate, watched solemnly. "They're beaten already," said the outspoken Wilbert Robinson, manager of the Brooklyn Dodgers.

But it was not power so much as consistency that gave the Yankees a four-game sweep of the Pirates. Ruth hit two home runs, but they were the only homers hit by either team. Steady batting, steady pitching, steady fielding won for the Yankees as the Pirates, for the most part, batted poorly, pitched poorly and fielded poorly. Maybe they *were* beaten before they started. Or perhaps they were not that good to begin with; they finished fourth a year later.

Serenity and success continued, and the Yankees won the pennant again in 1928, the second time in the decade that they won three in a row. But where everything worked perfectly all season in 1927, now it was the other way around. Lazzeri hurt his shoulder and was out for almost 40 games. Koenig missed 30 games at shortstop. Durocher, back from the minors, filled in for both, displaying his usual brilliance in the field and ineptitude at bat. Dugan's knee was crippled again and he missed 60 games in this, his last year with the club. Moore, after his season in the sun, was nothing: four wins, four losses (perhaps the scout was right). Late in the season Combs sprained his wrist and Pennock hurt his arm, and both missed the World Series. Ruether retired. Worst of all, Shocker fell seriously ill in the spring, was out all season and to everyone's dismay died in September at the age of thirty-eight.

It was not the same team, and yet by July 1 it was in first place by 13½ games, and it held on to a good part of that into August. Then the Philadelphia Athletics, a rising club, slowly ate away New York's margin and on Saturday, September 8, moved into the lead, a half game ahead of the Yankees. A four-game series between the two clubs started the next day. The excitement in New York was immense, particularly since the series began with a doubleheader on Sunday. Yankee Stadium was completely filled. Standees were everyplace. Thousands and thousands more were turned away from the gates before the game began. Barrow blithely announced that the crowd totaled 85,265, another of his innocent fabrications, but whatever the actual count, it was much the biggest crowd ever to see a baseball game to that time. And the Yankees beat the Athletics twice, 5–0 and 7–3, to go back into the lead. "We broke their hearts," Ruth said, although he himself did relatively little in either game. Next day, he broke a 3–3 tie in the eighth with a two-run homer, and that victory effectively ended the Athletics' threat.

Gehrig had another outstanding season (.374, 142 runs batted in), but his home run total subsided to 27, second in the league to Babe but only half Ruth's total. For more than half the season it seemed certain that Ruth was going to break the record again. By August 1 he had 42 home runs, which put him 26 games ahead of his 1927 pace, but he tailed off, hit only five the rest of August and seven in September and finished with 54, the fourth time he had hit more than 50 in a season and the second time he had done it two seasons in a row.

The edginess of the season, the injuries, Shocker's death, the challenge of the younger, stronger Athletics, all were forgotten when the Yankees clinched the pennant in Detroit a couple of weeks later. The players shouted their way back to their hotel, where Ruth rented three or four rooms with connecting doors and threw a party. The hotel could not supply a piano, so Ruth bought one for the party. Waiters came in and out all night with trays of food and bootleg liquor. At one point Ruth climbed on a chair, a beer in one hand and a sandwich in the other, and shouted, "Any girl who doesn't want to fuck can leave now." And, said a smiling old Yankee forty-five years later, very few of them left.

The exuberance of the party and the subsequent ride home to New York carried over into the World Series, which the Yankees won in four straight from the Cardinals to take happy revenge for the defeat in 1926. Ruth and Gehrig put on astounding performances. Babe had ten hits in sixteen at bats in the four games for a batting average of .625, still the highest ever made in a World Series. Six of his ten hits were for extra bases, and three were home runs, all in the same game—the second time he hit three homers in one game in a World Series. Gehrig batted .545, second only to Ruth's as the highest average in Series history, and had four home runs and nine runs batted in. The Yanks won, 4–1, 9–3, 7–3 and 7–3. The Cardinals were almost always behind, and not until the last game did they put up any kind of a struggle. Then they led, 2–1, into the seventh inning, the only run a homer by Ruth in the fourth that tied the score temporarily at 1–1. In the seventh he came to bat again against

Willie Sherdel, a lefthander who won 21 games during the season. Sherdel got two strikes on Ruth and when Babe turned his head to banter with his old adversary, Earl Smith, who was catching, Sherdel quick-pitched him, throwing abruptly to the plate without a windup for what appeared to be strike three. Quick pitches were legal in the National League, but Judge Landis and the two league presidents agreed that they would not be allowed during the World Series. Plate umpire Cy Pfirman therefore ruled it no pitch. Sherdel screamed in objection and charged off the mound, and Frank Frisch raced in from second base. Manager Bill McKechnie came from the dugout, followed by others, and they all jammed around Pfirman, shouting and arguing. The crowd was booing. Huggins came from the Yankee bench to make sure Pfirman did not change his mind.

Ruth, wallowing in innocence, backed out of the batter's box and took no part in the argument. He stood waiting with a big amused grin on his face, and when the Cardinals finally gave in and moved away he ostentatiously applauded them. Sherdel and he exchanged a few words. The crowd, still booing, threw torn up programs on the field and even a few bottles. Sherdel pitched again, missed the plate twice, and the count went to two and two. Again he and Ruth exchanged words, and on the next pitch Babe hit the ball into the right field stands for a home run that tied the score. He laughed as he ran around the bases and waved merrily to the sullen crowd. Sherdel was taken out and Alexander brought in, but this was not 1926. Gehrig, who followed Ruth to bat, hit a homer to put the Yankees ahead, and in the eighth inning Ruth hit another homer off Alexander, his third of the game.

A year and a half later Ruth was asked by a reporter what he and Sherdel had said to each other in the moments after the quick pitch and before the home run.

"I said the National League is a hell of a league," Ruth replied.

"What did he say?"

"Oh, he said it sure was, or something like that."

"Then what did you say?"

"I said put one right here and I'll knock it out of the park for you."

"What happened then?"

Ruth grinned. "He did and I did."

This happened four years before the famous called home run in Chicago. And Waite Hoyt said Ruth called a home run in Boston once. There was a loudmouth fan there named Conway, who was always at the ballpark and always needling the Yankees, particularly Ruth. His voice, loud and harsh, carried well in Fenway Park, which was usually pretty empty in those doldrum days (the years when the Red Sox finished last nine times in eleven seasons). On this day Conway's abrasive comments got to Ruth, who became visibly annoyed. He stepped out of the batter's box, looked at Conway and pointed to the right field seats. Then he stepped back in and hit a home run. Into the right field seats. When he crossed home plate he stopped, faced Conway and made a deep bow.

In St. Louis after the game he shouted, "I told those friends of mine in the bleachers I'd hit two home runs, and I hit three!" In 1969 K. E. Dougan wrote to Gary Valk of *Sports Illustrated* after an article appeared in the magazine arguing that Ruth's called shot in 1932 never happened. "Not having been there," Dougan wrote, "I have no opinion. However, I was a personal witness to either two or three home runs which Babe did call in one game. A friend and I skipped school and took a street car at 4 A.M. to get bleacher seats to the fourth game of the 1928 World Series. We sat in the left field bleachers behind Ruth. He took a lot of good-natured booing. About the middle of the game, as he took his position in left field, he held up the number of fingers for the next inning and pointed to the right field bleachers. And the next inning he hit a home run. As I recall, he did this twice during the game."

The three home runs were gloriously satisfying to Ruth, but there was one more thing for him in the game. In the last half of the ninth the Cardinals, behind 7–2, scored one run and had a man on base with two outs. Frisch was up, always a dangerous batter. Frank was batting lefthanded, but he hit a foul fly to the opposite field,

along the left field line. It looked as though it would drop harm-
lessly into the temporary field boxes that had been built in front of
the regular stands for the Series. But Ruth, playing left field,
sprinted across the foul line and along the wooden railing of the
boxes. The fans shouted at him and swatted him with programs and
newspapers but, still running, he reached in with his glove hand and
plucked the ball from the air for the final out of the Series. Without
breaking stride, he ran all the way into the dugout, holding the
gloved ball high in the air, waving it as though it were a trophy.

The train ride back to New York that night was a royal progress.
Ruth ripped shirts and pajama tops from everyone, including Jacob
Ruppert, who fled his compartment and tried to hide unnoticed in
an upper berth. The news that the Yankee train was coming was
flashed ahead, and all that night and the next morning, at every
little station stop between St. Louis and New York, crowds of people
gathered to watch the Yankees go by. Whenever the train stopped,
the people clamored for Ruth, and he would go to the door and
wave and say a few words.

CHAPTER 28

Kaleidoscope: Personality of the Babe

That was the apex of Ruth's career, the happiest moment of three years of great accomplishment and relative serenity. His life would never be as uncomplicated again, although nothing—not the deaths of people close to him, a second marriage, or the inevitable decline of his physical powers—was able completely to suppress his casual, carefree personality.

One day in 1930, before the first of a routine series of games in St. Louis between the Yankees and the Browns, Ruth was behind the batting cage talking with Bill Killefer, the Browns' manager, Tony Lazzeri and a reporter.

"Your face is getting fatter and fatter," Killefer said.

"Yeah?" said Ruth. He spat some tobacco juice. "Well, I don't hit with my face."

"Is the wife on the trip with you?"

"Sure."

"Having a hard time dodging the old phone calls?" Killefer said, grinning.

"Oh, go to hell."

"Who do you like in the Derby?" the reporter asked.

"I'm not playing the ponies."

"What books are you reading?"

"Books?" Ruth looked at him. "Reading isn't good for a ball-player. Not good for his eyes. If my eyes went bad even a little bit I couldn't hit home runs. So I gave up reading."

"You must do some reading. Who are your favorite authors?" The reporter pronounced it in the midwestern way, alien to Ruth's semi-southern ear.

"My favorite Arthurs? Nehf and Fletcher."

"Not Arthurs," the reporter said patiently. "Authors, writers."

"Oh, writers. My favorite writer is Christy Walsh."

"Seriously, what President of the United States do you admire most?"

"Well, I liked Harding a lot, and I liked Wilson a lot. Coolidge was all right. Hoover is okay with me, but Al Smith was my favorite for the job."

"What is the psychology of home runs?"

"Say, are you kidding me?"

"No, of course not. I just want an explanation of why you get so many home runs."

Ruth spat again. "Just swinging," he said.

"Have you ever had an idol, someone you thought more of than anyone else?"

"Sure he has," Lazzeri said. "Babe Ruth."

"Go to hell," Ruth said, and to the reporter, "Excuse me, it's my turn to hit."

When he finished he ducked under the stands for a few minutes and came back with a hot dog. He sat on the Browns' bench next to Killefer and the reporter.

"What was the biggest thrill you ever got out of a ballgame?" the reporter asked.

"Biggest thrill?" Ruth said. He bit off half the hot dog and gulped it down. "That's easy. It happened right here in St. Louis when I got three home runs in one World Series game and made that running catch off Frankie Frisch. Picked the ball right out of the stands. And

I got a thrill out of little Sherdel trying to sneak that strike over on me when I wasn't looking and then hitting one out."

"How much did you earn last year? I mean, from everything—baseball, exhibitions, testimonials, everything."

"A hundred and ten thousand dollars."

"Are you saving any money?"

"Lots of it," Ruth replied. He finished the hot dog. "I started a trust fund three years ago and I've got $120,000 in it right now. I got an older one with $50,000 in it. Right now I'm good for $500 a month for as long as I live."

"What are you going to do when your baseball days are over?"

"Take life easy," Ruth said. "Excuse me, I've got to hit again."

Later the Yankee batboy and mascot, Eddie Bennett, a hunchback, came down to the runway into the Browns' dugout. He was carrying a cup of some sort of whitish liquid.

"What have you got there?" Killefer asked.

"Some bicarbonate of soda for the Babe."

"How many hot dogs did he have?" Killefer asked.

"Three."

"How often does he do that?" asked the reporter.

"Every day," Bennett said, shaking his head. "Every day."

Ruth drank bicarbonate of soda every day in the dugout. He called it his milk. He began the habit one day after he gobbled down a couple of hot dogs too quickly and felt bloated just before game time. The trainer recommended bicarbonate. It made him feel good and he decided that was the ideal diet before a game: a couple of hot dogs and a glass of bicarb. He chewed tobacco and gum, smoked cigars and occasionally cigarettes or a pipe, took snuff in such vast amounts that some of the dust became impacted in his nasal passages. A doctor ordered him to quit taking it after that.

Before the game that day in St. Louis a photographer asked Ruth to pose for pictures and he willingly complied. He always went along. A photographer asked him one day to have his picture taken with "another champion, the greatest egglayer in Nebraska." He was handed a chicken and an egg. He posed amiably with the chicken cuddled in one hand, the egg in the other, a huge grin on his face and his eyes all crinkled up from laughing. He was relaxed with reporters, and would go out of his way to be cooperative with them, although he was often subjected to bizarre questions. "What do you think of the Chinese situation?" he was asked. "The hell with it," he replied. But when Will Grimsley of the Associated Press was a young reporter, Ruth patiently answered all his questions one day even though his teammates were yelling at him to hurry up.

On the road he always had a suite, sometimes in a different hotel from the one the team was staying at. He liked to lounge around in red slippers and a red robe, smoking a cigar. Dozens of people streamed in and out of the suite day and night. He always carried a wind-up portable phonograph with him on road trips. He loved to sing. Occasionally he would strum a ukulele. He was always shaved by a barber. ("That's what they're for, aren't they?") In St. Louis he liked to eat at a German restaurant that made barbecued spare ribs. Often, on the day the Yankees were leaving town, he'd go from the ballpark to the restaurant and order a mess of ribs and home brew and take it to the train. He would set up shop in a washroom and sell the ribs to the players for fifty cents a portion. He insisted on being paid too, but he also provided beer, and the players could have all the beer they wanted for their fifty cents.

He was apolitical, although he called himself a Democrat until Franklin D. Roosevelt ran for a third term, and apparently he never cast a vote in a national election until 1944. Yet he created a mild political furor in September 1928, when Herbert Hoover was running for President. Hoover appeared at the ballpark and a publicity man ran down to the Yankee clubhouse to get Ruth to come and pose with the Republican candidate.

"No, sir," said Ruth, "nothing doing on politics." He had been burned a few days earlier by a story saying he was supporting Hoover. He denied it, saying he was for Al Smith, and now he declined to appear with Smith's rival. But, graciously, he said, "Tell him I'll be glad to talk to him if he wants to meet me under the stands." No doubt here as to which was king.

Reporters with Hoover heard about all this, and it became a headline story: "RUTH REFUSES TO POSE WITH HOOVER." Christy Walsh almost died. Republican newspapers were threatening to drop Ruth's syndicated column. Walsh got in touch with Babe and hurriedly prepared a statement, ostensibly by Ruth, saying he regretted that because of a misunderstanding he had been unable to pose with the Republican candidate. He would be happy to, he declared, and a photo was duly taken of Ruth and Hoover together.

Despite the earlier publicity, Hoover's camp was happy to have the photograph, because Ruth's personality was pervasive. The crudity, the vulgarity, the indifference, the physical humor that bordered on brutality, the preoccupation with his own needs that ignored Hoover and hurt Helen—none of it mattered when Ruth smiled or laughed or moved or did almost anything. "He was one of those exciting people who make life fun, and who give more to life than they take from it," said Arthur Robinson, a New York sportswriter who was another of the Babe's ghosts. "God, we liked that big son of a bitch," said Hoyt. "He was a constant source of joy." When Roger Maris was chasing Ruth's home run record in 1961, Jimmy Dykes said, "Maris is a fine ballplayer, but I can't imagine him driving down Broadway in a low-slung convertible, wearing a coonskin coat." Dugan said, "What a fantastic ballplayer he was, the things he could do. But he wasn't human. He dropped out of a tree."

He was so alive, so attractive, like an animal or a child: ingenuous, unself-conscious, appealing. Frank Graham said, "He was a very simple man, in some ways a primitive man. He had little education, and little need for what he had." Tom Meany said he had the supreme self-confidence of the naïve. On a stifling hot day at the Washington ballpark he said to President Harding, "Hot as hell, ain't it, Prez?" He met Marshal Foch when that renowned French hero of World War I was making a tour of the United States early in the 1920s and said politely, "I suppose you were in the war?"

Introduced before a game to a man he had never seen before, Ruth said, "You sound like you have a cold." The man admitted he did. Ruth reached into the hip pocket of his uniform and pulled out a big onion. "Here, gnaw on this," he said. "Raw onions are cold-killers." During a blistering heat wave Ruth brought a cabbage into the dugout and put it in the team's old-fashioned water cooler, and each inning before he went on the field he took a fresh cabbage leaf and put it under his cap to keep himself cool.

Famous for not remembering names (when Waite Hoyt was leaving the Yankees in 1930 after eleven seasons as Babe's teammate in Boston and New York, Ruth shook hands and said solemnly, "Goodbye, Walter"), he had nicknames for other players, not necessarily complimentary nicknames. His teammates were Chicken Neck, Flop Ears, Duck Eye, Horse Nose, Rubber Belly. People he did not know or remember he called Doc or Kid, which he usually pronounced Keed, in the flashy slang pronunciation of the time. He called older men Pop, older women Mom. Younger women he needed no special name for. He usually called Claire Clara. He himself was called Jidge by the Yankees, a corruption of George that was apparently first used by Dugan.

His appetite was enormous, although accounts of it were often exaggerated. A report of one dinner says he had an entire capon, potatoes, spinach, corn, peas, beans, bread, butter, pie, ice cream and three or four cups of coffee. He was known to have eaten a huge omelet made of eighteen eggs and three big slices of ham, plus half a dozen slices of buttered toast and several cups of coffee. Ty Cobb, no stickler for accuracy in his memoirs of baseball life, said, "I've seen him at midnight, propped up in bed, order six club sandwiches, a platter of pigs' knuckles and a pitcher of beer. He'd down all that while smoking a big black cigar. Next day, if he hit a homer, he'd trot around the bases complaining about gas pains and a bellyache." He belched magnificently and, I was told, could fart at will.

He was, as noted, a sexual athlete. In a St. Louis whorehouse he announced he was going to go to bed with every girl in the house during the night, and did, and after finishing his rounds sat down and had a huge breakfast. In the early 1930s the Yankees signed a superior pitcher named Charlie Devens out of Harvard, who abandoned a promising major league career a year or two later to join his family's banking business in Boston. Devens joined the team in St. Louis, reporting in at the hotel. He was given the key to his room and went up and unpacked. His roommate, some secondary figure on the team, was not around. Just as he finished unpacking, the phone rang and a voice asked, "Devens?"

"Yes."

"Bring your room key with you and come down to the lobby."

Obediently Devens took his key and went downstairs. When the elevator doors opened at the lobby floor, there was Babe Ruth, a girl on each arm.

"You Devens?" Ruth asked.

Devens nodded. Ruth put out his hand. Devens looked at him dumbly.

"The key," Ruth snapped. Devens gave him the key and Babe and his friends swept into the elevator. Later Devens learned that when Mrs. Ruth was with Babe on road trips he occasionally pre-empted teammates' rooms for extracurricular activities.

There were inevitable stories that Ruth was exceptionally well equipped sexually, and a male nurse who took care of him in his terminal illness was impressed by the size of Ruth's genitals. But apparently any abnormality in size then was a product of illness. One teammate, asked if Ruth had an exceptionally big penis, frowned a little as he searched his memory and shook his head. "No," he said. "It was normal size, judging from locker room observation. Nothing extraordinary. Del Pratt's was. And Home Run Baker's. My God, you wouldn't believe Home Run Baker's. It looked like it belonged to a horse. But Babe's wasn't noticeably big. What was extraordinary was his ability to keep doing it all the time. He was continually with women, morning and night. I don't know how he kept going." He was very noisy in bed, visceral grunts and gasps and whoops accompanying his erotic exertions. "He was the noisiest fucker in North America," a whimsical friend recalled.

There is a story, probably apocryphal, about a time he and Meusel were barnstorming together. They shared a hotel suite. Meusel was half asleep when Ruth came in with a girl, went into his room and made love to her in his usual noisy fashion. Afterwards he came out to the living room of the suite, lit a cigar and sat in a chair by the window, smoking it contemplatively. When he finished the cigar he went back into the bedroom and made love again. And then came out and smoked another cigar. In the morning Meusel asked, "How many times did you lay that girl last night?" Ruth glanced at the ashtray, and so did Meusel. There were seven butts in the tray. "Count the cigars," said Ruth.

On the other side of the coin there is another story, about a barnstorming trip with Gehrig. Ruth came back to the suite boisterously drunk with two girls and went into the bedroom with both of them. During the night one of the girls came out to Gehrig and said, "You better come and see if you can straighten out your friend." Lou went into the bedroom and found Ruth sitting naked on the side of the bed, sobs racking his shoulders, tears running down his face. In bits, from Ruth and the girls, Gehrig discovered what was wrong. However successful he had been earlier in the night with his friends, Ruth was crying because he was unable now to service both girls.

Everything about him reflected sexuality—the restless, roving energy; the aggressive skills; fastball pitching; home run hitting; the speed with which he drove cars; the loud, rich voice; the insatiable appetite; the constant need to placate his mouth with food, drink, a cigar, chewing gum, anything. When he played poker, he liked to raise even when his cards did not justify a raise, and when he lucked into a pot he chortled happily. He was a fairly skillful bridge player, but he wanted to play every hand himself and often outbid his partner as well as their opponents. In retirement his favorite sports were golf and bowling; he liked to hit a golf ball a long way, and in bowling to keep track of the total number of pins he knocked down rather than his average score. He loved to win in whatever he did. He received absolute physical joy from cards, baseball, golf, bowling, punching the bag, sex.

He liked to fish and would go with Gehrig before their friendship became strained, but he was a better hunter than a fisherman. His physical stamina, superb eyesight and quick reflexes helped his hunting, and he also had a quality seldom in evidence anywhere else: extraordinary patience. Once in Georgia he stalked a wild turkey for seven hours before getting close enough to shoot. Then he picked it off the top of a tree with one shot.

Physically he was a paradox. He was big, strong, muscular, exceptionally well coordinated, yet he was often injured and he suffered from a surprising number of colds and infections. This would indicate a low resistance to disease, yet he had an amazing ability to recover quickly. He dramatized injuries; no player in big league history was carried off the field on his shield as often as the massive Bambino. But he could ignore both illness and injury and play superlatively well despite them.

In his later years Ruth was often babied by the Yankees. He and Jimmy Reese, a rookie second baseman who weighed seventy-five pounds less than the Babe, crashed into each other running for a fly ball. They staggered apart and fell to the ground, both apparently hurt. The trainer and others ran from the bench, past Reese's prostrate form, and gathered around Babe. When Lefty Gomez was a rookie, he was pitching batting practice in spring training. Hoyt came past the mound just as Ruth was stepping in to hit. "Nothing but fastballs right down the pipe," Hoyt told Gomez. "Don't get cute, kid. And for God's sake, don't hit him or you're gone."

In the summer of 1931, going after a fly ball, Babe smashed into a chicken-wire screen that was serving as a temporary outfield fence during renovations. A strand of loose wire ripped into his finger, cutting it badly and tearing the nail off. The trainer ran out, took one look and said Ruth would have to come out of the game. Holding the damaged hand with the other, his face screwed up in pain, Ruth limped all the way in from right field, even though his legs had not been hurt. In the trainer's room he was told the damaged nail would have to be cut away. "Not without gas," he declared. "Nobody's going to cut me unless I have gas." He made a great fuss before the nail was removed and the finger bandaged, and everybody laughed about the limp and the gas. But the next day he played, torn finger and all, and stole a base. His second wife reacted to the well-publicized stories about Mickey Mantle having to have his legs bandaged each day during his career because of his osteomyelitis by saying, "No one ever mentions that my husband played with bandaged legs practically every day of his career." Old teammates verified this. When Ruth slid into base he slid with abandon, and because he would not wear sliding pads under his uniform his thighs and hips were scraped raw by the rough pebbly soil of the old infields. His legs were richly decorated with raw "strawberry" wounds which persisted all season. He would have them doused with alcohol and wrapped in bandages and go on playing.

"He was very brave at the plate," Casey Stengel said. "You rarely saw him fall away from a pitch. He stayed right in there. No one drove him out."

His weight fluctuated throughout his career. When he signed with the Orioles he weighed about 185 and with the Red Sox he went up to 198 and then to 212 in a couple of seasons. He got down below 200 again, but not for long, and after 1919 his weight was seldom below 220. It soared to 240 in Cuba late in 1920 and stayed around 230 in 1921 and 1922. In the spring of 1923, after his first reformation, he was down briefly to 215, but a year later he was up to 230 again. In January 1925 he weighed 256 and was probably more than 260 at the time of his collapse in Asheville. Determined work at McGovern's gymnasium the following winter got him down to 212; thereafter his weight as a player varied from about 225 to 240, depending on the time of the year. But he continued to work with McGovern every winter, and he was in much better shape at that weight than he used to be. When he first went to McGovern during the winter of 1925–26 his chest measured 43 inches normal and 45 inches expanded; both his waist (49¾ inches) and his hips (47 inches) were larger than his chest. But in the winter of 1931–32, approaching his thirty-eighth birthday and weighing 235½, his waist was 38 and his hips 40, and his chest was 41 normal and 48 expanded.

Because of Ruth's bulk, Ruppert decided to dress the Yankees in their now-traditional pinstripe uniform and dark blue stockings.

The natty, clothes-conscious Ruppert felt the new uniform would make Ruth look trimmer. The Yankees also introduced uniform numbers to the major leagues in 1929. Ruth's number was number 3 because he batted third, Gehrig's 4 because he batted fourth, and so on.

When Ruth left the ballpark or the hotel, usually to meet a girl, he would say, "I'm going to see a party." He seldom if ever went to popular night clubs or famous restaurants. He much preferred out-of-the-way places where he knew the owner and could relax in relative peace and quiet. One of his favorites was a spot in northern New Jersey called Donahue's. The owner fixed up a private room for him where he could eat and drink and talk with his guests without being bothered by strangers. He seldom had many people with him, usually four or five at the most.

His voice was rich and warm, his accent very slightly southern. "Less go out to the *bowl* game," he would say, pronouncing ball that way and stressing it heavily. His speech was splattered with vulgarities. "Piss pass the butter," he would say childishly if he was dining with a teammate. Or, asked how he was feeling, he'd reply, "Pussy good, pussy good." In the early 1920s he saw a teammate on the street with a pretty girl. Next day he asked, "Who was that cunt you were with?" The teammate said, "For God's sake, Babe, that was my wife."

"Oh," Ruth said, "I'm sorry. I *knew* she wasn't no whore."

He was sitting around a table with several players and their wives in Hot Springs in 1923. "Excuse me," he said, getting up. "I've got to take a piss."

Herb Pennock, very much a gentleman and also very much a friend of Ruth's, followed Babe out to the men's room. "Babe," he said, "you shouldn't say that in front of the ladies."

"Say what?"

"Say piss like that. You just don't say that in front of women. You should say, 'Excuse me, I have to go to the bathroom,' or something like that."

"I'm sorry, Herb."

"Okay."

They went back to the table and sat down, and Ruth said to the women, "I'm sorry I said piss."

After Ruth came back from a trip to the Far East in the 1930s, a friend who had just been married came to visit, bringing along his new wife. Babe told them stories about the trip, including a long anecdote about a game in Manila.

"Then these Hawaiians tried to tell us—" he began.

"Not Hawaiians, Babe," said Mrs. Ruth, "Filipinos."

"Yeah, Filipinos." He went on and after another couple of sentences said, "Then this little Hawaiian—"

"Filipino," said Mrs. Ruth.

"Filipino. This little guy came over . . ." He went on to the end of the story, laughed uproariously and said, "Those Hawaiians thought they were pulling a fast one on us."

"Filipinos."

"Oh, Christ, call them Eskimos. Who gives a goddamn?"

He told another story about sitting next to Lefty Gomez' wife at dinner one evening on the trip. "They brought out this great caviar, and they started it around the table from one side of me. Lefty's wife was sitting on the other side. It goes all the way around the table, and there's only a little left when it gets to her, and she takes it all. 'Oh, I love this stuff,' she said. So I asked the waiter to bring some more, and they bring it and it goes around the table again, and damn if she didn't take the last bit again. She was sitting there eating it on bits of toast. My God, she ate so much of that stuff she looked like a seagull eating shit."

The friend was wondering uneasily how his lovely new wife was taking this, and he got Ruth to talking instead about his trophies. Babe gave them a quick guided tour. He pointed to one silver cup and said, "Look at this one. You know what I got it for?"

"No, what?"

"I won first place in a farting contest. Honest. Read the writing on it. Boy, I had to down a lot of beer and limburger to win that one."

The friend left the apartment a bit shaken. In the elevator he looked nervously at his wife. But she seemed exhilarated.

"What a fascinating man," she said.

"Ruth's language *was* pretty bad," Frick said, "but, you know, it's a remarkable thing. My wife is a very genteel lady, *very* genteel, yet she always enjoyed seeing Ruth, and we were with him a great deal in those years. In all the time we knew him, I cannot recall one instance when he ever said anything crude or obscene in front of her." Meany said he was with Ruth at a party on Long Island when Babe decided to tell a joke, something he rarely did. Before he began, he insisted that all the women leave the room. And the anecdote turned out to be fairly innocuous.

Many stories about Ruth were turned into legend by the encrustations of time. Here are three of them, with a factual basis for each. The story of Johnny Sylvester is one of the most famous in Ruth lore. The simplest version says that Johnny, a young boy, lay dying in a hospital. Ruth came to visit him and promised him he would hit a home run for him that afternoon. And he did, which so filled Johnny with the will to live that he miraculously recovered. The facts are parallel, if not so melodramatic. In 1926 eleven-year-old Johnny Sylvester was badly hurt in a fall from a horse and was hospitalized. To cheer him up, a friend of Johnny's father brought him baseballs autographed by players on the Yankees and the Cardinals just before the World Series that year, as well as a promise from Ruth that he would hit a home run for him. Ruth hit four homers in the Series, and after it was over paid a visit to Johnny in the hospital, which thrilled the boy. The visit was given the tears-and-lump-in-the-throat treatment in the press, and the legend was born. After that, few writers reviewing Ruth's career failed to mention a dying boy and the home run that saved his life.

The following spring Ruth was sitting with a couple of baseball writers when a man came up to him and said, "Mr. Ruth, I'm Johnny Sylvester's uncle. I just want to thank you again for what you did for him."

"That's all right," Ruth said, "glad to do it. How is Johnny?"

"He's fine. He's home, and everything looks okay."

"That's good," said Ruth. "Give him my regards."

The man left. Ruth watched him walk away and said, "Now who the hell is Johnny Sylvester?"

There is a legend that Ruth once hit a ball so hard that it went between the pitcher's legs and over the center fielder's head for a home run. In 1927 the Yankees played the Senators when Hod Lisenbee was pitching for Washington and Tris Speaker was playing center field. Lisenbee was in his first year in the majors and Speaker in his next to last. There was a runner on second taking a big lead, although he was keeping his eyes on both the shortstop and the second baseman. Speaker began a favorite maneuver of his: sneaking in from center field toward second base in the hopes of getting a quick throw from the pitcher and picking the runner off second. Lisenbee ignored Speaker's move and threw to the plate. Ruth hit a low line drive directly back at the pitcher, who leaped and lifted his right leg frantically to avoid being hit by it. The ball ticked the underside of his thigh as it went past. It hit the ground a few feet past second, took a huge bounce and went over Speaker's head. One of the other outfielders retrieved it, but Ruth got an extra-base hit out of it—not a home run.

And there is a legend, seldom printed but often talked about in baseball circles, that says Leo Durocher stole Babe Ruth's watch, which is not true. What is true is that Ruth did not like Durocher. When he saw Leo, a rookie, wearing a tuxedo in the lobby of a spring-training hotel, Ruth asked with considerable distaste, "Who's the little gink in the monkey suit?" He resented Leo's cockiness, and the two never got along, although Leo tried to—at first.

Durocher was in a hotel elevator late one night with a couple of other players when Ruth got on. "Oh, am I drunk," said the Babe. "Somebody's got to undress me and put me to bed. You guys have to help me."

The other players backed away rapidly, but Leo said, "I'll help you, pal."

"Thank you, pal," Ruth said. Leo helped him off the elevator and down the hall to Babe's room. The next morning Ruth decided that he was missing something—money in one version of the story, his watch in another. Although he was drunk on the town the night before and had been in the Lord knows what places, he blamed Durocher. As Leo said, in a half-angry, half-mocking tone, "Jesus Christ, if I was going to steal anything from him I'd steal his god-damned Packard."

Ruth continued to harass Durocher. One night on the train as he was getting undressed by his berth, he called to Durocher.

"Hey, Leo, you want to see something?" He held up a glittering bit of jewelry. "See that, Leo? Isn't that beautiful? That cost me seventy-five hundred bucks, Leo. I'm going to give it to Claire when we get to New York. Tonight I'm putting it under my pillow. And, Leo, I want it to be there when I wake up in the morning."

After that, Durocher disliked Ruth as much as Babe disliked him, although in a year or so their paths parted. After the 1929 season Durocher was sold out of the American League to Cincinnati. Explaining the sale, which was made when he was manager, Shawkey said, "You'll never see a better fielding shortstop than Leo, but he couldn't hit. And he was a little too much of an individual."

Ruth did not like Ty Cobb much either, primarily because of Cobb's bench jockeying, which was cruel and humorless. When the story about Ruth never changing his underwear got around the league during his early years with the Red Sox, Cobb would say the same thing whenever he saw Ruth: "You fellows smell something around here? Oh, hello, Babe." Ruth's usual reply to Cobb's gibes was a stream of obscenity. Cobb and some of the other Tigers were riding Ruth about the 1922 Series, and Cobb said, "We hear that little Johnny Rawlings ran you out of the Giant clubhouse. Is that true?" Ruth said, "It ain't a goddamned bit true, and you sons of bitches can go fuck yourselves." Cobb said that when Ruth extended himself he had a vocabulary that stood alone, even in the purple atmosphere of dugout and clubhouse. Ruth and Cobb had a fight of sorts on the field in 1924 when a free-for-all broke out between the

Yankees and Tigers, but they were separated before anything much happened. Ruth was not much of a brawler. His quick temper got him into a lot of mixups, but, according to Meany, he never won a fight. He never really lost one either. He had a lot of No Decisions. He seldom stayed angry very long.

Ruth's tendency to get into trouble, particularly during his first decade in the majors, gave rise to a fairly widespread opinion that he was subnormal mentally (Ban Johnson said he had the mind of a fifteen-year-old) or else was so primitive that he could not accept a moral code. "He was an animal," Dugan said. "He ate a hat once. He did. A straw hat. Took a bite out of it and ate it."

But Ernie Shore said, "You have to remember, he had grown up in that Catholic reformatory. When they let him out it was like turning a wild animal out of a cage. He wanted to *go* everyplace and *see* everything and *do* everything."

"Ruth recognized the difference between right and wrong," Frick said. "What he did not recognize, or could not accept, was the right of society to tell him what he should do, or not do."

He had a perceptive understanding of things in certain areas and, in his own way, a refreshing sense of taste. When he met Red Grange after the Illinois football hero turned professional in the mid-1920s, Ruth said to him, "Kid, don't ever forget two things I'm going to tell you. One, don't believe everything that's written about you. Two, don't pick up too many checks." Someone introduced him to Max Schmeling when he and the then heavyweight champion of the world happened to be riding on the same train. After Schmeling returned to his own compartment, a friend said to Ruth, "You should have asked him for his autograph." Ruth said, "Who the hell wants to collect that crap?" Frick said, "He drank a great deal and he was a ladies' man, but he never led a young ballplayer astray and he never took advantage of an innocent girl."

He understood clearly what he was doing when he batted, despite his habit of saying, "I just keep swinging," when people asked him the secret of hitting home runs. Once, seriously discussing his batting, he said, "I swing as hard as I can, and I try to swing right through the ball. In boxing, your fist usually stops when you hit a man, but it's possible to hit so hard that your fist doesn't stop. I try to follow through the same way. The harder you grip the bat, the more you can swing it through the ball, and the farther the ball will go. I swing big, with everything I've got. I hit big or I miss big. I like to live as big as I can." He held his bat at the very end, with his right hand curled over the knob. He had a big callus in the palm of his right hand as a result, along with the usual calluses that all batters have on their fingers and thumbs.

"He liked anything connected with playing baseball," Frick said, "but he liked home runs best. Whenever he hit one, he laughed. Sometimes before a game he'd say, 'I feel hitterish today. I'm due to hit one.' And if he did hit one, he'd talk about it long after the game."

He could be thoughtlessly cruel at times. Bud Mulvey, whose family used to own a substantial part of the Brooklyn Dodgers and still retains an interest in the Los Angeles Dodgers, remembered a baseball writers' dinner he was taken to as a boy. Ruth, retired by then, was there, and before the dinner he began to fool with Jackie Farrell, a tiny man literally half Ruth's weight, who later worked in the Yankee publicity department. Mulvey watched in distaste as Ruth playfully twisted Farrell's arm. "Jackie was really in pain," Mulvey said, "and Ruth was roaring with laughter. I never could like him after that."

Bob Condon, whose father knew Charlie McManus, the Yankee Stadium supervisor, was sometimes a backstage guest at the Stadium when he was a boy, which was relatively late in the Babe's career. Once, while a game was going on outside on the field, Condon was playing by himself in an open area under the stands behind the Yankee dugout. Ruth left the game for some reason, possibly a minor injury, and came angrily up the runway from the dugout. As he did, the ball Condon was playing with took a freak bounce directly into Ruth's path. The boy dove for it and fell flat in front of the Babe, who irritably shoved him out of the way with his foot. Kick may be too strong a word for the action, but substantially that is what Ruth did. "Stay out of the Babe's way," someone warned the tearful boy.

Alice Doubleday Rhodes recalled a time when Ruth played an exhibition in her small town when she was about ten. For some reason she accepted a dare to get Ruth's autograph, and well before the game she sneaked onto the field and walked to the Yankee bench. She had to ask, "Which one is Babe Ruth?" and this, to her confusion, made everyone laugh. He was pointed out and when she walked over to him he said, pleasantly enough, "You want to see me, sister?" She handed him her school notebook and a pen, a brand-new pen that had just been given to her for her birthday. "Here," she said. He signed his name, in "a beautiful, even hand" and gave her back her schoolbook and pen. "There you are, sister," he said. "Now don't go home and sell it." But she had promised to get autographs for her schoolmates too. She handed book and pen back to him and said, "Write some more. Write on all the lines." The other players broke up laughing. Ruth shrugged and slowly wrote his name on line after line until the page was filled. "That okay now?" he said, not smiling. He handed her the book and, looking out at the field, absentmindedly put the pen in his own pocket. Her marvelous birthday pen. She did not know what to do. Ruth looked at her coldly. "Something else on your mind, little girl?" he asked. She shook her head and said, "No, sir," and left. Chagrined and not a little afraid, it took her some time to get up the courage to tell her father what had happened, and she was totally unable to understand his hilarity when she did tell him. "Babe Ruth swiped your pen?" he howled.

Yet his affection for children was genuine, and it remained with him all his life. In 1943 he played a round of golf in the rain at the Commonwealth Country Club near Boston. As he was teeing up on the first hole he noticed two boys staring through a chain-link fence.

"Hey," he called to them. "You want to follow me around? It won't be any drier but it'll be more fun. You want to?"

The kids nodded. "Show them how to get into this joint," Ruth said to Russ Hale, the club pro. He waited until the boys reached the tee before he hit his drive, and he walked down the fairway with one arm around each, talking. He played nine holes in the rain, most of the time laughing and joking with the other men in his foursome but always returning to the kids to make sure they were enjoying themselves.

A decade earlier Jack Redding, who was to become librarian of the National Baseball Library at Cooperstown, caddied for him at Wheatley Hills on Long Island. "He'd give us a two-dollar tip if he won, a dollar and a half if he lost," Redding said. Was that a good tip? "Hell, yes," Redding said. "The usual tip was a quarter, or at best a half dollar. And on the thirteenth hole, where the refreshment stand was, that's where you tested your man. Some golfers would buy you a soft drink, some wouldn't buy you anything. Ruth always said, 'Get whatever you want.' "

He was a frequent and interested visitor to hospitals, orphanages, children's wards and the like. He could create a holiday spirit in a ward merely by being himself. Many of his visits were well publicized—Walsh saw to that—but they were not done for publicity. Ruth always, or almost always, made himself available to the press, but the publicity was coincidental. After someone made fun of all the newspaper copy he received from such visits, he avoided mention of them, and for every one that got public notice several more did not.

Stories about the time and trouble he took to call on the sick and distressed are innumerable. Even when he was ill himself, he continued the practice. A year or so before he died, racked with pain from the cancer that was to kill him, he went with Paul Carey to visit a man who had gone blind. After they left, Ruth said of the blind man, "Some guys get all the bad breaks, don't they?"

He liked seeing children the best. He enjoyed them. He was comfortable with them. "He's just a big kid" was a common description of him, and perhaps the only time he was truly at ease was when he was with children. With them there were no rules, no authority, no need to apologize, to explain, to explode, to drink, to fuck, to prove himself over and over. Without thinking about it, he knew who they were and they knew who he was. They got along. Like a child, he did not like to wait or plan for the right moment. He did not like to wait for anything. "It might rain tomorrow," he would say.

He did things impulsively, the way a child does. Children are emotionally neutral to things that deeply affect adults. Without malice, they casually hurt the feelings of a close friend. Without love, they do an act of exceptional thoughtfulness for a casual acquaintance. In his novel *Stop-Time* Frank Conroy wrote, "Like all children, I was unsentimental." Hoyt said of Ruth, "Babe was not a sentimentalist and generally made no outward demonstration of affection either by word or action."

This may explain a curious thing that Paul Carey, his great friend, said when he was asked about Ruth's feelings toward Claire. "I don't think the Babe really loved Claire," Carey said. "I don't think he really loved anybody."

CHAPTER 29

Death of Helen:
Marriage to Claire

On Friday night, January 11, 1929, a fire broke out in the home of Dr. Edward H. Kinder, a dentist who lived at 47 Quincy Street in Watertown, Massachusetts, one of the big towns around Boston that are really part of the city. Someone passing by saw the flames and called the fire department.

When the arriving firemen asked if anyone was in the house, neighbors said fearfully that Mrs. Kinder probably was. Dr. Kinder went to the fights at Boston Garden on Friday nights, they said, and their little girl was away at boarding school. When the flames were under some semblance of control, Fire Captain John Kelley made his way to the second floor of the small frame house. Crawling on hands and knees to avoid as best he could the heat and smoke, he pushed open a bedroom door. A woman in a nightgown lay on the floor near the door. Kelley grabbed her arm and pulled her out of the room and with another fireman carried her downstairs and outside. The firemen tried to revive her, but she was dead.

Dr. Kinder was paged at Boston Garden and told to return home at once. When he reached Quincy Street and saw his house and heard what had happened, he was stunned. He barely answered the questions put to him by Dr. George West, the medical examiner.

The death certificate signed by Dr. West said the dead woman's name was Helen Kinder, that she was a housewife and that her husband was Edward H. Kinder. This information appeared in newspaper stories tucked away on inside pages of the next day's Boston newspapers.

Dr. Kinder was stunned that night for another reason, beyond the fire and the death, for Helen Kinder was really Helen Ruth, and he knew the Babe would have to be told. Kinder and Helen had been living together for two years—the Sudbury farm, which was in Helen's name, had been sold—and his family was under the impression that they had been married in Montreal. Helen and Dorothy moved into the Watertown house with Kinder after he bought it on May 31, 1927, and the couple was listed in the Watertown city directory as man and wife. Kinder, a veteran of World War I, went to Tufts Dental College after the war, graduated in 1924, taught for a couple of years and set up practice late in 1926. He had one office in Back Bay Boston and another in Watertown. He and Helen were accepted without comment in the neighborhood, and Dorothy, about six when they moved in, was popular with other children. At the time of her mother's death she was at the Assumption School in Wellesley, Massachusetts. One wonders why she was away at school when she was not yet eight. Perhaps it is significant that four months earlier, on September 10, 1928, Helen was admitted to Carney Hospital in South Boston with another of her nervous breakdowns. The hospital recommended that she be transferred to Ring Sanitarium in Arlington, but on September 18 Helen left the hospital abruptly and returned to Watertown.

Kinder had remodeled the Watertown house, adding a sun porch downstairs and a sleeping porch upstairs. According to the fire examiners, the electric wiring added then was improperly installed. Circuits were overloaded, and fuses were too strong; when the circuits overheated, the fuses did not blow. The fire began in the living room near a wall outlet and went up through the wall into the floor of the bedroom, where it burned a hole so large that a radiator fell through to the floor below.

Helen's body was taken to an undertaker in Newton, and Kinder went to his parents' home in Boston. Plans were made to hold the funeral services on Sunday morning and the burial in the Kinder family plot in St. Joseph's cemetery in West Roxbury. On Saturday morning, according to his brother William, Kinder went to New York to find Babe Ruth and tell him what had happened to his wife. However, Ruth did not learn anything until very late Saturday evening, more than twenty-four hours after the fire, when he was with Claire at a small party at Joe Dugan's house in suburban Scarsdale, New York. He cried on the phone when he heard the news and decided to go to Boston at once. It was too late for the midnight train from Grand Central, but he was able to catch the through train from Washington at Penn Station at one-fifteen A.M. He phoned Boston and spoke to a friend named Arthur Crowley, asking him to meet the train. At seven-thirty in the morning, when Ruth arrived at Back Bay Station, Crowley was there. Ruth was tired and somber.

"It's pretty rough, Arthur. What do you know about it?"

Crowley knew nothing beyond what Ruth had told him. Babe wanted to go directly to Watertown, but Crowley persuaded him to check into a hotel first. They went to the Brunswick Hotel and got the same fifth-floor suite that Babe occupied when the Yankees were in Boston. At nine o'clock they went out to mass at St. Cecilia's Church, where Ruth, his head bowed, fingered a large brown wooden rosary all through mass. Back in the hotel they ordered breakfast in the suite, but Babe was not able to eat. He paced back and forth nervously, smoking cigarette after cigarette. He phoned another friend, a lawyer named John Feeney, who went immediately to Watertown and spoke to the police and then came to the hotel. He gave Ruth details of the fire and sketched a rough plan of the house to show him where and how Helen had died. Babe asked him to go to South Boston, where Helen's widowed mother, Mrs. Joanna Woodford, lived on West Fourth Street with two other daughters, Catherine and Nora. Feeney did, and brought Catherine and Nora to the hotel. They spoke to Babe and then went with

Feeney to Watertown, where they assured Police Chief John Mill-more that the death certificate was inaccurate and that Helen Kinder was indeed their sister and the wife of Babe Ruth.

Meantime, Babe, who had been awake for more than twenty-four hours, lay down in the bedroom of the hotel suite and slept fitfully for two or three hours. Feeney returned to the hotel with the Wood-ford sisters and then took them on home to South Boston before coming back to the hotel. By now the newspapers were aware of the story, and reporters jammed into the corridor outside Ruth's suite. Inside, Babe and Feeney worked on a statement, Feeney writing it out in longhand. He wrote several versions before it was the way Babe wanted it. At three o'clock they admitted the reporters. When all were inside and quiet, Ruth read the brief statement in a low voice. "My wife and I have not lived together for the last three years," he said. "During that time I have seldom met her. I've done all that I can to comply with her wishes. Her death is a great shock to me." That was it. When he finished, the fact-hungry reporters started asking questions, but Ruth, his voice quavering, said, "I won't answer any questions. I don't want to say anything more." He left the hotel with his friends and did not return that night.

The next day, Monday, more than two days after the fire, the revelation that the unknown Mrs. Kinder was the real Mrs. Ruth made sensational headlines. The accounts dwelled on the fact that she had been living with a man not her husband, and some tried to make something of the apparent discrepancies in Kinder's account. He usually went to the fights with his brother, but his brother said his seat was empty Friday night. Where had he been? Why had he informed the medical examiner that Helen was his wife if, as his brother said, he had gone to New York to tell Ruth? Why did his family believe he was married to Helen if he was not? He had disappeared Saturday morning. Had he really gone to New York, as his brother said? Where was he now?

Dr. Kinder appeared voluntarily at the Watertown police station Monday afternoon to clarify things. He had not "disappeared," he said, but had been staying with his parents. He had not gone to New

York but sent word to Ruth through a friend of Babe's. He had not been with his brother Friday night because he was sitting with James Coughlin, an old friend from the 101st Regiment. He did not remember telling the medical examiner anything after the fire, much less that Helen was his wife. He and Helen were not married and he had never told anyone, including his family, that they were. If anyone had made that suggestion, he said, it must have been Helen. And with that, Dr. Kinder retired again from public view.

The plans for a Sunday morning service and burial in the Kinder plot—the grave had been dug open—were canceled after Feeney spoke to the Watertown police, and the district attorney ordered the body, already embalmed, to be returned to the medical examiner for an autopsy. It was quickly determined that the cause of death given on the original certificate, "suffocation and incineration," was correct, but the Woodford family in the meantime had been talking freely with the press, and Helen's brother William, arriving late on the scene, said sternly that if there had been foul play he wanted everything brought out in the open. No one else in the family or among the police had raised the question, but William's comments were well publicized and the district attorney ordered a second, more detailed autopsy, even though he said flatly that there was no indication of anything but accidental death.

On Monday morning Catherine and Nora Woodford, accompanied by two police officers, identified Helen's body at the morgue. When they came out they were surrounded by reporters, but they would not answer any questions. "Leave the talking to the big boy," one of them said. Babe was saying almost nothing, but Arthur Crowley told reporters again that Babe had long been separated from Helen (he said three and a half years, which meant since just after the tearful scene at the Concourse Plaza in August 1925) but that whenever Babe was in Boston he would see her and take her to dinner. Crowley discussed new funeral plans with William Woodford and Mrs. Josephine McCarthy, another sister of Helen's, and they decided the wake would be at the Woodford home Monday night and Tuesday, the funeral mass at St. Augustine's in South

Boston on Wednesday and the burial that day in Old Calvary Cemetery in South Boston. The reporters were still pressing to talk to Ruth himself about the details of his wife's death, and late Monday afternoon, after Babe came back to the hotel, an impromptu press conference was held in the living room of his suite. Ruth sat in a chair, his hands fidgeting in his lap, his eyes red. He was wearing a black suit.

"Boys, I'm in a terrible way," he said, his voice low. "This thing has licked me. The shock has been terrible." Tears came to his eyes and his voice shook. "I hold nothing against my wife. She was the victim of circumstances. I still love her. I have fine memories of her." His voice broke, and there was a pause. "What I'm going to say I can say in very few words." He paused again and took a gulp of air. "Please leave my wife alone. Let her stay dead." Silence for a moment. "That's all I'm going to say."

He took a handkerchief and wiped his eyes and sat looking at the floor. After a moment or two one of the reporters said, "Can you tell us when and where you and Mrs. Ruth were married?"

Ruth lifted his head. "Yes, I certainly can," he said, his voice suddenly strong and calm. "We were married October 17, 1914, in Ellicott City, Maryland. And the priest who married us was Father Dolan."

"What about Dorothy, your daughter?"

Ruth shook his head. "I'd rather not say anything about the little girl."

The interview was over.

The medical examiner could not release Helen's body until reports of the second autopsy were complete, and the wake and the funeral were postponed again. The reports came through at last on Wednesday (again verifying the original cause of death) and the body was released to an undertaker in South Boston. Later Wednesday it was brought to the Woodford home. Hundreds of people moved in and out of the house during the evening. There were floral pieces from Lou Gehrig, Colonel Ruppert, Miller Huggins, Herb Pennock. Ruth came to the still-crowded house shortly after midnight, stayed a few minutes looking down at his dead wife, and left.

The funeral service was conducted in the house Thursday morning by Father Richard Burke of St. Augustine's and lasted only seven minutes. A memorial mass would be said the next morning at the church. There was no music. When the procession left the house for Calvary Cemetery, Ruth rode in a car with Helen's mother and her sister Josephine. Arthur Crowley, John Feeney and two other friends of Babe's were the pallbearers.

It was raining slightly when poor Helen, as upset and confused in death as she had been in life, was finally laid to rest. She was thirty-one.

Helen's death cleared the way for Babe and Claire to be married. They had known each other for almost six years, and for the past three had been very close. Ruth was on good terms with Claire's mother, went hunting with her brothers when they were around, and liked her little girl. It was as though he had found an instant family, the thing he had never really had. He did not fall in love with Claire because of her family, but it certainly filled a need. His own mother had been sick and sometimes unstable. His father was a busy, harassed man who solved a lot of problems by depositing Babe in St. Mary's. He seldom saw his sister. He received considerable attention (not all of it loving) the first few years of his life, as the first child of young parents, and then was abruptly deprived of it. No matter how much personal concern Brother Matthias had for young George, the boy was still one of hundreds at St. Mary's. No wonder he later demanded the attention and affection of the world. Everything exploded into athletic genius and sexual hunger, and he was forever seeking approval and gratification. This, of course, is cocktail-party psychiatry, but isn't it reasonable to suggest that Huggins, in clamping down so hard on Ruth in 1925, became in a way his father, and that Claire, who for all her physical and social attractiveness was sometimes a nag, became his mother? He was still free-wheeling in the fun and frolic part of his life, but after 1925 he was at least concerned with what both thought. There was no more trouble between him and Huggins, and despite occasional carpings and complaints at Claire there was never a serious rift or a question of separation.

What about Barrow as a father figure? Well, Barrow, despite his sternness, could not be to Ruth what Huggins was, because he never wholly accepted or admired Ruth. To Barrow, a ballplayer, even one as outstanding as the Babe, was supposed to be subservient to management. A complete egoist, he was never able fully to comprehend what Ruth was. Barrow was a strong executive and a smart baseball man who knew how to run a ball club. The first great Yankee team was pretty well assembled when Barrow joined the club late in 1920, but he was the man whose astute trades and purchases, particularly for pitchers, strengthened it even further. And he rebuilt it twice, first in 1925–26 and again in the 1930s. He was a baseball genius, but he was a tyrant, a despot, who deferred only to Colonel Ruppert. Once from his box in Yankee Stadium— this was in the flapper era of the 1920s—he saw a woman smoking a cigarette in the grandstand. That was outrageous to a man whose ideas of behavior were established before 1900. He called Charlie McManus, the stadium supervisor, and said imperiously, "Tell that woman to stop smoking." Angry at something the gentlemanly Bill Slocum wrote, he punched Slocum and knocked him across a desk.

It took Barrow a long time to get used to Ruth's home runs. On September 9, 1919, when Ruth was charging toward his first home run record and had the whole country excited about it, Barrow made one of the more impressive bad predictions of all time. He said in Boston, "After Babe has satisfied himself by hanging up a record for home runs that never will be touched, he will become a .400 hitter. He wants to establish a record of 30 or 35 home runs this year, and when he has done that he will start getting a lot of base hits that will win us more games than his home runs. He will just meet the ball and hit it to left field as well as Ty Cobb. He will not be trying to knock the ball out of the lot after this season. He will be content with his record because it will be far and away out of the reach of any other player the game is likely to develop."

Asked who the best of all baseball players was, Barrow always said, "Cobb was the finest hitter and Ruth the greatest slugger and gate attraction, but Wagner was the best ballplayer." Wagner was Barrow's discovery, and he never let anyone forget it, even when Ruth was winning pennants for him. But Miller Huggins, for all the arguments and fines, did like and admire Ruth, and once he had established his authority over him things went smoothly. As for Claire, she was beautiful, but so was Helen. She was presumably a splendid wife and partner in love, but surely in his adventures in bed Ruth had known splendid lovers. She was bright and intelligent and sophisticated, but so were other women Ruth had known. What she had beyond all this, I suggest, is what he wanted: She loved him in the demanding yet tolerant way that mothers do, perhaps bossing and nagging and correcting, but leaving no doubt that she loved him all the time despite his faults. She was strong and forceful, and she was his.

They were married when Ruth came north from spring training in 1929, three months after Helen's death. It was more or less an open secret that they would be married, although when he was asked if the rumors were true, Ruth said, "It's news to me." Pressed on the subject, he said, "Everybody knows all about my plans but me. I'm not getting married today, I'm not getting married this year. I haven't seen Mrs. Hodgson."

One of his friends among the sportswriters called on Ruth at Claire's apartment a few days before the season began. Ruth was living at the Hotel Alamac, but he was very much at home in the Hodgson apartment. He was wearing bedroom slippers and had a lounging robe over his trousers and shirt.

"Congratulations," said the friend.

"What for?"

"For getting a marriage license."

"My God, did they find that out?" He conceded that he and Claire would be getting married soon. "But, say, tell them fellows down on the sidewalk to lay off the pictures, will you? The girl's afraid of them damn flashlights."

Opening day of the season was April 17. Very early in the morning, before six o'clock, Babe and Claire and their friends, Mr. and Mrs. George Lovell of Scarsdale, arrived at St. Gregory's Roman Catholic Church on West 90th Street. It was raining, but a dozen or so neighborhood kids, who had their own sources of information, were waiting outside the church. With a sense of the importance of the moment, they did nothing but say, solemnly, "Hello, Babe," as the party passed. "Hello, boys," said Ruth, just as solemnly. Inside, by prearrangement, they met Father William M. Hughes, who married them. Babe was thirty-five, Claire not quite twenty-nine.

Afterwards they returned to the apartment, where they were joined by friends and a few reporters. "Where are you going on your honeymoon?" a reporter asked. Claire said, "We're not going on a honeymoon. We're going to go to work and win another pennant."

The party kept on all day but so, happily, did the rain, and the opening game was postponed until the next day. Claire went to the ballpark for the first time as Mrs. Babe Ruth. She sat in a box near the Yankee dugout, and when Ruth hit a home run he tipped his hat to her as he came around third base and blew her a kiss before he disappeared into the dugout.

"You'd better stop blowing kisses," she told him, "or you're going to be hearing about it from everybody in the league."

They brought Dorothy down from her school in Massachusetts to live with them. In a novel legal action, Claire adopted Dorothy, while Babe adopted Julia, and the two girls, some years apart in age, became, in effect, sisters. Claire was soon functioning as Babe's manager as well as his wife. She had been a strong influence on him for years anyway. Before he met her he had worn extravagantly expensive clothes, loud garish things, including a diamond horseshoe tie pin. Under her influence he continued to buy expensive clothes, but they were far more tasteful. After 1925 he was probably the best dressed man in baseball, except for that cap.

Claire put a control on his eating and drinking, at least at home. She did not cook herself, but she supervised his diet, cutting out starches and desserts but giving him plenty of meat and vegetables.

She introduced him to orange juice. "He didn't want it at first," she said in a 1934 interview. " 'Gee, Claire,' he said, 'I can't drink that stuff. It gives me indigestion.' I said, 'Nonsense,' and now he wouldn't be without a double portion every morning. He realizes now that mother knows best." She cut down on his drinking, deftly erecting a barrier that kept many of his old carousing friends out in the cold. She began to travel with him on the road trips the Yankees took and always went to spring training, which she did with the sanction of Ruppert and Barrow, who felt her constant presence would deter Babe from kicking over the traces. She and Babe always had a compartment on the team train (she would stay in it, discreetly out of sight, most of the time) and a suite in out-of-town hotels. The club, although approving, did not pick up the tab for any of this, which irritated Claire, who had a fine appreciation of money.

She put a hold-down on Babe's spending. They lived well and did not stint, but she kept an eye on where the money went. She took care of the bills and controlled the family checkbook. When Babe wanted cash, he would say, "Clara, write me a $50 check. I gotta get some cigars and a few things," Claire wrote so many $50 checks, she said in her autobiography, that she later used his endorsements of them as autographs to send to interested fans. But, she also said, the $50 checks at least cut down on the lavish tips he was in the habit of handing out when he carried hundreds of dollars around in his pocket.

Ruth's income was approaching a peak when they married, and despite the impact of the Depression, which struck before he and Claire were married a year, it remained high. Christy Walsh was still drumming up business ("I can't do anything without consulting my business manager," Ruth would tell those who came to him with deals. "You'll have to call him in New York"), but equally important were the friendships he came to develop with Paul Carey and Melvyn Gordon Lowenstein in New York and Emery C. Perry in Chicago, who watched over his financial situation and kept it healthy.

His salary had been raised to $70,000 a year in 1927, when he signed a three-year contract, and he was in the final year of that contract in 1929. He was thirty-five years old, but he was still at the height of his powers, and when the Yankees started the 1929 season by winning 13 of their first 17 games it looked as though the team was still strong too and was going to win a fourth straight pennant. But the Yankees went into a bad slump, fell behind the Philadelphia Athletics and never seriously threatened the Athletics the rest of the season. And Ruth hurt his wrist in May and developed a bad chest cold. He missed several games early in June as the cold grew worse. On June 7 he was admitted to St. Vincent's for examination, and after the doctors reported that there were heart murmurs, a rumor spread that he had died of a heart attack. Ruth came home from the hospital the next day and had the fun, almost obligatory in such circumstances, of saying, "I feel pretty good for a dead man." But he was told to rest for a while, and on June 9 he and Claire went to Maryland and spent a week on the Chesapeake near Annapolis, resting, fishing, lying in the sun. He took his own time coming back to New York, spending one day in Baltimore playing croquet and another in Washington visiting friends. On Tuesday, June 18, he took batting practice and on Wednesday he played a few innings. Not until June 20 was he back in the lineup to stay. He had been out for seventeen days, and when he returned, Gehrig was far in front in the home run race, with 19 to Babe's ten. But Ruth hit six in twelve days and by August 1 had 24 to Gehrig's 26. By September 1 he had 40, which means he hit 30 homers in ten weeks, and he ended the season with 46, nine ahead of Gehrig.

As for the Yankees, they finished 18 games behind the Athletics. Meusel was through as an outfielder, Dugan was gone, Koenig had lost the rare skills of 1926, 1927 and 1928, Pennock and Hoyt were no longer important pitchers, and Huggins, depressed at the way his team was going, was deathly ill. During the summer he developed an ugly carbuncle on his face below his eye and kept picking at it nervously. Three times he missed games because of illness and on Friday, September 20, he entered the hospital. The carbuncle was a symptom of erysipelas. His condition grew rapidly worse and five days later, on Wednesday afternoon, he died. The Yankees were playing in Boston, and the news reached the ballpark just as the fifth inning ended. Players from both teams gathered at home plate and observed a minute of silence as the flag was lowered to half mast. Ruth, asked for a statement after the game, said, "It's one of those things you can't talk about much. You know what I thought of Miller Huggins, and you know what I owe to him." He cried in the clubhouse, as did several of the players. When Tom Meany reported this by phone to his paper in New York, a copyreader said, "Come on, kid, stop overwriting." Meany said, "I can't help it. They were crying."

The Yankees came from Boston to attend services in New York. Huggins' three coaches, O'Leary, Shawkey and Art Fletcher, were pallbearers, along with Ruth, Gehrig, Lazzeri, Combs and Pennock. The body was taken to Cincinnati for burial. Pennock and O'Leary went along to represent the Yankee players. Barrow and Ruppert stayed in New York.

CHAPTER 30

The $80,000 Salary: A Better Year than Hoover

Art Fletcher, a Yankee coach who had played shortstop for Mc-Graw, ran the club for the handful of games left in the 1929 season after Huggins' death, but when Barrow asked him to become the manager on a permanent basis, he said no. He preferred to continue as coach, without the headaches of running the club. Ruth wanted very much to be named manager, but Barrow turned to Shawkey, who had been a coach under Huggins after his pitching days ended and who had managed in the minors. "Shawkey deserves the chance," he told Ruth, mentioning the new manager's apprenticeship as coach and minor leaguer. Ruth was not happy about it. He liked Shawkey and he grudgingly accepted the *fait accompli*, but he decided that as long as his contract was up and he needed a new one, he would hit the Yankees for a lot more money.

He worked hard again that winter in Artie McGovern's gym and before he went south to spring training early in 1930 he told Ruppert he wanted $100,000. Ruppert refused out of hand, offering only a $5000 raise to $75,000. Ruth turned this down, and for the first time since his 1919 dispute with Frazee he became a serious holdout. Walsh composed a letter for Babe's signature, detailing Ruth's financial situation and noting that "I'm good for $25,000 a year for life even if I quit baseball today." It was sent to the New York newspapers and to the Yankees. It received considerable play in the papers, but in the Yankee office it was ignored.

Ruth and Claire went to Florida and stayed at the Jungle Club in St. Petersburg, where Ruppert was staying too, and he worked out every day with the ball club. But the salary talks remained at an impasse. Babe came down to $85,000, but on a three-year contract, and Ruppert came up to $80,000 on two (and agreed to return the $5000 fine Huggins had slapped on Ruth in 1925), but that was as close as they came. Ruth was restless, and the night before the first exhibition game of the spring he felt particularly low. Things were so different. It was his first Yankee camp without Huggins and his first without a contract signed and in his pocket. He and Claire had some friends in for the evening, Alan Gould of the Associated Press among them, and Babe got to talking about the game the next day. Gould said, "Are you actually going to play, even though you're not signed?"

"Why not?"

"Why not? Well, suppose you break a leg? You think Ruppert is going to give you $85,000 then? Or even $80,000?"

"I never thought of that," Babe said. Later he got to mulling about it. He had a few drinks, not many, but enough to get his naturally impulsive nature into gear. By God, he decided, he wasn't going to break his leg in an exhibition game for nothing. He made up his mind. If he did not have a signed contract by noon the next day, he was going to hand in his uniform, quit the squad and go back to New York.

Word of Ruth's decision reached Dan Daniel of the *New York Telegram*. Daniel wrote the story and sent it to his paper, which played it big in its first edition late the next morning. About the time New Yorkers were reading that Ruth would quit the Yankees unless he signed by noon that day, Daniel and Frick and a couple of other writers ran into him near the Jungle Club. It was a beautiful morning. The sun was shining. Ruth was cheerful.

"What a day," Ruth said. "I hope I hit one this afternoon."

"What do you mean, hit one?" Daniel said. "You're not playing."

"Why not?"

"You can't. You haven't signed. You said you weren't going to play until you signed."

"Oh, that was last night," Ruth said.

"The hell it was last night," Daniel said. "I'm all over page one with it today."

Ruth shrugged. "I'm sorry, Dan. I changed my mind. I decided to stick with the club."

"And leave me holding the well-known bag. You ought to stick with what you said last night."

"Hell, there's no harm done," said Ruth.

"That's what you think," Daniel said. "You ought to stick to your word, Babe. If you're going to play this afternoon, you ought to sign. You and Ruppert aren't that far apart anyway."

Ruth looked at him. "You think I ought to sign?"

"Damn right."

"Okay. All right. Go find Jake, and I'll sign."

The writers deployed. Will Wedge of the *Sun* went to find Colonel Ruppert, who was taking a leisurely walk with an old friend of his named Colonel Alfred W. Wattenberg. Daniel raced to the Western Union office to clear the wires to New York for all the newspapermen. Frick and Slocum, the closest friends Ruth had among the writers, stayed with him to keep him from wandering off. After an interminable time, Wedge came back shepherding the two slow-moving colonels at all deliberate speed. Ruth and Ruppert greeted each other warmly, chatted for a few minutes in private, and Babe agreed to the $80,000 for two years. "What about the fine?" Ruth asked. Ruppert consulted with Barrow, who said, "If it's up to me, the fine stays." Ruth reminded Ruppert that he had promised it, and Ruppert gave in. "If Huggins had lived," he said, "you would not be getting this. But Miller is dead and he won't know."

And so Ruth had a two-year contract at $80,000. The impact of $80,000 in 1930 is lost against the background of the vast amounts paid today's professional stars. But here are verified figures for salaries earned a couple of seasons earlier by the 1927 Yankees, that team of superstars. After Ruth, at $70,000, the next highest paid player was Pennock, at $17,500. Meusel made $13,000, Dugan and Hoyt $12,000, Combs $10,000. Gehrig made $8000, Lazzeri $8000, Koenig $7000. Wilcy Moore, who won 19 games, got $3000. The President of the United States, as stories about Ruth so often point out, was paid $75,000 in 1931. The idea of a ballplayer making more than the President was almost incomprehensible. An apocryphal story, often told, says that someone asked Ruth if he thought it was right for him to be paid more than President Hoover and that Ruth replied, "Why not? I had a better year than he did."

He had a better year in 1930 too, hitting 49 home runs to beat Gehrig handily again, the fourth straight year Lou finished second in homers to the Babe. Ruth had one particularly explosive stretch in May when he hit nine home runs in a week, including three in one game. He had twice hit three in a game in the World Series, but this was the first time he did it in regular season play.

Otherwise it was not a memorable season. Shawkey, a sound baseball man, was faced with the never enviable job of taking a famous manager's place, and he had trouble with some of the players. He and Hoyt quarreled, and Waite and Mark Koenig were traded to Detroit. A bevy of infielders and outfielders tried to fill the gaping holes left behind by Koenig, Dugan and Meusel, without notable success. The pitching was poor. The Yankees finished a lackluster third, and Shawkey was fired. He had not expected to be and in September, after discussing next year's prospects with Ruppert and Barrow, suggested signing his new contract then. But Ruppert said, "No, we'll sign it in the winter, the way we did with Huggins."

As the season ended the Chicago Cubs fired Joe McCarthy, a strong, authoritative manager whom Barrow had long admired, and he sent Paul Krichell to Chicago to sound McCarthy out about managing the Yankees. McCarthy was willing, came to see Barrow and Ruppert in New York and was signed. Shawkey, who knew nothing about this, stopped in at the Yankee offices that same day, saw all the reporters and McCarthy and realized what had happened. The Yankees had a new manager even before the old one knew he was gone. "It was a dirty deal," Shawkey said years later.

Ruth felt the same way, except that he thought he should have been named to succeed Shawkey. He was hurt and bitter that he had been passed over again. "Did they have to go to the National League for a manager?" he kept asking. He went to see Barrow and Ruppert. Barrow seemed almost amused that the undisciplined Ruth was serious about wanting to manage, but Ruppert, always diplomatic, told the Babe that he did not believe in playing managers. He reminded his star player that he had a few good seasons left.

Ruth was hardly mollified. "Speaker was a playing manager," he argued. "Cobb was a playing manager. Hornsby was a playing manager." He resented McCarthy from the beginning and everyone knew it, including McCarthy. But the new manager, a shrewd man, accepted Ruth's antagonism without direct comment or reaction. He had his own ideas on how to run a ball club, and Ruth's flamboyance did not fit in. But he respected Ruth's bat and recognized his enormous popularity, and he saw to it that peace between them, however uneasy, was maintained. Ruth followed his own rules, but this was accepted by the other players. Jimmy Reese, whom Ruth took a liking for, remembered coming to the clubhouse late one day in Ruth's company. McCarthy, looking past Ruth at the rookie, snapped, "Reese, where the hell have you been?"

McCarthy got along very well with Gehrig and Combs and Pennock, now in his nineteenth season, and with Bill Dickey, the catcher, who became a regular in 1929 and was soon recognized as one of the best in baseball. He thought he might have trouble with Lazzeri, one of the old school and a good friend of Ruth's, but Tony worked well with McCarthy. There were post-Huggins players like Red Ruffing and Lefty Gomez, who became the stars of McCarthy's pitching staff, and Ben Chapman, a bad-tempered but talented player who came into his own when McCarthy shifted him from third base to the outfield. And he kept turning over infielders, getting Joe Sewell from Cleveland to play third base and eventually finding Frank Crosetti to fill the gap at shortstop that had been there since Koenig stopped being a star.

It was soon McCarthy's team without question. He established a discipline in the dugout, in the clubhouse, in hotels and on trains. He insisted the players wear jackets and ties on the road ("You're the Yankees," he kept telling them), and he told them to shave at home or in the hotel, not in the clubhouse ("This is your job. Shave before you come to work"). He would not let them play cards in the clubhouse, and when the club was traveling he insisted on nominal nickel-and-dime limits in poker and twentieth-of-a-cent-a-point stakes in bridge.

But he let Ruth alone, and the Babe behaved. He played hard and he had a superb season. Early in the year, in April, in Boston, he strained his foot sliding into third base. He got laboriously to his feet and stayed in the game, and when the next batter hit a moderate fly ball to right field he came pounding toward home in an attempt to score. The throw reached catcher Charlie Berry, who had been an All-America football player, at the same time Ruth did. Ruth slammed into Berry, was flipped upside down but landed near the plate, which he touched with one hand for the run. He seemed okay despite the collision, but in the outfield the next inning, when he turned abruptly to chase a fly ball, he yelped in pain and fell. He had done something to his leg when he hit Berry and he could not put his weight on it. It was diagnosed as a temporary paralysis of a nerve, and he was hospitalized for several days. When he came back to the team ten days later he was fine, and his batting became the stuff Barrow dreamed of in 1919. As June ended he was hitting .400 and leading the league, and he was near .390 much of the summer. But then he ripped his finger on the chicken-wire fence in the outfield and fell off to .373, second to Al Simmons' .390. And, after all his years of trying, Gehrig caught up to him in home runs, the two tying for the league lead with 46 each.

Life was not quite as lively as it had been, but it was still fun and Babe found a lot of it. He played against a House of David team in 1931 and put on a full set of false whiskers. Whenever he hit a home run off a new pitcher, he would call over cheerily, "Young man, you have just joined the Babe Ruth home run club."

But he also said, "It's hell to get older," and he was becoming wary of big hard-throwing pitchers. A good-looking rookie named Jim Peterson joined the Athletics in 1931. He came in to pitch against Ruth, and Mickey Cochrane, the Athletics' Hall of Fame catcher, told him, "Nothing but fastballs, but put everything you have on it." Peterson, regarding Ruth with more than a bit of awe, put all his 200 pounds behind a fastball, lost control of it and sent it directly at the Babe, who sprawled ignominiously in the dirt and jumped up, spluttering, "Why, you collegiate son of a bitch." He walked, and when Gehrig came to bat a moment later, Lou said placatingly to Peterson, "Now don't be nervous."

Ruth went hunting every winter and in 1931 came back from North Carolina with three wild turkeys, twenty ducks and a deer, and had them all delivered to his butcher. "Send a turkey to Ed Barrow," he told the butcher, "and take care of the ducks. But don't let anybody touch that deer. I don't want somebody monkeying with it and spoiling the skin. I'll come back and skin it myself."

Claire told him to let Anton, the butcher, skin the deer, but Ruth said, "Him? What does he know about skinning a deer? He'd ruin it. I want the skin made into a rug for Dorothy's room, and the job has to be done by somebody who knows how to skin a deer."

He went to Anton's with Rud Rennie, who watched as Babe put on a butcher's apron, accepted a knife and prepared to operate, lecturing as he did like a surgeon in a hospital amphitheater.

"The way we usually do this," he said, "is to hang the deer from a tree. But I'll have to do it the way it is. Now, we start here."

He jabbed the carcass and Anton emitted a shrill cry of protest. "No, no," he said, and without ceremony took the knife from Ruth and made the proper incision. Ruth said, "Oh," and Anton continued, Ruth watching with interest.

When the butcher finished, Babe asked, "Where did you learn to skin a deer?"

"In Austria. Where I come from there are many deer. People eat them all the time. I skin many deer."

"Hell, if I'd have known that, I'd have stayed home. Hey, cut out a roast and send it up to the house. Put those horns in a bag. I'll take them with me."

As he grew older, his hunting equipment became more elaborate. Ruth believed in roughing it in comfort, and often he would say, "You fellows go on out. I think I'll do my hunting on Mahogany Ridge today." Mahogany Ridge was the bar. One winter he took along his portable phonograph and fifty records, the old, heavy 78-rpm disks. He had a terrible time locating a container for the records and nagged Claire about finding something that would do.

"What about one of those big round cake tins?" he demanded.

"Haven't got a big round cake tin," she said. "Anyway, one wouldn't be enough."

"Well, call over and order half a dozen."

"Babe, cake tins don't come empty. They have cakes in them."

"All right," he said. "You can take the cakes out, can't you?"

She gave up and ordered four big cakes, complete with tins. The cakes were jettisoned, the records safely packed and Ruth left for his hunting trip with three guns, three suitcases and four cake tins.

Ruth went to Los Angeles in the autumn of 1931 to make some short baseball films, and there he said he intended to retire after two more seasons (he wanted to complete twenty years as an active player). Asked if he hoped to own a club some day, he said, "Nope, but I want to manage one." His $80,000 contract had expired, and he and Ruppert soon were in another hassle. Ruppert sent Ruth a contract for $70,000, a cut of $10,000. Babe said he would refuse to consider anything but another two-year contract at $80,000. But he was not on as strong ground as he had been two years earlier. The Depression was two years old; jobs generally were scarce, and salaries in those that were around were being cut. Babe said, "I haven't noticed the Yankees in any depression," but it had little effect. No one was going to waste sympathy on Ruth having to get along on $70,000. After two months of disagreement he and Ruppert came to terms in the foyer of the Rolyat Hotel in St. Petersburg. They talked alone before the big fireplace at one end of the long room, while at the other end a cluster of people watched and tried to hear what they were saying. After ten or fifteen minutes Ruppert sent for Colonel Wattenberg, who supplied a pen and witnessed the signatures. They had compromised again. Ruppert went up $5000 and Ruth came down $5000. And he agreed to take the $75,000 on a one-year contract.

The photographers posed them outside afterwards and had Ruth and Ruppert and Claire toss coins into a wishing well. Ruth said, "I wish for another pennant, so that I can play in ten World Series." Claire said, "I wish for many more Yankee contracts." Ruppert said, "I wish I had the money in that well."

CHAPTER 31

The Magnificent Moment:
The Called-Shot Home Run

Everything worked for the Yankees in 1932. The infield clicked, the outfield was strong, the catching outstanding (except when Dickey was under a thirty-day suspension for breaking a Washington outfielder's jaw with one punch in a dispute at home plate). The pitching was superb, and the hitting strong and consistent all year long. The team won 107 games and took the pennant by a wide margin.

Ruth pretty much decided when he wanted to play, which was most of the time, but more and more he left the game in the late innings and let young Sammy Byrd or Myril Hoag finish up for him. Ruth's caddies, they were called, or his legs. Babe, now thirty-eight, had a solid enough year, although it was distinctly below his traditional high level of accomplishment. For one thing, he lost the home run championship he had held (except for 1922 and 1925) since 1918. Jimmie Foxx of Philadelphia even threatened Ruth's record of 60, ending with 58. Babe was second, but far behind, with 41. He batted .341, not bad, scored 120 runs and batted in 137, not bad at all. But people like Foxx and Gehrig and Simmons were obviously better hitters than he was now. The only thing the Babe led the league in was bases on balls.

357

Twice he was out of the lineup for extended periods, the first time in the middle of July after he ruptured the sheath of a muscle in the rear of his leg as he chased a fly ball. He fell in a writhing heap and once again was carried off the field. He was in a hospital for a few days and out of action for the better part of two weeks. Later in the year, in September, he felt shooting pains in his right side during a game in Philadelphia. The Yankees left on a western road trip, pausing first for an exhibition game in Binghamton, New York, and there Ruth felt the pain again. By the time the club reached Detroit he was convinced he had appendicitis. He phoned Barrow in New York, spoke to McCarthy and, with Claire, hurried back to New York for a thorough examination. It may or may not have been his appendix—there was no operation—but he ran a low fever for several days and was kept in bed. Ten days after his return to New York and only ten days before the World Series with the Cubs was due to begin, he got into a uniform and worked out at Yankee Stadium. The team was still on the road and Babe batted against an amateur pitcher, but he was unable to put one ball into the stands. "I'm so weak I don't think I could break a pane of glass," he said, "but I'll be okay in a few days. They had me packed so deep in ice I haven't thawed out yet."

There was considerable doubt that he would be able to play in the Series, but he was in the Yankee lineup for the last five games of the year (he had only three hits in sixteen at bats), and when the Cubs faced the Yankees on Wednesday, September 28, there was Ruth in right field, batting third. This was the World Series that is remembered for Ruth's called home run, the single most famous facet of his legend, yet it was really Gehrig's series. Chicago had a good solid team, representative of the glowing period from 1928 through 1938 when the Cubs won four pennants and never finished lower than third. These Cubs could hit, and indeed they scored almost five runs a game against the excellent Yankee pitching staff, but their own pitchers, a redoubtable collection of first-rate performers (Lon Warneke, Charlie Root, Guy Bush, Burleigh Grimes, Pat Malone), were destroyed by the Yankees, who scored an average of more than nine runs a game. Gehrig had nine hits in the four games, including three home runs and a double, and he scored nine runs and batted in eight as the Yankees won, 12–6, 5–2, 7–5 and 13–6.

Yet Gehrig's exploits were obscured, as they so often were during his career, by a brighter sun, meaning Ruth. Along with being the highest scoring Series ever played, it probably had the most bench jockeying, and the Babe was in the forefront of it. Mark Koenig, who had dropped down to the minors after the Yankees traded him away, had been brought back up by the Cubs late in 1932 to fill a hole at shortstop; he fielded splendidly, batted .353 in 33 games and was a key figure in Chicago's drive to the pennant. But when the Cubs met just before the Series to decide how they would divide their share of the World Series pot, Koenig was voted only a half share. (Rogers Hornsby, who had been fired as manager almost two thirds of the way through the season, received nothing. A young outfielder named Frank Demaree, who was in only 23 games during the season but played center field and batted fifth in two Series games and hit a home run, was given a quarter share.)

The Yankees, led by Ruth, made great capital of Koenig's half share. "Hey, Mark," Babe boomed, "who are those cheapskates you're with?" Variations, richly embellished, followed and never let up. The Cubs struck back, mostly at Ruth, calling him fat and old and washed up, and they dragged out the old "nigger" cry. Guy Bush, a dark-haired, swarthy Mississippian, was Chicago's starting pitcher in the first game, and the Yankees yelled back, "Who are you calling a nigger? Look at your pitcher."

The jockeying continued at this high level as the Yankees won the first two games in New York. Then the Series shifted to Chicago, where thousands of people crammed into La Salle Street Station to see the ball clubs arrive. Ruth, accompanied by Claire, fought his way through the not unfriendly crowd to a freight elevator and then out to a cab. Motorcycle cops had to clear the way for the Yankees, and as Ruth and his wife entered their hotel a woman spat on them.

Such anti-Yankee feeling was isolated on the streets, but it was overwhelmingly evident at Wrigley Field before and during the third game of the Series. Ruth complained a week or so later that the Chicago press had brought the fans down on him with stories about the bench jockeying. "They wrote about me riding the Cubs for being tight and about me calling them cheapskates," he said indignantly.

"Well, didn't you?" he was asked.

"Well, weren't they?" he answered with irrefutable logic. Then he grinned and said, "Jesus, I wish I had known they only voted that kid Demaree a quarter share. Would I have burned them on that one."

Almost 50,000 people were jammed into every part of Wrigley Field, and most of them were yelling at Ruth. Whenever a ball was lofted his way in pregame practice, a lemon or two would come flying out of the bleachers. Each time, Babe picked up the lemons and threw them back. He was in a good mood. There was a strong wind blowing toward right field, and during batting practice he and Gehrig put on an awesome show, far more spectacular than the one in Pittsburgh five years earlier. Babe hit nine balls into the stands, Gehrig seven. Ruth yelled at the Cubs, "I'd play for half my salary if I could hit in this dump all the time." Gomez, the non-hitting pitcher, said, "With that wind, I could hit a home run today."

The jockeying between the two teams, or, to be more accurate, between Ruth and the Cubs, became more intense as the game began. Charlie Root was the starting pitcher for Chicago, but Bush and Grimes and Malone were on the top step of the Cub dugout, leading the verbal barrage on Ruth. Andy Lotshaw, the Cubs' trainer, yelled, "If I had you, I'd hitch you to a wagon, you potbelly." Ruth said afterwards, "I didn't mind no ballplayers yelling at me, but the trainer cutting in—that made me sore." As he waited to bat in the first inning, according to Richards Vidmer in the *New York Herald Tribune,* "He paused to jest with the raging Cubs, pointed to the right field bleachers and grinned."

The game started badly for the Cubs. Koenig had hurt his wrist in New York and was out the rest of the Series. His replacement,

Billy Jurges, fielded the first ball hit by the Yankees—a grounder by Earle Combs—and threw it all the way into the stands behind first base. Joe Sewell walked, and Ruth came to bat with men on first and second and no one out. Root threw a pitch outside for ball one, another one inside for ball two. Then he threw a fastball on the outside corner and Ruth, swinging at the ball for the first time in a game in Wrigley Field, hit a three-run homer into the right field bleachers to put the Yankees ahead, 3–0, before an out had been made.

Gehrig hit a homer in the third with the bases empty (and Ruth hit a fly to the right center field fence), but the Cubs rallied and in the fourth inning tied the game at 4–4. The tying run was scored by Jurges, who reached second base with a double when Ruth, to the great delight of the crowd, looked foolish missing a try at a shoe-string catch.

And so it was 4–4 in a rowdy game as the Yankees came to bat in the fifth. Another lemon bounced toward Ruth as he waited in the on-deck circle while Sewell went out. Boos and hoots rose to a crescendo as he stepped into the batter's box. The Cubs were on the top of the dugout steps, Bush cupping his hands around his mouth as he taunted Ruth. Babe grinned, then stepped in to face Root. The pitcher threw. It was a called strike. The crowd cheered, and the Cubs razzed Ruth louder than ever. Still grinning, holding his bat loosely in his left hand, he looked over at the Cubs and raised one finger of his right hand. Root pitched again, in close, for ball one. He pitched again, this time outside, and it was ball two. The crowd stirred in disappointment, and the razzing from the Cubs let up slightly. Again Root pitched, and it was called strike two. The crowd roared, and the Cubs yammered with renewed vigor. Bush was so excited he ran a step or two onto the grass in front of the dugout, yelling at Ruth. Grimes was shouting something. Ruth waved the exultant Cubs back toward their dugout and held up two fingers. Gabby Hartnett, the Chicago catcher, heard him say, "It only takes one to hit it." Root said something from the mound, and

Ruth said something back. Gehrig, who was in the on-deck circle, said, "Babe was jawing with Root and what he said was, 'I'm going to knock the next pitch right down your goddamned throat.'"

Root threw again, a changeup curve, low and away. Ruth swung and hit a tremendous line-drive home run deep into the bleachers in center field. Johnny Moore, the center fielder, ran back and stood there looking up as it went far over his head into the stands. It was the longest home run that had ever been hit in Wrigley Field. Ruth ran down the first base line laughing. "You lucky bum," he said to himself. "You lucky, lucky bum." He said something to Charlie Grimm, the Cubs' player-manager first baseman. He said something to second baseman Billy Herman. He shook his clasped hands over his head like a victorious fighter, and as he rounded third base, still laughing, he yelled, "Squeeze the eagle club!" to the now silent Chicago dugout. In a box near home plate Franklin D. Roosevelt, who was running for President against Herbert Hoover, put his head back and laughed, and after the Babe crossed home plate Roosevelt's eyes followed him all the way into the dugout, where he was mauled and pounded by his gleeful Yankee teammates.

Gehrig stepped to the plate, Root threw one pitch and Gehrig hit a home run. Two pitches, two home runs; the Yankees led, 6–4, all their runs coming on homers by Ruth and Gehrig. Root was taken out of the game, and it ended with the Yankees winning, 7–5.

The New York clubhouse roared with noise afterwards. Ruth yelled, "Did Mr. Ruth chase those guys back into the dugout? Mr. Ruth sure did!"

The next day Bush was Chicago's starting pitcher. When Ruth came to bat in the first inning, Bush hit him on the arm with a blistering fastball. Babe pretended to flick something off his arm as he trotted down to first base. "Hey, Lop Ears," he yelled to Bush, "was that your fastball? I thought it was a gnat." To Gehrig, he called, "Don't look for nothing, Lou. He ain't got it." And Bush didn't. He faced five men in the inning, got one out and was lifted from the game. Lazzeri hit two homers, Combs one, Gehrig batted in three runs, and the Yankees won, 13–6. Ruth had only one single in five at bats and in the clubhouse afterwards put hot towels on his arm, which was flaming red and badly swollen where Bush's gnat had bitten it. Doc Painter, the trainer, said that if the Series had gone another game, Ruth could not possibly have played in it. But despite the pain, Ruth was gloriously happy. He even went over to McCarthy and shook his hand. "What a victory!" he said. "My hat is off to you, Mac." A few days later, back in New York, he said, "That's the first time I ever got the players and the fans going at the same time. I never had so much fun in all my life."

Now. What about the legend? What about the story, often affirmed, often denied, that Babe pointed to a spot in center field and then hit the ball precisely to that spot? It is an argument over nothing, and the fact that Ruth did not point to center field before his home run does not diminish in the least what he did. He did challenge the Cubs before 50,000 people, did indicate he was going to hit a home run and did hit a home run. What more could you ask?

The legend grew, obviously, because people gild lilies and because sometimes we remember vividly seeing things we did not see. Most of the contemporary accounts of the game talked about Ruth calling his shot, but only one that I could find said specifically that he pointed at the fence. That, written by Joe Williams, sports editor of the Scripps-Howard newspapers, appeared in late editions of afternoon newspapers on Saturday, October 1, the day of the game. The headline over Williams' story in the *New York World–Telegram* said, "RUTH CALLS SHOT AS HE PUTS HOMER NO. 2 IN SIDE POCKET," and part of his account said, "In the fifth, with the Cubs riding him unmercifully from the bench, Ruth pointed to center and punched a screaming liner to a spot where no ball had ever been hit before." That is the only place in the story where specific reference is made to pointing to center field. Elsewhere in his copy Williams wrote, "The first strike was called, and the razzing from the Cub bench increased. Ruth laughed and held up one finger. Two balls were pitched and Babe jeered the Cub bench, the fans and Root, grinning broadly all the time. Another strike was called and Bush ran part way out of the dugout to tell the Babe that he was just a tramp. Ruth hit the next pitch farther than any other ball ever was hit in this park."

Westbrook Pegler, who wrote a column but not a running account of the game, said, "Bush pushed back his big ears, funneled his hands at his mouth and yelled raspingly at the great man to upset him. The Babe laughed derisively and gestured at him—wait, mugg, I'm going to hit one out of the yard. Root threw a strike past him and he held up a finger to Bush whose ears flapped excitedly as he renewed his insults. Another strike passed him and Bush crawled almost out of the hole to extend his remarks. The Babe held up two fingers this time. Root wasted two balls and Babe put up two fingers on his other hand. Then with a warning gesture of his hand to Bush he sent the signal for the customers to see. Now, it said, this is the one, look. And that one went riding on the longest home run ever hit in the park. . . . Many a hitter may make two home runs, possibly three, in World Series play in years to come, but not the way Ruth hit these two. Nor will you ever see an artist call his shot before hitting one of the longest drives ever made on the ground in a World Series game, laughing at and mocking the enemy, two strikes gone."

The story by Williams was the only one I found of those written on the day of the game that interpreted Ruth's gestures as pointing toward center, but two days later Paul Gallico of the *New York Daily News,* a rococo and flamboyant writer, wrote, "He pointed like a duellist to the spot where he expected to send his rapier home." A day after that Bill Corum of the Hearst newspapers wrote that Ruth "pointed out where he was going to hit the next one, and hit it there," but in his game account the day it happened Corum neglected to mention the fact.

Tom Meany, who worked for Williams and sat next to him at the game on Saturday, wrote a story the following Tuesday that said, "Babe's interviewer then interrupted to point out the hole in which Babe put himself Saturday when he pointed out the spot in which he intended hitting his homer and asked the great man if he realized how ridiculous he would have appeared if he had struck out. 'I never thought of that,' said Babe." But it is not clear in Meany's story if the phrase about pointing was in the question put to Ruth or was merely incorporated in the copy as a clarifying description.

Williams was a positive, opinionated observer and a vigorous journalist. Taking an opposite tack some months later, he suggested to Gehrig that Root let Babe hit the ball ("Like hell he did," said Gehrig). Meany was a fine reporter, a gifted writer and a superior raconteur of baseball anecdotes. I believe that Williams' strong personality and the wide circulation given his original story in Scripps-Howard newspapers as well as Meany's repeated accounts of that colorful World Series are what got the legend started and kept it going. That the pointing version was often questioned is shown in Meany's biography of Ruth, published in 1947. In it Meany wrote, "It was then the big fellow made what many believe to be the *beau geste* of his entire career. He pointed in the direction of dead center-field. Some say it was merely a gesture toward Root, others that he was just letting the Cub bench know that he still had the big one left. Ruth himself has changed his version a couple of times. . . . Whatever the intent of the gesture, the result was, as they say in Hollywood, slightly colossal."

Ruth told John Carmichael, a highly respected Chicago sportswriter, "I didn't exactly point to any spot. All I wanted to do was give that thing a ride out of the park, anywhere. I used to pop off a lot about hitting homers, but mostly among the Yankees. Combs and Lazzeri and Fletcher used to yell, 'Come on, Babe, hit one.' So I'd come back, 'Okay, you bums. I'll hit one!' Sometimes I did. Sometimes I didn't. Hell, it was fun."

His autobiography, published in 1947, not only says he did it but adds the embroidery that he began thinking about it the night before the game, after he and Claire were spat on when they entered their hotel. It says he was angry and hurt because of the taunts of the Chicago players and fans. It says that before the first pitch he pointed to center field and that when Root threw the ball, Babe held up a finger and yelled, "Strike one," before the umpire could call the pitch. And held up two fingers and yelled, "Strike two," after the second pitch. And before the third pitch, he stepped out of the box and pointed to the bleachers again. And then hit the third pitch for the home run. This version is the one that was substantially followed by Hollywood in the movie of Ruth's life that starred William Bendix, and as bad as the movie was it gave the legend the permanence of concrete.

Both autobiography and movie infuriated Charlie Root, who turned the film company down flat when they asked him to portray himself. "Not if you're going to have him pointing," he said. He refused to have anything to do with it, and he went to his grave denying that Ruth had pointed to center field. "If he had I would have knocked him on his ass with the next pitch," he always insisted. Yet Root's memory was hazy on detail. In the mid 1950s, he said, "George Magerkurth, the plate umpire, said in a magazine story that Ruth did point to center field. But to show how far wrong Magerkurth was, he had the count three and two when it was really two strikes and no balls. To me, the count was significant. Why should Ruth point to show where he was going to hit a ball when, with two strikes and no balls, he knew he wasn't apt to get a pitch he could hit at all?" But both Magerkurth and Root were wrong. The count was neither three balls and two strikes nor two strikes and no balls. It was two strikes and two balls. And Magerkurth umpired at first base that day, not behind the plate.

Such fuzziness of detail is evident in several contemporary accounts of the game. Pegler, quoted above, said the count went strike, strike, ball, ball, whereas it was strike, ball, ball, strike. Corum said the count was three and two, and so did the play-by-play account in *The New York Times*. Meany's biography and Ruth's autobiography both say, as Root did, that it was two strikes and no balls. Any lawyer will concede that honest witnesses see the same things differently.

Here are what some witnesses said about it.

Charlie Root: "Ruth did not point at the fence before he swung. If he had made a gesture like that, well, anybody who knows me knows that Ruth would have ended up on his ass. The legend didn't get started until later. I fed him a changeup curve. It wasn't a foot off the ground and it was three or four inches outside, certainly not a good pitch to hit. But that was the one he smacked. He told me the next day that if I'd have thrown him a fastball he would have struck out. 'I was guessing with you,' he said."

Gabby Hartnett, the Chicago catcher: "Babe came up in the fifth and took two called strikes. After each one the Cub bench gave him the business, stuff like he was choking and he was washed up. Babe waved his hand across the plate toward our bench on the third base side. One finger was up. At the same time he said softly, and I think only the umpire and I heard him, 'It only takes one to hit it.' Root came in with a fast one and it went into the center field seats. Babe didn't say a word when he passed me after the home run. If he had pointed out at the bleachers, I'd be the first to say so."

Doc Painter, the Yankee trainer: "Before taking his stance he swept his left arm full length and pointed to the center field fence. When he got back to the bench, Herb Pennock said, 'Suppose you missed? You would have looked like an awful bum.' Ruth was taking a drink from the water cooler, and he lifted his head and laughed. 'I never thought of that,' he said."

Joe McCarthy, the Yankee manager: "I'm not going to say he didn't do it. Maybe I didn't see it. Maybe I was looking the other way. Anyway, I'm not going to say he didn't do it."

Jimmy Isaminger, Philadelphia sportswriter: "He made a satiric gesture to the Cub bench and followed it with a resounding belt that had so much force behind it that it landed in the bleachers in dead center."

The *San Francisco Examiner*, October 2, 1932: "He called his shot theatrically, with derisive gestures towards the Cubs' dugout."

The Reach Guide, covering the 1932 season: "Ruth hit the ball over the center field fence, a tremendous drive, after indicating in pantomime to his hostile admirers what he proposed to do, and did."

Warren Brown, Chicago sportswriter: "The Babe indicated he

had one strike, the big one, left. The vituperative Cub bench knew what he meant. Hartnett heard Ruth growl that this was what he meant. Ruth, for a long while, had no other version, nor was any other sought from him."

Ford Frick, who was not at the game, tried to pin Ruth down on the subject when the two were talking about the Series some time later.

"Did you really point to the bleachers?" Frick asked.

Ruth, always honest, shrugged. "It's in the papers, isn't it?" he said.

"Yeah," Frick said. "It's in the papers. But did you really point to the stands?"

"Why don't you read the papers? It's all right there in the papers."

Which, Frick said, means he never said he did and he never said he didn't.

CHAPTER 32

Decline:
It's Hell to Be Old

The joyful glow from the 1932 World Series did not last long. It was obvious that Ruth was going to have to take another salary cut for 1933, and probably a big one. The Depression was at its worst, and, as Barrow let everyone know, the Yankees had to refund more than $100,000 to holders of tickets to the unplayed sixth and seventh games of the Series.

Ruth was unconcerned. "Jake and I will meet," he said, "and he'll say what he thinks I should get next season, and then I'll say. Then we'll talk a little while, and then we'll come to an agreement. It's always been like that. Jake and I never have much trouble getting together."

But when Ruth received his contract in the middle of January, he was outraged. He had been cut 33⅓ per cent to $50,000, a drop of $25,000. Babe phoned Barrow and said he was returning the contract and asked if it was okay if he told the papers about it. Barrow said, "No, I'd rather you didn't. I'll take care of that myself."

Ruth waited a few days but when nothing appeared in the papers he called the reporters in. "I don't mind telling you and the world that the offer is $50,000," he said, "and that's a cut of 25 grand, and that's some wallop." He muttered about Barrow. "I don't believe

Colonel Ruppert ever saw the contract, and I told Barrow that. Hell, I expected to receive a cut, but I can't believe Jake would go so far as a third off. I'll never sign for that."

Yet Ruppert had seen the size of the cut, and had approved it, although his only comment to inquiring reporters was "I have nothing to say, nothing to say, nothing to say at all."

A few days later Babe's anger subsided somewhat and he said, genially, "I can see a 10 per cent cut or even a 15 per cent cut, but 15 per cent is as low as I'll go. I expected a cut, but $25,000 is no cut, that's an amputation."

Someone raised the question of the Depression, salary cuts, unemployment, breadlines, and whether Babe had a right to complain about his salary. Ruth said, "Why shouldn't I kick? The Yankees made money last year, and I think I helped draw the crowds as much as I ever did. Oh, hell, we'll work this out in Florida. We always do."

He went south and played golf. He had a hole in one on the 185-yard third hole at Pasadena Golf Club near St. Petersburg and shot a 78 that day. He played a lot of golf, but nothing happened with his contract. One of those rumors that he was dead flashed around again, this one saying he had been killed in a plane crash. "Nah," said Ruth on the phone to a worried inquirer, "I haven't been in a plane in weeks. The worst accident I've had is that Yankee contract."

He and Ruppert met once in Florida, and Ruth offered to come down to $60,000. Ruppert refused to budge from his original offer of $50,000. Babe worked out with the club, but did not sign. The exhibition season began, and in the middle of March he and Ruppert met again. Babe, his resistance melting like a snowball in St. Petersburg, came down to $55,000. Ruppert still said no. He not only said no, he said, "If Ruth does not sign by March 29, he will not be taken north with the team. Furthermore, if he does not come to terms by then, the present offer of $50,000 will be lowered. Ruth has come down in his demands, but I told him I cannot possibly sign him for more than $50,000."

Four days later, on March 22, Ruth gave in and signed. Ruppert had the grace to let Ruth save face. "We have reached an agreement," the colonel told the press. "I asked Ruth what he wanted, and he said, 'I'll take $52,000.' I told him that was all right, and that ended the matter."

They both had compromised, said one newspaper. Ruth had come down $23,000 and Ruppert had gone up $2000. Yet there was little sympathy for Ruth. In March 1933 Franklin Roosevelt had just been inaugurated. Banks were folding. Savings were gone. And Ruth was still the highest paid player in the game.

He took another distinct step down competitively in 1933. He played about as much as he had in 1932, still using his caddies to spell him in the late innings and the second games of doubleheaders, but he batted only .301 and was slow and lumbering in the field. He had the consolation of hitting more home runs than Gehrig, yet with only 34 he was well behind Jimmie Foxx. The Yankees had a disappointing year. They were the same team as in 1932, but this time things did not click. The pitching was off, and Ruth was no longer an asset but a liability.

Still, he had a couple of memorable moments that season. The first All-Star Game was played in Chicago in July, and sentiment prevailed over current performances in picking the lineups. John McGraw managed the National League, Connie Mack the American, and Ruth played right field for Mack's side. In the third inning, batting against lefthanded Bill Hallahan in Chicago's big Comiskey Park, he hit a two-run home run, the first in All-Star Game history, and it was the American League's margin of victory in a 4–3 game. Ruth stayed in the lineup, his adrenalin flowing, and in the eighth inning made a spectacular catch of a long fly ball. It was his day.

Then, in the final game of the season, in Yankee Stadium against the Red Sox, he pitched again. His appearance was well ballyhooed, and 25,000 people came to watch. It was billed as a fitting climax to his twentieth season in the majors, since he would be pitching against his original team, the Red Sox. Ruth took the assignment seriously and worked to get his arm in shape. He was thirty-nine years old and had pitched only once in the previous twelve seasons, but he went all the way against the Red Sox and beat them, 6–5. He gave up 12 hits, 11 of them singles. He walked three. But in only one inning did the Red Sox really get to him. In the sixth, with the Yankees ahead, 6–0, after Ruth's 34th home run an inning earlier, Boston hit out five singles, four of them in a row, and scored four runs. But Ruth stopped them, gave up one more run in the eighth, held on and finished the game. Winning meant that he had never had a losing season as a pitcher.

The trainer worked on his arm between innings in the dugout, but an hour after the game it was stiff and sore. Happy but exhausted, he showered, dressed painfully and left the Stadium. Outside, thousands of fans were waiting. Instead of cheering, they applauded as he made his way to his car. Ruth tipped his cap, using his right hand because he could not lift his left.

In previous years he had said he was going to retire after 1933, his twentieth season, but now he elected not to. He still wanted to become manager of the Yankees, and he decided to stay around. His contempt for McCarthy, temporarily in abeyance after the 1932 World Series, became evident again. McCarthy's resentment of Ruth was equally evident. Mrs. Ruth and Mrs. McCarthy did not speak to each other. McCarthy told someone that Pennock had been as impressive as Ruth in the 1932 World Series (Pennock had pitched very well in relief in the two games in Chicago).

Ruth's obtuseness about the Yankee managing job was almost pitiful. It was obvious that Barrow was convinced he was incapable of managing, and Ruppert, with justification, depended heavily on Barrow's judgment in running the club. After the 1932 Series Ruppert, on Barrow's advice, gave McCarthy a three-year contract that was to run through 1935. Wishful rumors persisted that Ruth would take over when McCarthy's contract ran out, but he never had a chance.

His stubbornness in wanting to remain an active player with the Yankees and his forlorn hope that he would ultimately succeed McCarthy may well have cost Ruth a chance to manage the Red Sox. Boston had five different managers in six years, and Ruth was approached about the job in 1932. James Michael Curley, still a power in Boston politics, was trying to revive baseball in his city, and he pointed out to prospective purchasers of the Red Sox the attractiveness of Ruth as manager. They talked to Ruth, but it was during the 1932 season and Babe felt he was still a force on the Yankees. He did not want to leave the club, nor is it likely that the Yankees would have let him go then—at least not cheaply. The Red Sox post came up again in 1933, when Tom Yawkey, a multimillionaire, bought the club. Yawkey wanted to hire Ruth, but was persuaded not to by Eddie Collins, his general manager. There were reports that the White Sox were interested too.

After the 1933 season the Detroit Tigers definitely wanted him. The Tigers' attendance had been declining for several years, and Frank Navin, the Detroit owner, felt that Ruth as player-manager would certainly help the gate and possibly help the team on the field. He spoke to Barrow during the 1933 World Series about the possibility of obtaining Ruth. Barrow, after conferring with Ruppert, said something could be worked out. The Yankees were looking for a way to dump Ruth gracefully, and this seemed an ideal situation. He would still be in the league, which would help the box office, and Barrow was even able to wheedle Navin into throwing a useful outfielder into the deal. It all depended on Ruth now. Before he closed the deal, Navin wanted to talk to Babe and reach an agreement on the details. He asked him to come to Detroit. But Babe and Claire and Julia (Dorothy was too young and had to stay in school) were leaving on a trip to Honolulu, where Babe had several exhibitions lined up. Ruth said he would see Navin on his return.

"You're making a mistake," Barrow said. "You better go see him now."

"There's plenty of time," Ruth said. "The season doesn't begin for six months. I've got these things all set in Hawaii. I'll call him when I get back."

Navin, never a particularly genial man, was annoyed. Connie Mack was again breaking up his team—he had already sent Al

Simmons and Jimmy Dykes to Chicago—and Navin bought Mickey Cochrane from Mack and made him player-manager. Ruth made no comment. In Hawaii he played golf, laid a wreath on the grave of Alexander Joy Cartwright, the founder of American baseball, and complained after an exhibition game, "I guess I'm getting too old. Another year and I'll have to quit."

Ruppert and Barrow winced when they heard that. Another year of Ruth. He would be forty in February, he was old and he was brittle. He was hurting the team on the field, and Ruppert liked to win. He did not like second place. Ruth was contemptuous of his manager, had quarreled with the fiery young Ben Chapman and had a serious falling out with his old friend Gehrig. He had become an incubus.

Barrow had an idea. If Ruth wanted to manage, why not make him manager of Newark, the Yankee farm club in New Jersey? Tell the Babe that here was his chance to demonstrate his ability. The implication would be that he would be preparing himself to take over from McCarthy. Barrow was sure that in time Ruth would get bored with the job, or mess it up. In either case he could be eased out with a minimum of hard feelings, particularly from the public.

Ruth rejected the Newark job. "I'm a big leaguer," he said. "Why should I have to go down to the minors first? Cobb and Speaker didn't. Why do I have to?" A year earlier the Washington Senators had made their twenty-six-year-old shortstop, Joe Cronin, player-manager. "How about that kid in Washington? Did he have more experience than me?"

The Yankees again cut his salary drastically, Barrow preparing the way by talking loudly on a telephone when he knew Dan Daniel, who loved news beats, was within hearing. "I think $25,000 should be our top offer," he said, apparently to Colonel Ruppert. Daniel wrote the story, and $25,000 was the amount in the 1934 contract sent to Ruth. Babe made no extravagant statements, and he did not hold out. He went to see Ruppert at the brewery and meekly signed, although not for $25,000. In his customary post-meeting report to the assembled press, Ruppert said, "I asked the Babe if he would sign for $25,000, and he said he thought he should get $35,000. After further discussion, I agreed." Ruppert made it sound as though the Yankees had met Ruth's figure. But Ruth had taken another 30 per cent cut (32.5 per cent to be precise, after a 30.7 per cent cut the year before). In two years his salary had been chopped $45,000. And yet he was still the highest paid player in the majors. Most baseball salaries had been slashed. Gehrig, who made $23,000 in 1933, was given the same in 1934 with the promise that he would not be cut in 1935, which was flattering.

Ruppert was asked about stories that Ruth might succeed McCarthy when the manager's contract expired after the 1935 season. "The management of the Yankees was not discussed," Ruppert said. "McCarthy is still our manager and will remain so for the next two seasons. I have no plans beyond that, but we have no new managerial plans in view."

Larry MacPhail took over the operation of the Cincinnati Reds that winter, after Powell Crosley bought the club, and it was rumored that MacPhail wanted Ruth as manager. Nothing came of it. Babe put in another painful season with the Yankees, his abilities sadly diminished. He seldom stayed in a game to its finish. A month into the season a cold in his back kept him out for several days, and before the end of May it was generally accepted that this would be his last season as a player. In June he was hit on the wrist by a pitched ball and went into a slump in which he went to bat twenty-one times without a hit—and got the ball out of the infield only five times. But then he hit a grand slam home run and felt fine again. He played in the All-Star Game early in July and was the first of the impressive array of hitters—Ruth, Gehrig, Foxx, Simmons and Cronin—that Carl Hubbell struck out in succession.

Ten days later he was running from first to second when a ground ball hit by Gehrig struck him on the right leg just above the ankle. He dropped as though he had been shot. In the clubhouse, waiting for an ambulance to take him to the hospital for xrays, he said, "I shouldn't have been playing today. I was going to rest, and then I changed my mind and decided to play today and rest tomorrow. It's like fate. Damn! I'm going to get out of this game before I'm carried out."

He complained more and more about McCarthy. The Yankees were in second place again, well behind the Tigers, who, under Cochrane, were winning the pennant. One day in Detroit, bad-mouthing McCarthy to Dan Daniel and Frank Graham, he said, "Do you think he's a good manager?"

Daniel and Graham said yes, they did.

"Well, I don't. I think if we had a good manager we'd win this year."

The sportswriters reminded him that he himself had slowed down badly and was not doing much to help the team. In fact, he had not even played that day.

Ruth shook his head. "I don't care, I still say he's a lousy manager. If you can't see what's going on around here and see how he's fucking everything up, I don't know what the hell you've been looking at."

Late in August, after he hit the 700th home run of his career, he announced, "I'm definitely through as a regular player after this season." He said he would not continue as a pinch-hitter, something Ruppert had suggested earlier in the summer. "I don't want to be a pinch-hitter," Ruth said. "You get a chance to bat maybe once every seven days. It's one thing I don't intend to do." He said he would continue playing only if he was also a manager.

As the season came to an end—he batted a weak .288 and hit 22 home runs, which meant that Gehrig, who led the league with 49, finally had passed him—his appearances in various cities around the league were accepted as a farewell tour, and a goodish crowd came out to see him play his last game at Yankee Stadium. Not much fuss was made.

Before leaving to go to Detroit for the beginning of the World Series between the Tigers and the Cardinals, which he was covering with his ghostwriter for Walsh, he went to see Ruppert.

"Are you satisfied with McCarthy as your manager?" he asked bluntly.

"Why, yes," Ruppert said. "Of course I am. Aren't you?"

"No, I'm not. I know I can do a better job than he can."

"Really?" Ruppert, of course, was well aware of Ruth's burning ambition to manage the Yankees, and he knew the player resented McCarthy, but this was the first time the issue had been presented so bluntly. "Well, that's too bad, Ruth. I'm sorry, but McCarthy is the manager, and he will continue as manager."

"That suits me," Ruth said. "That's all I wanted to know."

He went off to the World Series, seething. After the fifth game, in St. Louis, he was walking along the platform at the railroad station with Joe Williams, Dan Daniel and Tom Meany. The conversation was general for a while and then Williams, always probing, asked, "What are your plans, Babe?"

"I'm going on that barnstorming trip to Japan," Ruth said, mentioning a trip to the Orient with Connie Mack and a group of American League players that had been in the works since the previous spring.

"No, I mean next year," Williams said. "Are you going to play again?"

"Hell, no," Ruth said. "I'm through with the Yanks. I won't play with them again unless I can manage. But they're sticking with McCarthy, and that lets me out."

Williams wrote the story, which created something of a sensation because Williams stressed the McCarthy-or-me angle. Newspapermen were amused that Ruth had scooped Bill Slocum, his own ghost, but the next day they gathered around for more details. It seemed official. Ruth's playing days were over. He wanted to manage. During the winter McCarthy, who still had a year to go on his contract, went to Ruppert and offered to resign. Ruppert said, "Don't resign, and don't worry. You're the manager."

Once again Yawkey wanted to hire Ruth. He felt, as many did, that Ruth belonged in Boston. Late in 1934, an overflow crowd packed Fenway Park to see Babe in his last appearance there, and the big turnout revived Yawkey's interest. But Collins was still stubbornly opposed. He knew that Joe Cronin, the Senators' youthful player-manager, was available, and in an astonishing deal the Red Sox bought Cronin for $250,000 and installed him as manager. This closed Boston to Ruth, but it opened up Washington. However, Ruth was too expensive a proposition for Clark Griffith, who ran the Senators under a tight rein. Money was the reason that Cronin, who was Griffith's son-in-law, had been sold. Griffith supposedly offered Babe a $15,000 salary and a cut of the gate, but Ruth wanted $30,000. The Senators turned to that safe, inexpensive journeyman, Bucky Harris.

Connie Mack had on eye on Ruth too. Mack was the impresario of the Japanese trip, but Ruth, it was announced, would be field manager of the touring team. There were fourteen players in the group: Lefty Gomez, Earl Whitehill, Clint Brown and Joe Cascarella, pitchers; Charlie Berry and Moe Berg, catchers; Lou Gehrig, Jimmie Foxx, Charlie Gehringer, Rabbit Warstler and Eric McNair, infielders; and Ruth, Earl Averill and Bing Miller, outfielders. Nonplayers were Mack, an umpire, a trainer and a traveling secretary, and most of the players had their wives along. Ruth brought Claire and Julia. The troupe left Vancouver, Canada, on the *Empress of Japan* on October 28 and stopped at Honolulu on the way to Japan. After Japan they played in Shanghai and Manila before splitting up. Ruth went on around the world and came home via Paris and London.

The reception in Tokyo was extraordinary, with Ruth by far the biggest attraction. He rode in an open car holding an American flag in one hand and a Japanese one in the other, while throngs in the streets waved American flags at him. All tickets to Tokyo's 60,000-capacity Meiji Stadium had been sold out for weeks in advance, and the same was true of Osaka's Koshien Stadium, which held 80,000. The Americans played 17 games in Japan and 22 in all on the trip. Ruth played every inning, hit 13 home runs and had a marvelous time. Moe Berg, the erudite catcher, a Princeton graduate who spoke several languages, told of escorting Babe to a geisha house. Ruth took it for granted that it was a whorehouse and began to undress. The subtlety of a geisha's ways were lost on him.

As for Mack, who was going to be seventy-five the following February, he was toying with the idea of retiring as manager of the Athletics and moving into the front office, and he liked the idea of Ruth becoming the field manager. Ruth's presence would help the sagging gate, and Connie had always got along well with Babe.

But little things happened. Worst was the feud with Gehrig. Babe had always patronized Lou, never really accepting him as a co-star. Gehrig did not seem to mind and, indeed, was a worshipful admirer of the Babe's for many years. Ruth took Gehrig with him on barnstorming trips and made a great deal of money for the younger player. In 1932, when Ruth and Gehrig and a couple of sportswriters were sitting around talking about the barnstorming days, Ruth said, "Hey, Dutchman, didn't I pay you $9000 for that trip in 1927?" Gehrig nodded. "Wasn't that more money than you made all year from the Yankees?" Gehrig nodded again. Ruth and Gehrig fished and hunted together, went to Army–Notre Dame football games together and for a while Lou was as close to Ruth as any teammate ever was. After the 1929 season Ruth proposed to Gehrig that they hold out together, arguing with great logic that if they presented a united front the club would simply have to pay what they wanted. Gehrig, the well-disciplined son of strict but loving parents, was scared of the idea and shied away from it. "I don't think so," he said. Ruth was always a bit contemptuous of him after that, as he was of Gehrig's spending habits. Ruth was a big spender and a lavish tipper. Gehrig was frugal, and his modest tipping was famous. As Rosy Ryan said, "Lou was a grand fellow, but a little close. They used to claim he cut his own hair." Someone said that when Ruth and Gehrig were bridge partners, "All you had to do was sit there and let the Babe double to hear Lou cry." Claire Ruth wrote, "Surely Babe was ridiculous when he left a ten-dollar tip where fifty cents would have been generous. But Lou's dimes were just as silly."

Ruth loved to go with Gehrig to visit Lou's mother at her home in New Rochelle. Once on a road trip he bought a scraggly little chihuahua pup and brought it home and gave it to her. Mrs. Gehrig named it Jidge, after Babe, and had the dog long after the friendship between the two players was over. Ruth often brought his daughter Dorothy with him when he visited the Gehrigs, and the little girl and Mom Gehrig, as she was universally called, got along fine. Dorothy, according to Claire Ruth, was the innocent reason for the bad feeling that developed between Babe and Lou. She was only eleven or twelve, still a little girl. Julia was five years older, quite tall, a young woman. Julia dressed with great élan, Dorothy scampered around like a tomboy. One day Mom Gehrig, who didn't much like Claire anyway, said to someone, "It's a shame she doesn't dress Dorothy as nicely as she dresses her own daughter." The remark got back to Claire, who blew her cork. She got mad, which made Ruth mad, and he said something angrily to Gehrig about his mother minding her own business. You didn't knock Mom Gehrig to Lou, who would take her on road trips with him once in a while. The two stopped speaking off the ballfield, their friendship at an end.

On the *Empress of Japan* during the voyage across the Pacific the Ruths and the Gehrigs (Lou had recently married) avoided one another. Even Julia, then eighteen, fed the feud. Walking on deck with a member of the party, she noticed Gehrig and turned away. "Don't stop," she said. "The Ruths don't speak to the Gehrigs."

At best, the ill feeling created awkwardness. At worst, it divided the group into factions, and Connie Mack noticed it. In Japan, when Gehrig and Earl Whitehill were late arriving at some sort of ceremony at seven-thirty in the morning, Ruth grew unnecessarily angry and threatened to send them both back to the States if either was late for anything again. Mack decided to change his plans. He stayed on as manager (for another sixteen years, as a matter of fact) and the following spring told Joe Williams, "I couldn't have made Babe manager. His wife would have been running the club in a month."

Babe and Claire continued their way around the world in December and January. Babe was appalled by Bali. "Boy," he said, "when you see those women, billed as the most beautiful in the world, walking down the street chewing red tobacco . . ." Bloody Mary chewing betel nut was still in the future. They came through the

Red Sea and the Suez Canal and across the Mediterranean. He skied at St. Moritz ("Can you ski?" an incredulous reporter asked. "Can I ski? I'm a champ at that game.") and spent a couple of weeks in Paris, where Claire was in bed most of the time with flu. He didn't like Paris. Nobody knew him. Mail came to him in care of the American Embassy, and the Embassy, instead of sending it around to his hotel, dutifully listed his name in the *Paris Herald Tribune* along with others for whom they were holding mail. "Don't they know who I am?" Ruth asked plaintively. He posed in a gendarme's hat for a press photographer and swung the gendarme's baton like a bat, but the gendarme did not know him either. He perked up when he visited a school for American children in Paris but grew depressed again when he saw how ignorant of baseball most of them were. "Poor kids," he said. "Imagine an American kid not knowing how to swing a bat."

In Paris he talked about baseball with an American reporter. "I had a chance to manage Cleveland," he said, "but I talked my way out of it. I made fun of Alva Bradley's ballpark. Everyone knows I should have gone to the Red Sox, but what can you do about it? Philadelphia? That's out of the question." He was noncommittal about the Braves. "One thing, though, if I can't manage a team, I'll quit. Nothing can make me change my mind about that. I've been in baseball twenty-one years, but I can get out easy enough. I have enough money to live on and I'm crazy about golf. Still, I can't understand why with sixteen clubs there isn't one manager's job open. Club owners can be awful funny when they want to. A ballplayer is supposed to be dumb and know nothing. When they get a ballplayer who thinks, they get suspicious."

He was much happier in England, the last stop before sailing home. He celebrated his forty-first birthday the day he arrived. (The famous birth certificate saying he was a year younger than he had always thought had been unearthed the previous September when Babe was getting ready for the trip, but he ignored it.) Everyone in London seemed to know who he was. Alan Fairfax, a former Australian cricketer, took him to an indoor cricket pitch and taught him the rudiments of the game. Babe tried to bat cricket style but shifted to his baseball stance and hit beautifully. "It's a better game than I thought," he said. Fairfax said, "I wish I could have him for a fortnight. I'd make the world's greatest batsman out of him." When the Ruths left for home, Jimmy Walker, the exiled mayor of New York, came to see them off.

Ruth arrived in New York on the S.S. *Manhattan* on Wednesday, February 20. He had been gone four months. In his absence things had been happening.

CHAPTER 33

Farewell to New York: Back to Boston

Judge Emil Fuchs owned the Boston Braves. Or at least he held title to a substantial portion of the ball club. He had obtained control in 1923 and had struggled along since, trying to keep the club alive. Fuchs was a Boston politician, an associate of James Michael Curley's, and an operator with ideas who seemed always to be in trouble and headlines. The Braves finished in the second division sixteen times in the seventeen years between 1917 and 1932, but under Bill McKechnie, whom Fuchs hired in 1930, they improved and in 1933 and 1934 finished fourth twice in a row. Unhappily, improvement coincided with depression. Attendance dropped and Fuchs was broke. In the autumn of 1934, while Ruth was exploring geisha houses, the National League called the Boston owner on the carpet, and for a while it seemed certain that they were going to reclaim the all-but-bankrupt franchise from him. Fuchs wanted to put a dog-racing track in Braves Field in the hope of making money from the place when the Braves were not playing at home, but this was shot down. There was a report that Charles C. Adams, a major stockholder of the Braves who was generally antagonistic to Fuchs, would supplant the judge, move the team to Fenway Park and make Ruth the manager.

Fuchs fought back, found the necessary financial support and convinced the league he could continue to operate. Curley, who had just been elected governor of Massachusetts, thought it would be a great coup to get Ruth back to Boston, and he urged Fuchs to hire him as manager. Fuchs responded negatively. "I like Ruth," he said, "and I'd offer him the job if it was open. But I'm committed to McKechnie. He's a most satisfactory manager, and he can stay with me as long as he's in baseball."

That closed out Ruth's chance to become a manager in 1935. Every job was filled. But Fuchs still needed something to hypo his attendance, and his thoughts inevitably returned to Ruth. He sounded out Ruppert and Barrow about the possibility of obtaining him as a player. There were a few stumbling blocks. One was that Ruth had loudly insisted that he would not sign another player contract, that he would be a manager or nothing. Another was money. Fuchs did not have any, at least not enough to buy the Babe from the Yanks, and Ruppert had said frequently that while he would release Ruth to take a job as manager, he would not let him go to another club as a player. Also, Fuchs was not sure he could pay the salary Ruth probably would want to forget about managing and return to playing.

Barrow, determined to get Ruth out of McCarthy's hair and off the Yankees, assured Ruppert that something could be worked out. Ruppert agreed, perhaps wishing he had not been so adamant about saying he would not let another club have Ruth for nothing. A complex plan was worked out that would get the Yankees off the hook, would let Fuchs obtain Ruth for nothing, would let him keep McKechnie as manager, would satisfy Ruth's managerial ambitions and would still get Babe onto the field again as a player.

This all evolved while Ruth was abroad and was not made public, but in the first week of February, shortly after the National League gave him clearance to continue running the Braves in 1935, Fuchs sent up a trial balloon. "I'm ready to make an offer for Ruth," he said in Boston, his glib tongue in his sly cheek. "We will make him assistant manager and give him an official position if he comes to the club, and he can play as often as he wants." That Ruth was aware of the negotiations was indicated in comments he made when he talked with reporters the day the *Manhattan* docked in New York. The sharp insistence voiced a few weeks earlier in Paris that he would quit if he could not manage was distinctly muted.

"I don't want to leave baseball," he said. "It's hard to think of leaving the game after so many years. I want to get back in uniform."

"Are you going to play again?"

"I'm not sure. I've got something under consideration that I can't talk about just now, in case I don't get what I want this season. I can't say what it is. All I can say is, it has to do with big league baseball."

"Are you going to sign a player contract?"

"I don't know. I might change my mind and play, I'm not sure. But if I do, it will have to be as a regular and not as a pinch-hitter."

"Do you think you could play as a regular again?"

"Depends on how I feel in training."

"Oh, you're going to spring training?"

"Well, I'm going to St. Petersburg anyway. I got to thaw out. I'm getting so damn old I feel like I belong there."

A few sportswriters surmised that Ruth was going to the White Sox. A rumor had come out of an Akron, Ohio, sports dinner that Joe McCarthy had attended saying a trade was pending between the White Sox and the Yankees, with New York getting Al Simmons for Ruth, who would become Chicago's player-manager. But Jimmy Dykes had been named player-manager of the White Sox a year earlier, and there was nothing to the rumor.

Ruth's boat docked on Wednesday. On Thursday he spoke to Ruppert, who explained the possibilities of the job with the Braves. On Friday he spoke on the telephone to Fuchs, who was still in Boston. Fuchs was used to dealing in complex matters, money arrangements, nebulous promises. Words like executive position, manager, next year, stock options, profits, ownership of the club, caressed Ruth's ear. Specifically, Fuchs told him he would be a vice-president of the Braves and would share in the club's profits; and the Braves' ticket sales, already promising, would jump when the fans learned the Babe had joined the club. Ruth would have first call on buying stock in this soon-to-be lucrative enterprise. He would be assistant manager to Bill McKechnie and in a year's time, maybe earlier, he would probably succeed McKechnie as manager, with Bill moving into the front office as general manager. He would be a regular, but he would play when he was able; he could pinch-hit on other days. His base pay would be $25,000, before the glittering profits, and that was much the highest salary paid on the Braves, including McKechnie's.

Ruth liked the sound of it, especially the part about managing, and asked Fuchs to put it all down on paper. The judge said he would. It took him a day to prepare it, but on Saturday he sent Ruth a long letter. It is, in its way, a masterpiece:

February 23, 1935

My Dear George:

In order that we may have a complete understanding, I am putting in the form of a letter the situation affecting our long-distance conversation of yesterday.

The Boston Braves offer you the following inducements, under the terms and conditions herein set forth, in order to have you sign a uniform contract plus an additional contract which will further protect you, both contracts to be filed.

1. The Boston club offers you a straight salary contract.

2. They offer you an official executive position as an officer of the corporation.

3. The Boston club offers you also the position, for 1935, of assistant manager.

4. They offer you a share of the profits during the term of this contract.

5. They offer you an option to purchase, at a reasonable figure, some of the stock of the club.

6. The details of the amounts agreed upon will be the basis of a separate contract which shall be a personal one between you and the club, and, as the case may be, with the individual officials and stockholders of the club.

In consideration of this offer, the Boston club naturally will expect you to do everything in your power for the welfare and interest of the club and will expect that you will endeavor to play in the games whenever possible, as well as carry out the duties above specified.

May I also give you the picture as I see it, which, in my opinion, will terminate to the best and mutual interest of all concerned.

You have been a great asset to all baseball, especially to the American League, but nowhere in the land are you more admired than in the territory of New England that has always claimed you as its own and where you started your career to fame.

The fans of New England have a great deal of affection for you, and from my personal experience with them are the most appreciative men and women in America, providing, of course, that you keep faith, continue your generous cooperation in helping civically and being a source of consolation to the children, as well as to the needy, who look up to you as a shining example of what the great athletes and public figures of America should be.

I say frankly, from my experience of forty years interest in baseball, that your greatest value to a ball club would be your personal appearance on the field, and particularly your participation in the active playing of exhibition games, on the ball field in championship games, as well as the master-minding and psychology of the game, in which you would participate as assistant manager.

As a player, I have observed and admired your baseball intelligence, for during your entire career I have never seen you make a wrong play or throw a ball to the wrong base, which leads us to your ability to manage a major league baseball club. In this respect we both are fortunate in having so great a character as Bill McKechnie, our present manager of the club, who has given so much to baseball and whom I count among my closest friends. Bill McKechnie's entire desire would be for the success of the Braves, especially financially, as he is one of the most unselfish, devoted friends that a man can have.

That spirit of McKechnie's is entirely returned by me, and I know by my colleagues in the ball club. They feel, as I do, that nothing would ever be done until we have amply rewarded Manager Bill Mc-Kechnie for his loyalty, his ability and sincerity, which means this, George, that if it was determined, after your affiliation with the ball club in 1935, that it was for the mutual interest of the club for you to take up the active management on the field, there would be absolutely no handicap in having you so appointed.

It may be that you will want to devote your future years to becoming an owner or part owner of a major league ball club. It may be that you may discover that what the people are really looking forward to and appreciate in you is the color and activity that you give to the game by virtue of your hitting and playing and that you would rather have someone else, accustomed to the hardships and drudgery of managing a ball club, continue that task.

So that if we could enter into the spirit of that agreement, such understanding might go on indefinitely, always having in mind that we owe a duty to the public of New England that I have personally learned to love for its sense of fairness and loyalty, and it is also in this spirit that I hope we may be able to jot down a few figures of record that will prove satisfactory to all concerned.

Sincerely yours,
Emil E. Fuchs, President

It fair takes your breath away.

Ruth was impressed, but he spoke to Ruppert again to ask one last time if Ruppert was satisfied with McCarthy and to see if there might not be some slight hope that he might yet become Yankee manager one day. Ruppert said again that McCarthy was the manager and would continue to be. He said Judge Fuchs had phoned him to give him the details of his offer to Ruth, and the colonel told Babe that it was a wonderful opportunity that he should not pass up.

Ruth was slightly hurt when he realized that the Yankees were perfectly willing to give him his release. ("Eager" would be more accurate; the newspapers, still in the dark about the deal, had noted how uncommonly cheerful Barrow had been lately.) But he liked

Fuchs's offer—vice-president, assistant manager, manager next year, share of the profits—and he did not notice the double talk in the letter. He made up his mind. If the Yankees did not want him, the hell with them. He would go to the Braves.

Later, when the Boston adventure was over, several of his friends said they had advised him against it. Ford Frick, who as the new president of the National League had dealt with Fuchs, noted that much of what Babe thought he had been promised was not in the contract. As someone said, "Babe never heard the fine print in the promises." Nor did he consult a lawyer. "Hell," an oldtimer said, "you didn't talk to lawyers about things like contracts." Frick affirmed this, recalling that in his first year in office, the National League's fee for legal services was less than $500.

Ruth, Ruppert and Fuchs met on Monday and reached an agreement, and on Tuesday afternoon, six days after Ruth's return, the Yankees called a press conference at Ruppert's brewery. The three principals jointly faced the reporters. Ruppert made a little speech about not standing in Ruth's way when he had an opportunity like this, and he mentioned all the years they had been together. Despite their occasional differences, he said, they had always been friends and, indeed, Ruth had once told Ruppert he was a second father to him.

"I should have said Santa Claus," said Ruth genially.

Ruppert smiled. He finished by handing Babe a piece of paper and saying, "Ruth, I give you your unconditional release and wish you the best of luck."

Ruth and Fuchs took over then, but Ruppert hopped back up a moment later to interrupt. He just wanted to remind everyone that the Yankees were not being paid anything, that Fuchs was getting Ruth and Ruth was getting what he wanted, while he, Jacob Ruppert, was not getting a cent.

Someone asked Ruth what his duties would be as vice-president.

"Well, uh . . ." Ruth said.

"Advisory capacity," said Fuchs. "He'll be consulted on trades and so forth."

"A vice-president signs checks," Ruppert said. "Everybody knows that."

The laughter obscured another question, which was "What is the difference between an assistant manager and a coach?"

Someone asked if Ruth, between his salary and his share of the profits, would make as much with the Braves as he had the season before with the Yankees.

"I think he will," Fuchs said. "How much did he get last year?"

"Thirty-five thousand."

Fuchs looked at the ceiling as though he were figuring something out in his head. "Yes," he said, "I hope he will—and more."

And so, after fifteen seasons, Ruth was no longer a Yankee. He was still a bit miffed that the Yankees had actually let him go, but otherwise he was as excited as a kid with a new toy. The day after the press conference he was telling friends he would be the manager in 1936. This got into the papers, and Fuchs, back in Boston, was annoyed. "Ruth should not have said that," he told a reporter who asked him if the Babe's statement was true. "It's embarrassing to the Braves, and it's embarrassing to McKechnie."

"Yes, but is it true? Will he be the manager?"

"I will let my letter to Ruth answer the question. The letter speaks for itself."

On Thursday Babe and Claire went to Boston for the formal signing and a huge dinner in his honor at the Copley Plaza. Even though temperatures were near zero, thousands of people jammed into Back Bay Station and fought with police in order to get vantage points from which to see Ruth. A cynic said it was the first exciting thing to happen in Boston since the Babe had been sold to the Yankees. The slight rift between Ruth and Fuchs seemed smoothed over. The judge said, "I never thought there was any room for doubt in what will be Ruth's connection with the Braves in 1936 if he wishes it. My letter to Ruth contains a paragraph that makes this plain. Ruth has an agreement that he will manage the club in 1936 if certain conditions develop. The pledge is not definite in the sense that it is irrevocably binding. Maybe Ruth won't want the job after a year as assistant manager. In that event he would be justified in declining, though he would still stay on as assistant manager and vice-president."

That was almost as good as the letter. It certainly impressed one Boston sportswriter, who reported, "Judge Fuchs officially confirmed that Ruth has signed with the distinct understanding that he will be manager of the club in 1936 if he wants it."

Managing was all that Babe could talk about. "Of course, if I become manager," he said on the train to Boston that morning, "I will insist on discipline. But I will not apply the whip. You can get more out of men by showing them a little consideration than you can by driving them. You must have the good will of the men under you, and you can't get it by brow beating. A slap on the back is worth more than criticism, and that's the way I intend to work."

A slightly sour note was interjected at the Copley Plaza dinner by the dissident Charles Adams, Fuchs's rival for control of the club. Adams made a blunt speech in which he said, apropos Ruth becoming manager, "Babe will have to show he merits the post before he receives the job. No one is fit to give orders until he can take them himself. Judging from Ruth's past career, we can hardly consider him of managerial caliber now. I certainly hope he will merit promotion to manager, but he has much to learn the next few months."

Ruth was not bothered by this. He praised McKechnie on several occasions during the week, and when asked at the Copley about possible friction between them, said, "I'm sure we'll get along lovely."

CHAPTER 34

The Last Act:
Opera Bouffe with the Braves

Babe was happy, Boston was happy, Fuchs was happy, Ruppert was happy, Barrow was very happy. McKechnie was not happy, but nobody was paying much attention to Bill at the moment. When spring training began, the euphoria continued. Ruth's reception in St. Petersburg when he arrived there by train on March 4 was tumultuous. He had been coming to St. Pete as a Yankee for ten years and had never had anything like it happen before. He had to fight his way through the cheering crowd to get to a cab.

In Boston there had been photographs of Babe in a business suit, next to a desk, being a vice president, and now in St. Petersburg there were pictures of him in a Braves uniform, next to McKechnie, being an assistant manager. The Boston uniform, trimmed with red piping, looked comical and cheap after the sober Yankee garb he had worn for so long, but it gave him a rebirth of glamour. People flocked to see him. When the Braves played the Yankees in St. Petersburg on March 16, they drew the biggest crowd ever to see an exhibition game in Florida. And the crowds kept coming, all through the spring, even though the Babe did not look good at all. He was fat—he weighed 245 when he came back from Europe, fifteen or twenty pounds above his usual post-Artie McGovern weight—and he did not take much of that off down south. He hit no homers at all in Florida, and McKechnie was having a problem about where to put his assistant manager on the field. Ruth's weight, piled on his age, made him almost immobile in the outfield. Because Baxter Jordan, the Braves' regular first baseman, was holding out, Ruth played first base most of the time. But where he had once been deft around that bag, now he was generally clumsy and uncertain.

When the club began trekking north, Ruth played better. He hit his first home run of the spring on April 4 in Savannah and on April 7 in Newark hit two more, one a huge clout that went nearly 500 feet. He played first base rather well that day too, but a day or so later Jordan signed and Ruth opened the season in left field.

Babe's flair for the dramatic was seldom more evident than it was on opening day, when 25,000 people turned out in chilly New England weather to see the Braves face Carl Hubbell and the Giants. Hubbell was the best pitcher in baseball at the moment (Dizzy Dean fans might disagree), but Ruth drove in a run with a single in the first inning, scored a second run himself a few minutes later and in the fifth inning hit a two-run home run. The Braves beat Hubbell, 4–2, and Ruth was responsible for all of Boston's runs. He also made a diving catch of a fly ball. Boston went out of its mind, and when Babe had a couple more hits in the second game of the season, everything seemed absolutely wonderful.

But nothing more happened. In the next month he added only two more hits, one run batted in, one home run. He had a bad cold and missed half a dozen games. Not once did he play an entire game. He walked several times but was slow on the bases. He was bad in the field. The Braves lost game after game and settled into last place. Attendance was down, and those who came were booing.

The great experiment was a flop. Ruth discovered that Fuchs's spellbinding talk about a share in the profits and a chance to buy stock were froth. There were not going to be any profits to speak of, and who wanted to buy stock in a losing business? His duties as vice-president seemed confined to attending store openings and other such affairs in order to get the publicity Fuchs said the club needed.

As assistant manager all he did was tell McKechnie when he was
able to play and when he was not. He soon found out that Bill had
no intention of resigning to become general manager, and that
Fuchs had no intention of forcing McKechnie out to make way for
Babe. The only thing that was any fun was holing up someplace
with Rabbit Maranville, the old shortstop who was playing out his
string with the Braves, and having a few drinks. Sometimes quite a
few drinks.

He and Fuchs did not get along at all. The Babe was angry and
chagrined—he felt like a sucker—because Fuchs, far from paying
him as much or more than he had earned with the Yankees, had
asked him to invest $50,000 in the club. Fuchs was annoyed because
Ruth was a dud on the field and increasingly uncooperative off it.
McKechnie was distressed because his ball club had become completely disoriented. Except for Ruth, it was almost precisely the same
team that had finished fourth, five games over .500, the year before.
Now it was in last place and getting worse.

Early in May Ruth and Fuchs quarreled. The judge had arranged
for Babe and other players to help in promotion deals around Boston
that were tied in with ticket sales. Ruth did not appear at one he was
supposed to go to, and the merchant involved returned 500 tickets
unsold. Fuchs was angry and bawled Ruth out. Ruth yelled, "You
attend to your end of the business, and I'll attend to mine. Mine is
on the field."

But on May 12, shortly after this, he told McKechnie and Fuchs
that he knew he was through as a regular player. He asked to be put
on the voluntarily retired list, a technicality that meant he would
still be the property of the Boston club but would no longer be on
the active roster. It indicated that he wanted to continue as part of
the Braves' organization. Fuchs persuaded him to stay on as an
active player, at least for the duration of the club's first trip through
the western half of the league, which was to begin in a few days.
"Those cities are all waiting to see you," Fuchs said truthfully.
"They've had big ticket sales for our games. They've got Babe Ruth

days planned. You can't quit now. You should wait until you come back after this trip before you think about it."

"I'm thinking about it now," Ruth said.

"All right. But promise me you'll make the trip. They've got a big day set in Cincinnati. They've got something planned in Philadelphia the day before Memorial Day. You've got to be there."

Noblesse oblige. The Babe said okay. He was going home to New York first, driving down with Claire and Dorothy, but he would take a train there and rejoin the club in St. Louis, the first stop on the trip. In New York he complained to his friends about the situation—about Boston, about the fans, who were booing him, about the sportswriters, who were criticizing him, about Fuchs.

"I made a mistake," he said. "I never should have signed. I'm all washed up. I'm quitting after this trip."

His comments got into the papers and back to Fuchs, who a few days earlier had gone into the Braves' clubhouse and castigated the players for their poor performance. He was irritated by Ruth's statements, but publicly he shrugged them off.

"I'd be mighty sorry if he retired," Fuchs said, "but perhaps this trip will restore his peace of mind. He's been ill, and his eyes have been bothering him. He's been playing when he really should have been resting. However, if he does not show decided improvement on this trip, he will retire to pinch hitting and coaching."

The trip was pretty bad, and so was Ruth. The Braves lapsed into a losing streak, and Babe's average was down to .155. He was unhappy and complaining again. "I've had trouble hitting because my eyes keep watering," he said in St. Louis. "It's this damned cold. I'm not going to quit, but I may ask to be voluntarily retired." In Chicago he had a good day, hitting a home run, his third of the season, and making two really fine catches in the outfield. The club moved on to Pittsburgh. In the first game with the Pirates, on a Thursday, he had no hits but sent one very long fly ball to the wall in deep right field, where Paul Waner made a leaping one-handed catch.

That night in Pittsburgh there was a big dinner at the Schenley Hotel for Maranville, who had his best years as a shortstop with the Pirates more than a decade earlier. Rabbit began in the majors two years before Ruth, and had starred in Boston with the Braves when Ruth was pitching for the Red Sox. In 1934 he broke his leg badly sliding home in a spring training game ("Give me a cigarette," he said, sitting at home plate, staring at his leg as he waited for the ambulance) and missed the entire season. Now forty-three, he was trying to come back, but it was obvious that he could not do it any more and that this was his last season. Thus the dinner. He and Ruth had been friends for years, and Babe was one of those who spoke at the dinner.

"I've known Rabbit for a long time," he began, "and I love him. I love him like my own brother." His eyes suddenly filled with tears, and his voice broke. He could not speak. There was an embarrassed silence. "Damn it," he muttered. He dabbed at his eyes with a napkin. The orchestra began playing and in a few moments Ruth was all right. He nodded at the orchestra and the music died away. As it did, the audience began to applaud, warm sentimental applause that splashed down on Ruth until he began to speak again. He ended his talk by saying, "Baseball cannot afford to lose Maranville. If it ever finds it has no place for him, that's the day you'll hear me criticize baseball."

This lament for his lost youth over, Babe went out on the town with Rabbit and a few other friends. The next afternoon as the Pirates were taking batting practice, a Pittsburgh sportswriter named Havey Boyle sat down heavily on the bench next to Pie Traynor, the Pirates' manager.

"You look like you had quite a night," said Traynor.

"I certainly did. Oh, boy." He shook his head sadly. "I'll tell you one thing, though. You won't have to worry about that big guy today. I was with him all night, and he didn't get to bed until after breakfast."

But the forty-one-year-old Ruth played anyway and batted four times. He hit a single and a long fly that Waner caught ten feet from the right field fence and another fly, just like the one the day before, that Waner took with a one-handed leaping catch against the wall. Both of them, the press box agreed, would have been home runs in any other park but Forbes Field, with its outlandishly spacious outfield.

Ruth played again the next day, Saturday, and hit a two-run home run in the first inning off Red Lucas. When he came to bat in the third inning, Lucas was gone, and the Pittsburgh pitcher was Guy Bush, Ruth's old bench-jockey rival from the Cubs. The last time they faced each other, in the 1932 World Series, Bush hurt Ruth by hitting him in the arm with a fastball. This time Ruth hit a two-run homer, his second of the game. In the fifth inning, against Bush, he hit a single that drove in a run. In the seventh Bush was still pitching. The bases were empty. Ruth hit a third home run.

Bush said, "I never saw a ball hit so hard before or since. He was fat and old, but he still had that great swing. Even when he missed, you could hear the bat go swish. I can't remember anything about the first home run he hit off me that day. I guess it was just another homer. But I can't forget that last one. It's probably still going."

It was unbelievably long, completely over the roof of the double-decked stands in right field and out of the park. Nobody had ever hit a ball over the roof in Forbes Field before. Gus Miller, the head usher, went to investigate and was told the ball landed on the roof of one house, bounced onto another and then into a lot, where a boy picked it up and ran off with it. Miller measured the distance from the first house back to home plate and said it was 600 feet. His measurement may have been imprecise, but it was still the longest home run ever hit in Pittsburgh.

Ruth went four for four with his three home runs and a single, and batted in six runs. The Braves lost the game, 11–7. The home run over the roof was the 714th and last of his career. It was also his last major league hit.

Duffy Lewis, Ruth's old Red Sox teammate, was the Braves' traveling secretary, and he told the Babe after the game that if he was going to quit, he ought to quit then, on top. Claire told Babe the same thing. "I can't," he cried. "I promised that son of a bitch I'd play in all the towns on this trip." And there was still Cincinnati and Philadelphia to go.

In Cincinnati on Sunday it was Babe Ruth Day, and the crowd was the biggest in Crosley Field since opening day. But the fire was gone. Ruth struck out three times and popped up. He pinch-hit on Monday, and on Tuesday left the game in the fifth inning, his knee sore and aching.

He played again the next day in Philadelphia before another Babe Ruth Day crowd and was presented with a huge floral baseball. He walked twice and struck out twice, and the Braves won to break an eight-game losing streak.

On Thursday, May 30, in Philadelphia, he was in the starting lineup in the first game of a Memorial Day doubleheader. He struck out in the first inning. In the field in the bottom of the first he hurt his knee going after a fly ball and left the game. He never played again. His career ended not with a bang in Pittsburgh but a whimper in Philadelphia.

The Braves lost both games that day in Philadelphia and lost another doubleheader the next day in Boston. Four defeats in two days, 12 in the last 13 games. Fuchs was sick with disappointment. The team was deep in last place, attendance had fallen off terribly, and it was hardly more than a matter of time now before he would lose the club. He had borrowed heavily on his stock in the Braves and the notes were due August 1.

It rained on Saturday, June 1. The Braves did not play, but Fuchs and Ruth had another argument. The judge was annoyed with Ruth for not appearing in either game of the doubleheader the day before. Ruth said his knee was bad and he could not play. He asked again to be put on the voluntarily retired list. Fuchs said no. The Braves were playing the Giants on Sunday, there was an exhibition game on Monday in Haverhill, Massachusetts, and the Dodgers were coming in for games on Tuesday and Wednesday. There was a promise of fair gate receipts.

There was an uneasy truce overnight, but on Sunday the blowup came. A thousand miles east of Boston, a sleek, gleaming new ocean liner called the *Normandie* was racing toward New York. It was the flagship of the French Line, and this was its maiden voyage. The excitement and interest the *Normandie* created in America in 1935 is impossible to understand in the jet age, but newspapers were filled with stories, and everyone was talking about it. It was sheer glamour. It was due to arrive in New York on Tuesday, and a grand reception was to be held aboard the ship that evening. Ruth was among those invited to the reception.

On Sunday Ruth spoke to Fuchs about the *Normandie* invitation. As long as he could not play anyway on Tuesday or Wednesday, he thought he would go to New York for the reception. "Nothing doing!" said Fuchs. "You stay here." Ruth said he would go to Haverhill on Monday for the exhibition, since it had been advertised that he would play. He could not run, but he'd play first base and if he hit one he'd hobble around the bases. But he could not play against the Dodgers, so what was the point of staying? Fuchs lost his temper and Ruth lost his. Babe sent a message to the press box, asking "the New York writers" to see him after the game in the Braves' clubhouse. As they filed in they saw Ruth in civilian clothes, looking solemn and angry, while behind him Rabbit Maranville, who had played second base, was stomping around cursing the official scorer for charging him with an error on a ball he had been unable to handle.

"I'm quitting," Ruth said to the reporters. He talked about his bad knee and the exhibition game and the Dodger games and the *Normandie*. He said he was going on the voluntarily retired list. The clubhouse, except for the unceasing Maranville, was uncomfortably quiet as he spoke, as though the players were embarrassed by his presence. One of the reporters asked McKechnie if there had been trouble between him and Ruth. "No," McKechnie said, "everything is and has been fine." Nobody believed him, yet when he was asked the question McKechnie was in the act of asking Ruth to autograph a box of baseballs for him. Whatever their personal relationship, there is no question that the manager found Ruth's presence on the club awkward and attributed his team's woeful performance to it. The Braves were 10 and 27 when Ruth quit, which is a .270 percentage and terrible. Yet from then to the end of the season the Braves were even more inept: 28 wins and 88 losses, a .241 percentage. Their overall record was 38–115, the worst won-and-lost record for a National League team in the twentieth century, worse even than Casey Stengel's 1962 Mets.

While Ruth was talking, a message came down to the clubhouse from Fuchs saying Ruth had been released as player and assistant manager and had been fired as vice-president. "I have given Ruth his unconditional release," the statement said, "and he is through with the Braves in every way."

"That's fine with me," Ruth said. "I'm glad of it."

Later he said Fuchs had double-crossed him. "His word is no good," Ruth said. "He doesn't keep his promises." Asked about his second contract with the Braves, the one as an executive, Ruth said, "I'll let it cease. I don't want another damn thing from him, the dirty double-crosser."

Fuchs said, "Ruth is a poor sport. He says I double-crossed him. I wrote him a letter saying I had lost a large sum of money on the Braves, which is true. Ruth would have been the manager some day if he had been a good soldier and hadn't asked for extra privileges."

The Babe replied, "I don't think it's fair after 21 years in baseball and after what I have given to the game for Judge Fuchs to question my sportsmanship. I'll match my record in baseball against his any day."

Fuchs issued a long statement in which he blamed the team's troubles on Ruth, saying he had violated club rules and otherwise behaved badly. He said McKechnie had asked him several days before to drop Ruth for the good of the team but that he, Fuchs, had refused to do it. McKechnie more or less corroborated the letter of this statement. "I think the Babe should have retired so that he wouldn't get hurt," he said. "On May 12 Babe wanted to leave the club, but Judge Fuchs told Ruth he should wait and try to leave on top, rather than when he wasn't going well. When we came home from our western trip I told Judge Fuchs that Ruth couldn't go on and that some action should be taken regarding his status."

Ruth left for New York the next morning; he was driving home with Claire and Claire's mother. First, according to Duffy Lewis, "He took a cab to the ballpark and said goodbye to the secretary and gave her a $100 bill." At the hotel there were no more than half a dozen people watching as he prepared to leave, but a wedding party saw him and threw rice and confetti on him. Ruth said, "I bet this is the first time anyone was ever showered with confetti after being fired."

Just before he left, McKechnie came to the hotel to say goodbye. Ruth said later, "I guess that answers Judge Fuchs's charges. If I'd have been doing what Fuchs has been accusing me of doing, I don't think McKechnie would have come down to say goodbye." He and McKechnie talked for a few minutes, and as it came time to leave they shook hands.

"I'm sorry to see you go, Babe," McKechnie said, "but I guess it had to come. I wish you all the luck in the world."

"I know you do, Bill."

That afternoon, with Ruth on his way to New York, Fuchs called McKechnie in for a conference, and after it the Braves released a statement signed by the manager that vigorously defended Fuchs and just as vigorously condemned Ruth. Boston sportswriters snickered that, while the signature was McKechnie's, the florid style was Fuchs's, and when Ruth saw the statement in New York he dismissed it with "Somebody must have forced Bill to say that. We got along fine."

He told reporters, "I can't go out there and play every day. I'm through in that respect. But I still can play a few days a week. I can go in there maybe on Saturday and Sunday. I can pinch hit. I'm not through with baseball. At least, I hope I'm not."

He phoned his friend Grantland Rice and bellowed, "Get out your golf clubs, kid. I'm ready for you now."

Rice talked jocularly with him for a minute or so and then asked, "What are you going to do now?"

"I'm going to play a lot of golf."

"No, seriously, what are your plans?"

"I'd still like to manage," Ruth said. "I hope to stay in baseball all my life. But there's nothing in sight."

CHAPTER 35

Retirement:
The Call That Never Came

It was all over. He had spent twenty-one full seasons and part of a twenty-second in professional baseball, more than half his life, and now it was done. There was nothing in sight in baseball for Ruth, and there never would be again, except for a brief period in 1938 when Larry MacPhail of the Brooklyn Dodgers hired him in mid-season as a coach to stimulate attendance. He was finished. He was like an ex-President, famous but useless, creating a stir whenever he appeared in public but curiously neutered, no longer a factor.

He played golf, he bowled, he hunted and he waited, but the call to manage never came. Claire Ruth bitterly attacked baseball for this after Ruth's death, implying that there had been a boycott, a black-ball of her husband. This was not technically true, but there was some truth in it. "Club owners can be awful funny," Ruth had said in Paris five months before the blowup with Judge Fuchs. "When they get a ballplayer who thinks, they get suspicious." When a ballplayer has trouble with management, especially in public, they get even more suspicious. A bad actor, they say. Temperamental. Hard to handle. None of the owners cared particularly for Fuchs, or had much respect for him, but he was an owner and Ruth was a player and they reacted against Ruth. In time they took to echoing

Barrow, who, when asked if Ruth was ever going to manage, said, "How can he manage other men when he can't even manage himself?" This became a cliché, petrified truth, and other people repeated it profoundly as though they had just thought it up. Even Bob Shawkey, asked thirty-five years later whether he felt Ruth could have managed, said earnestly, "How could he have managed when he couldn't manage himself?" Bill Slocum, Jr., said with heavy sarcasm that it was the only universally held opinion in baseball.

Could he have managed? Of course. Baseball likes to think there is some occult skill involved in running a ball club, but there isn't. Some men do it well and some don't, but there is no way of telling ahead of time. Men who seem eminently qualified, like Billy Herman and Eddie Stanky, can't pull it off, while others who were never thought of as managers (Yogi Berra, Hank Bauer) go on to win pennants. Some, like Pee Wee Reese, who appear to have every quality a good manager needs, are never hired, while others who do become managers and are awful blisters at it, like Rogers Hornsby, are hired and hired and hired again.

Ruth had certain obvious qualities. He was baseball smart, he was sure of himself, he was held in awe by his fellow players and he was undeniably good copy. He may not have been a success—most managers are not—but he should have been given the chance. During his active career in baseball more than twenty of his contemporaries, some older, some younger, were made managers without previous experience, among them Speaker, Cobb, Sisler, Hornsby, Johnson, Frisch, Cronin, Cochrane, Grimm, Dykes, Terry, Traynor. One or two were excellent. A few had initial success, usually in their first season or two as player-manager, and then petered out. Most were undistinguished. In any case, they stand as evidence that Ruth, so eager to manage, at least deserved a try.

But he did not get it. He lost several opportunities during his last years as a player when he stubbornly continued to campaign for the Yankee job in the face of Barrow's absolute determination that he would never manage the club. There was a great turnover in managers during those years. Of the sixteen men who were managing in 1932 when Babe hit the called home run in Chicago, only Mack, McCarthy and McKechnie had the same jobs when Ruth left Boston in 1935. It was the very bottom of the Depression and Ruth's salary tastes scared off some of the owners, but if Babe had been more receptive to the feelers, more perceptive and aggressive and less cavalier, he almost certainly would have landed one of the available positions.

When he left the Braves, and was completely available and presumably willing to accept anything, the job market tightened up. Only one managerial change was made during the 1935 season, none at all during 1936 and only two in 1937, a period of remarkable stability for big league managers. When jobs began to open up after 1937, Ruth had been out of the game for almost three seasons, a long time in baseball. It was not so much out of sight, out of mind as it was out of touch, out of mind. The times were passing Ruth by.

His long first summer out of the game ended with no signal at all from baseball. The one managerial switch was at Cleveland, where Walter Johnson was fired and was replaced by Ruth's old pal, Steve O'Neill. Asked if he had considered Ruth for the job, Cleveland owner Alva Bradley said no. Ruth, meanwhile, made it clear that he not only wanted but expected to manage. Nothing happened during the 1935 World Series, and later in the autumn he foolishly said in public that he would give the owners their last chance at him during baseball's winter meetings in December. "If they don't take advantage of the opportunity then," he said, "I'll look outside baseball for a job." That tore it.

He went to relatively few baseball games. There is a story that he called Barrow for passes to Yankee Stadium soon after he left the Braves and was turned down on the technicality that he was no longer a part of the Yankee organization or even a part of baseball, although this seems farfetched. But he was angered and hurt when he asked for tickets to the opening game in 1936 and was routinely asked by whoever handled his request to send a check. He was childish about free tickets. In 1939 one of the biggest attractions at the New York World's Fair was Billy Rose's Aquacade. Ruth wanted to see it and said to a friend, "You know Rose, don't you? Can you get passes?" It was a matter of pride.

He worked at being a husband and father, looking with disapproval at boys who called to see his daughters and scolding if they stayed out too late. Dorothy graduated from a private high school in New York in 1938, and a couple of years later Julia was married, with Ruth, impressively attired in morning clothes, a proper father of the bride. He listened to the radio a great deal and was a rabid fan of the shows that were on regularly year after year in that pre-TV era. He was having drinks with a friend in a New York bar one evening when he glanced at his watch and said, "Jesus, I've got to run." He grabbed his cap and coat and headed for the door.

"What's the hurry?" his friend said. "Have another drink."

"Can't," Ruth said. "*Gangbusters* is coming on."

He made a few exhibition appearances in 1935, one of the last with a semipro team in Dyckman Oval, a local field in New York City. It was not major league baseball by a long shot, but Ruth's appeal was dramatically evident in the overflow crowd. He played a great deal of golf, and played it pretty well. He usually shot in the high 70s, but occasionally got into the low 70s and a couple of times broke par. He played in an amateur tournament in Westchester County and finished 17th in a field of 226, one stroke ahead of Dick Chapman, who later became both U.S. and British amateur champion. He was long but wild off the tee and an erratic putter, but curiously enough for such a free swinger, his short game was deft and accurate. He was fun to play with. A partner found him in a deep bunker one day. Ruth looked up and said, "Didn't you hear me call for help? I should have brought a shovel."

About this time the name John Montague began to appear in the sports pages. No one knew quite who he was, except that he was a fabulous golfer. He lived in Hollywood, and he played golf with Hollywood stars. People told amazing stories about his skills. He could break par playing with a rake and a shovel. If his ball was against a tree and his shot to the green was blocked, he would hit the ball at right angles to the direction to the hole and purposely slice it so that it curved around and landed on the green. He was sensational, but hardly anyone ever saw him play.

Late in 1937 the mysterious Montague was persuaded to come into the open. A New York newspaper sponsored a charity match in which Montague and an excellent golfer named Sylvia Annenberg played Babe Ruth and Babe Didrikson, the noted woman athlete. The combination of Montague and Ruth aroused enormous public attention, and when the match was held at Fresh Meadows on Long Island, 12,000 people poured onto the course to watch them play. Golf was not a major spectator sport then, and there never before had been a crowd like it on an American golf course. "This is worse than the World Series," said Ruth, who was knocked off his feet on the fourth fairway by the surging crowd.

Montague the Obscure proved a good, if not fabulous, golfer whose tee shots consistently went 20 to 30 yards farther than Ruth's booming drives. But he was decidedly unnerved by the sight of thousands of faces staring back at him as he drove. The fairways grew narrower as the mob pressed forward to see better, finally shrinking to an alley no more than ten feet wide. On the sixth hole, Montague's drive beaned a spectator and his game began to fray. On the seventh, Didrikson put her head down like a fullback and plunged through the crowd to get to the green. On the par-three ninth, after the two Babes and Montague drove, the spectators ignored Sylvia Annenberg and raced for positions encircling the green. With an admirable display of poise and skill, Sylvia lofted her tee shot over the crowd and hit the pin; the ball fell a foot or so away from the cup, and most of the spectators thought it was a hole in one. After that the match was called, with Ruth and Didrikson each two up on Montague. Later it was learned that Montague's real name was Laverne Moore, and that one reason for his reluctance to appear in public was because he was wanted by police in upstate New York for some chicanery committed in his youth.

Golf became something of a passion with Ruth, and he played as often as he could. His home course was St. Albans on Long Island. Often, he would leave his apartment in the morning, stop at the butcher's on Ninth Avenue, pick up a nice steak, drive to the course, give the steak to the cook at the club and have two or three drinks at the bar while it was being prepared. He'd have a couple more drinks over the steak at lunch and then play golf. The way from the ninth green to the tenth tee at St. Albans went past the clubhouse, and Ruth's foursome would usually pause at the bar, where Ruth would have one or two more. And then go on to complete the round in 77 or 78.

Ben Curry, for years president of Leewood Golf Club in Westchester County, New York, said that when Babe had a date to play golf at Leewood or another club in that neighborhood he would sometimes leave his New York apartment a bit earlier than necessary. He would stop at Curry's house and sit on the porch and chat. Mrs. Curry would bring out a pitcher of ice water and a quart of Scotch. When Babe left for the golf course, the bottle would be half empty.

Yet Curry said Ruth was not an alcoholic. "He drank a tremendous amount, certainly more than most people," he said. "Now and then his liver would act up and the doctor would tell him to cut out booze for a while. And he would. He wouldn't drink at all, just soda pop and things like that. It never seemed to bother him that he couldn't drink. After a while, when he began to feel better, he'd start to drink beer, and eventually he'd be back to Scotch again."

Claire, who did not play golf, accepted but did not relish her role as golf widow. Sometimes Babe would win something in one of the competitions he played in and would be invited to stay at the club for dinner and the presentation of the prizes. He would ask his partner, usually someone Claire knew, to phone and tell her about the prizes and the dinner and explain that he would be a little late. This seldom sat well with Claire. She had been doing a little eating herself in the 1930s and had put on too much weight; her temper was edgy. On one occasion she snapped at the telephoning friend, demanding that Ruth be told to get home right away.

The Currys and the Ruths spent some time together one summer at a resort in New Hampshire, along with the Currys' son and another teenage boy. They had a relay race in the swimming pool one afternoon, with Curry and his son against Babe and the other boy. Curry said to Ruth, "I'll count to three, and then you and I start. Ready? One." Pause. "Two." Long pause. Ruth, tottering, dove into the pool. He climbed out, got set again and Curry counted. "One." Pause. "Two." Longer pause, and again Ruth dove in. "Come on, Babe," Curry said, "that's not fair. You're cheating. Now. You ready?" Babe nodded. Curry said, "Onetwothree," and dove in. Ruth caught him ("He was a good swimmer," Curry said), but the artificial handicap kept the race close.

"He was a lot of fun," Curry said. "He used to wrestle with the kids, rolling around on the floor with them. One night we got into a pillow fight. All of us—me, my wife, the boys, Babe, everybody but Claire. She wouldn't get into it." Curry grinned. "The boys chased Ruth into a closet and locked him in, and they wouldn't let him out. So Babe put that big behind of his against the door and pushed. There was a full-length mirror on the door, and it cracked. He was very strong. They let him out then."

It seemed a carefree time, but Ruth was discontent. He was not used to living a domestic life all the time. He went south to Florida each spring and looked in at the training camps, waving his cap at the players from his car and boisterously hollering, "Hiya, slaves!" But he missed baseball. It hurt that no one wanted him any more. His threat to find something to do outside the game was not serious. He did a few things now and then, radio broadcasts and the like, but nothing permanent.

He got into a couple of minor scrapes with his car. Coming home from St. Albans one night, he bumped into a car in front of him but did not stop. The other man took his license number and went to a police station. A call went out to stop a convertible coupe, New York license number 1N7235, last seen heading for the Queensboro Bridge. When Ruth stopped for a traffic light at the Manhattan end of the bridge, a cop poked a gun at him and told him to get out of the car. The police were as surprised to see Ruth as he was to see them, but they took him to the station house. Babe chatted amiably while they waited for the complainant to arrive, and a crowd of people gathered outside, passing the word, "Babe Ruth's been arrested!"

The only one who didn't seem to know him was the man he hit. When he arrived at the station, he shouted at Ruth and Ruth shouted back. The police calmed them both, and Babe said, "All right, all right. I don't want any trouble. Get your car repaired and send me the bill." The other man seemed satisfied until Babe added, "But don't go sending me a bill for a new car."

"There's a lot of damage," the man shouted. "My water works is leaking."

"Your water works?" Ruth laughed. "I thought I hit the back of the car."

"No, no. The whole car is smashed."

They all went out to look at the auto, which had a noticeably damaged rear fender. The police mediated, and Ruth and the other man exchanged names and addresses.

"Don't you know who he is?" someone asked the man, who was studying Ruth's name and address.

"Who?"

"That's Babe Ruth, the famous baseball player."

"Is that so?" the man said politely.

In June 1938 Babe and Claire went to Ebbets Field for the first major league night game ever played in New York City and saw Johnny Vander Meer pitch his second straight no-hit no-run game for Cincinnati. Vander Meer's feat was front-page news, but earlier in the evening the biggest excitement in the ballpark was the arrival of Babe. A stir ran through the crowd, and fans swarmed around him. Larry MacPhail, who had become executive vice-president of the Dodgers that year, was doing everything he could to pump life into the then-moribund franchise. He remembered the Babe Ruth Day he put on in Cincinnati three years earlier, and the crowd the Babe attracted. In New York MacPhail was challenging the iron grip on baseball that the Yankees and Giants held. Ruth, who in 1936 was one of the five original players elected to the Cooperstown

Hall of Fame (along with Cobb, Wagner, Mathewson and John-son), was still the biggest name in baseball. To have him in a Dodger uniform would be a coup. MacPhail discussed the idea with his manager, Burleigh Grimes, and with Leo Durocher, the Dodger shortstop who had been made team captain late in May. MacPhail was grooming Durocher to succeed Grimes, who was well aware that this was his last year as manager.

Larry talked to Ruth and offered him $15,000 to put on a uniform and be a coach for the rest of the year. The Vander Meer game was on June 15, Ruth met with MacPhail, Grimes and Durocher the next day and signed a contract. This time he said nothing publicly about becoming manager, but he knew Grimes would not be back in 1939 and he was privately convinced that he would take over the club then. However, MacPhail stated clearly when he signed Ruth that the Babe would not be considered for the job; and though there were the usual comments that as a coach he would be a big help to the young players, he really had only one duty: to appear on the field in uniform so the fans could see him. He took batting and fielding practice before games, played in exhibitions and coached at first base. "What else could he do?" Grimes said. "That's what we got him for."

His debut with the Dodgers was on June 19, a Sunday double-header with the Cubs, and it was a box-office success. Artistically, it was not so good, because Babe did nothing impressive in batting practice. But when he toddled out to the coaching lines in his familiar pitty-pat trot there was a great welcoming cheer. Except for Durocher, the players liked him and enjoyed his presence. His penchant for nicknames led him to call Dolf Camilli Cameo and Vito Tamulis Tomatoes. He told stories on the bench and made noise in the clubhouse. It was stimulating. Kiki Cuyler, a thirty-eight-year-old outfielder who had starred with the Pirates and the Cubs and was now in his last season, sat in a corner of the dugout watching him and said, "That guy is amazing. He even does some-thing to me." Grimes said years later, "When he spoke everyone listened, all but Durocher."

He was amiable, cheerful. In Boston he saw Donald Davidson, the midget clubhouse boy of the Braves, and said kindly, "Hey, kid, you want to play catch with me?" In Ebbets Field he was walking with Van Lingle Mungo, a pitcher, from the Dodger clubhouse along the runway under the stands to the dugout. Kids stuck programs through the fence and asked for autographs. "Go away," said Mungo, who was famous for his bad temper, but Ruth stopped and signed all the programs the kids shoved at him. He would stand outside the park after games for an hour signing autographs. Grimes said, "When you're a player, you see the same kids asking for autographs every day. And it's always the big ones who get up close. The little ones are shoved in the back. Ruth signed for all of them. He made sure the little ones got autographs too."

He began to hit a few in batting practice. He and Babe Phelps, the Dodgers' rotund catcher, who was almost Ruth's size, bet cigars on who could put more in the seats. He played first base in exhibition games. In Elmira, New York, he hit one between the outfielders for extra bases, but as he reached first base, where Jesse Haines was coaching, he puffed, "Go ahead, Jess," and switched places with him. Jess got to third with a triple, and no one minded the illegality. In Albany he hit a home run, although not without assistance. Bill McCorry, the Albany manager and later the Yankees' traveling secretary, heard that Ruth was having a little trouble with his eyes and he told his pitcher to keep the ball up where he could see it. The pitcher dutifully laid the ball in the right spot and after missing a couple of times, Ruth rode one out of the park.

He more than earned his salary from the crowds he attracted to the exhibition games he played, and it made people wonder if he could possibly play again in a major league game. Considine asked him about it soon after he joined the Dodgers. "Oh, sure," said Ruth, "but it would take me a month to get in shape. I'm fat as a pig."

During the summer the idea kept coming back to him, and he liked the thought of it. He'd touch on the subject with the sports-writers, who would then push it with Grimes. Toward the end of

August Ruth asked John McDonald, the Dodgers' road secretary, what would have to be done to put him on the active roster.

"Just tear up your coach's contract and sign you to a new one as player."

"Why don't you tell MacPhail to do it. If he does it September first, when the roster goes up to forty players, I won't be taking anybody's job, and maybe I can hit one or two in a game."

MacPhail might have been receptive to the idea—the Dodgers were finishing sixth again and could use a little lift at the gate—but Grimes was absolutely against it. "He's forty-three and he can't see," he said. "If he can hit, I can still pitch."

Years later Grimes said, "He was having trouble seeing out of one eye, and sometimes he couldn't see pitches. I know he had trouble when I threw batting practice. So we used to have Merv Shea, a catcher, throw to him. Shea just sort of flopped his arm when he threw, and it was easy to follow the ball. But put him in a game? He might have been killed."

As the season moved on, Ruth's expectations of succeeding Grimes slowly waned. The manager knew that Durocher was going to take his place, and he conceded that Leo was the logical choice. Leo felt the same way. As captain, he was functioning more like the assistant manager Ruth had been in name only with the Braves. Leo worked closely with Grimes but he treated Ruth with contempt and they had one serious run-in. Although he was on the coaching lines, Ruth did not relay signals from the manager to the batters and runners. Legend says he could not remember the signs and, as a result, messed up a play badly the first day he coached; thereafter he was bypassed. This implies that giving and taking signs was a complex process beyond Ruth's mental capacities. ("He couldn't even give signals," was another echoing criticism.) But no man who plays major league baseball for twenty years is incapable of handling the not terribly demanding process of comprehending and relaying the signals for take, hit, bunt, and so on. Ruth's attitude toward signals was that of the Grand Seigneur, not the dim-witted peasant. He tended to ignore them. As a Dodger coach he was not involved with them—Grimes often was on the coaching lines himself, at third base—and Babe spent most of the time waving his arms, clapping his hands and shouting encouragement. But a young reporter innocently wrote one day that Babe had called for a hit-and-run play that gave the Dodgers a 1–0 victory in the eleventh inning. Grimes, who had given the signal for the play, was annoyed and bawled out the reporter. So did Durocher, who, according to most versions of the story, was the batter in the case. Others say it was Cookie Lavagetto, and that Durocher became involved in the dispute as *amicus curiae,* so to speak. In any case, Leo got into a flaming argument with Ruth in the clubhouse. In an early autobiography, Durocher claimed that Ruth said he had been wanting to slap Leo down for a long time. They tangled and the scuffle left a mark under Ruth's eye. But Grimes said, "Durocher got mad, not Ruth. I grabbed Leo and pushed him back. It's not true about a punch hitting Babe. Not a hand was laid on him, though I guess Leo would have belted him if I hadn't stopped him."

Whatever good will Ruth's presence in uniform might have generated among owners looking for a manager was destroyed by the mocking talk about his inability to give signals, and the dispute with Durocher served as the *coup de grâce* to his dying hope of ever being one. Grimes was formally dismissed as manager on October 10. Durocher was formally hired on October 13. Once again Ruth retired from baseball, this time forever.

CHAPTER 36

The End:
Joe, I'm Gone

Colonel Ruppert died in January 1939. Ruth visited him in the hospital as he lay dying and was touched when Ruppert, who had never called him anything but Ruth, whispered, "Babe, Babe." Gehrig was dying, and at the Lou Gehrig Day ceremonies at Yankee Stadium on July 4th, Babe ended their long antagonism by impulsively putting his arm around Gehrig and hugging him.

Time was closing in. Playing golf with Ben Curry at Leewood, Ruth said, "I feel terrible," and lay down on the grass near the sixteenth tee. "His face was almost blue," Curry recalled. A car was brought out and Ruth was driven to the clubhouse, where he lay down on a bench and asked for a glass of water. A doctor had been called, and Curry was afraid to let him have anything before the doctor got there. He put a sip of water in a glass and gave it to him. Ruth said, "Damn it, give me a glass of water," and began to lift himself. He was given a full glass of water and drank all of it and drank another. After the doctor checked him out, he rested for a while and that night felt fine.

But it was apparently a mild heart attack, and a year or so later he had another. Late in 1941 he was invited to appear in *Pride of the Yankees,* a movie about Gehrig. His weight was nearly 270, and he dieted strenuously in order to be down to presentable size when work on the film began early in 1942. He lost forty pounds in a few months and became edgy and irritable. He had a minor but frightening auto accident in December that depressed him terribly, an odd thing for a man who had been in so many accidents. He caught a bad cold, and early in the New Year, suffering from the cold and nervous exhaustion, he was taken from his apartment on a stretcher and sent to the hospital. He recovered quickly and was off hunting for a few days before going to California for the movie.

In Hollywood he worked hard on the Lou Gehrig movie and did a fine natural job of acting, even to the point of putting his fist through a Pullman car window in a pennant celebration scene. But the stringent working schedule demanded by the film combined with his own normally late hours did not mesh well. He caught another cold and it developed into pneumonia. Again he was hospitalized and for a day or so was reported to be near death. But he was out of the hospital in two weeks, and by the end of April, with the movie finished, was home in New York, healthy and playing golf.

During World War II he did work for the Red Cross, bought $100,000 worth of war bonds, made appropriate comments about Hitler and Mussolini and the Japanese, voted against Franklin Roosevelt and appeared frequently at benefits. He played a series of three golf matches with Ty Cobb for war charities, losing the first, winning the second and losing the third. In August 1942 he appeared at a benefit affair in Yankee Stadium, where he batted against Walter Johnson. It was his first time in the Stadium as a player since 1934, and he was as excited as a kid about it, making sure his uniform was clean and pressed, his spiked shoes shined. Johnson threw seven pitches before Ruth lifted a high fly into the stands in right. The ball curved foul, but Ruth, always a showman, accepted it as a home run and ran around the bases while the crowd cheered. In May 1943 he was in uniform again for a game between two teams from the armed forces, both studded with professional players. Babe pinch-hit and walked. A couple of months later he managed a servicemen's team in another benefit at Yankee Stadium and put himself in as a pinch-hitter against Johnny Sain. He hit one long foul and then walked. A pinch-runner came out from the dugout, but Ruth waved him off. The next man singled and Ruth moved to second, but he pulled up lame and puffing. He accepted the pinch-runner then and half walked, half jogged off the field. It was his last appearance in a formal game.

He was in the hospital toward the end of the war for a cartilage operation on his knee. After the war he let his hope of managing come alive again. The Ruppert estate sold the Yankees to a syndicate headed by MacPhail, and Barrow was no longer running the team. Ruth phoned MacPhail and asked him for the job of managing the Yankees' Newark farm club. It was an embarrassing retreat from his long-held position that he was a big leaguer who did not have to go back to the minors as an apprentice, but he was being realistic. MacPhail said he would get back to him. There was no answer for a few weeks and then a letter came.

"That's bad news," Ruth said. "When it's good news, they telephone."

MacPhail did not want Ruth and told him so in a polite, circuitous note that ended with a plea for Babe to become involved in a sandlot baseball program sponsored by the city of New York. That was the final humiliation. He went back to golf, bowling and hunting.

In May 1946, when Jorge Pascual was trying to build up the Mexican League by enticing American major leaguers with offers of huge salaries, Ruth spent two weeks in Mexico City as Pascual's guest. He was called El Rey Jonronero in the Mexican newspapers. Now past fifty, he said quite plainly that he doubted he would sign any sort of a contract with Pascual, but he had a fine time anyway. He went to a bullfight, played golf, got sunburned, saw a few ballgames, swung at a couple of pitches in batting practice. He met fifty-eight-year-old Armando Marsans, a Cuban who had been an American League outfielder thirty years earlier when Ruth was still a pitcher. "You remember me?" asked Marsans, and Ruth's face lit up. "Sure I do," he said, and he did. Not the name, but the man.

Marsans was managing in one of the games Ruth saw, and when he refused to take a pitcher out of a game despite a rally by the other team, Ruth approved. "That's right," he called out. "Let him stay in there."

Because of the major leagues' antipathy for Pascual and the Mexican League, Ruth was asked if anyone tried to persuade him not to visit Mexico. "No," Babe said, "nobody asked me not to come. But that doesn't make any difference. I go where I please anyway."

Several months later Ruth began to complain of extreme pain over his left eye. He thought it was a sinus headache, but it hurt so much that in November he entered French Hospital in New York for a thorough examination. Not much attention was paid—he had been in and out of hospitals so often—but this time it was deadly serious. He had a malignant growth in the left side of his neck, in such a position that it nearly encircled the left carotid artery. When he was operated on, nerves had to be severed and the artery tied off, which adversely affected the left side of his head, including his larynx. Most of the cancerous growth was removed but some could not be, and he was given radiation treatment to control it.

The disease and its treatment debilitated him. He could not eat and had to be fed intravenously. He was in French Hospital for three months and lost eighty pounds. When he was discharged in February 1947, he went to Florida to rest in the sun. He regained enough strength to play golf a few times and go fishing, but the seriousness of his condition was evident in his appearance. In March, A. B. (Happy) Chandler, the new Commissioner of baseball (Judge Landis died in 1944) declared that Sunday, April 27, would be Babe Ruth Day in the major leagues. Ceremonies were held in all the parks, but the most significant was in Yankee Stadium.

Ruth returned to New York in time to be at the Stadium for his day. He wore his familiar camel's hair overcoat and camel's hair cap, but he was thin, his color a bad yellowish tan, his voice a disheartening croak. Almost 60,000 people were in the Stadium. There was the usual plethora of speeches, including one from a thirteen-year-old who represented boys' baseball. Ruth spoke too, bending forward slightly from the hips to bring his mouth close to the microphone. His speech was extemporaneous.

"Thank you very much, ladies and gentlemen," he began, the awful voice sounding even harsher as it came from the loudspeakers. "You know how bad my voice sounds. Well, it feels just as bad. You know, this baseball game of ours comes up from the youth. That means the boys. And after you've been a boy, and grow up to know how to play ball, then you come to the boys you see representing themselves today in our national pastime. The only real game in the world, I think, is baseball. As a rule, some people think if you give them a football or a baseball or something like that, naturally, they're athletes right away. But you can't do that in baseball. You've got to start from way down, at the bottom, when you're six or seven years old. You can't wait until you're fifteen or sixteen. You've got to let it grow up with you, and if you're successful and you try hard enough, you're bound to come out on top, just like these boys have come to the top now.

"There's been so many lovely things said about me, I'm glad I had the opportunity to thank everybody. Thank you."

He smiled and waved to the crowd and walked slowly to the Yankee dugout.

The unexcised part of the tumor continued to grow, and Ruth was in extreme discomfort through the spring of 1947. He did not know what was wrong with him, and no one told him. Considine said, "Those who knew him best, Mel Lowenstein and Paul Carey and Claire, believed that if he knew he had terminal cancer, it would destroy him. He'd go right out the window." For a time Ruth thought his teeth were infected, and he would wince with pain and mutter, "These damn teeth."

He was in constant pain that had to be relieved with morphine. He tried to work with Considine on his autobiography, but when he could not recall something he was trying to remember, he would break off the conversation and say, "Let's get the hell out of here and go hit a few." They would get into Ruth's Lincoln Continental and drive to the butcher shop on Ninth Avenue. Instead of ordering a steak to take to the golf course, Ruth would buy chopped meat, since he could not chew. In the shop he would pick up a cleaver and playfully threaten the butchers. "I'm going to chop your goddamned heads off," he'd say, to their evident delight. A girl, a nurse, would usually meet him in the butcher shop and ride out to the golf course, where she would walk around with them while they played. Sometimes at the club he felt so bad he would have only a soft-boiled egg, and he had trouble swallowing that. One day he looked at the egg in his misery and said, "To think of the steaks." For a time he continued to play eighteen holes, but as he grew weaker his games grew shorter. One day he teed up his ball, swung well and hit the ball cleanly. It carried straight down the fairway, but for only about 90 yards. Ruth stood on the tee watching it and cried, cursing through the tears.

By June 1947 the pain had become so bad that his doctors decided to treat the cancer with an experimental new drug, a synthetic relative of folic acid, part of the vitamin B complex. Treatment began on June 29, and Ruth showed such remarkable improvement that in September a paper on his case was read at an International Cancer Congress meeting in St. Louis. He began to travel around the country doing promotional work on American Legion baseball for the Ford Motor Company. He also had Lowenstein draw up papers creating The Babe Ruth Foundation, which was designed to help underprivileged children. Late in September MacPhail put on another Babe Ruth Day at Yankee Stadium to raise funds for the Ruth Foundation, and Babe was there to watch an oldtimers' game played by Ty Cobb and Tris Speaker and others. He had hoped to be strong enough to be able to pitch an inning, but he was not.

His dramatic improvement was apparently only a temporary remission of the cancer, and he continued painfully ill. When Ruth was in Cincinnati for the Ford people, Waite Hoyt and his wife visited him in his hotel. Claire met them at the door and brought them into the living room of the suite where Ruth was sitting on a couch, his head down, nodding from the sedatives he was taking.

On the table in front of him was a bottle of beer, which, Hoyt said, he drank for food. Babe lifted his head wearily.

"I'm glad to see you," he whispered.

They talked for a while, but he appeared so exhausted that Hoyt decided he and his wife should leave.

"We'd better go, Jidge."

Ruth nodded. "I am kind of tired," he said.

The Hoyts stood up to go, but Ruth whispered, "Wait a minute." Painfully, he got to his feet and went into the kitchen. From the refrigerator he took a small vase with an orchid in it and brought it back to the living room.

"Here," he said to Mrs. Hoyt. "I never gave you anything."

On Sunday, June 13, 1948, the Yankees celebrated the twenty-fifth anniversary of Yankee Stadium, and Ruth was invited to be there along with other members of the 1923 Yankees. Sick as he was, he was delighted with the idea. The Yankees held a banquet for all the old players at Ruppert's brewery the night before the game, but Ruth was not well enough to attend that. There was concern that he might not be at the Stadium either on Sunday because it was a dank, rainy day. But he came. The other old Yankees were already in the locker room when he arrived.

"Here he is now," one of them said in a low voice, and Ruth came in slowly, helped by Paul Carey and Frank Dulaney, his male nurse. His face split into a grin, a shriveled caricature of the beaming one he used to have, and in his croaking voice he spoke to his old team-mates, calling most of them by their nicknames. Dulaney helped him take off his street clothes and put on his uniform. The old teammates stayed away until he had his uniform on, and so did the photographers. Then they began to take pictures, with Ruth posing willingly. The old Yankees were gathered together for a group photograph. Ruth, stooped, smiling, stood in the middle of the back row. Joe Dugan, standing half behind him, had a hand on his shoulder, and so did Wally Pipp.

The oldtimers began to go out onto the field, and Ruth, accompanied by Dulaney and Carey, followed slowly down the runway to the dugout. It was early and Ruth paused in the runway, a topcoat slung over his shoulders to keep off the chill. "I think you'd better wait inside," said Dulaney. "It's too damp here." Ruth was led back to the clubhouse and stayed there until it was nearly time for him to appear on the field. Then he came down the runway again and into the dugout, where room was made for him on the bench. Mel Harder, a Cleveland coach who had pitched against Ruth, came over to say hello.

Ruth said hoarsely, "You remember when I got five for five off you in Cleveland and they booed me?"

Harder smiled.

"Line drives," Ruth croaked, "all to left field. And they booed the shit out of me."

All the other oldtimers had been introduced, the applause from the big crowd rising and falling as each name was called. It was time for Ruth. He got to his feet, letting the topcoat fall from his shoulders, and took a bat to use as a cane. He looked up at the photographers massed in front of the dugout. His name rang out over the public address system, the roar of the crowd began and, as W. C. Heinz wrote, "He walked out into the cauldron of sound he must have known better than any other man."

He walked slowly and he was smaller than Babe Ruth should have been. He paused for the photographers, leaning on the bat, looking up at the crowded tiers of people. Near home plate he was met by Ed Barrow, a month past his eightieth birthday, who hugged him. At the microphone Ruth spoke briefly, saying how proud he was to have hit the first home run in the Stadium and how good it was to see his old teammates. When the ceremonies were over and the other old players trotted out to their positions for a two-inning game, Ruth left the field at Yankee Stadium for the last time. He was helped down into the dugout and back along the runway to the clubhouse. The topcoat was put over his shoulders again, and he kept it on in the clubhouse. He felt chilly. The glow of the excitement was wearing off. Dugan, who played only one inning of the oldtimers' game, came into the clubhouse.

"Hiya, Babe," Dugan said, sitting down next to him.

"Hello, Joe."

"Can you use a drink?"

"Just a beer."

A small bar had been set up in a corner of the locker room, and Dugan got a drink for himself and a beer for Ruth and brought them back. They sat there a while, sipping their drinks.

"How are things, Jidge?" Dugan asked.

"Joe, I'm gone," Ruth said. "I'm gone, Joe."

He started to cry, and Dugan did too.

A week or so later, Ruth was in the hospital again. He did not want to go, and when it was time to leave for the hospital he refused to get out of bed. Frank Dulaney said, "He was in terrible pain. I tried to cajole him, but he shook his head. He wouldn't get up. I sat on the side of his bed and talked to him. I said, 'If you were my father, I'd make you go.' He got up then."

As Dulaney helped him up the steps of Memorial Hospital, Ruth said, "Isn't this hospital for cancer?" Dulaney answered, "Cancer and *allied* diseases." Ruth grunted.

He never was told he had cancer, but he certainly knew it, at least toward the end. When Jim Peterson took Connie Mack to visit him, Ruth said, "Hello, Mr. Mack. The termites have got me."

Ruth was ambulatory in the hospital, and when he felt strong enough he would go out for a drive. Early in July he paid his last visit to Baltimore, flying down for a charity game. It was rained out, but he had a chance to talk to Roger Pippen, who had been with him in Fayetteville in 1914. Back in his hospital room he watched baseball on television, a relatively new phenomenon, and was pleased by visits and mail. He received hundreds of letters every day. A few would be read to him and he would rasp his reaction. May Singhi Breen, a onetime radio star who, with her husband, the songwriter Peter DeRose, was close to Claire and Babe, took on the job of seeing to it that all the mail was answered. Many contained requests for autographs, and on days he felt well Ruth would ask for "my cards." These were postcards with his photograph, and he would sign a hundred or so at a time to keep a supply on hand. President Truman phoned him, and Betty Grable, whom he had met and liked in Hollywood, sent him a bottle of pine-scented cologne. He wanted the cologne in his bath water each day and sometimes he would grunt to Dulaney, "Toss a little around the room, Frank."

The last rites of the Catholic Church were administered on July 21, but Ruth rallied again after that. He left the hospital on the evening of July 26 to attend the premier of *The Babe Ruth Story*. He was very uncomfortable watching the film and left well before it was over. He seemed content back in the hospital, and he never left it again. "All my obligations are over," he said. "I'm going to rest now. I'm going to take it easy."

In August his condition steadily deteriorated. Claire stayed in a room across the hall, usually attended by a friend or by Julia or Dorothy. Few visitors were admitted, but Ruth, even though he was unable to say much, relished the visits. Paul Carey phoned Ford Frick one day and told him Babe would like to see him. Frick said the hospital was like a three-ring circus, with reporters and photographers waiting, and the death watch across the hall. He spoke to Claire for a moment and then went into the room.

"It was a terrible moment. Ruth was so thin it was unbelievable. He had been such a big man, and his arms were just skinny little bones and his face was so haggard. When I came in he lifted his eyes toward me and raised his right arm a little, only about three or four inches off the bed, and then it fell back again. I went over to the bed and I said, 'Babe, Paul Carey said you wanted to see me.' And Ruth said, in that terrible voice, 'Ford, I always wanted to see you.' It was just a polite thing to say. I stayed a few minutes and left and I spoke to Claire again across the hall and then I went home and the next day he was dead."

Acknowledgments

John Drebinger and Ford Frick knew Ruth well and told me a great deal about him. Bob Considine, Ben Curry and Bill Slocum, Jr., shared their special knowledge of certain aspects of Ruth's life. Of Babe's teammates, George Twombly, Ernie Shore, Bob Shawkey, Joe Dugan and Waite Hoyt were especially helpful, Hoyt most of all.

Ken Smith, Cliff Kachline and Jack Redding of the Baseball Museum and Baseball Library at Cooperstown disclosed rich mines of material and Redding was of particular help in locating many of the photographs that appear here. Jim Creamer's research on Ruth's years in Boston produced detailed information that was otherwise unobtainable. From Jim Bready of Baltimore came much about Ruth's family and boyhood. Frank Sleeper, Jack Tobin and Herman Weiskopf provided interviews with prime sources.

There were many others, but it would be impossible to mention each of them without making a list that would fill several pages. Here, I thank them all. Because this is a popular, not a scholarly, biography, there is no need for a bibliography, although I have mentioned several books in the text and will add here *The Baseball Encyclopedia* (Macmillan, 1969), which was continually helpful, and *World Series Records,* published annually by *The Sporting News.*

As for editors, that saintly breed of men, I thank Dick Johnston for his early encouragement, Andy Crichton for his comments and editorial suggestions, Andre Laguerre and Roy Terrell of *Sports Illustrated* for their tolerance and, above all, Peter Schwed for his kindness and patience.

Index

For a complete list of books available from
Penguin in the United States, write to Dept.
DG, Penguin Books, 299 Murray Hill Park-
way, East Rutherford, New Jersey 07073.

For a complete list of books available from
Penguin in Canada, write to Penguin Books
Canada Limited, 2801 John Street, Markham,
Ontario L3R 1B4.